CROP – The Comparative Research Programme on Poverty

The Comparative Research Programme on Poverty was initiated by the International Social Science Council in 1992. The major aim of CROP is to produce sound and reliable research-based knowledge which can serve as a basis for poverty reduction. CROP is organized around a broad international and multi-disciplinary research arena which allows entry to all poverty researchers and others interested in a scientific approach to poverty. CROP organizes regional and topical workshops and international conferences, initiates and co-ordinates comparative projects and publications, offers educational courses, and invites its members to consult for national and international agencies. More than fifteen hundred researchers and others have joined the CROP network, close to half coming from so-called developing countries and countries in transition.

As an international and inter-disciplinary research programme, CROP's objectives are to:

- consider how scholars working within different paradigms can develop a joint arena for multi-paradigmatic research
- compare different theoretical approaches so as to understand better their links and relationships
- consider how the social sciences can contribute to the understanding of poverty in a global context
- establish an international scientific network which will give impetus to a long-term programme
- generate and secure high-quality data of importance for different social science approaches
- create a body of scientific knowledge which can be used for poverty reduction.

CROP Publications

Poverty: Research Projects, Institutes, Persons, Tinka Ewoldt-Leicher and Arnaud F. Marks (eds), Tilburg, Bergen, Amsterdam, 1995, 248 pp.

Urban Poverty: Characteristics, Causes and Consequences, David Satterthwaite (ed.), special issue of *Environment and Urbanization*, Volume 7, No. 2, April 1995, 283 pp.

Urban Poverty: From Understanding to Action, David Satterthwaite (ed.), special issue of *Environment and Urbanization*, Volume 7, No. 1, October 1995, 283 pp.

Women and Poverty: The Feminization of Poverty, Ingrid Eide (ed.), The Norwegian National Commission for UNESCO and CROP, Oslo and Bergen, 1995 (published in Norwegian only), 56 pp.

Poverty: A Global Review. Handbook on International Poverty Research, Else Øyen, S. M. Miller, Syed Abdus Samad (eds), Scandinavian University Press and UNESCO, Oslo and Paris, 1996, 620 pp.

Poverty and Participation in Civil Society, Yogesh Atal and Else Øyen (eds), UNESCO and Abhinav Publications, Paris and New Delhi, 1997.

Law, Power and Poverty, Asbjørn Kjønstad and John H. Veit Wilson (eds), CROP Publications, Bergen, 1997, 148 pp.

Poverty and Social Exclusion in the Mediterranean Area, Karima Korayem and Maria Petmesidou (eds), CROP Publications, Bergen, 1998.

Poverty and the Environment, Arild Angelsen and Matti Vainio (eds), CROP Publications, Bergen, 1998.

The International Glossary on Poverty, David Gordon and Paul Spicker (eds), CROP International Studies in Poverty Research, Zed Books, London, 1999.

Transcending the Poverty of Rights: Latin America, Human Rights and the Eradication of Poverty, Willem van Genugten and Camilo Perez-Bustillo (eds), CROP International Studies in Poverty Research, Zed Books, London, 2001.

Poverty Reduction: What Role for the State in Today's Globalized Economy?

Edited by Francis Wilson, Nazneen Kanji and Einar Braathen

CROP International Studies
in Poverty Research

NAEP
CAPE TOWN

Zed Books
LONDON · NEW YORK

Poverty Reduction: What Role for the State in Today's Globalized Economy? was first published by Zed Books Ltd, 7 Cynthia Street, London N1 9JF, UK and Room 400, 175 Fifth Avenue, New York, NY 10010, USA in 2001.

Published in South Africa by New Africa Education Publishing, PO Box 23317, Claremont 7735, Republic of South Africa.

Distributed in the USA exclusively by Palgrave, a division of St Martin's Press, LLC, 175 Fifth Avenue, New York, NY 10010, USA.

CROP International Studies in Poverty Research

Copyright © CROP, 2001

Cover designed by Andrew Corbett
Set in Monotype Ehrhardt and Franklin Gothic by Ewan Smith
Printed and bound in Malaysia

A catalogue record for this book is available from the British Library

Library of Congress Cataloging-in-Publication Data: available

ISBN 1 85649 952 9 cased
ISBN 1 85649 953 7 limp
In South Africa
ISBN 1 919876 03 0

Contents

16 Redressing Urban Poverty in Post-apartheid South Africa

Christian M. Rogerson

Index

Tables and Figures

Tables

Figures

Acknowledgements

One of the major research projects within CROP, the Comparative Research Programme on Poverty, is a comparative study of the role of the state in poverty reduction (ROSA). As part of the project, workshops are organized in different regions to facilitate the participation of scholars from several countries and increase the comparative character of the study. The first workshop was held in Botswana in 1997, the second was held in South Africa in 1998, the third was held in Jordan in 1999 and the fourth in Ghana in 2000. The articles in this book were presented as papers and laid out for discussion in the first two of these workshops.

CROP wishes to acknowledge and thank the following institutions for organizational and economic support: University of Botswana, Gaborone; Botswana Institute for Development Policy Analysis (BIDPA), Gaborone; Bank of Botswana; University of Cape Town, South Africa; Southern African Labour and Development Research Unit (SALDRU), University of Cape Town, South Africa; the Norwegian Agency for Development Co-operation (NORAD); the International Social Science Council, Paris; UNDP and UNESCO.

Else Øyen
Chair of CROP

About the Contributors

Arnon Bar-On is associate professor in the Department of Social Work at the University of Botswana; before taking up this position he taught social work and social policy in Israel and in Hong Kong. His major interests and publications deal with the theory of social work, the goals and implications of community participation, social services for minority groups, non-governmental organizations, and street children.

Einar Braathen is a researcher at the Norwegian Institute for Urban and Regional Research (NIBR). A political scientist, he was previously a research fellow at the University of Bergen writing a doctoral dissertation on the politics of telecommunications development in Mozambique and Zimbabwe. Since 1995 he has been project leader for a study of the decentralization process in Mozambique. Since 1997 he has worked as a part-time programme officer for the Comparative Research Programme on Poverty (CROP) with responsibility for the workshops on the 'Role of the State in Poverty Alleviation' on which this book is based. His most recent work (edited with M. Bøås and G. Sæther) is *Ethnicity Kills? The Politics of War, Peace and Ethnicity in Sub-Saharan Africa* (Macmillan, 1999).

Debbie Budlender has worked for the Community Agency for Social Enquiry, a non-governmental organization specializing in social policy research, since 1988. Since 1997 she has been on a long-term part-time secondment to Statistics South Africa, the government statistical agency, where she works primarily on gender and employment issues. She has been the editor and co-ordinator of the South African Women's Budget Initiative since its establishment in 1995 and has worked in the area of gender analysis of government budgets in a range of other countries in Africa and beyond.

Hartley Dean is Professor of Social Policy at the University of Luton, England. He previously worked for twelve years as the director of an inner-London welfare rights agency. More recently, he has undertaken research and teaching at the universities of Kent and Luton in areas relating to poverty, exclusion, welfare rights and citizenship. His several publications include *Social Security and Social Control* (Routledge, 1991), *Dependency Culture: The Explosion of a Myth* (with P. Taylor-Gooby, Harvester Wheatsheaf, 1992), *Welfare, Law and Citizenship* (Prentice Hall, 1996) and *Poverty, Riches and Social Citizenship* (with M. Melrose, Macmillan, 1999).

Blandine Destremau holds a permanent researcher position at the French Center of Scientific Research (CNRS), and has been appointed to the Tours University Research Center, URBAMA, which specializes in Middle Eastern Studies. After a PhD dissertation dealing with the economic transformation in Yemen, she taught economics at various French universities and dedicated the bulk of her research work to issues concerning Palestine and the changing regional context. Since 1996 she has specialized in poverty research, and is presently spending a year in Yemen doing field work. Her publications include *Femmes du Yemen* (Peuples du monde, 1990), *Palestine, palestiniens: territoire national, espaces communautaires* (with Riccardo Bocco and Jean Hannoyer, Centre d'études et de recherches sur le Moyen-Orient contemporain, 1997) and *ESCWA (1974–1999): Twenty-five Years of Service to the Region's Development* (with Serge Nedelec, United Nations, 1999).

Kenneth Good has been Professor of Political Studies at the University of Botswana since 1990. He previously taught and carried out research at universities in Zambia, Zimbabwe, Papua New Guinea and Fiji. Among his recent publications are *Realizing Democracy in Botswana, Namibia and South Africa* (Africa Institute, 1997), and articles in the *Journal of Modern African Studies and Democratization*.

Dirk Hansohm has been senior researcher at the Namibian Economic Policy Research Unit (NEPRU) in Windhoek, Namibia, since 1994, and its training co-ordinator since 1998. His areas of specialization include macroeconomics, industry, trade, poverty, labour and small enterprise promotion. Previously he has worked at the University of Bremen and for international organizations in Nigeria, Sudan and Zimbabwe. His several publications include *Small Industry Development in Africa. Lessons from Sudan* (Lit, 1992) and *Schwarz-weisse Mythen. Afrika und der entwicklungspolitische Diskurs* (Lit, 1993).

Dr Nazneen Kanji is a part-time teacher in the Department of Social Policy at the London School of Economics and does independent research and consultancy work. She has lived and worked extensively in East and Southern Africa and spent seven years in the 1980s in Mozambique working with government and non-governmental agencies to develop social policy for vulnerable groups. More recently, she has carried out research on the effects of Structural Adjustment Policies at the household level and has been involved in poverty assessments and gender-focused research. She has published several journal articles and book chapters including 'Gender, Poverty and Structural Adjustment in Harare, Zimbabwe' (*Environment and Urbanization*, 1995) and 'African Urban Livelihoods: Straddling the Rural–Urban Divide' (co-authored) in S. Jones and N. Nelson (eds), *Urban Poverty in Africa* (Intermediate Technology Publications, 1999). In 1998, she took part in a study of the World Bank's poverty reduction strategies in Southern Africa, which forms the basis for her chapter in this book.

Charity K. Kerapeletswe is a PhD student in Environmental Economics at the University of York. She previously worked as a research fellow for the Botswana Institute for Development Policy Analysis (BIDPA), a non-government policy research institution whose main foci are policy analysis and capacity building. In the past she has worked and undertaken research at the National Development Bank, the Ministry of Agriculture and the Rural Industries Promotions Company (Botswana) in areas relating to rural development, welfare, poverty, gender and natural resource management. Her publications include *Study on Poverty and Poverty Alleviation in Botswana* (with BIDPA, 1997), *Botswana's Income Support and Stabilization Policies for Subsistence Farmers* (Kansas State University, 1995) and *Constraints Faced by Female-headed Households in Arable Agriculture* (with Ministry of Agriculture, 1991).

Archie B. Mafeje is Professor at the American University in Cairo. He holds a PhD in anthropology and sociology of development from the University of Cambridge. His publications include *Anthropology and Independent Africans: Suicide or End of an Era* (CODESRIA, 1996), *Economic and Demographic Change in Africa* (with Samir Radwan, Oxford University Press, 1995) and *African Philosophical Projections and Prospects for the Indigenisation of Political and Intellectual Discourse* (SAPES Books, 1992).

Julian May is a senior research fellow in the School of Development Studies at the University of Natal-Durban where he is the head of the centre's Population and Poverty Studies Programme. Prior to joining the university in 1997, he was the director of Data Research Africa, an independent research organization concerned with social and economic policy in post-apartheid South Africa. He is a member of the South African Interim Statistics Council and has served on numerous task teams for Statistics South Africa, including the census evaluation, national poverty survey and rural survey. He recently led a team of South African and international researchers working on the Poverty and Inequality Report commissioned by the office of the then Executive Deputy President of South Africa.

Tsholofelo Moremi is currently working at the Botswana Institute for Development Policy Analysis (BIDPA). Her interests in research are poverty, welfare and gender issues.

Alessandro Palmero, an Italian national, lived in Mozambique from 1992 to 1998. During that period, he worked for four years in the representation of the European Commission and one year in the Mozambican Technical Secretariat for Electoral Administration. An economist by training, Mr Palmero holds an M Phil in development studies from the Institute of Development Studies at the University of Sussex, where he currently is a D Phil candidate.

Camilo Perez-Bustillo is Research Professor at the State of Mexico campus of the Instituto Tecnológico y de Estudios Superiores de Monterrey (ITESM), where he gives courses in media studies, law and international relations. He is also a resident scholar at the Permanent Seminar on Chicano and Border Studies of the Social Anthropology Division of Mexico's National Institute of Anthropology and History (DEAS-INAH), the representative in Mexico of the US-based National Lawyers' Guild and Adjunct Professor at the Mexico City campus of United States International University (USIU), based in San Diego, California.

Brian Raftopoulos is a research fellow at the Institute of Development Studies, University of Zimbabwe. From 1996 to 1997 he was the chairman of the Poverty Reduction Forum (Zimbabwe), a policy discussion body composed of NGOs, state officials, academics and donors. He has also been a leading member of the National Constitutional Assembly, a major coalition grouping set up in 1997 and fighting for constitutional reform in Zimbabwe. He has published widely in the fields of labour and nationalist history, and Zimbabwean politics. He was also co-author of the 1998 UNDP Human Development Report on Zimbabwe, the theme of which was poverty.

Christian Rogerson is Professor of Human Geography at the University of the Witwatersrand, Johannesburg. He is the author of 200 articles on issues relating to small enterprise development, local and regional economic development and urban and regional studies in Southern Africa, including the volume *South Africa's Informal Economy* (Oxford University Press, 1991), which he edited with Eleanor Preston-Whyte.

Klaus Schade has been a research trainer at the Namibian Economic

Policy Research Unit (NEPRU) in Windhoek, Namibia, since March 1997. He has worked mainly on issues related to poverty in Namibia and macro-economic topics. He has been responsible for NEPRU's Quarterly Economic Reviews and the 1997/98 and 1998/99 edition of NEPRU's publication *Economic Review and Prospects*. He has also published articles in regional journals on the Namibian economy with Dirk Hansohm.

Brigitte Schulz is an associate professor of Political Science at Trinity College in Hartford, Connecticut, and also serves as co-ordinator of the major in Comparative Development Studies. Her areas of specialization are international political economy, with an emphasis on economies and societies in transition. She has written extensively on North–South and East–South relations, as well as on problems and challenges of post-communist transformations. She received her MSc from the London School of Economics and her doctorate from Boston University. She has published *The Soviet Bloc and the Third World: The Political Economy of East–South Relations* (Westview Press, 1989) and *Development Policy in the Cold War Era* (Lit, 1995), as well as two dozen articles and chapters in books.

Arne Wiig is a senior researcher at Chr. Michelsen Institute, Norway. For the last two years he has worked as a research trainer at NEPRU. His main research fields are international trade, industrial analysis and micro-credits. His doctoral thesis, from the Norwegian School of Business Adminis-tration, was on *Marketing Barriers Facing Developing Countries.*

Francis Wilson has taught for thirty years in the School of Economics at the University of Cape Town, where he founded and directs the Southern African Labour and Development Research Unit (SALDRU). He is the author of a number of books, chapters and articles including *Labour in the South African Gold Mines* (Cambridge University Press, 1972) and *Up-rooting Poverty: The South African Challenge* (W. W. Norton, 1989) with Mamphela Ramphele. More recent articles are on 'Human Capital Forma-tion and the Labour Market in South Africa' and 'Reflections on Work in a Sustainable Society', published in the *American Economic Review* and the *Ecumenical Review* respectively. He has also written an essay on global-ization for a forthcoming book comparing the United States, South Africa and Brazil. He was chairman of council at the University of Fort Hare from 1990 to 1999 and also first chairman, 1996–99, of the National Water Advisory Council.

1

Introduction: Poverty, Power and the State

Francis Wilson, Nazneen Kanji and Einar Braathen

What new insights about the relationship between the state and the poverty of huge numbers of citizens do we have as we move from the 1990s into the new millennium? What role can the state play in alleviating or reducing poverty? Or is the state itself part of the problem? Within the context of Africa, to what extent is the social and economic stagnation of so many states since 1990 due primarily to external factors such as the terms of trade and the policies imposed by international finance institutions? Beyond conventional considerations of technical and organizational know-how, what political and cultural dimensions of the state have to be taken into account when considering *how* the state should help shape the activities of the society? What should be the role of the grass roots in development? How is the concept of citizenship incorporated in poverty reduction programmes? How is the role of power best analysed when considering strategies to eradicate poverty? What is the meaning of pro-poor governance? And is it possible?

Answers to these questions cannot be sought simply at a theoretical level. Much depends on the particular form of the state, the environment within which it is operating, and the history from whence it sprang. At the same time, is it not possible to draw insights from specific realities which can be generalized to provide a deeper understanding across a wide range of countries, if not the world as a whole?

In an attempt to provide some answers to these questions, the Comparative Research Programme on Poverty (CROP) has initiated a process of which this book is itself part. As a result of the papers delivered and the discussion which flowed from them it has been possible to bring together a volume focusing on these questions primarily, but not exclusively, within the context of Southern Africa as the new millennium begins.

Why Southern Africa? Over the past decade this region has been subject to a combination of changes which were themselves related to major political and economic shifts at the global level. The fall of the Berlin Wall in 1989 symbolizing the collapse of communism; the increasing pace of trade liberalization marked by the end of the Uruguay Round of the GATT negotiations in 1994 followed by the establishment of the World Trade Organization in 1995 and the subsequent downward pressure on tariffs; the further intensification of globalization inherent in the massive increase, during the early 1990s, of unrestricted flows of short-term capital around the world; and the huge acceleration in the speed of information flow brought about by the growth of the internet in the same period, all combined to change not only the environment in which the countries of Southern Africa operated but also the political and economic realities inside those countries themselves. At the same time the countries of the region have been at the forefront of a wide range of diverse attempts involving the state in tackling poverty.

Impact of Global Trends

For South Africa and Namibia the dramatic political changes of the early 1990s were accompanied by the no less profound economic changes inherent in the founding of the World Trade Organization, the huge increase in the transnational flows of capital, and in the information revolution epitomized by the exponential growth of the world wide web. Thus in Namibia, hard on the heels of independence in 1991, came mounting pressure for trade liberalization whose benefits were by no means clear to Africa in a world where the powerful OECD markets of Western Europe, North America and Japan maintained high levels of agricultural protection. And in South Africa there was the remarkable coincidence of the very month, April 1994, in which the country held its first democratic elections being the one in which the global agreement was signed in Marrakesh thus ending the Uruguay Round of trade negotiations and opening the door to the establishment of the World Trade Organization less than a year later.

Following a preoccupation with macro-economic stability and economic growth in the South in the 1980s, the 1990s saw a renewed focus on poverty reduction and social development. Although of course, as Dirk Hansohm and his colleagues make clear in their essay on Namibia in Chapter 9, all macro-economic issues such as trade policy must be carefully examined for their impact on poverty and inequality. The major agenda of many international inter-governmental meetings and UN conferences in the 1990s focused on social and environmental issues. Social policy at the national level, particularly in Africa in countries dependent on aid, has been increasingly shaped by global institutions. In the 1980s the World Bank played a major role in redefining the relationship between the state and the market in meeting social needs. In Chapter 7 the nature of the dialogue between the World Bank and the state in the formulation of poverty reduction strategies is examined by Nazneen Kanji in her critique of the Bank's policy in three countries of the region. Despite ongoing debates concerning the causes, there is consensus that social indicators stagnated or worsened and income inequalities increased in many countries in Africa during the implementation of structural adjustment packages, promoted and supported by the IMF and the World Bank.

In our increasingly globalized environment, the importance of global institutions has grown, with a wide spectrum of supra-national institutions, such as the UN, EU and NGOs such as Oxfam, attempting to influence social policies at the national and international levels. Definitions and strategies for social development continue to be a locus for political and ideological struggles, although there has been a marked shift away from the neo-liberal emphasis on economic growth and 'trickle down' to reduce poverty. An important critique of aid and its place in the structure of the international economy is made by Brigitte Schulz in Chapter 6, examining particularly the bilateral flows from Germany to Africa.

There is a range of views on the definition and scope of social policy. Some view it in a narrow sense, as state and NGO activity designed to intervene in the market, only when necessary, in the interests of social protection and social welfare. Others argue for a much wider perspective, where social policy is concerned with public action to address all social problems which are brought to national and international agendas by powerful interest groups (Wuyts et al. 1992). There is a parallel debate over poverty definitions with some definitions closely tied to lack of income and basic services while others argue strongly for a multidimensional view of poverty which includes the lack of economic, social, political and environmental assets and resources. In Chapter 8, Blandine Destremau shows how in Morocco the apparently technical question as to the definition of poverty can be used to evade or to confront the existence of vested interests whose analysis is, of course, fundamental to any implementation of effective anti-poverty policies.

A shift seems to occur away from residual approaches to social policy that recommend that limited public resources be targeted on the most needy sections of the population. Although there is no sign of a return to extensive involvement of the state in social welfare, the discourse which seems to be gathering strength is one that recommends pluralism and partnerships between the state, the private sector and civil society. The taxonomy of social development strategies discussed by Hartley Dean in Chapter 4 provides an extremely useful point of departure for understanding the strategies of individual countries in Africa, depending on historical context, social and political forces and the degree of influence of organizations such as the World Bank.

Despite the shifts, there is still a tendency both by governments in Africa and the international finance institutions to separate out economic and social policies and to underestimate the importance of the linkages. The realm of social policy tends to be confined to social services and social protection for 'vulnerable groups' rather than examining the social consequences of a range of economic policies which affect labour, land and other assets as well as the distribution of costs and benefits of particular development policies.

Still, the discourse on 'good governance' by Einar Braathen and Alessandro Palmero in Chapter 13 provides important linkages to a poverty reduction agenda. However, the question of how to 'mainstream' poverty issues into all other policies has not yet been fully dealt with, and the problems of operationalizing poverty as a key parameter for economic policy as suggested by the World Bank in its thrust for 'broad-based growth' has been controversial (see Chapter 7 by Nazneen Kanji).

While economists, led by the World Bank, have recently recognized the importance of social networks, trust and co-operation between people – increasingly called 'social capital' – the tendency is to emphasize its importance for economic growth processes and income poverty reduction in addition to 'physical' and 'human' capital. In other words, economic development is still often seen as a goal in itself rather than as a means to social development – the social well-being of the population as a whole. This is not to underestimate the importance of 'social capital' nor the concern that norms of reciprocity and sharing have been undermined by economic stress. Rather, it is to point out the danger of using 'social capital' as a new 'magic bullet' or missing ingredient for poverty reduction when the experience of the last few decades should have taught us that no such bullets exist!

All this shows that poverty is inextricably and structurally entwined with dimensions of power at the national and international levels. The role of the state cannot be glossed over in any analysis or action that seeks to move further in dealing with poverty reduction. But in any consideration of power or of the state it is necessary to understand the history and the particularities of each specific context.

Southern Africa: Differences and Commonalities

Table 1.1 helps to summarize some of the basic facts about the fourteen countries bound, albeit loosely, by their membership of the Southern African Development Community (SADC).

TABLE 1.1 Some characteristics of the fourteen countries of the SADC

Country	Population		Urban pop. (%)		GNP/cap. 1998		GNP/cap. growth (%) 1997/98	GNP/cap. av. annual growth (%) 1985–94	Gini index	HDI rank 1997	Life expectancy (at birth; years)	
	1998 (mil.)	dnsty[1]	1980	1998	$	@PPP[2]					1970	1997
Angola	12	10	21	33	340	840	4.8	-6.1	...	160	37.0	46.5 +
Botswana	2	3	15	68	3,600	8,310	3.5	6.6	...	122	51.6	47.4 –
Congo DR	48	21	29	30	110	750	0.7	-1.0	...	141	45.1	50.8 +
Lesotho	2	68	13	26	570	2,320	-5.4	0.6	56.0	127	48.4	56.0 +
Malawi	11	112	9	15	200	730	-0.7	-0.7	...	159	40.2	39.3 –
Mauritius	1	571	...	...	3,700	9,400	4.5	5.8	...	59	62.2	71.4 +
Mozambique	17	22	13	38	210	850	9.2	3.8	...	169	41.9	45.2 +
Namibia	2	2	23	39	1,940	4,950	-1.2	3.3	...	115	47.5	52.4 +
Seychelles	0.08	175	...	...	6,450	10,530	-1.3	4.8	...	66	...	...
South Africa	41	34	48	50	2,880	6,990	-1.2	-1.3	59.3	101	52.8	54.7 +
Swaziland	1	57	...	...	1,400	3,580	1.8	-1.2	...	113	45.9	60.2 +
Tanzania	32	36	15	26	210	490	0.6	0.8	38.2	156	45.3	47.9 +
Zambia	10	13	40	44	330	860	-4.0	-1.4	49.8	151	46.3	40.1 –
Zimbabwe	12	30	22	34	610	2,150	-2.2	-0.5	56.8	130	50.3	44.1 –
TOTAL	191											

Sources: World Development Reports 1996 and 1999/2000; Human Development Report 1999.

Notes: 1. Density per square kilometre.   2. Purchasing Power Parity

This table excludes far more than it includes but even so it serves to illustrate just how diverse are the countries on which we are focusing in even one region of the world. In terms of population the countries of the SADC range from the islands of the Seychelles with fewer than 100,000 inhabitants to the vast Congo (twice the area of South Africa) with 48 million persons. Population density per square kilometre ranges from two persons in arid Namibia to no fewer than 571 in Mauritius which is more than double that of Burundi and nearly 75 per cent higher than that of Rwanda whose densities are often seen as an underlying cause of the social explosions that have taken place there in recent years. The proportion of urban dwellers ranges from 15 per cent in Malawi to 68 per cent in Botswana which in percentage terms has, during the last quarter of the twentieth century, experienced one of the most rapid processes of urbanization in history. Measured in US dollars the per capita income (GNP) ranges from a low of $110 in the Democratic Republic of the Congo, via $2,880 in South Africa, to $6,450 in the Seychelles. The most recent growth rate, for the year 1997/98, ranged from −5.4 per cent for Lesotho, troubled by serious political instability leading to a controversial occupation by South African troops, to +9.2 per cent in Mozambique basking in the glow of peace and national reconstruction. Over the decade 1985–94, average annual growth rates varied between -6.1 per cent in Angola to +6.6 per cent in Botswana.

These growth rates do not, as we know, tell the whole story. In South Africa, for example, despite rapid growth in earlier decades the democratic government inherited a country with one of the highest levels of inequality in the world.[1] And in Botswana the rapid growth of average per capita income in the post-independence period has, thus far, masked the appalling impact of AIDS which has reduced life expectancy at birth in 1997 to four years *lower* than it was in 1970. In Zambia and Zimbabwe life expectancy over the same period was reduced by six years. Nor does there seem to be any end in sight, either for the countries where AIDS has already made its impact so visible nor in neighbouring countries, such as South Africa, where in 1999 all the signs point to a catastrophic epidemic in the near future.

It is perhaps useful to distinguish between those countries in the region which underwent fundamental political change during the post-Second World War process of decolonization before the disintegration of the Soviet Union in 1989 and those, such as Namibia and South Africa, for which the ending of the Cold War and a global shift in the balance of power was a prerequisite for the ending of racist rule by settler minorities. The post-colonial experience in the region has varied enormously: ranging from the independence of the Congo/Zaire in 1960, through Tanganyika/Tanzania

1961, Mozambique 1975 to Zimbabwe 1980; from Angola's unending civil war to Botswana's proud record of rapid and sustained economic growth combined with stable democratic government.

In Mozambique, for example, a combination of pressures from both the global and the grass-roots level led to the ending of the civil war in which destabilization by South Africa's apartheid forces had played such a destructive role. By the early 1990s Mozambique was all set on a post-war policy of reconstruction but in a global economic environment very different from the one fifteen years previously when a newly victorious Frelimo government had sought to pioneer a process of state-led 'national rebuilding' with the backing of a powerful Soviet Union.

In Zimbabwe the early political and economic successes of the democratically elected Mugabe government after 1980 in such areas as health, education and small-scale agriculture could not be sustained and, on adopting the IMF/World Bank's structural adjustment package (based largely on containment of state expenditure plus liberalization of trade), the conditions of the poor worsened, particularly in the 1990s.

Seen in this perspective, Southern Africa is not merely one small corner of the poorer part of the developing world tucked away at the bottom end of Africa. It contains within its boundaries many of the most significant opportunities, problems and contradictions with which nation-states, economic regions, and the world as a whole are grappling as people seek to come to terms with the reality and challenge of mass poverty at the beginning of the third millennium.

While they are different in so many ways, it is also important to recognize how much the countries of the SADC region have in common. If we exclude the special cases of the small island republics of Mauritius and the Seychelles, all the countries of the region, indeed of the entire continent, lie in the bottom range of countries ranked by their Human Development Index: from South Africa (101) to Mozambique (169) on a global list headed by Canada (1) and ending with Sierra Leone (174).

These countries share more than second-order ranking in the Human Development Report, though. Many of them were bound together not only by the investment flows and the lines of rail built to facilitate the extraction of minerals from the sub-continent to Western Europe and North America, but also by the intra-regional oscillating movement of workers caught in a long-term migrant labour system that drew workers to the single-sex mine compounds of the Witwatersrand from all over Southern Africa. As early as the mid-1890s no less than 60 per cent of the black workers on the gold mines came from Mozambique and over the next century tens of thousands of men came every year from south of the Save river to dig for gold. So, too, over the years, Lesotho, Malawi and other

TABLE 1.2 Geographical sources of African labour on mines affiliated to the South African Chamber of Mines, 1906–94

Country	1906		1936		1966		1986		1994	
	'000s	(%)	'000s	(%)	'000s	(%)	'000s	(%)	'000s	(%)
South Africa	18	23	166	52	131	34	315	60	203	55
Mozambique	53	65	88	28	109	28	58	10	51	14
Lesotho	2	3	46	15	64	17	109	20	87	24
Malawi etc.[1]	6	9	3	1	56	15	20	4	0	0
Botswana	0.3	0.4	7	2	19	5	20	4	12	3
Swaziland	0.6	0.7	7	2	4	1	14	3	15	4
TOTAL	81	100	318	100	383	100	536	100	368	100

Source: Chamber of Mines, Wenela, and Teba annual reports; South Africa Survey 1996/97, p. 356.

Note: 1. During much of the period between 1936 and 1966 migrant miners from 'North of Latitude 22° South' included men from Northern Rhodesia (Zambia), Tanganyika (Tanzania), South West Africa (Namibia) and (unofficially) Angola but by the mid-1960s almost all the 'tropicals' came from Malawi.

countries became locked in to the development of South Africa. Table 1.2 points to the extent to which labour flows helped bind the region together as a single economy.

This is not the place to analyse the impact of Southern Africa's peculiar system of oscillating migration on the overall pattern of development.[2] We pause simply to note three things: first, that its existence faced all the post-colonial, post-apartheid governments of the region with major dilemmas regarding transnational migration policy; second, that its impoverishing consequences added a major dimension to the challenges of economic development faced particularly by the 'sending' countries and provinces; and third that migrant labour forms, '[t]he key social link between the two spheres' of the bifurcated state (Mamdani 1996: 218; see also p. 190).

State Power

Mahmood Mamdani's seminal work, *Citizen and Subject* (1996), focuses particularly on South Africa's (internal) migrant workers to clarify his analysis of the legacy of late colonialism on contemporary Africa. Drawing on the consequences of the colonial experience for South Africa, Uganda and Kenya, Mamdani illuminates the importance of the distinction between the direct and indirect rule exerted by the colonial powers in Africa: 'Organized differently in rural areas from urban ones, the state was Janus-faced, bifurcated. It contained a duality: two forms of power under a single hegemonic authority. Urban power spoke the language of civil society and civil rights, rural power of community and culture' (p. 18). It is this duality, born of the common experience of colonialism, which the states of Southern Africa inherited and which confronts them with such a formidable challenge:

> The core agenda that African states faced at independence was three-fold: deracializing civil society, detribalizing the Native Authority, and developing the economy in the context of unequal international relations ... Of this threefold agenda, the task undertaken with the greatest success was deracialization ... the task undertaken with the least success was democratization ... The failure to democratize explains why deracialization was not sustainable and why development ultimately failed. (pp. 287–8)

This political failure is dealt with in three chapters in this book: by Archie Mafeje in his analysis of the predatory state (2); by Brian Raftopoulos in his examination of Zimbabwe (10); and by Braathen and Palermo in their discussion of Mozambique's recent history (13). The past decade has seen many contributions to the discussion of the state in Africa. There seems to be consensus that in general the state has impeded development and poverty reduction. This non-developmental state has been variously labelled as 'rent-seeking'; 'predatory'; 'patrimonial'; 'shadow'; 'balloon' and so on.[3] However, the weakness of these approaches is, first, that they tend to be based on Eurocentric ideal-types of state without due reference to the specific history and post-colonial agendas shaping the African state (Mamdani 1996: 11–12). Second, they take its coherence for granted, ignoring the differences across sectors and small periods of time. The state in Africa is usually a hybrid mixing 'progressive' and 'regressive' elements, combining pockets of effectiveness with tunnels of ineffectiveness, adapting 'modern' to 'traditional' logics and so forth. The notion of a neo-patrimonial state tries to recognize the mixed character of the state whose exact composition has to be ideographically analysed (Medard 1996).

Compared to states in the West, neo-patrimonial states tend to be weakly institutionalized in the sense that the public and private spheres are weakly separated. Bureaucratic and patrimonial norms co-exist. Although this kind of state is seldom as socially progressive as it pretends to be, it is able to extract and redistribute resources, but this extraction and redistribution is privatized. In redressing the colonial legacy of racially inherited privilege, the independent states (as argued by Mamdani 1996: 20–1) created a specific patrimonial path of redistribution which divided the indigenous majority along regional, religious, ethnic and at times familial lines. This privatization of public resources has three consequences (Medard 1996):

first, political-administrative power, instead of having the impersonal and abstract character of legal-rational domination associated with the modern state, is a personal power; second, politics becomes a kind of business for it is the acquisition of political resources that provide access to economic resources; third, mass politics is structured around vertical clientistic relationships. In sum, the result is authoritarian and incompetent states that rarely respond to public pressure. Furthermore, corruption – in the use of formal political institutions for personal gain – is endemic in the way politics is practised (Mamdani 1996).

It is the insight into the role of undemocratic and corrupt political structures which helps to explain the emerging insistence in the region on 'pro-poor governance'. In addition to the three chapters mentioned above, the chapters focusing on Botswana and on South Africa, by Kenneth Good (3), Arnon Bar-On (12), Charity Kerapeletswe and Tsholofelo Moremi (11), Julian May (14) and Debbie Budlender (15) have a good deal to say on issues related to governance in particular with regard to the participatory role of poor people themselves in efforts to reduce poverty. In Mozambique, South Africa, Botswana and Zimbabwe this emphasis lies at the heart of the emerging critiques of state policy. Good and Bar-On in their quite different chapters both focus particularly on the dangers of the gulf emerging in both South Africa and Botswana between the ruling elite and those who remain poor. The issues of 'governance' and of 'citizenship' represent two different but complementary approaches to the reform of African policy-making, as explained below.

The analysis of power is fundamental to any examination of poverty and the two chapters concerned with countries far outside the SADC – Morocco in North Africa and Mexico in Latin America – were included specifically because they illustrate the importance of this understanding. Camilo Perez-Bustillo (5) uses the Mexican experience to illustrate the importance (and shortcomings) of Mamdani's analysis.[4] Perez-Bustillo's essay is particularly interesting for showing how the insights gained from analysing the inability of so many postcolonial African states to play a constructive role in the reduction of poverty can be used in Latin America and then further sharpened.

Issues of power and representation are critical here: whose views are represented at decision-making levels? This leads directly into a consideration of governance structures and citizen participation.

Governance

Whose problems are included and whose are excluded? Which groups are marginalized in particular contexts, in relation to identities based on class, race, ethnicity and/or gender? As Deacon et al.(1997) point out, the influence of postmodernism has highlighted the tension between the universalism of social policy analysts and a new sensitivity to diversity and difference; the challenge is to facilitate the universal meeting of diverse human needs. More than economic growth and social stability is required. Pro-poor governance it is argued must also include dimensions of equity, institution-building, and 'poor people's participation in the definition of public policy and resources allocation'.[5]

People are more powerful and effective in influencing policy when socially organized, and organizations of civil society are increasingly seen by international development agencies as important to keep governments accountable and transparent. In Southern Africa, how strong and how inclusive are civil society organizations?

A pessimistic view, voiced for example by Edwards (1999), is that with the exception of South Africa and a few others, African societies lack intermediary organizations to link the grass roots with government, impeding communication, transparency and accountability. This situation deprives states of information to make decisions, erodes the capacity of civil society to act as a counterweight to wayward government and does not give support to policy-makers who face tough choices.

In a more optimistic vein, democratic decentralization, as discussed in the essay on Mozambique (see Chapter 13), shows how state action might provide such links through local self-government, and create public arenas and agendas that are closer to people's social realities.

In South Africa, civil society was well organized in the struggle against apartheid and the chapters on South Africa in this book provide examples of productive partnerships between government and civil society since 1994, as well as warning us that the situation is changing with dangers of co-option – as Budlender points out in her discussion of the Women's Budget Initiative. Both Julian May in his overview of the impact of the Reconstruction and Development Programme and Christian Rogerson in his assessment of the Mandela government's pro-poor urban strategy point to important lessons that can be learnt from the successes and failures of the latter half of the 1990s.

NGOs have mushroomed in Southern Africa over the past fifteen years but many are too dependent on foreign aid and very involved in delivering services to be of much use in keeping states accountable. On the other hand, Raftopolous's chapter on Zimbabwe (10) provides a useful discussion of coalitions of civil society organizations which pressure government on specific policies and programmes. There is a growing body of evidence that organizations of civil society have provided a 'voice' for people living in poverty as well as supporting their immediate needs for livelihoods.

However, a single emphasis on strengthening the role of civil society without disaggregating and understanding the huge variation in organizations of civil society, might only produce a cheap and 'safety-net'-oriented substitute for effective public policy.

Active partnerships for poverty reduction require, as Kanji argues in Chapter 7, a change in the mind-set and organizational culture of international as well as national development agencies, where the more powerful agencies, in particular, have to be prepared to engage in dialogue rather than policy prescription and to apply the same rules of accountability and transparency to themselves as they do to states in Southern Africa.

Above all, it requires commitment to a new, universal approach to citizenship rights.

Citizenship

In this volume Dean's and Perez-Bustillo's chapters explore the nature of citizenship and examine which groups are included and excluded from citizenship rights. 'Those who would address poverty in contemporary Africa', writes Dean, 'can no more avoid the relevance of citizenship (and its social dimension) as a concept than they can deny the power of transnational capital.' An important point made by Dean, based on empirical research, is that human experience of global capitalism creates conditions in which people's implicit preferences are for security against poverty, not freedom to become rich. Bustillo deals with cultural conceptions of citizenship but culture is not viewed as a static phenomenon but as dynamic and reflecting differences in power at community level. This point is also explored by Bar-On in discussing Botswana.

Apart from the chapter by Budlender, one issue which is only touched on in this book is a gender perspective on citizenship. It has been argued elsewhere[6] that the construction of citizenship is based on participation in the public sphere – participation in the labour market is a key to social citizenship rights. This immediately poses problems for women because of the unequal division of labour between women and men in so many societies and the fact that women have to balance responsibilities in the private sphere with their involvement in earning an income in the public arena. Time is a resource for citizenship and for most women, particularly low-income women, time is a scarce commodity. In most countries in the world, we are a long way from equal citizenship rights for mothers and carers and formal political systems which are accessible to informal political groupings.

Certainly, a tendency on the part of both development agencies and many academics to romanticize civil society ignores the reality of fundamentalists and anti-democratic groups. This is because civil society is treated as if it has nothing to do with citizenship and the political, social, cultural and economic rights of every citizen and group.

Conclusion

And so we return to a question with which we began. Is the state in Africa part of the solution or part of the problem? Or, to put it another way, is the social stagnation in Africa, from the point of view of an individual state, during the so-called 'lost decades' of the 1980s and 1990s best understood as having been caused by external or internal factors? How do the global economic structures and processes (on the one hand) and the national political–institutional structures and processes (on the other) affect each other? Contrary to the usual stereotype of North–South discussions, it is worth noting that, in the chapters dealing with this issue, it is the author from the South (Mafeje) with his focus on the 'predatory state' who emphasizes internal political factors while the author from the North (Schulz) underlines the external global factors. Indeed, there is truth in both arguments and we need to move beyond the simple either–or dichotomy of North vs South in analysing these questions. There is no doubt of the asymmetry in various power relations across the North–South divide. The terms of trade; the context of loans and indebtedness; the rules of the game as played by the multinational corporations are all strongly influenced by the vested interests of powerful coalitions based in the North. But we cannot ignore how these vested interests are supported, voluntarily or involuntarily, by internal social and economic forces within countries in the South. In many of the modern postcolonial states of the South dominant groups have become entrenched. They have found autonomous arenas and instruments to adapt to the existing pattern of global interdependence in ways that are beneficial to themselves. Finally, in order not to lose sight of the complexity of the full picture, it is important to take note of two other obvious aspects of the reality: first, the existence of poverty and inequality in North as well as South; and second, the diversity of the interactions between North and South that have created many different networks that pursue competing goals and agendas.

The evidence from Southern Africa suggests that even when state pro-poor policies are relatively well-developed, their successful implementation is dependent on wider social and cultural forces and the degree of their 'embeddedness' in a specific society. Institutional factors are critical. Nor can pro-poor policies at the national level be effective if global economic pressures force states, in order to stay competitive, to eliminate the costs of ensuring social development. In other words, pro-poor policies have to take account of factors at both the local and the global level.

It is tempting at this point simply to say that new strategies are essential and to echo what is fast becoming a cliché concerning the need for a third way, between state-led and market-led development. It is perhaps more useful if less dramatic to focus attention on the detail in the chapters that follow. While active citizenship and partnerships are critical in developing the nature and viability of a 'third way' into the new millennium, the most important lesson perhaps is as much about the need for sustained implementation of equitable social policies as it is about the need for 'new' policies.

Notes

1. The Gini Coefficient ranged from 39 per cent (0.39) in Tanzania to 59 per cent (0.59) in South Africa.

2. See, for example, Wilson and Ramphele 1989: 198–201.

3. For an assessment of the various contributions see Chapter 1 in Braathen et al. (eds) 1999, upon which our analysis of the neo-patrimonial state draws.

4. See the discussion by Dean in Chapter 4.

5. See Chapter 13 by Braathen and Palmero.

6. See, for example, Lister 1997.

References

Braathen, E., M. Bøås and G. Sather (eds) (1999) *Ethnicity Kills? The Politics of War, Peace and Ethnicity in Sub-Saharan Africa.* London: Macmillan.

Deacon, Bob with Michelle Hulse and Paul Sutton (1997) *Global Social Policy: International Organisations and the Future of Welfare.* Beverly Hills, CA: Sage.

Edwards, Michael (1999) *Future Positive: International Cooperation in the 21st Century.* London: Earthscan.

Lister, Ruth (1997) *Citizenship: Feminist Perspectives* London: Macmillan.

Mamdani, Mahmood (1996) *Citizen and Subject: Contemporary Africa and the Legacy of Late Colonialism.* Kampala: Fountain Publishers; Cape Town: David Philip; London: James Currey.

Medard, Jean-François (1996) 'Patrimonialism, Patrimonialization, Neo-Patrimonialism and the Study of the Post-Colonial State in Subsaharan Africa', in Henrick Secher Marcussen (ed.), *Improved Natural Resource Management: The Role of Formal Organisations in Informal Networks and Institutions.* Occasional Paper no. 17, Roskilde University, Denmark.

Wilson, F. and M. Ramphele (1989) *Uprooting Poverty: The South African Challenge* New York: W. W. Norton.

Wuyts, Marc, Maureen Mackintosh and Tom Hewitt (1992) *Development Policy and Public Action.* Oxford: Oxford University Press and Open University.

2

Conceptual and Philosophical Predispositions

Archie Mafeje

In the wake of globalization processes which have engulfed the modern world, it has become imperative for those who wish to deconstruct hegemonic forms of knowledge and conceptions of reality to interrogate them in a sustained way with the intention of making authentic representations, and of instituting original research protocols and new and more liberating ways of doing things. Putting aside the question of whether we can with equanimity speak of the 'state' in sub-Saharan Africa, it would appear that what is at stake is 'poverty alleviation' and the role therein of the powers that be, irrespective of whether in common parlance they pass as 'states' or 'governments'. Like any other concept, 'poverty alleviation' has its own social history and genesis. Accordingly, it would be more than appropriate to try and contextualize it before we discuss its applicability or otherwise in an economic and political setting such as obtains in Africa today.

Intellectually and programmatically, the evolution of development policies within the international community and the identification of target groups provide a background against which to measure progress, if any, and to evaluate current practice which might be at variance with professed objectives or simply inadequate or even misconceived. In this regard, it is important to note that the development of the concept of 'poverty alleviation' was a result of disillusionment with 'trickle-down' theories of the 1960s. These supposed that development at the national level would automatically improve the well-being of all sections of the population. Experience soon showed that even in those cases in the Third World where growth occurred, by and large it did not benefit the poor. In sub-Saharan African the situation was doubly worse. Not only have the economies stagnated since the end of the 1960s but more ominously the number of people who live in absolute poverty increased rapidly. The latter was true of Latin America and most of Asia as well, despite measurable growth. This led in the late 1970s to the recognition of 'poverty alleviation' as a development objective in itself.

This was first articulated by the UN agencies and found its most concrete expression in the ILO World Employment Programme which was inaugurated in 1976 and which emphasized the need to promote the productive capacity of the poor. Likewise, in 1977 IFAD was given a special mandate to 'increase food production, reduce undernutrition and alleviate rural poverty'. These new policy perspectives were crowned by the FAO World Conference on Agrarian Reform and Rural Development (WCARRD) which was convened in Rome in July, 1979 to discuss 'the global problem of poverty and hunger'. In the ensuing Declaration of Principles and Programme of Action, the FAO was mandated to develop strategies and programmes for dealing with the problem. These were consolidated in the well-known FAO document, the Peasants' Charter (1981), which aimed to promote equity and popular participation in development. These new policy orientations within the UN family coincided with the advocacy of equal rights for the small producers by the World Bank under the leadership of the redoubtable Robert McNamara in the late 1970s. It is, therefore, observable that by the end of the decade there was some unanimity between the UN agencies and the World Bank.

However, this did not last long. As the economic and agricultural crisis deepened, at least in Africa during the 1980s, a critical divergence in policy between the World Bank and the UN agencies emerged. This was precipitated by the introduction of the Structural Adjustment Programmes (SAPs) in Africa from the beginning of the 1980s. The SAPs effectively reversed the previous philosophical trend towards equity and solicitude for the poor by putting at the centre of its programmes not people but 'market forces'. For Africa the necessary rationalizations for such a dramatic change of policy had been provided in the famous Berg Report, *Accelerated Development in Sub-Saharan Africa: An Agenda for Action* (World Bank 1981). By betting on the economically strong and by arguing against any affirmative action by African governments, the World Bank was in fact forsaking the small producers and the poor and reverting to the old orthodoxy of 'trickle-down' theories or use of macro-economic indices for measuring development. All this proved extremely controversial and overwhelming in its impact.

The Berg Report was an intended negation of the strategy and ameliorative policy objectives proposed by African governments in the Lagos Plan of Action in 1980. African governments, most of which were under severe pressure nationally and internationally, were aware of this but most were unwilling to forgo the loans offered by the World Bank, despite their conditionality. Nevertheless, by 1989 disenchantment with the SAPs had begun. In a high-level conference convened by the Economic Commission for Africa (ECA) in Addis Ababa in April 1989, attendant

African ministers of economic planning expressed dissatisfaction with the programmes and protested that they were 'at variance with African reality'. This is as if African governments had not had sufficient warning from disinterested observers or had not been offered alternative strategies. Most significant among the latter were the United Nations Programme of Action for African Economic Recovery and Development (UN-PAAERD) 1986–90 and the FAO strategic document, *African Agriculture: The Next 25 Years* (1986). The original concern with the plight of small producers and the poor had been maintained in the development perspective projected in these documents. As such, they represented an implicit critique of the SAPs of the World Bank. They were soon followed by explicit critiques of the World Bank programmes, among which was the Khartoum Declaration of 1988 which emphasized the 'human dimension of Africa's economic recovery and development'. Of particular concern here were what were described as 'vulnerable groups', meaning women and children, under the influence of UNICEF.

Appropriately enough, and for the first time, the most devastating critique of the World Bank SAPs came from the ECA when it launched its alternative proposal in 1989 in a document entitled *African Alternative Framework to Structural Adjustment Programmes for Socio-Economic Recovery and Transformation* (AAF-SAP). The document constituted a direct intellectual and political challenge to the World Bank and served as a reminder to African governments not to have abandoned the Lagos Plan of Action. It urged African governments to ensure development with equity on the continent. In an accompanying technical document, entitled *Statistics and Policies* (1989), it disputed the scientific claims of the World Bank regarding 'adjusting countries' in Africa. Using weighted averages and 1980 as the baseline, instead of the unweighted averages used by the World Bank and 1985 (an exceptionally good year) as its baseline, the ECA was able to show that 'during 1980–1987 the performance of Sub-Saharan African countries with strong SAPs was the worst of any group; a negative annual average growth rate of 0.53 percent contrasted with a positive 2.00 percent for countries with weak structural adjustment programmes and a relatively strong positive rate of 3.5 percent for non-adjusting countries in Sub-Saharan Africa'.

It is fashionable nowadays to refer to the 1980s as the 'lost decade' in African development. But, given the findings of the ECA which the World Bank was never able to refute, it is clear that the loss was not entirely attributable to policy choices made by Africans. Instead, the indications are that, if the African governments had been guided by the Lagos Plan of Action in their policy orientations, all might not have been lost. However, the importance of the ECA intervention is that not only did it reaffirm what African governments thought in 1980 but also succeeded in putting back on the agenda the issue of growth with equity in Africa.

Unable to blunt these African initiatives, and as a response to the ECA public criticism of its programmes, the World Bank found it expedient to modify its stance in a policy document entitled *Poverty, Adjustment, and Growth in Africa* (1989). Although initially this was offered as a palliative to its critics, the World Bank had as yet to face the more fundamental question in the 1990s as to whether its SAPs in Africa were at all redeemable.

Since the end of the 1980s there has been a growing consensus that the World Bank's SAPs have been an unmitigated failure in Africa, in that they did not bring about any visible economic growth and far from alleviating poverty they increased it. This was partly due to the conditionality of the IMF which hurt the most vulnerable groups, as they lost any benefits they might have been deriving from government subsidies. While there is a general agreement on the evaluation of the SAPs, there is however lack of consensus on the underlying causes of their failure. The general view among African intellectuals and governments, despite apparent compliance by most in the 1980s, is that the SAPs are misconceived in that they seek to apply Euro-American development models in Africa. It is claimed that this is particularly true with reference to the role of the state in development and to agricultural/agrarian policies in particular.

Consequently, there is now an insistence on the role of a democratic developmental state in Africa (ADB 1995) and a persistent warning against unstudied individualization of land rights and of agricultural production under African social conditions. This view is not shared by those who uphold the validity of the neo-classical economic model of development and who attribute the failure of the SAPs largely to severe macro-economic disequilibria in African economies and general lack of technical skills for forging appropriate policy instruments in Africa, as compared to Asia and Latin America (Lele 1987). This is an issue which might be worth addressing independently of the fate of the SAPs since there is ample evidence of economic mismanagement by African governments since the end of the 1960s. Whether this in itself is proof of the technical incompetence of African technocrats, who after thirty years of independence are still playing second fiddle to consultants and experts from the North, is hard to say. In turn and apart from possible political domination, this could also be a reflection of the lack of the necessary intellectual clarity and political commitment among African leaders.

In the context of the above review, it would be interesting to find out precisely when and why CROP adopted the concept of 'poverty alleviation', though it is doubtful that it could have arisen outside the intellectual and philosophical/ideological climate which prevailed from the late 1970s to the early 1990s in the international community which, as is known, is dominated by the North. But it has to be acknowledged that even the northern pace-setters move at different speeds and often respond to different impulses within their immediate socio-political environments. For instance, it is obvious that there are differences in the philosophical/ideological assumptions which underlie the World Bank/IMF 'poverty alleviation' programmes and those of the neo-liberals within the UN system, and between the Social Democrats and Christian Democrats in Europe. However, these are never aired openly in international arenas since they could be a source of embarrassment and it might prove unpolitic to broach them. If we were to fail to do so even in academic fora, however, then there would be no future for us as intellectuals or scientists.

Looked at from the African perspective, the concept of 'poverty alleviation' is a reflection of social imperatives in *developed* countries and a culmination of the rise of the welfare state, especially in Western Europe. Nevertheless, its antecedents are to be found in the reaction against the great depression of the 1930s and the large-scale deprivation caused by the Second World War. It took the genius of Lord Keynes to point out that mass poverty was a liability in a developed economy in so far as it restricted the 'propensity to consume' among the majority of the population. If this is the economic foundation of the welfare state, as one suspects, then 'poverty alleviation' in affluent societies in which labour productivity is so high that it underwrites the 'propensity' of the great majority of the citizens to consume, then 'poverty alleviation' becomes nothing more than a mopping-up operation, namely, guaranteeing a decent livelihood for the lowest 20 per cent of the lower 20 per cent of the population i.e. 4 per cent according to Professor Solomon Cohen, a mathematician at Erasmus University (former Rotterdam School of Economics). From this perspective, 'poverty alleviation' is at best a product of welfare economics and at worst charitable neo-liberalism. Logically, the latter has to be so because the term 'alleviate' means to lessen, or make less severe, pain or suffering and assumes the existence of the wherewithal to do so. But, then, can we assume economic development universally?

Given the general state of underdevelopment outside Western Europe, North America and now South-East Asia, the answer to the above question must be 'No'. This in itself became a rationalization for the adoption of ameliorative policies by the developed countries or the so-called international community. In some ways this is a perverse reaction because it evades the problem of uneven development among nations and within nations. As far back as 1977 when I worked as a consultant to the Division for Development in Africa (DDFA) in FAO, I questioned the philosophical and practical implications of the concept of 'poverty alleviation' among agencies whose mandate was to promote development, especially in under-developed countries. I was told by the chiefs in FAO that it was best to ameliorate poverty as far as possible while waiting for development to occur. In practice, over the last twenty years neither poverty alleviation nor development has occurred in Africa, Latin America and South Asia.

According to the World Bank (1990), in 1985 an estimated 1,115 million people in developing countries lived in poverty i.e. about one-third of the total population of the developing countries. Nearly half of these lived in South Asia, but sub-Saharan Africa had about one-third as many poor people. Its share of the poor rose from about 16 per cent in the 1960s to 35 per cent in 1985. Worse still, it is estimated that by the year 2000 out of a total population of 410 million as many as 280 million people will live in poverty in the region. The Middle Eastern and North African countries have the next highest rate of poverty, followed by Latin America, the Caribbean and East Asia. Interestingly enough, this leaves out only one area in the Third World, South-East Asia, which, as is known, is the fastest developing region in the world and it is expected that it would have 'eliminated' poverty by the end of the century. Even if I, like the devil, quote the Bible for my own purposes, the inescapable conclusion that can be drawn from these figures is that poverty breeds poverty and that, as the example of South-East Asia shows, pervasive poverty is not a problem of amelioration but of development. Herein lies the difference between petty-reformism and radical change.

From 'Poverty Alleviation' to 'Poverty Eradication'

In human societies there is a greater predisposition towards petty-reformism or continuity than towards radical change, which often threatens instability and, therefore, a general sense of insecurity. This is particularly true of those groups or classes which enjoy hegemonic power nationally and internationally. Almost as an ideological reflex, opinion-leaders from the West often spurn anything that smacks of radicalism. Yet, radical and at times ruthless reforms is what brought western countries to a super-ordinate position. Therefore, it can be said that despite the tendency towards conservatism in society, under certain circumstances radical change can be the only way to guarantee that which is denied and to release latent social energies.

Although conjecturally it might appear that the necessity for change is a result of an impersonal dialectic between a variety of social, political and economic factors, in reality its subjects are those who are frustrated by present social existence or are its objects. In this sense new policy depar-tures or significant shifts in conventional paradigms are a reflection of underlying social struggles. The implicit argument here is that shifts in intellectual paradigms are neither accidental nor due to factors which are internal to them, as Thomas Kuhn suggested as far back as 1962. Therefore, it is of great relevance to contemplate the question why the international community, in the form of the UN and through the agency of UNDP, after twenty years of experience has shifted from the paradigm of 'poverty alleviation' to 'poverty eradication' as proclaimed by UNDP in 1997.

The immediate reason for the Gestalt-shift on the part of the international community is undoubtedly failure and the concomitant political/ideological pressures for the preferred model of development in the West to justify itself. According to the IFAD report on *The State of World Rural Poverty* (1992), nowhere in the Third World have the 'poverty alleviation' programmes, as were originally conceived, realized their objectives, namely, poverty amelioration and redistributive justice. Instead, rural poverty continued to rise, except in the new industrializing countries (NICs) of South-East Asia. In the meantime, the World Bank in its 1990 report on poverty had acknowledged that in sub-Saharan Africa, East Asia and Latin America poverty had either dramatically or significantly increased between the 1960s and 1980s; and that in the Middle East and Western Europe the situation 'more or less remained unchanged' (no specific reference was made to the USA which of all the developed countries has the dubious distinction of having the highest and still growing rate of absolute poverty).

The Bretton Woods institutions themselves had recognized (not to say acknowledged) the failure by the end of the 1980s. In 1989 the IMF, in its publication *World Economic Outlook*, introduced the concept of 'high quality growth' which laid emphasis on 'equitable growth', paying particular attention to the plight of the poor and vulnerable groups. To this end, the IMF took the initiative to open a dialogue with the UN agencies which were becoming increasingly critical of the development policies of the two Bretton Woods institutions. Reflecting the same mood, in the same year as the IMF the World Bank published its well-known capitulation document, *Poverty, Adjustment, and Growth in Africa*. These new policy departures were most welcome by the UN agencies, as is clearly shown by the UNDP *Human Development Reports* of 1990 and 1991.

It is not at all surprising, therefore, that in 1997 the UNDP can with confidence fly high banners declaring the death of 'poverty alleviation' programmes and the inauguration of 'poverty eradication' programmes which emphasize the role of the poor themselves in the process. This change of paradigm had already been anticipated by some of the UN agencies, notably IFAD and ILO. In touting what it called the 'new paradigm', IFAD declared in its 1992 *World Rural Poverty* report:

The new development paradigm conceives of poverty alleviation not just as a mechanism to get the poor to cross a given threshold of income or consumption, but as a sustained increase in productivity and an integration of the poor into the process of growth. For this, the poor must have access to resources, and the policy and institutional framework should be such as to enable them to utilise resources effectively. (IFAD 1992: 20; emphasis in the original)

Interestingly enough, this is reminiscent of Mojca Novak's review of the poverty concepts used by African contributors in the *Handbook on International Poverty Research* published by CROP in 1996. This is what she had to say:

More specifically, it has been argued that the poverty concepts employed should transcend the limitation to the micro level, which focuses primarily on personal income and expenditure. Poverty should be seen in the context of access to all forms of resources and facilities provided by or within a nation, and therefore socio-economic factors ought to be taken into consideration as well. The macro-level perspective of poverty conceptualization may not have matured. As a criticism, however, it may accelerate productive development in this respect. (Novak 1996: 56)

While in its text IFAD used 'poverty alleviation' and 'poverty elimination' interchangeably, it is clear that it was adopting a developmentalist approach with the underdeveloped countries in mind and by advocating mobilization of the poor for enhanced production in the belief that 'the gap between the potential and actual productivity of the rural poor is much greater than that of the non-poor'. The ILO, which in its World Employment Programme had been straining at the leash under the impact of the SAPs, simply advanced creation of employment opportunities for the poor and the unemployed as the best way of 'alleviating' poverty. Even so, it took the ILO a very long time to recognize that self-employment in the 'informal sector' was another way of creating employment opportunities, provided the poor have a *choice* between selling their labour-power or using it on their own behalf, without any threat to their livelihood. The latter could come in the form of denial of access to resources, legal restrictions, lack of infrastructure and supporting services. Yet, in the present economic and political crisis in sub-Saharan Africa this is the fastest-growing sector in most countries (Mafeje and Radwan 1995).

It is apparent that the Gestalt-shift from the 'poverty alleviation' to the 'poverty eradication' paradigm was the culmination of much discussion in high places within the international community. It is not clear to what extent the academic community was involved in the process. Those engaged in poverty research, such as the CROP network, might be able to enlighten us. In the meantime, we note that from the beginning of the millennium 'poverty eradication' is the buzz-word within the international community. Although it is predictable that the Bretton Woods institutions and the UN agencies will not, as in the case of 'poverty alleviation', bring about any 'poverty eradication', there are no immediate theoretical and philosophical objections to the notion of 'poverty eradication' at this stage of human and technological development. Indeed, it is an affirmation of the moral principle cherished by socialists and social democrats. In the circumstances it would be a pity if the pragmatism of 'poverty alleviation' advocates leads to the confirmation of the capitalist natural theology that inequity and a certain amount of poverty are inevitable in human societies. On the contrary, it is arguable that in modern societies 'poverty eradication' is within the realm of the possible. For the affluent societies this is almost a truism and for the underdeveloped countries it is an aspiration worth working for. What remains is the social question of agency. Who will do it? It is fair to state that while the Bretton Woods institutions and the UN agencies will not do it or are not in position to do it, by sanctioning a more enabling social and political environment, however reluctantly, they create opportunities for those who are motivated to bring about genuine change. In the normal run of things these would be socially disadvantaged people and their representatives or governments. Here, we enter a difficult and treacherous terrain, namely, the question of class interests. The interests of governments and of different classes and leaderships in society do not necessarily coincide. It is with this view in mind that we approach the question of the role of the state in 'poverty alleviation' in Africa.

The Role of the State in 'Poverty Alleviation' in Africa

For the purposes of this chapter I will assume the existence of a state and governance in Africa. Universally, the modern state is held responsible for the well-being and welfare of its citizens. Traditionally, this takes the form of social services. Otherwise, it was only under the welfare state that these services were extended to employment creation in the guise of indicative planning and welfare benefits for the poor. Indeed, under classical capitalism these two functions were regarded as the province of the private sector, namely, entrepreneurs and charitable organizations, the church in particular.

Consequently, in spite of the effective intervention of the welfare state during the post-Second World War economic boom in Western Europe, the belief that these were not rights but only charitable interventions which were dispensable under certain conditions persisted. In the last two decades this is best exemplified by the rise of Thatcherism and Reagonomics, and the dismantling of the welfare state by the Christian Democrats/Conservatives in Western Europe under conditions of recurrent economic recessions since 1966. It is conceivable that the crusade for 'poverty alleviation' since the late 1970s was not only an assertion of the rights of the poor but also a rearguard action against the economic policies of the Right in the West. The neo-liberals and social democrats in Western Europe (not in America which is for all intents and purposes a philosophical desert) are acutely aware of this but in general have been forced into a retreat. On the other hand, the international community has so far adopted a stoic stance precisely because there is a bigger world to save from alienation under the New World Order.

Needless to say, African states are hardly involved in these debates and boast of no national 'poverty alleviation' programmes, except Botswana. Even Botswana is a doubtful case in the long run because it relied on surplus revenues to ameliorate poverty, especially in the rural areas, without addressing fully the issue of increased and sustained productivity among the rural poor as part of the agrarian question. According to the evidence gleaned from recent studies (as yet unpublished) by some Botswana researchers, such as Drs O. Selolwane, P. Molutsi and I. Mazonde, it is clear that poverty in rural Botswana has increased to a point where some villages have totally lost economic viability and social cohesion due to lack of access to any productive resources under changed demographic conditions. Worse still, as a perverse reaction, in some instances receiving 'poverty allowances' is gradually becoming a way of life preferable to eking out a meagre livelihood under conditions in which returns to labour have fallen far below tolerable limits.

It transpires, therefore, that if in the short run the 'poverty alleviation' programmes of the Botswana government had proved successful, in the long run they offered no lasting solution to the problem of rural underdevelopment and increasing rural poverty. This was to be expected because of lack of real investment in agriculture and overdependence on minerals. According to the World Bank (1990), during the diamond boom in the 1980s when the economy was growing at an annual rate of 15 per cent, Botswana registered an annual growth of -0.6 per cent in agriculture. In its 1986 survey, *African Agriculture: The Next 25 Years*, FAO reported the same (-0.7 per cent). In the present circumstances in which diamonds have proved not to be for ever, correcting such a palpable structural distortion might prove intractable, given especially the unfavourable climatic and ecological conditions in Botswana.

As far as other sub-Saharan states are concerned, there is no evidence that any of them has initiated national 'poverty alleviation' programmes since their inception twenty years ago. A few responsive governments among them adopted what may be called egalitarian policies whereby they tried to combine growth with equity. Among these may be mentioned Tanzania, Uganda and Burkina Faso during Sakara's short-lived regime. This model was not favoured by the West because, according to its neo-classical orthodoxy, it retarded the development of market forces and hindered rapid capital accumulation. In the case of Tanzania it took the IMF six years to whip Nyerere's government into line (Singh 1986). But the same policies which were severely condemned in the wake of the SAPs are now implicit in the newly evolved concept of 'poverty eradication'. Indeed, as was mentioned earlier, since the end of the 'lost decade' in Africa the IMF and the World Bank have been making similar noises. Both have been courting Museveni's government whose country has shown a steady annual growth rate of 5–6 per cent since the mid-1980s, of which 40 per cent is accounted for by rapid growth in the informal sector (Livingstone 1992). This raises questions about the sincerity of the Bretton Woods institutions and about the validity of their previous arguments against policies which aim at promoting growth with equity. Or has the change in the ideological climate since the collapse of Eastern European socialism rendered such questions irrelevant?

On the whole, it is not surprising that most African states did not institute any 'poverty alleviation' programmes or adopt egalitarian develop-ment policies. Most of them are underdeveloped dictatorships whose economies have experienced a growing problem of accumulation since 1969 which reached critical proportions in 1979 when virtually all sub-Saharan economies (with the exception of Botswana and Gabon) experienced negative growth. Hardly any surpluses existed for financing development and social services, let alone 'poverty alleviation'. Competition for access to scarce resources among the ruling elites degenerated into a succession of *coups d'état* from 1969 onwards. In the 1980s and 1990s this erupted into bloody civil wars in several African countries. Under these conditions, columns of refugees, starvation and death became an indelible part of the African scene. In the circumstances the role of the state in 'poverty alleviation' had become totally untenable, an illusion born under different skies. In reality, what the African peoples, poor or not so poor, are faced with is a predatory state which is preoccupied with its own survival. Therefore, any amelioration or transformation of the conditions of life in Africa presupposes the emergence of a democratic state.

Even if for the sake of argument we were to imagine that we could find some benevolent dictators in Africa, at this historical juncture we would still be confronted with insurmountable economic problems. African countries are generally poor with per capita incomes ranging between 200 and 300 US dollars (Botswana and Gabon are the only two exceptions to have broken the $1,000 threshold). According to the World Bank (1994), thirty-two of the forty-seven poorest countries in the world are in sub-Saharan Africa, i.e. about two-thirds of the countries in black Africa. Universally, sub-Saharan Africans have no *real* wealth, i.e. money which makes money. They are all still caught up in the cycle of primitive accumulation from commodity–money–commodity. Among other things, this means that even the better-off Africans hardly invest; instead, they indulge in conspicuous consumption. At the state level they have displayed a singular lack of ability to convert surplus revenues (where they exist in the mineral-rich countries, including Botswana) into *capital*. As a reflection of the same inability, the productive sectors of their economies such as agriculture/pastoralism and nascent industry are marked by very low labour productivity. A combination of these disabilities has rendered African economies unviable and highly susceptible to negative external economies.

It is a striking anomaly that after nearly forty years of independence sub-Saharan Africa is bereft of any national bourgeoisie which is capable of reproducing itself socially by augmenting added-value and not by relentless plunder of state revenues. The negative impact of all these social aberrations is that at the present historical juncture there is a near collapse of state and economy in most of sub-Saharan Africa. In 1990 the World Bank summed up the situation as follows: 'In Sub-Saharan Africa per capita incomes are not likely to rise in the first half of the decade, although growth of about 1 percent a year is forecast for 1995–2000. The combination of low income growth and high fertility rates implies that the number of poor in the region is likely to swell rapidly' (World Bank 1990: 16). Thus, 'poverty alleviation' is out of reach for most African countries and as such does not even enter the considerations of their embattled regimes.

What of 'Poverty Eradication'?

The above critique could easily be interpreted as a confirmation of the Afro-pessimism which is so rampant within the international community and press. This would be a big mistake for there are grounds for believing that of all the undeveloped regions, Africa is in the best position to eradicate poverty. At stake here is the conception of different alternatives for development and the social meaning of what is called 'resources'. At the physical level sub-Saharan Africa is the best-endowed region in mineral resources and has the most favourable (wo)man/land ratio in the world, notwithstanding the fact that in general its soils have a relatively low carrying capacity (FAO 1986). Socially, sub-Saharan Africans enjoy greater equity than is found in other regions. In the agrarian sector they have equitable access to land (except in Southern Africa) and the direct producers have effective social control over their means of production or livelihood, i.e. they are not dominated by feudal landlords, haciendados or latifundistas, only by extractive and remote national governments. Politically, their chances of overthrowing their dictatorial but weak governments are greater than those of their counterparts in Asia, the Middle East and Latin America, as is demonstrated by the 'democratization' movement in Africa.

Also, African agricultural producers, who constitute the vast majority in any single African country (except in South Africa and Zimbabwe), are not as backward technologically as is often supposed. In a pioneering and highly technical study sponsored by FAO from 1980 to 1986 to assess what was termed the PSC (the potential population-supporting capacities) of the agricultural land resources of developing countries, the computer correlations showed that: 'Land-use intensity actually estimated to prevail implies that African agriculture uses land at cropping intensities close to those compatible with the intermediate level of technology of the PSC study ... However, the yields actually prevailing are decidedly closer to those of the low technology of the PSC study' (Alexandratos 1995: 160). In the same study it was estimated that former Zaire alone, if it used all its available land resources at prevailing levels of technological intensity, could support a population of 410 million people (i.e. an equivalent of the total African population by the year 2000). This finding was not welcomed by the policy-makers in FAO since it cast doubt on the prevailing orthodoxy about 'modernization' of technology being the key to the development of agriculture in Africa. Above all, it contradicted the suppositions of what was meant to be a blueprint for African agriculture, namely, *African Agriculture: The Next 25 Years* which had just been released with a fanfare. Thus, inevitably, an intriguing scientific puzzle was sacrificed for the sake of preconceived models sanctioned by the international community.

Prima facie the PSC finding did nothing more than simply signify that physical factors, in this case technology and land endowment, were not the immediate reason for the observable steep decline in agricultural productivity in Africa since the end of the 1960s. On the other hand, it posed a great challenge in that it was an invitation to look outside the conventional paradigm for possible explanations. As it happens, some radical African researchers had already been doing so, as is shown by what came to be known as the 'Dar Debate' of the early 1970s, the Kenya Debate of the late 1970s and early 1980s, the Zimbabwe Debate of the late 1980s, and to a lesser extent the Nigerian Debate in the aftermath of the Land Use Decree of 1978 and the ill-fated Green Revolution of the 1980s. From these various investigations social and economic factors emerged as the underlying causes of the so-called agricultural crisis in Africa. These included (1) discriminatory government investment policies against small producers or peasants in favour of big farmers; (2) overtaxation of the former by African governments through marketing boards paralleled by exemptions or rebates for big farmers; and (3) lack of support services for small producers (especially women) and poor social services in the rural areas compared to urban areas (urban bias).

These arguments are incontrovertible, but there are also standard counter-arguments to them. On the question of investment, it is often stated, as an article of faith, by adherents of neo-classical theory that 'large-scale' farmers are more efficient and more responsive to technological innovations, and that their propensity to save is greater than that of small producers. As regards the issue of overtaxation, it is simply argued, as a logical necessity, that you do not tax that which you seek to promote. Large-scale farmers are the biggest earners of sorely-needed foreign exchange. Regarding support services, it is argued, as a matter of rationality, that it is more rewarding to concentrate on a few good or progressive farmers than to spread your personnel too thin on the ground, by trying to cover a multitude of less productive small farmers who are often scattered over very wide areas. These are largely eurocentric arguments and might be contradicted by experience from elsewhere.

For instance, there is no evidence that big farmers in black Africa are more efficient than smaller ones. Second, if large-scale farmers were bigger foreign exchange earners until recently, the small female cultivators in Africa were and still are the biggest food producers. The latter observation is not invalidated by the fact that there are mounting food deficits in African countries. If anything, it is an argument for giving this category of producers preferential treatment instead of marginalizing them. Likewise, it cannot be proved that big farmers in Africa are more responsive to technological innovations than smaller farmers. In the present agricultural crisis, big farmers in general responded to the collapse of international markets for traditional export crops by pulling out of agriculture altogether, instead of diversifying away from such crops as a matter of expediency. In contrast, middle peasants in countries such as Kenya adjusted to the crisis by switching to high-value crops, dairy farming and poultry; so did small-scale female producers in countries such as Senegal and Zimbabwe. This would indicate that technological responsiveness has nothing to do with size of farmers but rather with the cost of innovation. In this context, poor peasants are necessarily handicapped and naturally are disinclined to take risks. In a more enabling environment this need not be the case. With a certain amount of encouragement, peasant producers in Kenya and Zimbabwe readily switched to hybrid maize varieties while their brethren in Malawi, faced with a cynical government, consciously avoided such a move.

Concerning the propensity to save, once again it cannot be proved that African big farmers actually save more than poorer peasant farmers. According to a study conducted by Dr E. Aryeetey (1993), the probability is that poor peasants save more as a percentage of their income than big farmers. However, the essential difference is that the peasants' savings are intended as insurance against unexpected economic exigencies. Therefore, they remain unmobilized for long periods of time. Looked at from this angle, the problem is not savings but economic insecurity. This provides further arguments for government support in the form of loans, seeing that commercial banks think of poor farmers as unbankable. Unlike landless peasants in Asia and Latin America, poor peasants in Africa have a claim to land resources and their land rights are often protected by their families or lineages. Such surety makes them thoroughly bankable and an economic asset if given the opportunity to be productive. In Malawi, Kydd and Hewitt (1986) found that the rate of repayment of government loans by poor peasants exceeded 94 per cent. To drive home the point about the bankability of the poor, reference could be made to the famous Grameen Bank in Bangladesh which experienced a 100 per cent loan recovery from poor women or to the Employment Guarantee Scheme of Maharashtra in India which made it possible for thousands of unemployed rural poor to be productive through food aid (IFAD 1992: 12).

The above considerations predispose us not towards 'poverty alleviation' but towards a 'trickle-up' strategy for development whose immediate objective is elimination of poverty. It is, however, important to note that here the emphasis is not on the time perspective but on treating poverty elimination as basically development from below. This makes perfect sense in regions such as sub-Saharan Africa where the vast majority of the population is poor but has access to land. In its report, IFAD (1992) argued persuasively that not only is the productivity of the rural poor easily raised by modest investment, but that the marginal capital:output ratio is much lower for the poor rural producers than for more capital-intensive large-scale farmers. Taking into consideration marginal capital productivity (i.e. the reciprocal of the capital:output ratio) between the two sub-sectors, the authors of the report posited that one unit of resources invested in the peasant sub-sector would generate greater savings than if it were invested in the capital-intensive sub-sector. They further suggested that, given a situation in which the poor are the vast majority, the diminishing return to capital would not be as significant in the poor sector as in the non-poor sector.

The thrust of these inspiring arguments is that in situations where the poor predominate it is more efficient to invest in them than in the non-poor who are prone to absorb more resources than can be economically justified. In other words, not only is it cheaper in terms of capital outlay (including foreign exchange) to invest in the undercapitalized majority but also it helps to mobilize their only form of wealth: labour. This is a guarantee for self-development and a necessary foundation for national development. In this context bourgeois arguments about scattered and unproductive marginal producers lose all relevance, as they do not take into consideration the real social, economic and human costs of poverty. In the context of sub-Saharan Africa, pervasive poverty is fundamentally a problem of development and is amenable to 'trickle-up' development strategies. By refusing to recognize this, African governments have thereby forfeited any claim to legitimacy.

References

ADB (African Development Bank)/UNDP/World Bank (1990) *The Social Dimensions of Adjustment in Africa: A Policy Agenda*. Washington, DC: ADB/UNDP/World Bank,
— (1995) *Africa and the Future*. Special Issue, 7, 2 (December).

Alexandratos, N. (1995) 'Food-Production Potential of African Lands and Projections to 2000', in Mafeje and Radwan (eds), *Economic and Demographic Change in Africa*.

Aryeetey, E. (1993) *Saving Among the Rural Poor in Ghana*. Proceedings of the Fourth CROP Conference, Paris, 16–18 April.

Collier, P. and P. Horsnell (1995) 'The Agrarian Response to Population Growth in Kenya', in Mafeje and Radwan (eds), *Economic and Demographic Change in Africa*.

Dey, J. (1984a) *Women in Rice-farming Systems. Focus: Sub-Saharan Africa*. Women in Agriculture, Series 2. Rome: FAO.
— (1984b) *Women in Food-production and Food Security in Africa*. Women in Agriculture, Series 3. Rome: FAO.

Dommen, A. (1988) *Innovation in African Agriculture*. Westview Special Studies in Agriculture, Science, and Policy. Boulder, CO: Westview Press.

Ewusi, K. (1990) *Land Reform and Rural Poverty in Africa*. Working Paper no. 19. Rome: IFAD.

FAO (1986) *African Agriculture: The Next 25 Years*. Main Report and Land Resource Base. Rome: FAO.

IFAD (1992) *The State of World Rural Poverty*. Rome: New York University Press.

ILO (1990) *The Challenge of Employment, Rural Labour, Poverty and the ILO*. Geneva: ILO.

IMF (1989) *World Economic Outlook*. Washington, DC: IMF.

Kesseba, A. M. (1989) 'Technology Systems for Resource-poor Farmers' , in A. M. Kesseba (ed.), *Technology Systems for Small Farmers*. Boulder, CO: Westview Press.

Knudsen, O. et al. (1990) *Redefining the Role of Government in Agriculture for the 1990s*. Discussion Paper no. 105. Washington, DC: World Bank.

Kydd, L. G. and Hewitt, X. (1986) 'Malawi after Six Years of Adjustment, 1980–1985', *Development and Change*, 17, 3 (July).

Lawrence, P. (1988) 'The Political Economy of the "Green Revolution" in Africa', *Review of African Political Economy*, 42.

Lele, Urna (1987) *Structural Adjustment, Agricultural Development and the Poor: Some Observations on Malawi.* Washington, DC: World Bank.

Lele, Urna and R. E. Christiansen (1989) *Markets, Marketing Boards, and Cooperatives in Africa. Issues in Adjustment Policy.* MADIA Discussion Paper no. 11. Washington DC: World Bank.

Lewis, B. C. (ed.) (1981) *Invisible Farmers: Women and the Crisis in Agriculture: A Women in Development Monograph.* Washington, DC: Agency for International Development.

Lineberry, W. P. (ed.) (1989) *Assessing Participatory Development: Rhetoric Versus Reality.* Boulder, CO: Westview Press.

Lipton, M. (1989) *New Seeds and Poor People.* London: Unwin Hyman.

Livingstone, I. (1992) 'Poverty Reduction in the Industrial Sector in Uganda', unpublished UNDP Mission Report on Poverty Reduction in Uganda.

Low, A. (1986) *Agricultural Development in Southern Africa: Farm Household Economics and the Food Crisis.* London: James Currey.

Mafeje. A. and S. Radan (eds) (1995) *Economic and Demographic Change in Africa.* Oxford: Cladendon Press.

Novak, M. (1996) 'Concepts of Poverty', in Øyen et al. (eds), *Poverty.*

Øyen, Else, S. M. Miller and Syed Abdus Samad (eds) (1996) *Poverty: A Global Review. Handbook on International Poverty Research.* Paris: UNESCO; Oslo: Scandinavian University Press.

Pankhurst, D. and S. Jacobs (1988) 'Land Tenure, Gender Relations, and Agricultural Production: The Case of Zimbabwe's Peasantry', in J. Davison (ed.), *Agriculture, Women and Land: The African Experience.* Boulder, CO: Westview Press.

Pearce, R., E. Amono and L. Honny (1989) *The Impact of Economic Recovery Programmes on Smallholder Farmers and the Rural Poor in Sub-Saharan Africa: Ghana Case-Study.* Rome: IFAD.

Rhoades, R. (1989) 'The Role of Farmers in the Creation of Agricultural Technology', in Robert Chambers, Arnold Pacey and Lori Ann Thrupp (eds), *Farmer First: Farmer Innovation and Agricultural Research.* London: Intermediate Technology Publications.

Rukuni, M. and C. K. Eicher (1987) *Food Security for Southern Africa.* Harare: University of Zimbabwe.

Sahn, D. E. and L. Arulpragasam (1991) *Development through Dualism? Land Tenure, Policy, and Poverty in Malawi.* Cornell Food and Nutrition Policy Programme, Working Paper no. 9. Ithaca, NY: University of Cornell.

Sahn, D. E. and A. H. Sarris (1991) 'Structural Adjustment and the Welfare of Rural Smallholders: A Comparative Analysis from Sub-Saharan Africa', *World Bank Economic Review*, 5, 2.

Saito, K. A. and C. L. Weidemann (1990) *Agricultural Extension for Women in Africa.* World Bank Discussion Paper. Washington, DC: World Bank.

Sarris, A. H. and H. Shams (1992) *Ghana under Structural Adjustment: The Impact on Agriculture and the Rural Poor.* New York University for IFAD, Rome.

Sen, A. (1982) *Poverty and Famines: An Essay on Entitlement and Deprivation.* Oxford: Oxford University Press.

Sen, A. and J. Dreze (1989) *Hunger and Public Action.* WIDER Studies in Development Economics. Oxford: Clarendon Press.

Singh, A. (1986) 'Tanzania and the IMF: The Analysis of Alternative Adjustment Programmes', *Development and Change*, 17, 3 (July).

Teka, T. and T. Nicola (1984) *Poverty Alleviation: The Case of Ethiopia.* Rome: FAO.

UNDP (1990, 1991) *Human Development Report 1990* and *1991*. New York: Oxford University Press.

(UN) ECA (1989a) *African Alternative Framework to Structural Adjustment Programmes for Socio-Economic Recovery and Transformation*. Addis Ababa: (UN) ECA.

— (1989b) *Statistics and Policies. ECA Preliminary Observations on the World Bank Report: 'Africa's Adjustment and Growth in the 1980s'*. Addis Ababa: (UN) ECA.

Wilson, F. (1996) 'South Africa: Poverty under Duress', in Øyen et al. (eds), *Poverty*.

World Bank (1989) *Poverty, Adjustment, and Growth in Africa*. Washington, DC: World Bank.

— (1990) *Poverty. World Development Report 1990*. Washington, DC: World Bank.

— (1994) *World Development Report 1994*. Washington, DC: World Bank.

3

Democracies and Poverty: Links and Associations

Kenneth Good

Political and economic frameworks are salient, for they constrain and limit, or, conversely, favour and facilitate, the amelioration of poverty. The avoidance of poverty, and the inequalities which accompany it, is funda-mental to human needs and rights. Everyone should have access to food, clothing and shelter, and acquire the foundations for self-determination. 'Bread first, then morals', as Brecht wrote.[1]

While all established democracies today are located within capitalist systems, not all democracies, now or earlier, are or were the same. In liberal (or representative or electoral) democracy, the predominant form of the late twentieth century, it is hard to address poverty as an issue demand-ing attention. Where that system is associated with *laissez-faire* capitalism, it is more difficult still. The United States is the leading liberal polity, and it is the home, and global progenitor, of an extensively deregulated market economy. The richest liberal capitalism is also the most inequitable in the advanced capitalist world, where injustice is the lot of the proliferating underclasses of blacks, Hispanics and poor whites.[2] Other contemporary democracies, such as social democracy in Western Europe, have notably lower levels of inequality and fewer people in poverty. Participatory demo-cratic forms, in actuality in ancient Athens, in the Leveller impulse in early capitalist England, and in the mass movement in South Africa in the 1980s, were significantly different again. But the ascendant American liberal capitalism threatens more egalitarian models elsewhere. The evidence suggests that where deregulation and downsizing are uncritically embraced, poverty alleviation is abandoned.

American Capitalism

The United States, towards the end of the 1990s, was wealthy and highly productive; on the assessment of the brokerage firm Merril Lynch, it was 'Paradise Found: The Best of All Possible Economies'.[3] Within this apparent prosperity, however, the situation of most working people was worsening. The average weekly earnings of 80 per cent of ordinary working Americans fell by 18 per cent between 1973 and 1995, from $315 a week to $258 a week,[4] the latter representing a less than adequate sum. According to Andrew Hacker, a three-person family living on $235 a week – the federally defined poverty threshold in 1995 – earned just enough to provide for subsistence in rural but not urban areas.[5] He felt that $25,000 per annum (or $480 a week) was a more plausible estimate of the minimum income a family would need to survive and to offer some opportunities to their children. One-third of all full-time jobs in America paid less than $20,000 a year. Half of the jobs for male workers paid below $28,000, barely enough to provide a minimal standard of living for a family.[6]

While the United States has been the only advanced society in which productivity has steadily risen over the past two decades, the incomes of eight out of ten of its people 'have stagnated or fallen'.[7] Output per person of all non-farm workers in the private sector rose by 25 per cent between 1973 and 1995, while the real hourly earnings of production and other non-supervisory workers fell by 12 per cent.[8] The poorest fifth of the population saw their share of aggregate household income fall, from 1975 to 1995, from 4.4 per cent to only 3.7 per cent. And the share of the fourth quintile also fell (from 10.5 per cent to 9.1 per cent), as did that of the middle fifth (17.1 per cent to 15.2 per cent), and the second fifth's as well (from 24.8 per cent – their highest share ever over the sixty years from 1935 – to 23.3 per cent).[9] The large majority of the population was steadily, remorselessly losing out. On Hacker's figures, some 64 per cent of wage-earners, in the mid-1990s, received incomes of less than $25,000 per annum.[10]

The terms of trade for the acquisition of social basics like housing were worsening too. In 1970 the price of an average new house had represented twice a young couple's income; towards the late 1990s it was four times that sum. In 1970, 66.3 per cent of Americans lived in detached single-unit homes, but by 1990 only 59 per cent did so; those living in trailers or mobile homes had more than doubled over the time to 7.2 per cent. Car prices, in the land of the automobile, have risen too: a new car represented 38 per cent of a young couple's income in 1970, but with in-built high-tech refinements it required about a 50 per cent outlay two decades later.[11] According to Hacker, 'the chief accommodation' that most workers have made when living on annual incomes of $21,000 or less is to 'postpone marriage and having children' as this was seen to be 'too expensive'.[12]

Not all of course were worse off. While the vast majority were getting poorer, a small minority in this highly productive society were becoming markedly richer. The household income of the top or best-off fifth had risen (1975 to 1995) from 43.2 per cent to 48.7 per cent. Best-off of all, however, were those within the top 5 per cent of households, whose income share had gone up from 15.9 per cent to 21 per cent. At the very top there was both room and great riches. About 68,000 families, near the end of the 1990s, had incomes of $1 million a year, five times as many as in 1979 (adjusted for inflation).[13] Moreover, while there were thirteen billionaires in America in 1982, there were 170 in the late 1990s.[14]

Hacker's 68,000 families included, in 1995, some 2,500 corporate officers, 1,500 men and women in Wall Street securities firms, and smaller numbers of lawyers, athletes, film stars and a few physicians. Of these, 'Wall Street money managers' and certain chief executive officers (CEOs) had done extremely well. In the early 1980s they had earned as much as $6 or $7 million annually. By the late 1980s and early 1990s, some were acquiring $100 million and eventually $1 billion in a single year. One such was George Soros who made $1.5 billion in 1995. A single year also saw Michael Eisner, chairman of the Walt Disney company, paid $203 million;[15] another, 1997, brought him remunerations worth $400 million.[16]

The inequalities accompanying this great wealth are huge. When Eisner acquired his $203 million, the state of Texas provided an annual welfare stipend to a mother with two children of $2,130. Inequalities are also worsening. The pay-cheques of corporate chairmen in 1975 were forty times larger than that of a typical worker, but in 1995 the same differential had reached 190.[17] Estimates of inequalities differ in details. Another found that the average CEO of a '*Fortune* 500' company earned forty-one times more than a factory worker in 1960, but gained 157 times as much in 1995. Figures provided by trade unionists showed that the average manager obtained 326 times more than the average factory worker near the end of the 1990s, while the same ratio had been only 44:1 in the 1960s.[18] An 'overclass' had arisen, and the gap between rich and poor in the American paradise was matching Brazilian levels.[19]

The meaning and significance of the figures were not in question. Among the world's advanced capitalist countries, the United States had 'the most glaring income gaps'.[20] Britain, too, in the 1990s was a 'far more unequal society than 20 years ago', and the country had been divided into 'a handful of economic giants in a sea of poverty-stricken dwarves'.[21] Other comparable capitalist countries were markedly different from the United States. In Japan, the ratio between a CEO's earnings and those of a factory worker – as with the above – was 17:1.[22] The top quintile of income earners in capitalist South Korea received only six times the amount that the bottom fifth obtained. On an index of income inequality in fourteen largely European and North American countries, Finland was first (the most equitable) Sweden was second, and the United States ranked fourteenth.

The United States was worst for double, cumulative reasons: as Hacker says, 'partly because its rich receive more than their counterparts in other countries, and mostly because those who are poor get so much less'.[23]

Inequalities are deep and deepening in the United States not because of a capitalist 'hidden hand', nor because of democracy as such. Finland, Sweden and Japan, for example, were patently both capitalist and democratic, and newly industrialized South Korea was democratizing. Specific policies were chosen and implemented by American corporate and political elites to bring Simon Head's 'new, ruthless economy' into being. Hacker points to 'the [underlying] structure and the culture of the nation's economy', and to tax-breaks granted to the very wealthy near the beginning of the Reagan presidency.[24] Head notes that a 'huge transfer of wealth from lower skilled, middle class American workers to the owners of capital assets and to a new technological [elite]' had occurred.[25] John Gray identifies contemporary American capitalism as characterized by 'hire-and-fire', 'slash-and-burn' and 'winner-take-all' values and techniques.[26] Widespread deregulation has been followed, outsourcing (of supplies, services and production processes) and downsizing strongly emphasized. Outsourcing tends to have the effect, according to Head, of lowering the skills-level of a firm's core workforce, reducing their wages and undermining trade union organization.[27] Downsizing is most obviously directed towards taking jobs and wages from that 80 per cent of the American population – the creation of 'disposable work and disposable workers'.[28] But it also has the effect of transferring a large part of what was saved to the corporate chiefs. The CEOs of the twenty-two biggest downsizing American firms in 1995 saw the combined value of their share options upsized by $36.6 million on the day their layoffs were announced.[29] Dunlap, the CEO of the Sunbeam Corporation, became known, through the mid-1990s, as Chain-Saw Al for the way 'he downsized thousands of workers while earning millions of dollars for himself'.[30]

Downsizing and outsourcing were the newest supplementations to existing legal mechanisms that discriminated against the worker-losers. Daniel Lazare notes that entire categories of workers, often the most vulnerable and exploited, are effectively barred from unionizing. Even in the 1990s, thousands of workers were still fired each year in the United States for unionizing.[31]

American Liberal Democracy

The ruthless economy is contained within what Abraham Eisenstadt accurately defines as 'the paradigmatic liberal polity'.[32] Liberal democracy is essentially a system which is emphatically value-free. It aimed, in the first great wave of democratization, when socialism and social democracy were on the agenda in Europe, at incorporating the masses into politics, as Weber put it, in an orderly way; not through 'irrational' interventions like strikes and demonstrations, but in voting for competing elites in periodic elections.[33] The ideals of justice and equality were shorn-off as dangerously ideological, while Lockean beliefs in the rights of individual property ownership remained. The former were in any case irrelevant to what democracy represented; in Schumpeter's influential terms, simply a 'political method', an 'institutional arrangement', for determining the governors. Weber's 'law of the small number' prevailed.[34] Elitism accompanied by popular passivity, as Lipset recognized, distinctively characterized the liberal form of democracy.[35]

American democracy, elitist, non-activist, value-free, is the extreme form of the liberal democratic variant.[36] Its law is 'essentially the law of property relations',[37] and its 'civil servants, judges, and politicians' have at times 'regarded the economy as an object for extortion'.[38] While universal male suffrage was introduced early in the western states, 'the majority of the [country's] population did not place any value on an honest administration, or ... never collectively manifested this'.[39]

Consistent with the winner-take-all principle, the society 'prizes winners and despises losers'.[40] Injustice easily results. When most countries in the European Union imprison fewer than 100 persons per 100,000 inhabitants, the United States incarcerates more than six times this number, rivalling at the end of the 1990s only Russia for the world's highest imprisonment rate.[41] America's rate of incarceration in 1994 was fourteen times greater than Japan's, and it was rapidly growing. The numbers of people locked up near the end of the 1990s was three times greater than the total of 1980; as of mid-1995, 1.1 million people were in jail. Bondage, according to Scott Christianson, as variously slaves, indentured servants, bonded labourers, and prisoners, has played a central role in building the American Republic from the beginning. The motives of profit and of punishment mutually propelled this process, and popular support for mass incarceration, over the centuries, has been constant.[42]

America's rate of violent crime was similarly high.[43] America alone in the western world 'enthusiastically endorses the death penalty'.[44] It is currently executing people, says Lazare, at the rate of one every five days,[45] and it is one of only six countries which enforces the death penalty for crimes committed under the age of eighteen years.[46] American prisons are 'extraordinarily barbaric places where homosexual rape and sex slavery are considered by the authorities and a complaisant public to be appropriate, if unregulated punishment'.[47] On top of the existing motivations of profit and punishment, the 1990s, says Gray, saw recourse 'to a policy of mass imprisonment as a surrogate for the controls of communities which un-regulated market forces have weakened or destroyed'.[48]

Imprisonment also served to deprive weak and vulnerable people of their political rights. In mid-1994, notes Christianson, nearly 7 per cent of all black men nationwide were imprisoned. In New York State simultaneously nearly one in four young black men were under the control of the criminal justice system. Because incarcerated persons were universally prevented from voting, and the laws in thirteen of the most populous states stripped felons of the vote, a disproportionately large share of African American men were, by implication, disenfranchised.[49] Other estimates deepen and extend the political dis-empowerment. Some fourteen states actually ban convicted felons from voting for life; twenty-nine ban them while on probation; and thirty-two ban them while on parole. The result is that some 3.9 million Americans are temporarily or permanently dis-enfranchised, of whom 1.4 million are black men.[50]

The economic losers are treated with no greater concern. Experts of corporate re-engineering, such as Michael Hammer and James Champy, write with frankness about the 'abject terror' and the 'total inner panic', of workers about to learn of their redundancy. Nowhere do they recognize that employees have interests which should be subject to negotiation and compromise. Nor do they write of pay; if it is discussed, says Head, it is in isolated, bilateral encounters with the employer, where the latter 'generally has the upper hand'.[51]

Capitalist America, for Adam Przeworski, is 'an inhumane society', interlinked closely with its paradigmatic liberalism.[52] Its highest inequalities, and huge prison populations, are supported by one of the lowest voter participation rates in the world. Even presidential elections are unusual if half of the eligible electorate participates. The 'Great Communicator' Ronald Reagan, for instance, received votes from only 28 per cent of those eligible in 1980, and Bill Clinton entered the White House in 1992 with 24.5 per cent of the electorate supporting him. The Republicans led by Newt Gingrich won an historic mid-term Congressional victory in 1994 with 39 million voters behind them, 35 million voting Democrat, and with another 112 million eligible Americans staying home.[53]

The influence of wealth in circumstances of high inequalities and low popular participation easily becomes dominant and decisive. In the 1998 election cycle, 'the candidate who outspent his opponent emerged victorious in 95 per cent of House [of Representatives] races and 94 per cent of Senate races. In more than 60 per cent of House districts, the winner outspent the loser by 10 to 1.'[54] A majority of today's senators, notes Michael Lind, are millionaires.[55]

Poverty and inequalities are not easily discussed in such a non-functioning democracy. Popular discontent, notes Gray, is mainly expressed in movements on the fringes of political life. For Merril Lynch, Francis Fukuyama and many others, the free market is synonymous with the American paradise and its liberal polity. The huge costs of the free market, widening and deepening though they are, are 'taboo subjects' in the national discourse.[56]

Regulated/Stakeholder Capitalism

Though American triumphalism suggests otherwise, there are in fact different forms of capitalism, as there are historically different democracies. These differ from the American model significantly, not least on the issues of the ends of the capitalist endeavour and on who participates in corporate policy-making. Stakeholder capitalism is a generic shorthand term which embraces distinct though overlapping models: chiefly Britain's post-war welfare state, Scandinavian social democracy, the German social market, and the East Asian interventionist strategy.[57] What these have in common has been summarized as follows:

> What goes under the name of capitalism varies a lot from country to country, even among rich economies. A big difference is in attitudes to public companies; in particular, in views about their duties and responsibilities beyond their obvious objective of producing goods and services ... In Japan and much of continental Europe ... firms often accept broader obligations that balance the interests of shareholders against those of other 'stakeholders', notably employees, but including also suppliers, customers, and the wider 'community'.[58]

Much of the distinctiveness of European social democracy was in the breadth of its aims and aspirations. Its core demands in Germany in 1891 were the democratization of society, a welfare state and the regulation of the labour market.[59] The Social Democratic Party in Sweden through the 1930s laid the foundations for the post-war Western European model of social democracy – the compromise between labour and capital, as Donald Sassoon describes it, and the establishment of successful institutional structures for permanent negotiations between employers, trade unions and government on labour and social policies.[60] What was being attempted was the melding of what liberalism separates and frees – the economic and the political dimensions of society, the regulation of capitalism in the interests of a more effective democracy. British Labour's mandate in 1945, says Sassoon, was to introduce a fairer society, where excessive inequalities would be removed, while those that persisted would not deprive anyone of certain basic social rights, such as employment, health-care and education.[61]

In 1938 in Britain, the top 10 per cent of the population received 34.4 per cent of all post-tax income, while by 1949, partly as a result of wartime egalitarianism, this ratio had been reduced to 27.1 per cent. Sassoon stresses that what the social democratic welfare state promoted was an equality of the highest standards, not an equality of minimal needs.[62] From around 1945 to 1975 the European form of capitalism afforded social democracy a key role. With growth and full employment, a large proportion of the surplus produced was allocated by political means, not by market forces, to health, education, transport, child-care and old-age protection. These measures served to stabilize capitalism and, he adds, enabled acceptance of regulation on minimum wages, paid holidays and similar provisions which legislation, backed by trade union demands, imposed.[63]

The German social market, social democracy, and the East Asian model have today different socio-political arrangements for accommodating the interests of CEOs and shareholders with those, notably, of workers, but the outcomes of such participative and consultative processes are distinctively different from those found in America.

Inequalities of income, as suggested already, are unusually low in Japan, Taiwan and South Korea, and Sweden has the second most equitable income distribution on Hacker's index. On data presented by Przeworski, the percentage of people in poverty after taxes and transfers, near the end of the 1980s, in Norway was 4.8; in Sweden 5.0; in Britain 12.1; and in the United States 16.9.[64] The German social market, states Gray, 'enfranchises stakeholders – employees, local communities, bankers, sometimes suppliers and customers – in corporate governance'. Workers in firms with over 800 employees are assured of representation on supervisory boards. Its capitalism accords a lower weight to share values than do American and British free-market economies. When workers lose their jobs, as they now do, they receive about two-thirds of their working incomes in unemployment benefits (cf. about one-third in Britain, even less in America). He quotes the chairman of the leading electronics firm Siemens, Heinrich von Pierer, saying: 'The hire and fire principle does not exist here and I never want it to.'[65]

Yet the values and institutions of stakeholder capitalism, in Europe and East Asia, are now under serious threat from the slash-and-burn, hire-and-fire techniques emanating from the United States: global *laissez-faire*, notes Gray, 'is an American project'. Social democracy and social market capitalism 'are inherently incompatible', he believes, with unrestricted global free trade. For full employment and decent wages, a government needs to develop socio-economic policies specifically designed for that end,[66] as the welfare state's experience has indicated. Growth reduces poverty only if the pattern of that growth is from the outset intended to benefit the poor, either directly through increased employment and incomes, or indirectly through good social services.[67] Earlier free-market capitalism did not foster social justice,[68] and unregulated globalization fiercely opposes it.

Ruthless capitalism on a global scale undoubtedly threatens the institutions and values of the stakeholder systems, but they survive where corporations, the state and a functioning democracy want them to. In the Netherlands in 1998, 'employers, trade unions and government co-operated closely'. Unemployment was a relatively low 5.5 per cent – though with the proportion of part-time workers twice that of Germany's – and observers spoke of a 'Dutch miracle' characterized by both 'growth and social cohesion'.[69]

Athenian Democracy, the Levellers, and Rousseau

American liberalism's claim to represent the one true model of democracy is historically, palpably false. Originating in an insurrectionary uprising by the lower classes in Athens at the end of the sixth century BC, a popular and participatory democracy was brought into being which existed for almost two centuries (508 to 322 BC), and has seen no equals since. Democracy here represented 'political power wielded actively and collectively by the demos', the latter being all residents of the state who '[we]re culturally defined as citizens, regardless of their class or status'.[70] Women, resident foreigners and slaves were not citizens; but the exclusion of women was well-nigh universal until the twentieth century, and black Americans, for example, did not begin to acquire political rights until the 1960s. Such exclusions were arguably of lesser significance than the issue of the inclusions in citizenship in class and status terms. Athens was slave-owning and imperialistic, and it 'upheld a stern ethical code predicated on duty to self and community',[71] but the issue is not whether it was attractive or always just, but the reality of its democracy. Michels and Weber successfully purveyed the view, during the democratization movement around the First World War, that real democracy was impossible. Athenian democracy, 'revolutionary in its energies, dynamic in its practices, and remarkably stable', constitutes the negation of this unproven elitist assumption.[72]

Elites of wealth and education existed in Athens, which was a class society. They were politically active and litigious, and critical in speech and writing. But they were not, states Josiah Ober, a politically dominant elite. Democracy had been brought into being through a largely 'leaderless' uprising, and the ordinary citizens established political, legal and ideological power thereafter. Their judges handed down huge fines, banishment and death for those caught breaking the rules and, Ober observes, Athenian political life was 'hard, often unkind'.[73] But it was also voluntary, and the elite individual could choose to pay his taxes and liturgies like others did and keep out of politics. He was free to criticize democracy, as none did more severely in conversation and writing than Plato, but not to take his case into the public domain or encourage others to overthrow the system, as Socrates did.[74] The educated held undoubted advantages in public speaking, but Athenians, says Ober, believed in the wisdom of mass audiences; special education was not considered necessary for collective decision-making, since growing up in the democratic polis was seen as an education in itself.[75]

Athenian political institutions also expressed direct popular power. It was exercised by ordinary citizens in the Assembly, which routinely drew between 6,000 and 8,000 participants. A meeting's agenda was drawn up by the Council of 500, whose members were selected by lottery and were forbidden to serve more than two annual terms – a large and rotating membership was not conducive to strong institutional identity or domination. Assembly meetings were presided over by a lotteried 'president-for-a-day' who announced the agenda items. Any citizen was free to speak, for only as long as his fellows were willing to listen to him. A simple majority, usually by show of hands, decided the outcome. All important business, including foreign policy and taxation, was decided in this way. Attendance at Assembly meetings, and most important official positions, was remunerated on a daily basis, so that no citizen would be excluded on financial grounds.[76]

People's courts, meeting almost daily, heard both private and public suits. Litigants faced a jury of some 200 or 500 citizens chosen by random drawing. The jurors were also the judges and, after hearing both claimants, they decided by majority vote in a secret ballot. Most official positions were, in fact, chosen by random lot, and all citizens aged above thirty were expected to staff an office. Only a few specialists, including military commanders and financial magistrates, were elected on renewable annual terms. Elections were seen by Athenian democrats as an aristocratic method, conferring, as in contemporary America, advantages upon the well-born, prominent and wealthy.[77] Executive and popular power were thus fused.

The conception of citizenship in Athens was profound. The democratic uprising had been preceded by prohibitions on debt-slavery and by legal reforms which, says Ober, made Athenians 'potentially responsible for one another's welfare'. Ordinary men began to see themselves not as clients of great families but as citizens.[78] After 508 the juror tended to be deeply suspicious of the wealthy as a class. Democratic ideology and power 'encouraged voluntary redistribution of wealth and limited the political effects of wealth inequality'.[79] There was taxation and the large fines imposed in the courts. Ellen Meiksins Wood stresses the fact that, while Athens was a slave society, 'the majority of citizens were people who worked for a living'.[80] The status enjoyed by free labour in democratic Athens has, she says, never been higher, before or since. What was most distinctive was found in the 'union of labour and citizenship' and 'specifically in the *peasant-citizen*'. The polis was a form of political organization which 'united landlords and peasants into one civic and military community'.[81] This was no formal or passive unity as has been seen. Democracy co-existed with slavery, but it also inhibited the concentration of property, and 'it limited the ways in which slavery could be utilized, especially in agriculture'. Peasant-citizens were able to use their political power in Athens to resist the exploitation and domination of the rich.[82]

The historic significance of Athens for Meiksins Wood is that it was an active, participatory and a majoritarian workers' democracy all at once. But the cultural status of labour changed most significantly, she believes, with the rise of capitalism. With John Locke's notions of 'improvement' and productivity, the virtues of labour no longer resided with the labourers themselves, but became the attributes of capitalists – who did not let resources lie idle but put them to work productively. The devaluation of labour and the empowerment of capitalists as true producers were also potent conceptualizations.[83] Locke not only fathered liberalism. He facilitated in addition the present arrangements wherein a formal democracy – citizens merely as masses periodically voting (or rather not voting) for representatives/elites – leaves inequalities and class exploitation intact.

Part of the significance of the Levellers' movement was that they emerged when liberal capitalism was first being emplaced and through revolutionary means. They arose out of the great clash between new parliamentary and rising capitalist forces, on the one hand, and old absolutist and feudal power, on the other. The Levellers represented chiefly a radical element within the New Model Army, a popular revolutionary force. They lasted no more than the last four years of the 1640s, but they spoke, at their height, when the parliamentary forces were not fully consolidated, for many of the victorious soldiers, mustered thousands of signatories to petitions, and prompted large demonstrations in London.[84] The leaders were men of limited education and property, and the rank and file were small traders, artisans and apprentices.[85]

They demanded franchise reform, religious tolerance and the abolition of arbitrary power, whether located in the king, the Lords or, as they saw it becoming, in the House of Commons itself. Their underlying ideas were political equality and popular sovereignty. They expressed a radical Protestant belief in individual responsibility, believing it was imprudent and wicked to surrender control over one's fate to political leaders. True political authority derived only from the consent of the people,[86] and they endeavoured to draft and promulgate a basic constitution, the *Agreements of the People*.[87] The Levellers, David Wootton emphasizes, never saw themselves as prospective rulers, but as spokesmen for a set of rules which should govern popular participation.[88]

Oliver Cromwell had led the army in a popular cause, but he and the other grandees were deeply opposed to popular sovereignty and equality. Calls for a widening of the franchise were not to be trusted. If the poor could outvote the rich, said General Ireton, the officer's spokesman at Putney, 'why may not those men vote against all property?'[89] For the parliamentary leadership, people like Rainborough had gained quite enough already. They had seen the end of arbitrary rule by one man, and had won the right to be governed by constitutional parliamentary rule.[90]

Parliament's victory saw tyranny replaced by oligarchy, buttressed by constitutionalism. Sovereignty lay not with the people but in abstractions such as 'the King in Parliament'. Liberalism entered political discourse not only as a restriction on state power, but also, says Meiksins Wood, as a *substitute* for democracy.[91] The framers of the United States constitution, she adds, subsequently worked in this tradition of oligarchic constitutionalism with a democratic façade.[92]

Rousseau's work is distinctive for its close concentration upon the meaning and significance of participation, and the importance of equality in a good democratic society. Participation and freedom are closely related. Whereas Locke, following Hobbes, had defined freedom as being left alone (that is, negatively, the absence of constraint), Rousseau saw it totally differently as involving self-determination. We are free when we ourselves choose the principles which we follow in life, 'for the impulse of appetite alone is slavery, and obedience to a law which we prescribe to ourselves is freedom'.[93]

Extensive inequalities caused moral degradation, and prevented a sense of common interest from developing in a society. Equality and democracy might grow together, however, through the active participation of the citizenry. Unlike Locke's emphasis on a citizen's merely tacit consent to government,[94] Rousseau proposed an active agreement frequently renewed. Participation would promote a sharing of values and experiences among the citizenry, and represent the basis for equality and democracy.[95] As in Athens, democracy meant for him not simply a form of government, but a whole society founded on the principle of social equality.[96]

Active participation of all citizens was the basis of the good society; and the state or government was the agency for implementing the people's decisions (and could be variously organized). Popular decision-making would be binding on all citizens equally.[97] Social interaction would therefore be highly affirmative and interventionist, in sharp contrast again with liberalism's quietist and negative freedom. As the Levellers had sensed in the 1640s, the freedom that mattered most to the poor in England was the freedom to escape from poverty; they could not attain this alone and unaided, since it necessarily involved challenging property owners.[98]

South Africa

It was South Africa's uniqueness that through the 1980s tens of thousands of people endeavoured to participate directly in politics,[99] to determine for themselves the direction of their lives, and to construct in the process a popular and just democracy. The origins of the movement stemmed out of the quickening industrialization and urbanization of the country, and the formation of a large and eventually skilled African working class.[100] In 1973, 100,000 workers in the Durban area went on strike, and such 'largely spontaneous' mass actions served to vitalize trade union organization from the ground up.[101]

The movement gained its substantive organized form with the launching of the United Democratic Front (UDF) in August 1983. The UDF was 'an unprecedented political organization' that linked together 'hundreds of affiliated student, youth, civic and other [groups]'.[102] The impetus for the formation of the UDF came from 'a coalescence' of different forces and factors, some of which were 'completely autonomous' of the African National Congress (ANC).[103] Equally unprecedented protest and confrontation, chiefly in black townships, soon occurred.[104] More significantly, the movement also 'transformed people's lives and often set up democratic political structures independent of (and directed against) the state'.[105]

While the UDF sometimes found itself, in a time of great upsurge and rapid change, 'trailing behind the masses', as its national secretary, Popo Molefe, himself admitted,[106] it quickly stressed the need for people to be critical of, and to have control over, their leaders. As was stated in *Isizwe*, the main journal of the UDF, in 1985: 'One thing that we must be careful about ... is that our organizations do not become too closely associated with individuals ... No person is a leader in a democratic struggle such as ours simply because he or she makes good speeches ... No individual may make proposals on the people's behalf – unless mandated by them.'[107]

The formation of the Congress of South African Trade Unions (CO-SATU) in 1985 strengthened and broadened the popular base of the UDF, as what was termed social movement unionism leapt forward. COSATU promoted the politicization of trade unions and their collaboration with the UDF.[108]

In early 1987 Murphy Morobe, the UDF's acting publicity secretary, comprehensively described the participatory democracy growing in South Africa.

> We in the [UDF] are engaged in a national democratic struggle ... [It] involves all sectors of our people ... a democratic South Africa is one of the aims or goals of our struggle ... [But] democracy is [also] the means by which we conduct the struggle. This refers to the democratic character of our existing mass-based organizations ... By developing active, mass-based democratic organizations and democratic practices within these organizations, we are laying the basis for a future democratic South Africa.
>
> The creation of democratic *means* is for us as important as having democratic *goals* as our objective ... What is possible in the future depends on what we are able to create and sustain now. A democratic South Africa will not be fashioned only after transformation of political power to the majority has taken place.
>
> A democratic solution in South Africa involves all South Africans, and in particular the working class, having control over all areas of daily existence – from national policy to housing, from schooling to working conditions, from transport to consumption of food ... When we say that the people shall govern, we mean at all levels and in all spheres, and we demand that there be real, effective control on a daily basis.
>
> In other words, we are talking about direct as opposed to indirect political representation, mass participation rather than passive docility and ignorance, a momentum where ordinary people can do the job themselves.

'Rudimentary organs of *people's power*', he said, had begun to emerge in the form, for example, of street and defence committees and shop-steward structures, and he identified the 'basic principles of our organizational democracy': (1) elected leadership: periodically re-elected and recallable; (2) collective leadership; (3) mandates and accountability; (4) reporting and reporting back; (5) criticism and self-criticism. These were, he stressed, 'fundamental weapon[s] of our struggle'.[109]

The UDF and COSATU in the 1980s testified to the validity of the proposition that it is the urban working class which is 'the most frequent proponent of the full extension of democratic rights'.[110] The forces arrayed against the full extension of democracy in South Africa were considerable. Heavy state repression by the late 1980s had succeeded in weakening the popular movement,[111] but the established ANC leadership, in exile and in prison, had also indicated that it had very limited respect for the UDF's basic principles of organizational democracy. By 1989 it was clear that some ANC leaders – most flagrantly typified by Winnie Mandela – were undoubtedly above criticism.[112]

With the release of the imprisoned ANC leaders and the return of the exiles, the issue of preparation for state power quickly dominated all else in the nationalist movement. By 1994 democracy was officially re-presented in standardized form as voting for majority rule.[113] The 1990s have witnessed, says Michael Neocosmos, 'a systematic (and astonishingly rapid) process of political demobilization'.[114] When democracy was further interpreted by the ANC government as, significantly, the formation of a black middle class from above,[115] the liberal elite–mass dichotomy was emplaced.

Nevertheless, the extent of the demobilization in South Africa should not be exaggerated; much remained. COSATU and the South African Communist Party are strong, allied and largely autonomous forces, both supported by the fact that in South Africa, between 1985 and 1995, trade union membership rose by 126.7 per cent, one of the largest growth-rates in the world.[116] COSATU's 'deliverable membership' near the end of the decade, in political support of the ANC or in other directions should it choose, was 1.8 million.[117]

Passivism, and a large gulf between the ruling elite and the mass of the population, have characterized Botswana's democracy since independence in 1966.[118] When South Africa was estimated as possessing some 54,000 civic groups shortly before the 1994 elections,[119] Botswana had perhaps 200 with some potential for becoming an active civil society.[120] Political participation can fall even below liberal American levels – at the referenda to approve a number of important political reforms in October 1997, voter turnout averaged only 17 per cent.[121] Poverty and inequalities were structural features of the political economy,[122] and wide values of deference – women to men, the young to the old, the poor to the rich and powerful – have accompanied them.[123]

Botswana has both the wealth and the state capacity to reduce poverty substantially, should the elite have chosen this as an original developmental goal. Consistent with the values of liberal democracy, the ruling elite have not addressed poverty-eradication directly (1966–98),[124] and the people have yet to insist that they do so.

Democracies and Poverty

The broad picture is fairly clear. Liberal democracy tolerates poverty and severe inequalities because of its symbiosis with *laissez-faire*, winner-take-all capitalism and its diminution of citizenship. Participatory democracy upholds broad egalitarian ideals, and is usually opposed by ruling elites, including those in the liberal democracies, largely for that very reason. If there is very little direct democracy in most contemporary societies, the reasons, Anthony Arblaster has suggested, are political rather than practical or technical: those who occupy positions of power and authority 'simply do not want it, and actively resist any attempt to bring it into being'.[125]

Notes

1. See Anthony Arblaster (1990) 'Bread first, then Morals', in David McLellan and Sean Sayers (eds), *Socialism and Morality*. London: Macmillan.

2. Joyce Carol Oates, 'A Lost Generation', review of William Finnegan's *Cold New World: Growing-Up in a Harder Country*, *New York Review of Books*, 16 July 1998.

3. Noted by Jeff Madrick, 'In the Shadows of Prosperity', *New York Review of Books*, 14 April 1997.

4. Figures adjusted for inflation. John Gray (1998) *False Dawn: The Delusion of Global Capitalism*. London: Granta, p. 114.

5. Andrew Hacker (1997) *Money: Who Has How Much and Why*. New York: Scribner, p. 62.

6. Ibid., p. 238, and Madrick, 'In the Shadows', p. 41.

7. Gray, *False Dawn*, p. 114.

8. Simon Head, 'The New, Ruthless Economy', *New York Review of Books*, 29 February 1996.

9. Hacker, *Money*, pp. 48–9.

10. Ibid., p. 51.

11. Ibid., pp. 60–1.

12. Ibid., pp. 59–60.

13. Ibid., pp. 49 and 72.

14. *The Economist* (London), Editorial, 30 May 1998, p. 13.

15. Hacker, *Money*, p. 53 and Chs 4 and 5 (his analysis is reviewed in Madrick, 'In The Shadows').

16. *The Economist*, 1 March 1997.

17. Ibid., p. 53.

18. Figures provided on the website www.paywatch.org and quoted in *The Economist*, 30 January 1999, p. 57.

19. 'Own correspondent' quoting the work of Michael Lind and others in *Business Day* (Johannesburg), 20 September 1995.

20. Hacker, *Money*, p. 52.

21. A report by the Institute of Fiscal Studies, reviewed by Kamal Ahmed, in the *Guardian* (London), 28 July 1997.

22. *Business Day*, 20 September 1995.

23. Hacker, *Money*, pp. 53–4.

24. Ibid., p. 49.

25. Head is quoting Felix Rothatyn, a senior investment banker; 'New, Ruthless Economy', p. 47.

26. Gray, *False Dawn*, pp. 93 and 115.

27. At Chrysler, General Motors and Ford in the 1970s, two-thirds of the hourly

workforce were members of the United Auto Workers. In the mid-1990s, with out-sourcing, only one-quarter of the components workforce were union members. This deunionization 'had a devastating effect on the earnings of workers throughout the auto industry'. Head, 'New, Ruthless Economy', p. 48.

28. Words of Bill Bamberger and Cathy Davidson, quoted in a review of their book, *Closing: The Life and Death of an American Factory* (New York: DoubleTake/W. W. Norton), in *The Economist*, 13 June 1998.

29. A report by the Institute for Policy Studies also noted that downsizing recently involved big companies such as AT&T, Kmart, BellSouth and Lockheed Martin, which were mostly profitable; *The Economist*, 27 April 1996, p. 56. Greed rather than rationality appeared the prime principle at work.

30. Meyer Friedman, quoting from the *New York Times Weekly*, 'Letters', *New York Review of Books*, 8 October 1998.

31. Daniel Lazare (1998) 'America the Undemocratic', *New Left Review* (London), 232 (November/December), p. 7.

32. Abraham S. Eisenstadt (1993) 'Political Corruption in American History', in Arnold J. Heidenheimer et al. (eds), *Political Corruption: A Handbook*. New Brunswick and London: Transaction, p. 546.

33. David Beetham (1985) *Max Weber and the Theory of Modern Politics*. Cambridge: Polity Press, p. 105.

34. Political democracy, said Weber, would not alter the dominance of 'small groups'; the essential role of the masses was to respond to the initiatives of the leaders. Beetham, *Max Weber*, pp. 105–6.

35. Schumpeter and Lipset's views are enlarged upon in K. Good (1998) 'Development and Democracies: Liberal v. Popular', *Africa Insight* (Pretoria), 27, 4.

36. French liberalism draws on a different tradition, not of complacent property ownership but of a radical republican liberty, equality and fraternity. Anthony Arblaster (1984) *The Rise and Decline of Western Liberalism*. Oxford: Basil Blackwell, Chs 11–12.

37. Eisenstadt, 'Political Corruption', p. 546.

38. Jacob van Klaveren (1993) 'Corruption: The Special Case of the United States', in Heidenheimer et al. (eds), *Political Corruption*, p. 563.

39. Ibid., p. 558.

40. John Carlin, 'From America', *Sunday Independent* (Johannesburg), 17 May 1998.

41. Review of Vivien Stern's 'A Sin Against the Future: Imprisonment in the World', *The Economist*, 16 May 1998.

42. Scott Christianson (1998) *With Liberty for Some: 500 Years of Imprisonment in America*. Boston: Northeastern University Press, pp. 275–95, and review, 'A Land of Bondage', *The Economist*, 13 February 1999.

43. For example, in 1993 the male homicide rate was 12.4 per 100,000, compared with 1.5 for the European Union, and 0.9 for Japan; for rape, the figures were 1.5 in Japan, and 42.8 in the United States. Gray, *False Dawn*, pp. 116–18.

44. Carlin, 'From America'.

45. Though executions per million people are far higher in small, authoritarian Singapore, the rate of execution there since 1994 is one every nine days. *The Economist*, 3 April 1999, p. 53.

46. The others are Iran, Nigeria, Pakistan, Saudi Arabia and Yemen. Lazare, 'America', p. 6.

47. Carlin, 'From America'.

48. Gray speaks too of the 'hollowing-out' of its social institutions, *False Dawn*, pp. 116 and 119.

49. Christianson, *With Liberty*, p. 281.

50. *The Economist*, 3 April 1999, p. 40.

51. Hammer and Champy's first book, *Re-engineering the Corporation* (1993), sold nearly two million copies, and their ideas became 'familiar to most high corporate executives'. Head, 'New, Ruthless Economy', pp. 49–50.

52. Adam Przeworski (1993) 'The Neo-Liberal Fallacy', in Larry Diamond and Marc Plattner (eds), *Capitalism, Socialism and Democracy Revisited*. Baltimore and London: Johns Hopkins University Press, p. 40.

53. Assessment and figures of James S. Fishkin (1995) *The Voice of the People: Public Opinion and Democracy*, New Haven and London: Yale University Press, pp. 45–7.

54. This campaign spending amounted to an estimated $1 billion, but included only the money that was regulated by the Federal Election Commission. The unregulated money spent by interest groups and political parties in support of particular candidates may have totalled an additional $345 million. 'Did money talk? Is water wet?', *The Economist*, 7 November 1998.

55. Michael Lind (1999) 'Why There Will be no Revolution in the US', *New Left Review*, 233 (January/February), p. 105.

56. Gray, *False Dawn*, pp. 120 and 130. Fukuyama has purveyed the view, in an article entitled 'The End of History', then in a book reaffirming his thesis, that 'democratic capitalism' constitutes the 'final form of human government', and its global reach 'the triumph of the Western idea'.

57. The use of the term 'stakeholder' by Tony Blair's New Labour is looser and non-specific.

58. *The Economist*, 10 February 1996.

59. In path-breaking moves Germany had introduced health insurance in 1883 and a general pension scheme for age and invalidity in 1889. Donald Sassoon (1996) *One Hundred Years of Socialism*. London: Fontana, p. 137.

60. Ibid., pp. 42 and 44.

61. Ibid., p. 123.

62. Ibid., pp. 141 and 149.

63. Ibid., p. 445.

64. Przeworski concluded that 'the only countries in the world in which almost no one is poor after taxes and transfers are those that pursue social democratic policies', 'Neo-Liberal Fallacy' pp. 48 and 53.

65. Gray, *False Dawn*, pp. 93–4. No date is given for von Pierer's statement.

66. Keynes showed that full employment is not the natural outcome of a market equilibrium. Gray, *False Dawn*, pp. 85–6 and 90.

67. In the recent recognition of the World Bank (1997) *Taking Action to Reduce Poverty in Sub-Saharan Africa*. Washington, DC: World Bank, p. 8.

68. It produced constant crises with terrible political effects such as global war, dictatorships and massive unemployment. Sassoon, *One Hundred Years*, p. 446.

69. *The Economist*, 2 May 1998.

70. Josiah Ober (1999) *The Athenian Revolution*. Princeton, NJ: Princeton University Press, p. 19.

71. Ibid., p. 11.

72. Ibid., pp. 5 and 19.

73. Ibid., pp. 11, 24 and 28.

74. Ibid., pp. 28–9.

75. Ibid., p. 26.

76. John Dunn (1993) 'Conclusion', in John Dunn (ed.), *Democracy: The Unfinished Journey 508 BC to AD 1993*. Oxford: Oxford University Press, pp. 241–2, and Ober, *Athenian Revolution*, pp. 23–5.

77. Dunn, *Democracy*, p. 242.

78. Ober, *Athenian Revolution*, p. 38.

79. Ibid., p. 27.

80. Ellen Meiksins Wood (1995) *Democracy Against Capitalism: Renewing Historical Materialism*. Cambridge: Cambridge University Press, p. 183.

81. Ibid., pp. 185 and 188. Her emphasis of peasant-citizen.

82. The goddess Athena was patron of both the arts and crafts, Meiksins Wood notes, but the greatest testimony to the status of free labour in Athens was seen in Plato's vehement reaction against it. Ibid., pp. 190–2.

83. Ibid., pp. 200–1.

84. David Wootton (1993) 'The Levellers', in Dunn (ed.), *Democracy*, p. 72.

85. Iain Hampsher-Monk (1991) 'Levellers', in David Miller et al. (eds), *The Blackwell Encyclopaedia of Political Thought*. Oxford: Basil Blackwell, p. 283.

86. Their spokesman, Colonel Thomas Rainborough, during the army's Putney debates in November 1647: 'I think that the poorest he that is in England has a life to live as the greatest he; and ... the poorest man in England is not at all bound in a strict sense to that government that he has not had a voice to put himself under.' Quoted in Wootton, 'The Levellers', p. 74.

87. Hampsher-Monk, 'Levellers', pp. 283–4.

88. Wootton, 'The Levellers', p. 79.

89. Quoted by Hampsher-Monk, 'Levellers', p. 284.

90. Meiksins Wood, *Democracy Against Capitalism*, p. 230.

91. Ibid. Her emphasis again.

92. Ibid., p. 231. Alexander Hamilton, for instance, affirmed that 'society naturally divides itself into the very few and the many', and James Madison believed that it was nature's design to create 'unequal faculties of acquiring property'. Quoted in Hacker, *Money*, p. 48.

93. The democratic idea of freedom is one of self-determination, derivative of Rousseau's *Social Contract*. John Schwarzmantel (1994) *The State in Contemporary Society*. London: Harvester-Wheatsheaf, p. 32.

94. Deemed to have been given when, for example, a man passed the age of twenty-one, or when he travelled unmolested on the highway.

95. Arblaster supports Rousseau's perception that severe inequalities would prevent the development of a common interest in a society, and undermine the foundations of democracy. Anthony Arblaster (1987) *Democracy*. Milton Keynes: Open University Press, pp. 77–8.

96. Ibid., p. 81. The absence of big inequalities was a prerequisite for Rousseau's good society.

97. Roger D. Masters (1991) 'Rousseau', in Miller et al., *Blackwell Encyclopaedia*, p. 457.

98. The Diggers, their more radical off-shoot, attempted to find the solution in working common lands for themselves, until they were dispersed by mob violence.

99. Unique in Africa assuredly, and possibly also by comparison with the 'transition to democracy' in Central Europe.

100. The number of Africans working in manufacturing rose from 308,000 in 1960 to 781,000 in 1980. Between 1965 and 1975 the number of blacks in secondary schools increased nearly fivefold, while between 1980 and 1984 they doubled again to over a million. Michael Neocosmos (1996) 'From People's Politics to State Politics: Aspects of National Liberation in South Africa, 1984–1994', *Politeia* (Pretoria), 15, 3, p. 78.

101. Ibid., p. 95.

102. Jeremy Seekings (1991) '"Trailing Behind the Masses": The United Democratic Front and Township Politics in the Pretoria-Witwatersrand-Vaal Region, 1983–84', *Journal of Southern African Studies*, 18, 1, p. 93.

103. The ANC was perhaps just beginning to emerge from a concentration upon externally-directed armed struggle in which it ignored domestic political action. Howard Barrell (1991) '"The Turn to the Masses: the African National Congress" Strategic Review of 1978–79', *Journal of Southern African Studies*, 18, 1, pp. 66 and 92. Dale McKinley argues, however, that the ANC leadership remained elitist and non-accountable and 'ignored the very people in whose name [the] struggle was conducted'. Dale McKinley (1997) *The ANC and the Liberation Struggle*. London: Pluto Press, p. xi.

104. Seekings, 'Trailing', p. 93.

105. Neocosmos, 'People's Politics', p. 77. Steven Friedman noted too that the ongoing struggle for workers' rights in the factories had 'given birth to a new type of politics ... rarely seen among the powerless ... [one] which stresses the ability of ordinary men and women ... to act to change their world'. Steven Friedman (1987) *Building Tomorrow Today: African Workers in Trade Unions, 1970–1984*. Johannesburg: Ravan Press, p. 8.

106. Seekings, 'Trailing'.

107. Quoted in Neocosmos, 'People's Politics', p. 87.

108. Ibid., p. 97.

109. Murphy Morobe (1987) 'Toward's a People's Democracy: The UDF View', part of a speech made on Morobe's behalf, May 1987, *Review of African Political Economy*, 40, pp. 81–5; all emphasis was Morobe's.

110. Dietrich Rueschemeyer, Evelyne Stephens and John Stephens (1992) *Capitalist Development and Democracy*. Cambridge: Polity Press, p. 6.

111. Neocosmos, 'People's Politics', p. 111.

112. Ibid., p. 87. That accountability was little more attractive than criticism is argued in K. Good (1997) 'Accountable to Themselves: Predominance in Southern Africa', *Journal of Modern African Studies*, 35, 4. Martin Meredith describes the country's foremost nationalist leader as follows: 'He confides in few people'; 'he tends to be autocratic'; and 'the company to which he is most attracted is that of the rich and famous; status impresses him'. Martin Meredith (1997) *Nelson Mandela: A Biography*. London: Penguin Books, pp. 1–3.

113. Re-presented by both the ANC and the National Party, as Waldmeir's supposed

'miracle' took place. Patti Waldmeir (1997) *Anatomy of a Miracle: The End of Apartheid and the Birth of the New South Africa*. London: Viking.

114. Neocosmos, 'People's Politics', p. 76.

115. Ibid., p. 102. The formation of the new 'patriotic bourgeoisie' is considered in Good, 'Accountable to Themselves', pp. 554–5.

116. Robert Taylor, quoting figures of the International Labour Organization, *Sunday Times*, 9 November 1997.

117. Vuyo Mvoko, *Business Day*, 8 July 1998.

118. K. Good (1999) 'Enduring Elite Democracy in Botswana', in *Democratization* (London), 6, 1 (Spring).

119. Of which total 'about 20,000 could be considered to be development-oriented'. Wilmot James and Daria Caliguire (1976) 'Renewing Civil Society', *Journal of Democracy* (Baltimore), 7, 1, p. 61.

120. Patrick Molutsi, 'The Civil Society and Democracy in Botswana: An Overview'. Paper presented at the Conference on Civil Society and Democracy in Botswana, Democracy Research Project, Gaborone, 25–27 October 1995, p.11.

121. There were three important proposals: to establish an independent electoral commission; to extend voting rights to citizens resident outside Botswana; and to lower the voting age to eighteen. It should perhaps be noted that the government-controlled print and radio media ran a 'No' campaign. *Gazette*, 8 October 1997.

122. A basic argument in Good and Molutsi, 'The State and Poverty in Botswana'. Paper presented to the first CROP workshop on 'The Role of the State in Poverty Alleviation', Gaborone, October 1997.

123. For Legong Raditlhokwa, student apathy in Botswana is 'a structurally determined behaviour' emanating from values manufactured and perpetuated in 'aspects of village culture, the school system, economic expectations, political leadership and state bureaucracy'. The young have been 'systematically programmed to dream only of marginal positions in the echelons of the system', and are 'perpetually made to feel inferior and incompetent by political leaders'. 'Time to Break the Passive Cycle', *HEDU Bulletin* (University of Botswana), 11 (October 1994), pp. 7–8.

124. Which is not to say that a number of remedial programmes do not exist, for example, efficient drought relief, a parsimonious destitute's programme, and a small old-age pension. See, e.g., K. Good (1999) 'The State and Extreme Poverty in Botswana: the San and Destitutes', *Journal of Modern African Studies*, 37, 2 (June).

125. Arblaster, *Democracy*, p. 89.

4

Poverty and Citizenship: Moral Repertoires and Welfare Regimes

Hartley Dean

Central to any discussion of the role of the state in poverty alleviation is the contested concept of citizenship. Theories of citizenship bear, on the one hand, upon questions of status and the meaning of poverty itself, and, on the other, upon social practices and the basis of the interventions directed to the prevention or relief of poverty. This chapter sets out to do two things. First, I wish to identify the underlying moral discourses or 'repertoires' on which our understandings of citizenship are based; here I shall be concerned not so much with the abstract formulations of intellectuals as with the meanings and values which underpin popular beliefs and aspirations. For this I shall draw upon evidence from a research study recently conducted in England, but I shall relate this to certain features of participatory poverty assessments in Africa. Second, I wish to articulate this analysis of moral repertoires with, on the one hand, the different kinds of political strategy for poverty alleviation that are pursued by different kinds of state or welfare 'regime', and, on the other, with different theories of social development that have been applied in the African context. My object is to contribute to an understanding of the part which popular commitment to citizenship values may play in sustaining effective social policy.

Conceptual and Theoretical Traditions

It is necessary to begin with an outline of the competing philosophical and political traditions which have constituted citizenship as a conceptual or theoretical category. There has been a daunting proliferation of recent literature on citizenship theory (for example, Culpitt 1992; Roche 1992; Turner 1993; Oliver and Heater 1994; Twine 1994; Steenbergen 1994; Lister 1997). The approach I shall outline here is one which seeks first to develop a distinction between two principal traditions, the contractarian and the solidaristic (for a fuller account see Dean with Melrose 1999), but then goes on to demonstrate how those different traditions can be inflected towards either more or less egalitarian interpretations. It is in this context that accounts of the rights of citizenship and of exclusion from citizenship can be addressed.

The relevance of poverty for citizenship was evident over 2,000 years ago to Aristotle. Though the Athenian city-state which gave birth to the concept of citizenship was *in practice* highly elitist and exclusive (but see Good, Chapter 3 in this volume), Aristotle recognized that, if the logic of the principle of democratic self-government were pursued, it ought *in theory* to lead to mob rule; his fear was that 'in democracies the poor have more sovereign power than the rich: for they are more numerous' (Aristotle 1981: 362). In the event, the development of citizenship has yet to accord sovereign power to the poor, though the emergence of the modern Enlightenment project portended two possible ways in which the issue of sovereignty might be resolved. One of these envisaged a form of social contract in which sovereign power is negotiated between the individual citizen and the state; this is the solution posed by classical liberal theory. The other sought to subordinate sovereignty to solidarity and the need for citizens to achieve social integration and mutual cohesion; this is the solution of civic republicanism. The three Enlightenment principles embodied in the French revolutionary slogan – '*liberté, egalité, fraternité*' – in fact expressed what Hobsbawm has called 'a contradiction rather than a combination' (Hobsbawm 1962: 284). The contractarian conception of citizenship which sought to protect the liberty of the individual subject is inimical to the solidaristic conception of citizenship which seeks to promote fraternity or belonging. Neither conception, as we shall see, is necessarily concerned to uphold equality or combat poverty.

In the Northern world,[1] therefore, as modern civil and political regimes developed from the eighteenth century onwards they have tended to draw on one or a combination of two strategies (cf. Mann 1987). One strategy was essentially constitutionalist, subscribing to a contractarian notion of citizenship by which individuals are subject to the rule of law and constitutional governance; it is the strategy which came to typify the Anglo–Saxon world. The other was essentially corporatist, subscribing to a solidaristic conception of citizenship by which the interests of individuals are brokered through negotiated compromise between different sources of coercive power; it is the strategy which came to typify the continental European world. In both kinds of regime administrative state power developed in ways which made it possible for governments to alleviate poverty. Here it is necessary to introduce the important contribution to citizenship theory which has been made by T. H. Marshall (1950).

Marshall, writing specifically about Britain, contended that, in the twentieth century, citizenship had come of age. In addition to the civil and political rights which had been important to achieve emancipation from despotism, the welfare state had ushered in an array of social rights – rights to health-care, education and income maintenance – which would ensure that every citizen could enjoy a broad equality of status and opportunity. Citizenship, he argued, required a social element to be meaningful or effective. The power that is accorded to the free market through civil rights and the rule of law needs to be constructively balanced by democratic rights, while the conflicts and privations to which market forces may give rise should be tempered by rights to social welfare. The idea of a 'social dimension' that complements the economic and political dimensions of citizenship has since become common currency within the discourse of supra-national bodies like the European Union (EC 1994).

However, in seeking to develop a social dimension and a common approach to poverty alleviation the European Union has been beset by the essential tensions which exist between the two conceptions of citizenship. As Room (1995) has pointed out, the concept of poverty reflects a characteristically liberal concern with distributional issues, while corporatist concerns are characteristically with processes of 'social exclusion' and relational issues. Seminal theorists of poverty such as Townsend (1979) have sought to define relative *poverty* in relation to *exclusion* from social participation and this allows for an uneasy compromise or conflation between the two conceptual traditions (see also Levitas 1996). That conflation, while permitting politicians and academics from both sides of the traditional divide to co-operate on the alleviation of poverty and social exclusion, tends to mask the significance of another important distinction: that between egalitarian and non-egalitarian approaches to citizenship's social dimension; that between approaches to social welfare which would secure either formal or substantive equality between citizens on the one hand and those which would preserve or constructively regulate social hierarchies on the other.

How relevant are such debates to the African context? Commentators from very different ends of the ideological spectrum have rightly warned against the assumption that Enlightenment values forged over the past two centuries in the North should be reflected in the workings of the nations of the South (Lal 1997) and against the analytical distinctions that would reduce African history to a history by analogy with that of the Northern world (Mamdani 1996). Mafeje (see Chapter 2 in this volume) cogently argues that the very concept of 'poverty alleviation' – as opposed to the more radical objective of poverty eradication – characterizes the thinking of Northern welfare regimes. At the normative level, without doubt,

T. H. Marshall's conception of welfare citizenship was ameliorative rather than transformative: he sought to civilize capitalism, not transcend it. At the analytical level, however, he contributed a seminal insight into the way that citizenship can sustain capitalism. A similar point has been made from a critical neo-Marxist perspective by Offe: 'the owner of labour power first becomes a wage labourer as a citizen of a state' (Offe 1984: 99). Citizenship is not merely some ambiguous Northern ideal; its substantive logic inhabits the very processes by which capitalism has attained global hegemony. To the extent that poverty may be said to be 'ideologically indispensable to capitalism' (Seabrook 1985: 12), those who would address poverty in contemporary Africa can no more avoid the relevance of citizenship (and its 'social dimension') as a concept than they can deny the power of transnational capital.

Nevertheless, capitalism does not fashion citizenship in any single or distinctive form. Citizenship develops in response to a range of influences, including war, migration and the impact of social movements: it may be imposed from the above, but it can also be seized from below (Turner 1986; 1990). To have any purchase in everyday life, citizenship must have popular as well as political meaning. In this context, there is one other important theoretical contribution to our understanding of the relationship between poverty and citizenship. It has been suggested by John Scott (1994) that the extremes of poverty and wealth – or of deprivation and privilege – constitute the boundaries of the ordinary public realm that constitutes citizenship. To this extent, the basis of citizenship as a common ideal rests in identification with the 'ordinary', while those who are excluded from conventional lifestyles and social participation by poverty and those who exclude themselves by virtue of extreme wealth are the 'other'. Though Scott, following Townsend, has argued that there are certain 'catastrophic boundaries in the distribution of resources' (Scott 1994: 173) which separate both poor and rich from ordinary citizens, I have argued elsewhere (Dean 1992) that poverty can be as much a discursive construct as an objective condition; that it can also be a symbolic signification of 'otherness'. The boundaries may defy clear or objective determination, but citizenship as an intersubjective construct may be most commonly understood in relation to that 'imagined community' (cf. Anderson 1983) that is constituted within the boundaries established by our perceptions of poverty on the one hand and of wealth on the other.

'Bottom-up' Discourses of Poverty and Citizenship

It was with such considerations in mind that a colleague and I recently undertook an empirical investigation that sought to locate perceptions of social inequality and citizenship at the level of everyday experience and popular discourse.[2] This was a qualitative study involving in-depth interviews with seventy-six working adults from various parts of England, with disposable incomes ranging from well below half the national average ('the poor') to well above twice the national average ('the rich'). The object was to investigate the respondents' perceptions, attitudes, fears and aspirations in relation to issues pertaining to poverty, wealth, the welfare state and the meaning of citizenship. Though they were primarily discursive, the interviews included for benchmarking purposes selected questions drawn from Runciman's (1966) study of relative deprivation and from the British Social Attitude Surveys (see Taylor-Gooby 1990; Lipsey 1994; Brook et al. 1996). The findings should be understood in the context that, though Britain is a relatively affluent country, it is also one of the most unequal societies in the world (Barclay 1995; UN 1996; Bradshaw and Chen 1997).

First, it became clear that a fear of poverty extended up the income scale to respondents on middle and even high incomes. Poverty tended to be regarded, even by 'the poor' themselves, as a distant horror which usually happens to other people, but it manifested itself as a cause of everyday worry. Second, the extent to which respondents feared poverty exceeded the extent to which they aspired to wealth. Wealth had a certain fascination – it would be fun to be free from everyday constraints – but many respondents, even among 'the rich', made it clear that they valued comfort above riches. Third, as in Runciman's study thirty years before, respondents were seldom able to locate themselves within the social distribution of incomes. Asked to place themselves on a scale between rich and poor, few were able to do so with any degree of accuracy. In particular, respondents with middle to higher incomes tended grossly to underestimate their relative standing, a finding which cast light on their underlying sense of insecurity (cf. Pahl 1995) and their worries about poverty.

This last finding also casts light on the fact that, in their attitudes to redistributive state welfare, respondents tended to exhibit an apparently contradictory mixture of guarded altruism and pragmatic instrumentalism (cf. Rentoul 1989; Brook et al. 1996). To a degree, it would seem, in an unequal society people may in reality be subject to the same 'veil of ignorance' about their relative material standing as that which Rawls (1972) had sought artificially to impose upon the imaginary participants in his famous thought experiment. Ontological insecurity might incline people just as much as calculative rationality to subscribe to certain principles of social justice. By implication, people's preference is likely to be for a form of citizenship which protects against poverty before it secures the opportunity to pursue wealth. It remained the case, however, that, although respondents generally valued key elements of the solidaristic or collectivist principles on which the welfare state was established, they were also predisposed to ideological principles which would underpin more individualistic self-sufficiency. Close examination of the respondents' underlying discourses revealed a complex picture. For example, as might be anticipated, respondents who were poor were more in favour of state redistribution than those who were rich but, paradoxically, the poor were less inclined to indulge in solidaristic rhetoric than were the rich and, denying that they *themselves* were poor, were often more inclined to be judgemental about the behaviour of those *other* people whom they defined as poor.

Although the context and purposes of the study were very different, elements of the findings up to this point bear certain similarities with findings from participatory poverty assessments in Africa. The concept of participatory poverty assessment is associated with the 'Basic Needs' approach to social development (Wisner 1988) and, although this fell out of favour in the 1980s, in the 1990s participatory poverty assessments have re-established themselves as a qualitative investigative technique by which to define the task of poverty alleviation – as it were, from 'the bottom up'. It would be wrong to draw too many parallels, since the nature of poverty in Africa is fundamentally different from that in European countries: quite apart from macro-economic and geo-political considerations, such factors as seasonal cycles, the urban–rural divide, generational and gender dynamics all bear far more acutely upon the manner in which poverty and wealth are popularly perceived. Taking as examples the assessments conducted in Zambia (Norton et al. 1994) and South Africa (May et al. 1998) we can none the less observe three important findings that resonate with those of our study. First, ordinary Zambians and South Africans are likely to place greater store on 'well-being' and security – of food supply, employment and so on – than upon income alone. Second, the horizons by which their expectations are set and their definitions of what constitutes 'wealth' are in relative terms remarkably modest. Third, attitudes to 'other' poor people are often conservatively judgemental and based on victim-blaming explanations of poverty.

African participatory poverty assessments are subject to certain methodological limitations, however. First, the process of 'wealth ranking' which is used in the assessments can have particular immediacy in a small village setting, for example; the intimacy of the social structure makes it far easier to locate oneself than in the anonymity of a cosmopolitan Northern society, but, precisely because of this, the exercise can be inhibiting for the participants. Second, although the studies explore Africans' definitions of poverty, it is seldom clear from the reports cited above whether or in what circumstances the concepts with which participants were working were those they would apply to themselves, as opposed to those they might apply to their neighbours. Third, in so far as a full picture of the survival strategies pursued by participants might often necessarily depend on admissions regarding informal and/or illegal economic activities, the accuracy of the data may in some instances be doubtful. Finally, questions of accuracy also arise to the extent that popular discourse can be both complex and artful; participants may well 'borrow' elements of a dominant discourse expressly for the benefit of the investigators.

James Scott's studies of everyday peasant resistance in Malaysia (1985; 1990; and see Jordan 1993 for a commentary) illustrate the ways in which subordinate groups may not only engage in low-risk acts of petty sabotage against their perceived oppressors, but may skilfully draw on the discourses of the powerful when framing their claims against those in authority. The ingenious application of officially approved language and the reinterpretation or subversion of the agendas of administrators or researchers constitute one of the 'weapons of the weak', yet this need not preclude the use of other discourses; the 'hidden transcripts' of popular vernacular, which even ostensibly 'participative' techniques may struggle to reveal. The prima-facie evidence from poor people in a variety of situations suggests that their resistance against the conditions which perpetuate their poverty tends to be inherently 'conservative' in nature (see, for example, Dean and Melrose 1997).

It is important, therefore, to develop techniques that can access such 'hidden transcripts' and discover their potential. We need to find ways of unpacking the diverse range of discursive repertoires on which people draw in relation to their 'citizenship'; that is, to their membership of unequal society. This was something we sought to develop in the study outlined above. In fact, our respondents were seldom able to engage coherently with the concept of 'citizenship'. Almost a third said they did not know what being a citizen meant or that it didn't mean anything very much, and others could define citizenship only in its narrowest sense by equating it with nationality. The horror with which respondents regarded poverty and the sceptical fascination with which they regarded wealth were far more tangible than their concepts of citizenship. Even among many of those who clearly were relatively 'poor' or 'rich', it was their own sense of distance from the extremes of poverty and riches, coupled with their aspiration to a 'comfortable' lifestyle, which defined their inclusion within the pale of social convention; as citizens, not by virtue of civic status, but because they believed themselves to be neither rich nor poor, but ordinary (cf. John Scott 1994). Nevertheless, respondents could and did convey what they understood with regard to rights and responsibilities and the nature of their and other people's relationships as individuals to society.

Moral Repertoires and Popular Discourse

It is through such discourses that people disclose the different ways in which they negotiate the everyday realities of living in an unequal society. They are unlikely to engage explicitly with discourses of citizenship, so much as to relate pragmatically to questions bearing upon their own comfort and security. In this respect the study concerned itself not so much with the expressed opinions of the respondents as with the way in which those opinions were constructed out of everyday experience and discourse. For the purposes of this analysis we drew, in part, on an argument developed by Offe (1993) that there is a range of different 'moral repertoires' upon which society at large may draw in order to validate any particular pattern of rights and obligations. Offe drew his taxonomy of repertoires somewhat arbitrarily from an analysis of dominant Northern political and philosophical traditions – distinguishing Utilitarian, Kantian and communitarian moral repertoires. However, we derived our taxonomy analytically from a study of our interview transcripts.

It was evident that the important differences between respondents in the study related partly to the substance of the explanations or justifications they used, and partly to the strategies of understanding and expression (or 'voices') upon which they were able to call. Popular discourse is, by its nature, a complex mixture of competing explanations and voices and it is these which inform the various ways in which individuals bind themselves in to social structures. In order to construct a taxonomy of the popular discourses through which dominant moral repertoires are constituted, we called on the work of two very different theorists: the sociologist Anthony Giddens and the anthropologist Mary Douglas.

Giddens (1990; 1991; and see also Beck, Giddens and Lash 1994) has been responsible for developing the concept of 'reflexive modernisation'. His original formulation of the concept was linked to a discussion of social processes under conditions of 'late modernity'. He was concerned with the reflexivity that is required of individuals in the late modern age if they are to place their trust in advanced technical and administrative systems and maintain social relations across increasingly indefinite spans of time and space; and with the anxiety that is entailed in the maintenance of self-identity and ontological security in a society full of social hazards, environmental risks and economic uncertainty. It is possible to articulate Giddens's particular concepts of reflexivity and ontological security with the concepts of 'grid' and 'group' in the work of Douglas (1978). 'Grid' and 'group' are the dimensions in Douglas's system of cultural typologies. 'Grid' relates to the extent to which systems of classification in a society are either shared or private; to which codes of discourse are either restricted

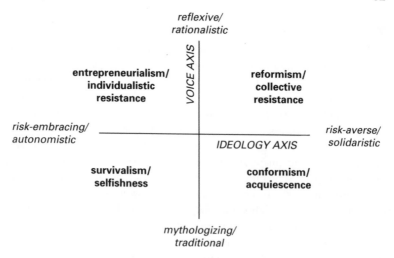

reflexive/
rationalistic

VOICE AXIS

entrepreneurialism/
individualistic
resistance

reformism/
collective
resistance

risk-embracing/
autonomistic

IDEOLOGY AXIS

risk-averse/
solidaristic

survivalism/
selfishness

conformism/
acquiescence

mythologizing/
traditional

FIGURE 4.1 A taxonomy of moral repertoires

and tradition-bound or elaborated and radical. 'Group' relates to the extent
to which individuals in society are either controlled by other people's
pressure or are free to exert pressure on others; to which they are either
integrated through reciprocal group social relations or largely independent
(or alienated) from them.

I would argue that, where Douglas is describing the ways in which some
individuals, groups or societies may come to depend less on ritual and more
on elaborated communicative codes, Giddens would speak of reflexivity.
Where Douglas is describing the ways in which some individuals, groups
or societies become less bounded by collective power and more alienated,
Giddens would speak of loss of ontological security and of increased risk.
Figure 4.1 incorporates Douglas's and Giddens's respective theoretical
distinctions as intersecting dimensions or continua. The taxonomy represented in Figure 4.1 supersedes the notions of grid and reflexivity with the
more general concept of *voice*, to which I have made reference above: this
is represented along the vertical continuum or axis. The taxonomy supersedes the notions of group and ontological security (or its converse, anxiety/
risk) by articulating them with the realm of *ideology*, as the medium though
which individual perceptions of social existence are apprehended or shaped;
this is represented along the horizontal continuum or axis.

This represents a taxonomy of the discourses or repertoires relating to
the risk of social inequality under global conditions of 'late modernity'. At
issue here is the extent to which people drew upon reflexive or mytho-

logizing modes of expression on the one hand or to which they draw upon autonomistic (i.e. behaviourally situated and pro-risk-taking) or collectivist (i.e. structurally situated and pro-ontological security) modes of explanation on the other. So, for example, respondents who drew on autonomistic modes of explanation would characteristically blame poverty on the poor themselves. Of these, those who drew on reflexive modes of expression were characteristically *entrepreneurial* – for them, the way to resist poverty is through individual merit and the seizing of opportunity; but those who drew on mythologizing modes of expression were characteristically *survivalist* – for them, resisting poverty is a matter of good luck and of keeping ahead of the competition. In contrast, respondents who drew on collectivist modes of explanation would characteristically regard the poor as the victims of social circumstance. Of these, those who drew on reflexive modes of expression were characteristically *reformist* – for them, resisting poverty is a matter of social justice and is a policy question; but those who drew on mythologizing modes of expression were characteristically *conformist* – for them, though the poor might be deserving of help, poverty was an inevitable occurrence.

The taxonomy is a classification of discursive repertoires, not personal characteristics. Nevertheless, it was possible to assign each of the respondents in our sample in terms of the overall balance of discourses within their individual interview transcripts to one of the four quadrants in Figure 4.1. In daily speech we all of us draw on a multiplicity of often variable and sometimes contradictory discursive repertoires but, by taking account of the relative extent of different discourses within the text generated by each interview and identifying the dominant discourse, it was found that the sample could be distributed between the quadrants of the taxonomy in broadly equal proportions. From this it is possible to conclude (see Dean 1998) that, surviving within popular discourse in Britain, there is a paradigm which accepts a role for the welfare state, and that the values necessary to support that paradigm have by no means been eclipsed. However, it can equally be argued that popular discourse is capable of sustaining a variety of approaches to welfare provision and poverty alleviation – not only in Britain, but elsewhere in the world. My purpose in this chapter is to reflect more generally upon the relationship between moral repertoires in popular discourse and the contrasting political assumptions that underpin different welfare state regimes and social development strategies.

'Top-down' Discourses of Poverty and Citizenship

The discursive repertoires on which people draw in apprehending the nature of social inequality do not exist within a political vacuum and it is

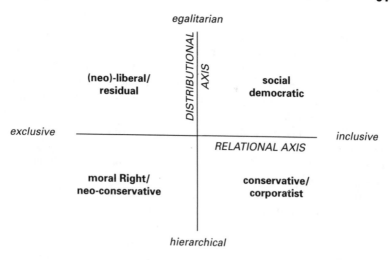

FIGURE 4.2 A taxonomy of welfare state regimes

necessary at this point to return to my earlier discussion of the conceptual and theoretical traditions of citizenship. I wish to argue that it is possible to map the moral repertoires of popular discourse against a related but different taxonomy which is much more explicitly concerned with competing conceptions of citizenship.

I have attempted to show that what distinguishes different approaches to citizenship is, on the one hand, differing understandings of the *relations* between the individual and the collectivity; a distinction between liberal/contractarian ideas (which are, by implication, exclusively focused upon participating individuals) and republican/solidaristic ideas (which are, by implication, inclusively focused upon the collectivity). On the other hand, there are also differing evaluations of the constitutional basis on which social *distribution* occurs; a distinction between egalitarian and hierarchical values. In Figure 4.2 these distinctions are represented as the axes of a taxonomy of different types of welfare regime: the relational dimension is represented along the horizontal axis and the distributional dimension along the vertical axis. Three of the regimes so identified correspond to the welfare regimes identified through empirical analysis by Esping-Andersen (1990). Though the validity, scope and rigour of Esping-Andersen's seminal typology of welfare regimes have been widely debated, it still provides a valuable heuristic model on which to build. The regimes, of course, are ideal types and, just as individual discourse may draw on a mixture of repertoires, so the strategies adopted by political parties and nation-states may represent a synthesis drawn from different quadrants of the taxonomy.

The (neo-)liberal or residual welfare regime would be the embodiment of the 'night-watchman state'. It would be only formally egalitarian, but substantively exclusive in the sense that it would aspire to be rigorously meritocratic. The role of the state would be minimized so as to give free play to market forces. The responsibilities of the state would be confined to those required in order to guarantee individual freedom and equality of opportunity. The regime would not, however, guarantee equality of outcome and would be tolerant of poverty and social exclusion. To the extent that provision would be made for the relief of poverty, this would be undertaken with a view to the maintenance of civil order and the conditions necessary for a market economy. The liberal welfare regime is broadly equated in Esping-Andersen's typology (1990) with Anglo-Saxon welfare states. To the extent that such a regime has a moral basis, Offe (1993) has characterized this as 'utilitarian' in that it would defend welfare on the basis of a calculus of second order material benefits (such as economic efficiency) and the avoidance of collective evils (such as epidemics or social unrest).

The social democratic welfare regime, potentially, would provide the most comprehensive form of welfare state. It would be both substantively egalitarian and substantively inclusive in the sense that it would seek to make universal provision for all citizens. The role of the state would be maximized so as to ameliorate or negate the adverse consequences of market forces. The responsibilities of the state would be extended so as to ensure broad equality in terms of both status and resources. The regime would be concerned to redistribute resources so as to prevent the occurrence of poverty. The social democratic welfare regime is broadly equated in Esping-Andersen's typology with the Scandinavian welfare states. To the extent that such a regime has a moral basis, Offe has characterized this as 'Kantian' in that it would defend welfare in terms of a principled commitment to universal and inclusive rights and obligations (and rests on an assumption that free will depends on moral choices which transcend self-interest).

The conservative, or corporatist welfare regime, would represent the most paternalistic form of welfare state. It would be substantively hierarchical but only formally inclusive in the sense that it would make extensive provision for most citizens while sustaining established social relations of power. The state would act as broker between competing sources of power – in particular the interests of capital and labour – bringing them together as 'social partners' rather than as coercive adversaries. The regime would be concerned to supervise the distribution of resources and generally to prevent poverty in the interests of social cohesion and the preservation of the status quo, but would neither ensure equality, nor protect the interests of marginalized or powerless social groups. The conservative welfare regime is broadly equated in Esping-Andersen's typology with continental European welfare states. To the extent that such a regime has a moral basis, Offe has characterized this as 'communitarian' in that it would defend welfare on the basis of a particular set of external preferences and draws on the principle of solidarity exclusively to protect the welfare of a defined community. Here Offe clearly had in mind the kind of traditional communitarianism associated with Christian Democracy, rather than the newer, US-influenced, strand of communitarianism to which I shall refer below.

The moral Right or neo-conservative welfare regime would be an authoritarian or coercive welfare state. It would be both formally hierarchical and formally exclusive in the sense that it would aspire to sustain a traditional moral order. The state would countenance welfare interventions only to the extent that they might deter undesirable forms of individual behaviour or enforce desirable ones. The regime would promote a social order based on inequality and would be concerned neither to relieve nor prevent poverty. Esping-Andersen does not identify this as a regime type on the basis of his empirical evidence, but such a regime is logically possible in analytical terms. If it were to have a moral basis, it could perhaps be characterized as 'Hobbesian' in that it would not so much defend welfare as harness the power of the state to regulate the supposedly anarchic and amoral disposition of the populace.

The classic Bismarckian and Beveridgean welfare states of the Northern world drew respectively upon a corporatist and a social democratic strategy, or – in practice – a combination of both; virtually all welfare states were to some extent hybrid regimes. More recently, the attempts to remould welfare provision according to monetarist principles during the height of the Thatcher/Reagan era exhibited elements of both a neo-liberal strategy and a neo-conservative strategy (e.g. Gamble 1988). To a varying extent, both in Britain and the USA, not only were attempts made to curtail welfare provision, but welfare took on a more authoritarian face. In the current era, the Thatcher/Reagan orthodoxy is being displaced, some would argue, by an emerging Blair/Clinton orthodoxy (e.g. Jordan 1998). It is an orthodoxy that has quite explicitly been influenced by a new strand of socially conservative communitarian thinking (Etzioni 1994; and see Driver and Martell 1997; King and Wickham-Jones 1999) that draws in rather complex and contradictory ways upon libertarian elements of neo-liberal strategy and authoritarian elements of conservative strategy. While emphasizing a role for state intervention, especially on the supply side of the economy, it is concerned that the rights of citizens should strictly reflect their observance of duties and obligations to the community. It is seeking in one sense to be both formally egalitarian and formally inclusive, though it remains to be seen what the substantive effects upon either dimension might prove to be.

The Moral Basis of Social Development Strategies

Northern orthodoxies have inevitably found their equivalent in the discourses of development agencies and, particularly, the Bretton Woods institutions. Mafeje (in Chapter 2 of this volume) demonstrates how in the 1980s elements of the emerging Thatcher/Reagan orthodoxy came to represent a significant element in policy prescriptions made for developing countries by the IMF and the World Bank (see also Deacon 1997). In the 1990s, it is suggested, the Blair/Clinton othodoxy is growing in dominance and in its hegemonic influence around the globe. The context for this growing influence is a trend which Deacon (1997) identifies as the beginnings of a 'globalisation of social policy and a socialisation of global politics'. Following the collapse of the Cold War and of communism, the threat of global migration and the essentially transnational nature of social and environmental concerns have meant that social policy questions may be becoming more central to the preoccupations of the world's business and political elites. Alleviating poverty might be on the global political agenda, but this is an age when it is generally accepted that the 'golden age' of welfare state protectionism is past (Esping-Andersen 1996) and prescriptions for welfare reform are informed by a perceived need to limit public spending and sustain labour market flexibility. The 'new paradigm' espoused by IFAD and cited by Mafeje (Chapter 2 of this volume) conceptualizes poverty alleviation as a 'mobilization' or 'integration' of the poor in the cause of economic growth. The poor must be helped to accept responsibility for their own destiny, but in the context of a world order that depends on economic growth. Implicit here it seems to me is an acceptance of the economic liberal agenda and the socially conservative communitarianism that is the hallmark of the Blair/Clinton orthodoxy. The 'new paradigm', therefore, is not so much new as a recombination of old paradigms.

Midgley (1993; 1995; 1997) has developed a three-fold classification of the principal social development strategies, characterizing these as enterprise or market-led strategies, founded in the 'trickle-down' theory of economic development; statist or planned development strategies, founded in the kind of welfare economics which neo-liberal critics excoriate as the prevailing 'dirigiste dogma' of a left-wing intellectual establishment (Lal 1997); communitarian or community development strategies, founded in the 'trickle-up' theory of economic development. Midgley himself believes it is possible and indeed necessary to achieve a synthesis of these strategies,

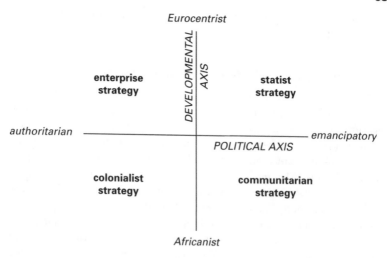

FIGURE 4.3 A taxonomy of social development strategies

but his analysis is also important for the way in which his categories can be loosely mapped on to the taxonomy of welfare state regimes developed above: the enterprise strategy equates with the neo-liberal approach; the statist strategy with the social democratic approach; the communitarian strategy with the conservative approach. If there were a strategy equivalent to the neo-conservative approach, it might perhaps be not so much a development strategy as the traditional colonialist strategy.

To round off the analysis presented in this chapter, therefore, I shall attempt to recast Midgley's taxonomy of social development strategies. In a way similar to Midgley, Mamdani (1996) has sought a synthesis between different theoretical approaches to what he characterizes as 'Africa's impasse'. The impasse he wishes to transcend is 'between modernists and communitarians, Eurocentrists and Africanists' (Mamdani 1996: 3). This distinction constitutes the developmental dimension that I use as the vertical axis in Figure 4.3. For the horizontal axis I use a different distinction made by Mamdani – that between emancipatory and authoritarian modes of politics – though I would seek to interpret this in terms of what Foucault (1977) has defined as a '*bio*-political' dimension: the 'emancipatory' extremity of the axis is essentially pro-populationist and, if not explicitly revolutionary, it is concerned to unlock the potential promised by the African people; the 'authoritarian' extremity is essentially anti-populationist and, if not explicitly Malthusian, it is concerned to contain the threat posed by the African people.

The object at this juncture is to present, not necessarily a menu from which to choose or even synthesize an effective poverty alleviation strategy, but a model through which to understand or 'critique' the anatomy of current discourses. My thesis is that advocates of social development tend in practice to draw upon a mixture of discourses drawn from these repertoires. The more eurocentrist discourses tend either to enterprise strategy and the imposition of Structural Adjustment Programmes, or to statist strategy and the application of universalist premises derived from social-democratic welfare economics. What might be defined as Africanist discourses tend either to embody the legacy of neo-colonial strategies of indirect domination through the manipulation of customary power (see Mamdani 1996), or various forms of communitarian or 'participatory' approaches to poverty amelioration.

Conclusion

The issue for this chapter is the extent to which the contortions of political and theoretical discourse correspond to the notions of moral rights and obligations within popular discourse. Popular discourse, as I have shown, is no more coherent or consistent than political discourse. What is more, its substance will be subject to variations in different countries and cultures. It is an empirical question that participatory poverty assessments in Africa might yet directly address, but I would hypothesize on the basis of insights tentatively contained within existing evidence that certain elements of the taxonomy represented in Figure 4.1 might be broadly translatable to any society that is subject to social inequality. Unequal societies may sustain:

- Discourses which favour 'enterprise', meritocracy and a liberal/select-ivist conception of poverty alleviation, based on the idea that free markets will allow created wealth to 'trickle down' to benefit the poor.
- Discourses which favour 'reform', social justice and a social democratic/ universalist conception of poverty alleviation, based on the idea that poverty can be prevented through comprehensive state provision.
- Discourses which favour 'conformity', social cohesion and a con-servative/communitarian conception of poverty alleviation, based on the idea that the state should underwrite the capacity of the community to protect itself from poverty (or else encourage or even compel it to do so).
- Discourses which favour mere 'survival', order, fatalism and a neo-conservative indifference to poverty alleviation.

These discourses will co-exist in tension with each other and the issue for policy-makers and activists who are concerned to promote the role of the state in the alleviation of poverty is not one of how to manipulate public opinion in favour of some chosen strategy, but of how popular discourse interprets the nature of citizenship. If resistance to poverty and the basis for an accommodation with the ascendant world order can indeed be seized from below rather than imposed from above, it is a question of how the moral repertoires within popular discourse are to be translated into authentic forms of political consensus. Good's call for 'participatory democracy' (Chapter 3 in this volume) must presuppose a form of citizenship capable of resolving such tensions within popular discourse and, in the process, of embracing a social as well as a political dimension.

It should also be remarked that the particular discourses outlined above, though they may be dominant, are not the only possible discourses. There is, for example, no scope in the taxonomy developed in this chapter for radical socialist, feminist or ecological moral repertoires. Nor is there much scope here for aspirational forms of 'global citizenship' that might transcend the established bounds of existing nation-states and political communities (see Falk 1994). This is an inherent limitation of the model. Advocates of a politics of discourse hold out the possibility that radical forms of democracy would enable alternative intellectual critiques to permeate popular discourses (e.g. Laclau and Mouffe 1985), but as Doyal and Gough (1991) point out, even a fully democratized civil society would require forms of social regulation in order to maximize the health and autonomy of its people. By implication, it would require a form of citizenship which could articulate the freedom of the individual with the interests of the collectivity, and which could furnish comprehensible parameters in relation to social structures and differences. Clearly, political and popular discourse can and should be inflected towards new possibilities, but the old conundrums remain.

I have sought to demonstrate the complexity and ambiguity of our dominant moral repertoires. However, my argument is that, in spite rather than because of any hegemonic political discourse, popular discourse in an unequal society has elements that incline towards a desire for social justice. Reformist moral repertoires are not dominant in popular discourse any more than social democratic values are dominant in current political discourse, but neither are they extinct. Whether in an English suburb or a South African township the chronic insecurity, uncertainty or *risk* (see Beck 1992) which characterizes human experience of global capitalism create conditions in which people's implicit preference is likely to be for security against poverty, not the freedom to become rich.

The alleviation of poverty, therefore, requires an understanding of the importance of citizenship theory. It is also necessary to understand the equivocal nature of popular commitment to citizenship. Certainly, it is possible to dismiss the relevance of citizenship as a bourgeois fiction; as a system of fetishized categories which obscure the nature of our self-alienation as members of civil society from our own 'social humanity' (see Marx 1845); as a notion which reduces the reciprocity of social life to a narrow calculus of rights and duties. It is possible that under more transparent and less exploitative social relations it would be possible for our rights to reflect our political demands for emancipation and for our duties to reflect the logic of our interdependency. The fact remains, however, that as long as there is poverty we must critically engage with the basis on which citizenship has been or is being constructed or reconstructed within different welfare regimes around the world; with the various ways in which 'the poor' may therefore be excluded from citizenship; and the substantive means by which the 'social dimension' of citizenship can be realized through social development strategies directed at the alleviation of poverty.

Notes

1. For the purposes of this chapter I shall adopt the convention that characterizes 'Western civilization'/ 'developed nations'/ the 'First World' by reference to the Northern hemisphere or 'the North', and 'developing nations'/the 'Third World' by reference to the Southern hemisphere or 'the South'. It is none the less important to remember that there are some significant 'western-style' welfare state regimes to be found in the Southern hemisphere.

2. The study was funded by the UK Economic and Social Research Council under Award Ref: R000236264 and undertaken by the author with Margaret Melrose at the University of Luton between 1995 and 1997. A more detailed account of the study and its findings may be found in Dean with Melrose 1999.

References

Anderson, B. (1983) *Imagined Communities*. London: Verso.

Aristotle (1981) *The Politics*. London: Penguin.

Barclay, Sir Peter (1995) *Inquiry into Income and Wealth*, Vol. 1. York: Joseph Rowntree Foundation.

Beck, U. (1992) *Risk Society: Towards a New Modernity*. London: Sage.

Beck, U., A. Giddens and S. Lash (1994) *Reflexive Modernization*. Cambridge: Polity Press.

Bradshaw, J. and J. Chen (1997) 'Poverty in the UK: A Comparison with Nineteen Other Countries', *Benefits*, 18, January.

Brook, L., J. Hall and I. Preston (1996) 'Public Spending and Taxation', in R. Jowell, J. Curtice, A. Park, L. Brook and K. Thompson (eds), *British Social Attitudes, the 13th Report*. Aldershot: Dartmouth.

Culpitt, I. (1992) *Welfare and Citizenship: Beyond the Crisis of the Welfare State?* London: Sage.

Deacon, B. with M. Hulse and P. Stubbs (1997) *Global Social Policy: International Organisations and the Future of Welfare*. London: Sage.

Dean, H. (1992) 'Poverty Discourse and the Disempowerment of the Poor', in *Critical Social Policy*, 12, 2.

— (1998) 'Popular Paradigms and Welfare Values', *Critical Social Policy*, 18, 2.

Dean, H. and M. Melrose (1997) 'Manageable Discord: Fraud and Resistance in the Social Security System', *Social Policy and Administration*, 31, 2.

Dean, H. with M. Melrose (1999) *Poverty, Riches and Social Citizenship*. London: Macmillan.

Douglas, M. (1978) *Natural Symbols*. London: Penguin.

Doyal, L. and I. Gough (1991) *A Theory of Human Need*. London: Macmillan.

Driver, S. and L. Martell (1997) 'New Labour's Communitarianisms', *Critical Social Policy*, 17, 3.

Esping-Andersen, G. (1990) *The Three Worlds of Welfare Capitalism*. Cambridge: Polity Press.

— (ed.) (1996) *Welfare States in Transition*. London: Sage.

Etzioni, A. (1994) *The Spirit of Community*. New York: Touchstone.

European Commission (EC) (1994) *European Social Policy: A Way Forward for the Union*. Luxembourg: European Commission.

Falk, R. (1994) 'The Making of Global Citizenship', in Steenbergen (ed.), *The Condition of Citizenship*. London: Sage.

Foucault, M. (1997) *Discipline and Punish*. London: Penguin.

Gamble, A. (1988) *The Free Economy and the Strong State*. London: Macmillan.

Giddens, A. (1990) *The Consequences of Modernity*. Cambridge: Polity Press.

— (1991) *Modernity and Self-Identity: Self and Society in the Late Modern Age*. Cambridge: Polity Press.

Hobsbawm, E. (1962) *The Age of Revolution 1789–1848*. New York: Mentor.

Jordan, B. (1993) 'Framing Claims and the Weapons of the Weak', in G. Drover and P. Kerans (eds), *New Approaches to Welfare Theory*. Aldershot: Edward Elgar.

— (1998) *The New Politics of Welfare: Social Justice in a Global Context*. London: Sage.

King, D. and M. Wickham-Jones (1999) 'Bridging the Atlantic: The Democratic (Party) Origins of Welfare to Work', in M. Powell (ed.), *New Labour, New Welfare State? The 'Third Way' in British Social Policy*. Cambridge: Polity Press.

Laclau, E. and C. Mouffe (1985) *Hegemony and Socialist Strategy*. London: Verso.

Lal, D. (1997) *The Poverty of 'Development Economics'*. London: Institute of Economic Affairs.

Levitas, R. (1996) 'The Concept of Social Exclusion and the New Durkheimian Hegemony', *Critical Social Policy*, 16, 2.

Lipsey, D. (1994) 'Do We Really Want More Public Spending', in R. Jowell, J. Curtice, L. Brook and D. Ahrendt (eds), *British Social Attitudes: The 11th Report*. Aldershot: Dartmouth.

Lister, R. (1997) *Citizenship: Feminist Perspectives*. London: Macmillan.

Mamdani, M. (1996) *Citizen and Subject: Contemporary Africa and the Legacy of Late Colonialism*. Princeton, NJ: Princeton University Press.

Mann, M. (1987) 'Ruling Class Strategies and Citizenship', *Sociology*, 21, 3.

Marshall, T. H. (1950) 'Citizenship and Social Class', in T. H. Marshall and T. Bottomore (1992) *Citizenship and Social Class*. London: Pluto.

Marx, K. (1845) 'Theses on Feuerbach', in *Marx-Engels Gesamtausgabe*, Vol. 1, Section 5; translated extract in T. Bottomore and M. Rubel (1963) *Karl Marx: Selected Writings in Sociology and Social Philosophy*. London: Penguin.

May, J. with H. Attwood, P. Ewang, F. Lund, A. Norton and W. Wentzal (1998) *Experience and Perceptions of Poverty in South Africa*. Durban: Praxis.

Midgley, J. (1993) 'Ideological Roots of Social Development Strategies', *Social Development Issues*, 15, 1.

— (1995) *Social Development: The Developmental Perspective in Social Welfare*. Thousand Oaks, CA: Sage.

— (1997) *Social Welfare in Global Context*. London: Sage.

Norton, A., D. Owen and J. Milimo (1994) 'Participatory Poverty Assessment: Synthesis Report', in *Zambia Poverty Assessment*, Vol. V. Washington, DC: World Bank.

Offe, C. (1984) *Contradictions of the Welfare State*. Cambridge, MA: MIT Press.

— (1993) 'Interdependence, Difference and Limited State Capacity', in G. Drover and P. Kerans (eds), *New Approaches to Welfare Theory*. Aldershot: Edward Elgar.

Oliver, D. and D. Heater (1994) *The Foundations of Citizenship*. Hemel Hempstead: Harvester Wheatsheaf.

Pahl, R. (1995) *After Success: Fin-de-siècle Anxiety and Identity*. Cambridge: Polity Press.

Rawls, J. (1972) *A Theory of Justice*. Oxford: Oxford University Press.

Rentoul, J. (1989) *Me and Mine: The Triumph of the New Individualism?* London: Unwin Hyman.

Roche, M. (1992) *Rethinking Citizenship: Welfare, Ideology and Change in Modern Society*. Cambridge: Polity Press.

Room, G. (ed.) (1995) *Beyond the Threshold, the Measurement and Analysis of Social Exclusion*. Bristol: Policy Press.

Runciman, W. B. (1966) *Relative Deprivation and Social Justice*. London: Routledge and Kegan Paul.

Scott, James (1985) *Weapons of the Weak: Everyday Forms of Peasant Resistance*. New Haven: Yale University Press.

— (1990) *Domination and the Arts of Resistance: Hidden Transcripts*. New Haven, NJ: Yale University Press.

Scott, John (1994) *Poverty and Wealth: Citizenship, Deprivation and Privilege*. Harlow: Longman.

Seabrook, J. (1985) *Landscapes of Poverty*. Oxford: Basil Blackwell.

Steenbergen, B. van (ed.) (1994) *The Condition of Citizenship*. London: Sage.

Taylor-Gooby, P. (1990) 'Social Welfare: The Unkindest Cuts', in R. Jowell, S. Witherspoon and L. Brook (eds), *British Social Attitudes: The 7th Report*. Aldershot: Gower.

Townsend, P. (1979) *Poverty in the United Kingdom*. London: Penguin.

Turner, B. (1986) *Citizenship and Capitalism: The Debate over Reformism*. London: Allen and Unwin.

— (1990) 'Outline of a Theory of Citizenship', *Sociology*, 24, 2.

— (ed.) (1993) *Citizenship and Social Theory*. London: Sage.

Twine, F. (1994) *Citizenship and Social Rights: The Interdependence of Self and Society*. London: Sage.

United Nations (1996) *The Human Development Report*. Oxford: Oxford University Press.

Wisner, B. (1988) *Basic Human Needs and Development Policies*. London: Earthscan.

5

'The Right to Have Rights': Poverty, Ethnicity, Multiculturalism and State Power

Camilo Perez-Bustillo

What possible relationship could there be between the Zapatista revolt against 'neo-liberalism' in Mexico, centred in the Mayan indigenous communities of the south-eastern state of Chiapas (and similar movements elsewhere in Latin America), and popular democratic resistance movements of the poor in Africa centred in similarly marginalized racial or ethnic groups (as in the South African, Kenyan, Congolese and Ugandan cases discussed by Mahmood Mamdani in his seminal *Citizen and Subject*, or the case of the San/Basarwa/Bushmen in Botswana)?[1] The central assumption of this chapter is that these approaches shed light on parallel issues in Mexico and Latin America, and suggest bases of comparison that provide valid points of departure for broader analysis of the inter-relationship between issues of poverty and of racial/ethnic marginalization and social exclusion on a global scale.

This chapter will seek to: (1) explore Mamdani's framework of analysis regarding the relationship between poverty, ethnicity and state power as reflected in his African case studies; (2) attempt its application to parallel experiences of colonialism, marginalization and exclusion in Mexico and Latin America from a comparative perspective; and (3) suggest some points of departure regarding 'multiculturalism' as a possible basis for the definition of some common ground between African and Latin American studies in this context.

The chapter's approach is inter-disciplinary, but rooted primarily in a conception of issues of poverty as inextricably linked to questions regarding state power and its strategic exercise and deployment in a framework of systemic relations (Destremau 1998) in which debates about notions of social justice, equity and democracy are inextricably embedded. This approach also assumes that these relations have become 'globalized' by an increasing transnationalization of capitalist hegemony (in its 'neo-liberal' variant), at the same time as there has been a global resurgence of affirmations of heterogeneity (e.g. 'multiculturalism') through the increasing social and political mobilization of racial, ethnic, cultural, linguistic and religious identities (Amin 1997; Barnet and Cavanagh 1994; Castells 1997; Gurr 1993; Horowitz 1985).

The convergence of these two processes – economic globalization and the resurgence of 'communal' identities – is the crucial grounding for more abstract debates about the extent to which increasingly globalized international human rights norms (both those traditionally categorized as 'civil and political'– assumed to be primarily of an 'individual' character – on the one hand, and 'economic, social, and cultural' rights– ostensibly of a primarily 'collective' character – on the other), and international law itself, are in fact universal, integral and indivisible, and potentially prefigurative of an emergent 'law of peoples' (Rawls 1993), 'radical democratic' global 'rule of law' (Habermas 1998) (Villoro 1997), or 'globalization of law' (Feest 1999).

The Bifurcated State – and Society – in both Africa and Latin America

Mahmood Mamdani's critique of mechanistic applications of both modernization and dependency theory and later of poststructuralism to the study of complex political phenomena in African societies is both generally applicable to Latin America, and specifically so in the context of exploring the relationship between the failures of 'development' and democratization in both contexts, and particularly regarding the importance of ethnic cleavages in 'explaining' such failures. In this context the issue in both regions is how to understand the ways in which contemporary cleavages reflect a combination between the weight of colonial legacies, regional processes of post-independence state formation, and the contemporary impact of 'neo-liberalism' and Structural Adjustment Policies.

The assumption here would be that, in sum, the subjection of Latin America's indigenous peoples to entrenched patterns of socio-economic, political and cultural marginalization and exclusion reflects a 'bifurcated' process of state formation akin to that critiqued by Mamdani in the African context, and which results in the relegation of these groups to a kind of second-class citizenship parallel to that diagnosed by Mamdani in his South African, Kenyan, Congolese and Ugandan case studies.

The colonial experience Mamdani is especially critical of the way in which the colonial 'bifurcation' of the state and the economy between the spheres directly and indirectly dominated and penetrated by colonial power distorts the development of the classic kind of 'civil society' and 'public sphere' envisioned by Hegel, Gramsci and Habermas, *inter alia*, and ultimately undermines the possibility of achieving an authentically democratic 'rule of law'. Instead, the exclusionary 'civil society' and incomplete 'rule of law' which result from such 'bifurcation' serve to perpetuate and reproduce the colonial legacy – and render hegemonic its contemporary neo-colonial ('neo-liberal') equivalents – rather than provide the necessary and desirable basis for its radical democratic transformation. As a result, both 'development' and democracy are frustrated, and feed the explosiveness of latent racial/ethnic cleavages that threaten to derail the process of building a new society capable of being more just and inclusive.

For Mamdani, South Africa provides the best illustration of the way in which (British) colonial rule combined features of direct (Cape Colony) and indirect (Natal) rule (Mamdani 1996: 17). In a parallel sense I would argue that Mexico is paradigmatic for Latin America in terms of the way in which Spanish colonial rule also combined both direct and indirect features which combined to lay the structural basis for current inequities as to the status of the region's indigenous peoples. Similar contemporary patterns and histories with respect to the marginalization and exclusion of indigenous peoples are especially pronounced in Guatemala, Colombia, Ecuador, Bolivia, Peru and Chile.

There is a parallel, increasingly influential school of thought to that of Mamdani in Latin America that finds the origin of contemporary inequities in the region (such as those between indigenous and non-indigenous sectors of the population) in the combined legacies of European colonialism (primarily Spanish and Portuguese), and in the way in which post-independence regimes reproduced and perpetuated this legacy through their mechanistic application of what they understood to be nineteenth-century European liberalism. This school of thought argues that the principal legacy of Spanish colonial rule was to lay the foundation for a kind of state power abstracted from any real sense of nationhood, and where statehood in fact preceded nationality (Basave 1992). This was then compounded by the top-down imposition of a uniform definition of nationality ('Mexican', 'Peruvian', 'Colombian', etc.) that came to be literally at war with the indigenous nations existent prior to the imposition of colonial domination (Villoro 1998; Florescano 1997). This neo-colonialist approach to nation-building by Creole (mixed-race or 'mestizo') elites assumed all the necessary ideological trappings first of nineteenth-century positivist 'Order and Progress', and then of twentieth-century 'modernization' and 'development'. More recently, this accumulated legacy of inequity has then been magnified and multiplied by the 'necessary' social costs of 'neo-liberal' macro-economic policies, once again assimilated as the supposedly unavoidable path to western-style 'First World' status.

In this view, there was an initial 'bifurcation' (as Mamdani characterizes it) under Spanish colonial rule between settler and native spheres, where in effect civil society and thus full citizenship were presumed reserved for the 'civilized' (in Latin America the Spanish conquerors and their descendants, or 'creoles', and successors as the result of new settlement), who exercised an unmediated, centralized despotism over the urbanized indigenous population, and a decentralized, indirect despotism over the rural native population through structures of 'customary' power. In Latin American historiography generally (and specifically in the work of Mexican historians), these two spheres have been described as '*la republica de españoles*' (the republic of Spaniards) and '*la republica de indios*' (the republic of Indians) respectively (Lira 1996). Here, as in Africa, civil society became 'racialized', and indigenous communities 'tribalized'. In his extraordinary book *Mexico Profundo* (Bonfil Batalla 1994), Bonfil in fact argues that the colonial division of Mexican society into these two spheres has been perpetuated since independence, and more recently, since the Mexican Revolution, in the contemporary division of the country into a '*Mexico Profundo*' (deep Mexico) still primarily rooted in pre-Hispanic Meso-American civilization, and a '*Mexico Imaginario*' (imaginary Mexico) oriented primarily to 'western' civilization.

Returning to the colonial version of this 'bifurcation', for Mamdani the differentiation between the settler and native spheres of exercise of colonial power is both a division between the urban and the rural as well as between a hypothetical 'mainstream' minority enjoying citizenship rights, and a discriminated but 'incorporated' majority either denied such rights entirely (such as the right to vote or to own property) or enjoying only their 'pantomime' in a second-class 'customary' version. In this way colonial 'civil society', and the rule of law itself, is 'racialized', and vestigial elements of pre-colonial 'Native Authority' become 'tribalized', and all in the service of maintaining colonial rule (Mamdani 1996: 19).

In the Mexican context the parallel carries over to a distinction between cities or towns as the realm of the 'republic of Spaniards', and the spatial relegation of the 'republic of Indians' to either predominantly indigenous neighbourhoods ('*barrios*', e.g. 'townships'?) within cities or towns and/or to wholly indigenous rural communities (e.g. Bantustans?). A corollary of this spatial differentiation in Mexico has been the tendency which has been maintained since the period of Spanish colonial rule for the seat of municipal authority to be located in predominantly non-indigenous towns which in turn hold sway over many different smaller, predominantly indigenous communities on their periphery. The net result in either the urban or rural context, as in apartheid South Africa, was that a foreign minority population was accorded unaccountable power over a subjugated native majority in both structural and spatial terms. And, as Mamdani notes, revolt by the latter sooner or later becomes inevitable as a way of rendering accountable a power which presumes its own impunity (Mamdani 1996: 11).

In Mexico, as noted by Mamdani regarding Africa, 'peasant communities' reproduced themselves 'within the context of a spatial and institutional autonomy' (Mamdani 1996: 17) made possible by the 'indirect' nature of decentralized colonial despotism in the countryside. This is in fact the generally accepted explanation for how many pre-Hispanic indigenous identities were able to survive Spanish colonial rule despite initial genocide due both to colonial violence and exposure to previously unknown illnesses. But the price of survival as indigenous peoples was the fragmentation of their pre-Hispanic identities as 'nations' (Mexica, Maya, Zapotec, Mixtec, etc.) into an ethos of 'communities'. As a result these pre-existing nations became subsumed into colonial entities which in turn formed the basis of post-independence nation-states whose borders had no direct relationship to territories occupied by ethnic groups such as the Maya (who ended up divided among Mexico, Guatemala, Belize and Honduras). Similarly, for Mamdani one of the principal characteristics of the 'tribalization' wrought by European colonists in Africa is the reduction of ethnic and/or national identity to a sense of belonging to a localized tribe, often latently or actually at war with others (e.g. Rwanda and Burundi).

Gradually the most humanistic (yet no less colonialist, in general) sectors of the Catholic Church won the early debates over the extent to which indigenous people in the Americas were human or had souls or not, and assumed more direct control over the daily life of rural indigenous communities than the incipient colonial state could have from its centres in urban settler enclaves. In effect, in the Latin American state the colonial 'mode of rule' (Mamdani's expression, 1996: 294) was bifurcated or perhaps triply dispersed between its urban/rural, settler/native and rule of law/customary dimensions on the one hand, and the distribution of power over the indigenous population between the colonial state, colonial land-owners and the Catholic Church respectively. The most direct expression of power over indigenous people in structural terms during the colonial period was exercised by land-owners and by the Church (itself a major land-owner and exploiter of indigenous labour), but this power was also, in Mamdani's terms, a vehicle for indirect colonial rule, which thus still amounted to a 'single hegemonic authority' (p. 18).

A key aspect of the exercise of this colonial power in both the Latin American and African context was the supposed 'freeing' of land from its customary native possessors and transformation into a commodity susceptible to accumulation by the colonizers, and the 'bonding' of the native labour needed to wrest its fruits. As Mamdani notes in the African context, this process assumed a key role for 'autonomous peasant communities that would regularly supply male, adult, and single migrant labor to the mines' (Mamdani 1996: 17). Mayan indigenous highland communities in Chiapas and Guatemala have typically played the same kind of role as purveyors of cheap agricultural labour and indentured servitude for coffee plantations and cotton producers on the coast since the nineteenth century at least (Benjamin 1995).

This kind of structured exploitation was accompanied by a sophisticated cultural apparatus in both Africa and Latin America as well. According to Mamdani, it was Great Britain that was 'the first to marshal authoritarian possibilities in indigenous culture. It was the first to realize that key to an alien power's achieving a hegemonic domination was a cultural project: one of harnessing the moral, historical, and community impetus behind local custom to a larger colonial project' (Mamdani 1996: 286). Mamdani's slip here into a perhaps inadvertent Anglocentrism clearly attributable to his focus on the African (and perhaps South Asian?) colonial experience can serve as a possible prod highlighting the need for more comparative analysis regarding Africa incorporating possible insights from the Latin American context.

I would argue that it was actually the Spanish who pioneered the exploitation of the hegemonic possibilities of indirect colonial despotism through the 'cultural project' of Catholic evangelization, and socialization, of indigenous communities throughout the Americas, but most archetypally in colonial Mexico and Peru (each of these incorporating territories way beyond the boundaries of the nation-states currently known by these names). In this way and through its territorial, military and economic domination and exploitation, the Spanish colonial state was able to 'incorporate' America's indigenous peoples into its 'mode of rule' while still excluding them from access to any power over its wealth or resources.

The post-independence phase The parallels between the Latin American and African experience suggested by Mamdani's analysis continue in the post-independence phase. For Mamdani, the three major challenges of this phase in Africa are (1) the 'deracialization' of civil society (e.g. the extirpation of its 'original sin' of racial exclusion; Mamdani 1996: 19); (2) the 'detribalization' of 'Native Authority'; and (3) the development of the economy of the new state in the adverse context of 'unequal international relations' (p. 287). For Mamdani, the greatest success of the new states in Africa since independence has been deracialization (defined by 'conservative' regimes as 'indigenization' and by 'radical' regimes as 'nationalization'), but tragically as civil society has become deracialized, the overall exercise of power has become tribalized due to the new states' failure (across the political spectrum, regardless of their supposed 'conservative' or 'radical' orientations) to dismantle the 'bifurcation' between the urban and rural sectors of African societies entrenched by colonialism (pp. 289–90). In this way the failure to detribalize nourished the emergence of 'patrimonialism' as a neo-colonial 'mode of rule'.

The fundamental dilemma of the decolonization process in Africa thus has been to seek to achieve 'deracialization without democratization', with the result that whatever 'deracialization' took place was not sustainable. In Mamdani's view it is precisely the 'failure to democratize [that] explains why deracialization was not sustainable and why development ultimately failed' (Mamdani 1996: 288). All of this relates to the failure of African decolonization processes to tackle successfully the reform of the 'bifurcated' state inherited from colonialism, and for our purposes here this is crucial because such a state is structurally incapable of uprooting the conditions which produce and magnify inequalities in the distribution of wealth and power within postcolonial African states. Such inequalities are especially 'explosive' (p. 289) when they coincide with racial and ethnic differences, as in Mamdani's case studies of South Africa, Uganda and Kenya. Such unreformed, tribalized (or retribalized) neo-colonial, patrimonial states are thus also incapable of playing a constructive role in the alleviation, reduction or alleviation of poverty. On the contrary, their tendency is to be parasitical and feed upon it as a way of reaffirming and reproducing their own exclusionary power.

Without reform in the local state, the peasantry locked in the hold of a multiplicity of ethnically defined Native Authorities could not be brought into the mainstream of the historical process. In the absence of democratization, development became a top-down agenda enforced on the peasantry. Without thoroughgoing democratization, there could be no development of a home market. This latter failure opened wide what was a crevice at independence. With every downturn in the international economy, the crevice turned into an opportunity for an externally defined programme of globalization. The result was both an internal privatization that recalled the racial imbalance that was civil society in the colonial period and an externally managed capital inflow that towed alongside a phalanx of expatriates – according to the UN estimates, more now than in the colonial period (Mamdani 1996: 88).

Here, too, there are important parallels with political conditions in Mexico that helped lay the basis for the Zapatista revolt, for example (and with similar conditions elsewhere in Latin America that feed parallel responses by the most excluded sectors of the population, such as the Movimento Sim Terra in Brazil). Setting aside a certain underlying determinism in Mamdani's argument (which I will return to later in terms of its weaknesses), his idea of how 'development' (employed uncritically here by Mamdani, another weakness in his argument) became a 'top-down agenda enforced on the peasantry' resonates in terms of Chiapas, Mexico, and perhaps Latin America more generally. Specifically his critique of the African neo-colonial state rings very true for a parallel critique of the expression of the same historical and social forces at work in Mexico in the context of the one-party regime of the Institutional Revolutionary Party (PRI) which emerged from the Mexican Revolution (1910–20).

As Mamdani's critique of the African post-independence state develops, it comes closer and closer to the Mexican experience, particularly as it highlights the attempt by early post-independence single party regimes to forge initially 'noncoercive' links between the rural and urban sectors as a way both 'to contain social and political fragmentation reinforced by ethnically organized Native Authorities' and to resist slipping into a 'civil society-based clientelism' (Mamdani 1996: 290). The option then became to 'depoliticize civil society' as a potential source of threats to continued hegemony, with methods of rule that 'came to rely more on coercion than on persuasion' (p. 290). The net result of what Mamdani characterizes as a 'forced developmental march' that was 'enforced from above on a reluctant peasantry', 'was to exacerbate tensions between the rural and the urban' (p. 290). The single party then makes the transition from 'a mobilizing organ into a coercive apparatus' (p. 291).

This summary is applicable in general terms to the transition of the PRI from the embodiment of the first twentieth-century social revolution to an instrument of bureaucratized authoritarian despotism with corporatist features (government-controlled trade unions, peasant organizations, business associations and mass media) between the 1920s and the 1970s. In the background of this transition, amid its 'hidden transcripts' (Scott 1990), is the story of an artificial, supposedly uniform, urbanized European-style nation-state superimposed upon an underlying, negated reality of persistent ethnic, linguistic, cultural and religious diversity rooted in the pre-Hispanic indigenous past, as well as a complex web of syncretism fusing elements of indigenous, African and Hispanic social and cultural practices, complicated more recently by pervasive cultural influences from the USA. Parallels could be drawn here as well to the complexity of the African heritage in general, but specifically as the result of both Dutch and British colonialism in South Africa, together with the emergence of a distinct Afrikaner culture (with its own medley of influences), and the presence of East Asian immigrant communities, in South Africa (and similar examples of diversity elsewhere as in the former Portuguese colonies, or that of German influence in Namibia).

According to Mamdani, the post-independence state is caught in a trap then between two differing forms of despotism: a decentralized form which exacerbates underlying ethnic divisions, with an apparent solution in greater centralization, or a centralized despotism which tends to exacerbate urban–rural divisions, and whose apparent solution is decentralization (or even state fragmentation or division, e.g. Eritrea and its separation from Ethiopia) (Mamdani 1996: 291). The only constructive way out of this trap, which leads back to despotism at either extreme according to Mamdani, is an overall process of democratization that requires striking a complex and challenging 'balance between decentralization and centralization, participation and representation, autonomy and alliance' (p. 298) capable of transcending and/or reconciling a series of related binary opposites such as 'rights vs. customs' and 'civil society vs. community' (p. 34). To accomplish this requires the simultaneous transformation of the exercise of power in both the urban (rule of law/civil society) and rural (customary/tribal) spheres, for otherwise a 'bifurcated reform strategy' will succeed only in re-creating a bifurcated state.

Poverty, ethnicity and democracy Sometimes the democratizing impulse comes from unexpected directions. The final step in my exploration here of the possible connections between phenomena such as the Zapatista revolt in Mexico and popular resistance movements of poor and marginalized racial/ethnic groups in Africa (South Africa, Congo, Uganda, Kenya) is centred on exploring the relationship between such movements and the overall agenda of democratization in both Africa and Latin America in the context of issues of 'multiculturalism'.

'Democracy' is understood here as a multidimensional framework of rights of equal participation in the distribution of power among political, economic, social and cultural domains of human activity which are interdependent (Sachs 1997; Sen 1997). From this perspective, rampant poverty, social exclusion and deepening inequity are the worst enemies of an authentic, non-formalist democracy. This definition in turn assumes that state policies intended to combat poverty, exclusion and inequity must themselves be democratized, and that such democratization of social policy must include affirmative recognition of rights of equal citizenship, self-determination and autonomy on the part of groups marginalized at least in part because of their communal identities (this is my working definition of 'multiculturalism', as well, for the purposes of this chapter).

What, then, is the relationship between ethnicity, democracy and revolt, according to Mamdani? Here emerge the most important apparent divergences between his diagnosis of the unfinished agenda of democratization in Africa, and current trends in Mexico and Latin America exemplified by the Zapatista rebellion. His most startling assertion from a Latin American perspective is that 'Europe did not bring to Africa a tropical version of the late 19th century European national state. Instead it created a multicultural and multiethnic state' (Mamdani 1996: 287). This is a broader version of his more precise argument earlier in the book that tribalism in Africa was not the 'effect' of colonialism but rather the 'very essence' of colonial rule (p. 185).

Mamdani's concept of a 'multicultural and multiethnic state' as a colonial vestige that must be extirpated is evidently very different from the demand *for* such a state employing the same words in a completely different sense promoted by the Zapatistas and other similar movements among indigenous people throughout Latin America that have emerged with great force in the last few years. Is any common ground possible here?

Despite the apparent rigidity of his judgement of 'multiculturalism' here as a perpetuation of colonialist 'tribalism', Mamdani's analysis in fact is more nuanced and less determinist than might appear at first blush. Even though he argues that 'tribalism' was the very essence of western colonial rule in Africa, he also affirms that ethnicity in Africa must also be understood at least in certain cases as a 'form of anti-colonial revolt' (Mamdani 1996: 185). In other words, he does not reduce ethnicity in Africa as a political, social and cultural force to 'tribalism' alone, nor does he reduce it to a purely colonialist function. This distinction is crucial.

Furthermore, Mamdani eloquently dismisses essentialist approaches to ethnicity in African studies: 'In assuming that only those ethnicities are real which have always existed, they presume ethnicities to be trans-historical phenomena and thereby miss the fact that ethnicities have a social history. This is why, rather than conceiving of an ethnicity as simply "invented" by statecraft or imagined by intellectuals, it would make more sense to speak of the "making" of an ethnicity' (Mamdani 1996: 185), referring among others to the approaches of Benedict Anderson and E. P. Thompson to questions of nationalism and class identity. He then concludes: '[i]f this much makes sense, then one need neither be singularly alarmed by the mere sound of ethnic movements nor be moved into embracing them uncritically' (p. 185).

He is nevertheless clearly troubled by what he perceives to be the underlying shift and intellectual agenda behind the

> changing vocabulary of Africanist social science: from a study of tribalism to that of tribalism to that of identity. Each succeeding term gives the phenomenon increasing respectability by casting it within a more acceptable, human, and universal frame. Whereas the sound of TRIBALISM was un-deniably pathological, ETHNICITY is more placid, part of a value-free

vocabulary on the way to reconciling itself with the object it claims to describe; but IDENTITY has more of the ring of a personal quest, if not quite the sound of a battlecry.

Yet here, too, his ultimate conclusion, linking ethnically based and peasant movements together as examples of 'particularism', is more nuanced: 'it is not possible to grasp the democratic content of peasant movements without transcending the unilinear modernist perspective that counterpoises social particularism to state universalism' (Mamdani 1996: 185). Here, as with ethnicity, Mamdani's aspiration is to fashion an approach to the analysis of peasant communities and peasant movements which 'neither glorifies nor dismisses' them (p. 186). This is precisely the approach taken by Neil Harvey as to both ethnicity and indigenous peasant movements in his recent detailed exploration of the origins and implications of the Zapatista revolt in Mexico (Harvey 1998).

Either Mamdani is fighting too many battles here simultaneously on too many battlefronts, or his argument has several inter-related layers that must be sorted through. The best explanation is the latter, because it is what is clearly reflected in his assessment of several specific cases which he uses to flesh out his overall arguments regarding African ethnicity and popular movements of resistance.

The theoretical framework he sets up for his case studies regarding the role of race and ethnicity in African popular resistance movements is very critical of the dualistic tendency in African studies either to characterize 'ethnically defined movements (tribalism)' as some kind of 'primordial carry-over, a traditional or atavistic residue, to be cured or erased with the march of modernity' (referring to the work of Geertz and Throup), or 'as the result of a modern conspiracy, either external or local' (referring to Southall, Mafeje and Saul, to varying degrees). In this way ethnicity ends up being perceived as either an ahistorical 'original sin' pushing from below, or as a 'kind of cancer introduced from without and above'. The common ground between these two extremes (which in part reflect a Right/ Left split) is that both agree that 'tribalism is a curse of which Africa must be rid' (Mamdani 1996: 187–8).

Mamdani is specifically critical here of the resultant tendency to dismiss the seriousness and complexity of ethnic demands under either extreme posture sketched above, specifically noting an example of such attitudes in the context of the presentation of a paper by K. Datta and A. Murray: 'The Rights of Minorities and Subject Peoples in Botswana: A Historical Evolution'. Mamdani disapprovingly notes in this context how 'the only comment the paper could draw from conference participants [in Botswana] was that "the authors' emphasis on minority rights was divisive rather

than promoting national unity which should be everyone's concern"'
(Mamdani 1996: 324, fn 6).

In the same vein he quotes Samora Machel's well-known statement,
'[F]or the nation to live, the tribe must die' (Mamdani 1996: 135), and then
critiques it as evidencing the same kind of despotic, centralizing tendency
expressed in the drive towards a 'single party, a single trade union, a single
cooperative movement … a single movement of women or youth' or the
imposition by decree of a 'single body of substantive law' (p. 135).

Here we return to Mamdani's concern with the 'bifurcated' character
of despotic power in Africa. He draws a stark contrast between the situation
of the urban and rural poor with respect to their access to the exercise of
rights:

> Unlike the urban poor who live within the confines of the modern civic
> power – the law-defined boundary of civil society – whose predicament may
> be grasped as a de jure legal equality compromised by a de facto social
> inequality, a formal access to legal institutions rendered fictional in most
> cases by the absence of resources with which to reach these institutions, the
> situation of the rural poor is not that of lack of access or reach, but the
> actual law (customary law) and its implementing machinery (Native Author-
> ity) that confront them. (Mamdani 1996: 137)

Although he never explicitly puts together the pieces of his argument
regarding civil society and customary law (Ch. III) with his argument regarding race, ethnicity and resistance movements (Ch. VI), I would argue
that the only way to interpret and apply them in a manner which is
internally consistent would be to acknowledge, as I think he suggests above,
that it is possible, within his framework, for a 'bifurcated' centralized
despotism to assume either a racial (as it did under colonialism and
apartheid) or ethnic (as it does under conditions of rampant tribalism)
character, and that such a regime may manifest itself both de jure and de
facto. In sum I would argue that the Zapatista revolt, for example, is
precisely a movement of resistance to such a regime imposed in Mexico
against the country's indigenous peoples.

Mamdani's analysis of case studies of popular resistance movements in
the Congo, Kenya, Uganda and South Africa (plus snippets from elsewhere)
essentially supports an argument that movements of this kind which are
(1) locally based or regional in character; (2) rooted in specific ethnicities;
and which in fact (3) promote a 'comprehensive programme of social
transformation' seeking the democratization of the whole country, render
either or both of the two dominant schools of thought as to ethnic
movements in Africa inoperative. This is so because neither of the two
approaches (ethnicity as either vestige or conspiracy) is able to account for

the possibility of localized ethnic resistance movements articulating broad–based demands in support of overall democratization, which in effect turn the assumptions of the orthodox tribalist thesis (a localized ethnic movement raising demands for the sole benefit of its own group) on its head.

From Mamdani's perspective the Mau Mau of Kenya, the Mulelist guerrilla struggle in post-Lumumba Congo, the anti-apartheid movement of urbanized migrant labourers in South Africa, and the Ruwenzururu 'peasant guerrilla movement' on the Uganda/Zaire border between 1962 and 1980, share the above-described characteristics (regionalization, racial/ethnic character, national demands), and are illustrative of the inherently non-predetermined, 'contradictory character of ethnicity' under varying conditions (Mamdani 1996: 189). In terms of the Mau Mau he adopts Frank Furedi's analysis which stresses that despite the movement's origins and dominant characteristics 'as an authentic voice of the Kikuyu have-nots' under British rule, it became the vehicle whereby an anti-colonial mass movement could emerge and act independently of its traditionally hegemonic middle-class leadership and 'put to question the existing socio-economic structures of society' (p. 188). Mamdani is insistent about this:

> Stepping aside from the question of whether Mau Mau was a strictly Kikuyu movement or whether it gained significant support from various Kenyan nationalities, does not the larger significance of Mau Mau lie in its social basis and its demands? Did not the social base of the Mau Mau in the 'Kikuyu have-nots' and its struggle for 'land and freedom' [Zapata's identical call to arms during the Mexican Revolution] underline its democratic content as opposed to its particularistic concern? Its thrust toward equality as opposed to privilege? Its significance for the majority (the 'have-nots') liberating and unifying as opposed to repressive and divisive? (Mamdani 1996: 189)

The Mulelist guerrilla movement in eastern Congo, which he touches on only briefly, similarly both fought for 'a comprehensive programme of social transformation' and was centred in, and never succeeeded in expanding beyond, its origins and base among the Mbunda and Penda peoples (Mamdani 1996: 189).

In the South African context, Mamdani explores at length the complexities of race, ethnicity and labour status in the context of the role played by migratory labourers in the anti-apartheid movement and their relationship to other sectors of the movement (trade unions, community-based movements in the townships, the ANC and Inkatha, *inter alia*). He also notes the way in which although anti-apartheid revolts in the tribal homelands were 'everywhere an anti-chief [e.g. anti-Native Authority/Bantustan] phenomenon' (e.g. the Pondoland revolt), 'not all chiefs were attacked everywhere'.

Here a key distinction was made between the need to uproot 'tribalized' Native Authorities and their figureheads who were in complicity with the apartheid regime and who enjoyed the rewards of official patronage through the Bantustan system; between 'bad and good chiefs, between those who gave in to the temptation for individual enrichment and those who stood alongside their communities, even if out of fear for their lives if they did not; in sum between those who violated real custom and those who upheld it' (Mamdani 1996: 195).

Thus, the struggle was not simplistically against 'traditional' or 'tribal' authority in itself, but against its perversion, co-optation and manipulation by apartheid (as previously by colonialism).

In fact, 'real custom', authentic tribal traditions and authorities not incorporated into apartheid's hegemonic 'mode of rule' could in fact serve as the basis for attacking false 'traditionalism' in the congealed form of the Bantustans. The rationale here is exemplified by the peasants of Sekhukhuneland who argued that 'a good chief is a traditional chief'. And what is a 'traditional' chief? A chief who 'is a chief by the people' (*Kgoshi de kgoshi ka batho*, in the local language), that is, 'a leader in some measure accountable to the peasant community' (Mamdani 1996: 195). In the Mayan tradition of accountability by rotational leadership to community assemblies, since taken up by the Zapatistas as the central tenet of their political discourse, the parallel concept is '*mandar obedeciendo*' (to govern by obedience to community mandate) (Harvey 1998). In effect, then, in this context in both Africa and Latin America (or at minimum in the cited cases of South Africa and Mexico), to be most traditionalist – most 'tribalized', in the authentic and not distorted colonialist and pro-apartheid sense – is also, under certain circumstances, to be most democratic.

The 'plasticity of tradition' (Mamdani 1996: 256) in the service of the democratic anti-apartheid struggle is also evidenced, according to Mamdani, by the use of leaflets and other propaganda both in African languages (especially Sotho and Zulu) and in English as part of the 'stay away' struggles in the wake of the regime's attempt to impose Afrikaans as a medium of instruction in black schools, which led to the Soweto uprising of 1976 (p. 250). Similarly, 'ethnically organized burial, stockveld, or cultural societies' in the townships and migrant hostels played an important role in promoting cohesion in the anti-apartheid struggle among displaced native communities but 'did not necessarily isolate their members from urban influences' (p. 193).

The parallel in the Mexican context would be the role played by '*mayorazgos*' and '*mayordomias*' (traditional syncretic Catholic/indigenous fraternal societies organized around cults to patron saints associated with specific communities) among migrant indigenous and peasant communities in Mexico City, and the importance of migration from the highlands communities of Chiapas into the Lacandon jungle region that created the basis for multiethnic peasant movements demanding land which would have been more difficult to organize in the ethnically stratified home communities. A similar dynamic is highlighted with respect to the 'multi-ethnic' character of the National Resitance Army/Movement (NRA/M) of Uganda's Luwero Triangle, built on an alliance between the Banganda and Banyoro nationalities (Mamdani 1996: 207). The role of migration in facilitating organizing is highlighted both by Mamdani with respect to South Africa ('migrants become organizers, taking the message of organizing with them', p. 193), and by Harvey (1998) with respect to the Zapatistas in Chiapas. Mamdani himself notes as well the parallels between the challenges of urban organizing in Mexico City and Durban, with the squatter population of the latter considered second only to that of the former (Mamdani 1996: 275).

In South Africa there was no automatic initial contradiction between promoting racial and ethnic solidarity among the victims of apartheid as part of the struggle against its overtly racist and ethnocentrist policies. Later contradictions would emerge, however, as the struggle for the political, social and cultural space of the migrant hostels became crystallized into a battle for hegemony first between Inkatha and the African National Congress, and then between Zulus and non-Zulus, and most recently during the post-apartheid phase since 1994, as Afrikaner political discourse has honed its demands for the respect of the 'cultural rights of minorities', if not in support of 'multiculturalism' itself.

Mamdani draws similar inferences to those regarding the Mulelist guerrillas in Congo and the Mau Mau, from the Ruwenzururu peasant guerrilla movement centred along the Uganda/Zaire border between 1962 and 1980. The movement was 'organized in response to intense nationality oppression that led to land deprivation, language exclusion, and job discrimination through most of the colonial period' against the Bakonzo and Bamba nationalities living on the slopes of Mt Ruwenzori. According to Mamdani, 'although its political leadership came mostly from middle class intellectuals like teachers, the social impetus came from the poor peasantry of the mountains' (Mamdani 1996: 197). In these terms the movement is indistinguishable from that of the Zapatistas in Mexico who share all of the characteristics described here.

Especially crucial at this juncture is Mamdani's additional notion that ethnicized movements of democratic resistance of this type also unleash virtual 'civil wars' within their own ethnicities precisely because of the democratic, predominantly non-particularistic character of their demands: 'between the mountain dweller and the plains dweller, between initiatives anchored in poor peasants and rich peasants, between those organizing an armed struggle and those calling for peaceful methods of resolving conflicts' (Mamdani 1996: 198). In this way the Ruwenzururu movement implied at the same time 'a recasting of the relations internal to the peasantry and a reorganization of the peasant community' (p. 198). The parallels with the characteristics, and effects, of the Zapatista movement on the peasantry of the Chiapas region – and on indigenous and peasant communities throughout the rest of Mexico – are once again surprisingly close (Harvey 1998). They extend as well to the democratic character of each movement's overall national demands, in addition to their demands for equal treatment in ethnic terms (Mamdani 1996: 198–200; Harvey 1998).

Mamdani then relates the nature of the democratic demands supported by the Ruwenzururu Movement to that of the National Resistance Army/ Movement (NRA/M) of Uganda. Both 'came up with a similar innovation in the arena of rights: the right of peasant communities to organize as communities and to hold state officials accountable as communities', a distinct departure from traditional western liberal notions that claim that democracy is itself founded (perhaps exclusively) on individual rather than collective rights (Mamdani 1996: 201).

This community-based approach to the promotion and protection of fundamental civil and political rights

> was a response to a dual context. On one hand, market relations had yet to penetrate and disintegrate communities fully, so that they may in turn be re-created through voluntary associations; the place of work coincided in the main with the place of residence; the family was still a unit of not just consumption and reproduction, but also production; circumstances of birth prevailed over choice of association in shaping one's life possibilities ...
>
> In this context the right of association would have an extremely limited practical significance if understood only as an individual right. To be meaningful, it had to be interpreted as a right of residence-based communities, not just individuals. This innovation was of particular significance to those who lived on the margins of civil society. (Mamdani 1996: 201 and 202)

There are also important traps here, however, whereby localized resistance movements of this kind are cornered into accepting localized solutions that short-circuit the broader horizons of their overall national democratizing demands. In the case of the Ruwenzururu, for example, the net result of their struggle was neutralization by the state via the concession to them essentially of a localized form of ethnic autonomy (Mamdani 1996: 211). This has been one key aspect of the Mexican state's strategy towards the Zapatistas, constantly seeking to minimize them as a localized movement among the most marginalized sector of the population in the country's poorest state; all of these, however, also being factors which the Zapatistas have sought to use (with mixed success) to propel themselves to national importance and international recognition.

In conclusion, for Mamdani the truly critical and fundamental questions we need to ask 'when assessing the democratic content' of ethnically-based, localized resistance movements of the poor raising broad democratic demands is '[d]o they tend toward realizing equality or crystallizing privilege? Are they generalizable to other ethnic groups or can they be realized only at the expense of others? In other words, when do they signify a struggle for rights and when a demand for privilege?' (Mamdani 1996: 203). The most critical need for such movements if they are to be successful in pressing their broader democratic demands is for them to find the organizational means to transcend 'the many ways in which power fragments the circumstances and experience of the oppressed population' (p. 272).

The same kinds of questions were raised by Good and Molutsi's paper ('The State and Poverty in Botswana') at the 1997 Gaborone workshop regarding the 'underclass' status of the San/Basarwa/Bushmen people of Botswana 'as the most exploited and impoverished of all', and by the 1998 UNDP *Human Development Report*'s references to disparities between urban and rural sectors in Namibia, and specifically regarding differential rates of poverty according to language group (65 per cent among the San vs 8 per cent among English-speakers, 10 per cent among German-speakers, 11 per cent among speakers of Afrikaans, and 21 per cent among the dominant Tswana-speaking elite) (UNDP 1998: 30, 34). According to Good and Molutsi, the dominant characteristics of the San's 'continuing dispossession' in contemporary Botswana include 'their unique absence of land rights ... wideranging sociocultural disabilities, and their lack of autonomous political organizations with which to articulate their demands at the national level'. They conclude by suggesting that, from a comparative perspective, the San are 'clearly far worse off than other indigenous minorities such as the Sami of Norway and Australian aborigines'.

Conclusions

My principal interest in undertaking this detailed exploration of Mamdani's ideas is to demonstrate their potential for enriching our understanding of the parallel issues of poverty, ethnicity and state power in the Latin American and specifically Mexican context. His framework, though, needs additional grounding in terms of some of its broader theoretical aspects in order for such a transference (and ultimately the search for common ground between African and Latin American studies) to be successful and productive.

Concretely the task would be to situate Mamdani's approach in a broader exploration of the ways (strategies, discourses, practices) in which states and societies throughout the world have constructed 'ethnicity' and related forms of differentiation and social relations, and discourses of 'rights', on the basis of 'racial', cultural and linguistic identity, and regarding how these structures and processes of differentiation are reflected in patterns of social exclusion and marginalization that amount to second-class citizenship, both de jure and de facto (Silver 1995). The focus then would be on how such structures and processes of differentiation relate to, and have become interdependent with, global issues of poverty, human rights and social justice, and specifically on how they have been structured, reflected and reinforced by both national and international juridical norms, discourses and processes, and by the complex relationships between the definition and achievement of such norms and the emergence of new movements of resistance among such marginalized groups. In this context, the insights of James Scott, E. P. Thompson, Eric Hobsbawm and Michael Taussig, among others, as to the ways in which the upsetting of customary understandings of social justice and equity ('moral economy') provide the necessary basis to legitimize rebellion by marginalized groups are of particular relevance.

The most critical absence in Mamdani's framework for the purposes of this chapter is the developing literature regarding the relationship between poverty, democracy and 'multiculturalism'. According to Canadian philosopher Will Kymlicka, his concept of 'multicultural citizenship' is applicable to societies where collective rights based on membership in a particular group (defined by race, ethnicity, language, religion, etc., but also by subjection to discriminatory conditions of socio-economic marginalization and exclusion) enable individuals belonging to such groups not only to be treated as equal citizens but as citizens whose differential status has been legitimized (e.g. through programmes of 'affirmative action' or 'positive discrimination', bilingual education and voting rights, proportional representation, regional and/or local autonomy and other forms of federalism, decentralization or 'devolution', special rights for minority language use and development, etc.).

The idea is then of a democracy built on the recognition, rather than the negation, of difference (Kymlicka 1996). Such an approach is more common, according to Kymlicka, than is usually acknowledged by orthodox western liberal theorists of democracy. Examples of varying types would range from Canada and the United States to the United Kingdom, Spain, Belgium, Switzerland, Norway, Denmark, Israel/Palestine, Ethiopia,

Eritrea, South Africa, India, Australia and New Zealand, among others, including several Latin American countries that have recently adopted or are in the process of adopting constitutional and/or other legal reform measures along these lines in terms of indigenous peoples (Mexico, Guatemala, Nicaragua, Colombia, Ecuador, Paraguay, most notably). This is precisely what Mexican philosopher Luis Villoro, a key adviser to the Zapatistas, defines as 'radical democracy', drawing in part on Habermas (Villoro 1997).

A closely related concept is that of 'cultural citizenship' first developed by anthropologist Renato Rosaldo and then expanded upon in a book edited by Bill Flores and Rina Benmayor (1997), and that of 'ethnic citizenship' developed by Peruvian anthropologist Rodrigo Montoya (1996). According to Rosaldo and Flores (1997), '[c]ultural citizenship refers to the right to be different (in terms of race, ethnicity, or native language) with respect to the norms of the dominant national community, without compromising one's right to belong, in the sense of participating in the nation-state's democratic processes'. Their work reflects the lessons and experiences of community-based movements for civil rights and equity among the Mexican immigrant, Chicano and Latino movements in the USA. Montoya's formulation of the concept in the very different context of indigenous people's struggles in Peru, is virtually identical.

Concepts such as 'multicultural', 'cultural' and 'ethnic' citizenship provide an ethical and political basis for questioning the extent to which apparently 'democratic' outcomes of traditional western liberal 'majority rule' in fact comport with more fundamental democratic principles or sound social policy in a multicultural society where socio-economic outcomes (income, wealth, employment, access to quality education, healthcare, housing) are stratified on the basis of membership in 'disfavoured' groups. This is clearly the same kind of critical spirit that is behind Zapatista demands for the social, economic, political and cultural inclusion of Mexico's indigenous peoples, and that is reflected in the new post-apartheid South African Constitution with its recognition of eleven official languages and of the state's obligation to act 'to redress the results of past racially discriminatory laws and practices' (see Sections 6, 9, 29, *inter alia*), and in recent constitutional reforms in both Ethiopia and Eritrea. It is also the same spirit that informs the demands of the popular resistance movements of racially and ethnically excluded groups in Mamdani's case studies of South Africa, Kenya, Congo and Uganda.

Ultimately, then, the most effective, democratic approach to issues regarding the interaction of poverty, human rights, social justice and marginalized racial, ethnic, cultural and linguistic identities is one which highlights the cultural dimensions of development processes along the lines suggested by the report recently issued by UNESCO's World Commission on Culture and Development, *Our Creative Diversity* (1998) (Arizpe 1997). From this perspective, effective, equitable anti-poverty efforts are not possible in societies stratified by differentiated identities in the absence of meaningful incorporation into their formulation, implementation and evaluation of notions of 'cultural', 'ethnic' and 'multicultural' citizenship. Only such a 'multiculturalist' approach can lay the basis necessary for those groups and individuals relegated to second-class citizenship status to recover their full dimensions as critical, participatory, deliberative subjects with 'the right to have rights' (Arendt 1949, quoted in Jelin 1996 and Harvey 1998).

Note

1. See, for example, the paper by Ken Good and Patrick Molutsi, 'The State and Poverty in Botswana', presented at the workshop on the 'Role of the State in Poverty Alleviation', Botswana, October 1997. An amended version of the paper entitled 'The State and Extreme Poverty in Botswana: the San and Destitutes', has been published in the *Journal of Modern African Studies* (37, 2, June 1999).

References

Amin, Samir (1997) *El Eurocentrismo: critica de una ideologia*, Mexico: Siglo XXI.

Arendt, Hannah (1949) 'The Rights of Man: What are They?', in *Modern Review*, 3, 1 (Summer).

Arizpe, Lourdes (ed.) (1997) *Our Creative Diversity*. Report issued by UNESCO's World Commission on Culture and Development. Mexico City: UNESCO.

Barnet, Richard and John Cavanagh (1994) *Global Dreams: Imperial Corporations and the New World Order*. New York: Simon and Schuster.

Basave, Agustin (1992) *Mexico mestizo: Analisis del nacionalismo mexicano en torno a la mestizofilia de Andres Molina Enriquez*. Mexico City: Fondo de Cultura Economica.

Benjamin, Thomas (1995) *Chiapas: Terra rica, pueblo pobre: Historia politica y social* Mexico City: Grijalbo.

Bonfil Batalla, Guillermo (1994) *Mexico profundo: Una civilizacion negada*. Mexico City: Grijalbo.

Castells, Manuel (1997) *El Poder de la Identidad, Vol. II of La Era de la Informacion: Economia, sociedad, y cultura*. Mexico City: Siglo XXI.

Destremau, Blandine (1998) *The Systemic Relations of the State and Poverty*. Background paper for the CROP workshop on 'The Role of the State in Poverty Alleviation III'.

Feest, Johannes (ed.) (1997) *Globalization and Legal Cultures: Oñati Summer Course* Oñati: International Institute for the Sociology of Law (IISL).

Flores, William V. and Rina Benmayor (eds) (1997) *Latino Cultural Citizenship: Claiming Identity, Space, and Rights*. Boston: Beacon Press.

Florescano, Enrique (1997) *Etnia, estado y nacion: Ensayo sobre las identidades colectivas en Mexico*. Mexico City: Aguilar/Nuevo Siglo.

Gurr, Ted Robert (1993) *Minorities at Risk: A Global View of Ethnopolitical Conflicts*. Washington, DC: United States Institute of Peace Press.

Habermas, Jurgen (1998) *Facticidad y validez: Sobre el derecho y el Estado democratico de derecho en terminos de teoria del discurso*. Madrid: Editorial Trotta.

Harvey, Neil (1998) *The Chiapas Rebellion: The Struggle for Land and Democracy*. Durham, NC and London: Duke University Press.

Horowitz, Donald L. (1985) *Ethnic Groups in Conflict*. Berkeley and Los Angeles: University of California Press.

Jelin, Elizabeth (1996) 'Citizenship Revisted: Solidarity, Responsibility, and Rights', in Elizabeth Jelin and Eric Hershberg (eds), *Constructing Democracy: Human Rights, Citizenship and Society in Latin America*. Boulder: Westview Press.

Kymlicka, Will (1996) *Ciudadania Multicultural: Una teoria liberal de los derechos de las minorias*. Barcelona: Paidos.

Lira, Andres (1996) 'La extraña anomalia. Realidades indigenas en el Mexico del Siglo XIX', in Alicia Hernandez et al. (eds), *Cultura y derechos de los pueblos indigenas de Mexico*. Mexico City: Arcivo General de la Nacion/Fondo de Cultura Economica.

Mamdani, Mahmood (1996) *Citizen and Subject: Contemporary Africa and the Legacy of Late Colonialism*. Princeton, NJ: Princeton University Press.

Montoya, Rodrigo (1996) 'La ciudadania etnica como un nuevo fragmento en la utopia de la libertad', in Pablo Gonzalez Casanova and Marcos Roitman Rosenmann (eds), *Democracia y estado multietnico en America Latina*. Mexico City: La Jornada ediciones/Centro de Investigaciones Interdisciplinarias en las Humanidades-UNAM.

Rawls, John (1993) 'The Law of Peoples', in S. Shute and S. Hurley (eds), *On Human Rights: The Oxford Amnesty Lectures* New York: Basic Books.

Rosado, Renato and William V. Flores (1997) 'Identity, Conflict, and Evolving Latino Communities: Cultural Citizenship in San Jose, California', in Flores and Benmayor (eds), *Latino Cultural Citizenship*.

Sachs, Ignacy (1997) 'Overcoming Growth without Development?' in Louis Emmerij (ed.), *Economic and Social Development into the 21st Century*. Washington, DC: Interamerican Development Bank/Johns Hopkins University Press.

Scott, James (1990) *Domination and the Arts of Resistance: Hidden Transcripts* New Haven, CT: Yale University Press.

Sen, Amartya (1997) 'Development Thinking at the Beginning of the 21st Century', in Louis Emmerij (ed.), *Economic and Social Development into the 21st Century*. Washington, DC: Interamerican Development Bank/Johns Hopkins University Press.

Silver, Hilary (1995) 'Reconceptualizing Social Disadvantage: Three Paradigms of Social Exclusion', in Gerry Rodgers, Charles Gore and Jose B. Figueiredo (eds), *Social Exclusion: Rhetoric, Reality and Responses*. Geneva: International Institute for Labour Studies/United Nations Development Program.

UNDP (1998) *Human Development Report 1998*. New York: Oxford University Press.

Villoro, Luis (1997) *El poder y el valor: Fundamentos de una etica politica* Mexico City: Fondo de Cultura Economica.

— (1998) *Estado plural, pluralidad de culturas*. Mexico City: Paidos/UNAM.

6

Poverty and Development in the Age of Globalization: The Role of Foreign Aid

Brigitte Schulz

The world is changing in fundamental ways. The end of the Cold War also ended the bipolar global order that had largely determined international relations for more than four decades. Ongoing changes in communication, transportation, production and exchange relations have had an even more profound effect on the way in which people around the world order their daily lives. This new 'information age', not even two decades old and accelerating at a breakneck speed, has intensified global linkages and economic interactions to such an extent that 'globalization' has become the object of intense scholarly scrutiny.

This globalization process has been enormously uneven and has further widened the gap in global power and wealth. The assets of the wealthiest three individuals in the world now exceed the combined GNP of the forty-three least developed countries. Total income of the bottom 41 per cent of the world's people is less than that reported by the 200 wealthiest individuals. This fundamental asymmetry between the global North and South is starkly expressed in other numbers: 1.3 billion people live on incomes below the equivalent of US $1 (1987 PPP$) a day, almost the same number lack access to safe drinking water, nearly a billion are illiterate, and some 840 million people are chronically hungry and malnourished because they lack access to food.[1] Put yet another way: '80% of the world's population lives on about 15% of the world's total GNP. These figures suggest that about 4300 million people live on an annual average per capita income of around $750, a little over $2 a day.'[2] This geography of hunger expresses itself in radically shortened lifespans, political and economic marginalization, and an existence of spiritual and material deprivation.

Foreign aid, or official development assistance (ODA), is popularly seen as an instrument designed to help narrow the gap between North and South and thus to overcome these conditions of material deprivation. The 'donors' in this North–South flow of funds and resources are eager to support this view, stressing their commitment to 'develop' the poor countries in Africa, Asia and Latin America via various ODA programmes. Much has been written about the past failures of the development project as it emerged with decolonization. It is the central thesis of this chapter that present discourse and practice involving aid to developing countries continues down this road of failure because it dispenses advice that is largely incompatible with the challenges presented by globalization to governments in the North and South alike. The empirical base for this assertion rests on an analysis of current prescriptions for 'development' offered by a bilateral official aid organization, the German development ministry (Bundesministerium für wirtschaftliche Zusammenarbeit und Entwicklung – BMZ), as well as a respected multilateral aid organization, the United Nations Development Programme (UNDP).

The Mission of Foreign Aid

The self-proclaimed purpose of foreign aid programmes is most often couched in moral terms. The BMZ, for example, explains its mission as an 'ethical/moral obligation' to offer help to those in need, an 'ethical/ humanitarian' act of political obligation that transcends national borders.[3] From its beginnings, however, ODA was more than humanitarian assistance; it constituted an integral part of the donors' overall foreign policy objectives. Given the global division of labour, the maldistribution of incomes and resources, and the needs of the donor countries' economies for markets and raw materials, ODA became an instrument for shaping the politics and economies of recipient countries towards a particular end. That end was expressed in W. W. Rostow's *Stages of Economic Growth: An Anti-Communist Manifesto* to be an advanced capitalist society having reached the pinnacle of human existence; i.e. a 'mass consumption society'. Not coincidentally, Walt Rostow lived and worked in the United States of America and his vision of 'modernization' was clearly informed by life in the USA. ODA programmes, either implicitly or explicitly, presented this vision as a window into the future of all poor countries willing to follow the advice of 'development experts'.

As the title of Rostow's book suggests, however, there was yet another strand that constituted the core of ODA programmes: anti-communism. From the beginning of 'foreign aid' in the immediate post-Second World War year, the conflict between the capitalist West and the communist East played a key role. On 8 May 1947, the US Secretary of State, Dean Acheson, explained his country's aid efforts in the following way: 'Free peoples who are seeking to preserve their independence, and democratic

TABLE 6.1 Total external debt, 1980 and 1995 (in billion US $)

	1980	1995
Low- and middle-income countries *of which:*	616	2,066
Sub-Saharan Africa	84	226
East Asia and Pacific	64	404
South Asia	38	157
Europe and Central Asia	87	425
Middle East and North Africa	83	216
Latin America and Caribbean	257	636

Source: World Bank Development Report 1997

institutions and human freedoms against totalitarian pressures, either internal or external, will receive top priority for American aid.'[4]

What was initially conceived of as a massive transfer of public funds from the United States to Europe soon became the cornerstone of relations between the West and postcolonial countries in the so-called Third World. Since most of the funds were given in form of loans rather than non-repayable grants, the pursuit of western prescriptions for 'modernization' and 'development' contributed to the massive indebtedness of the recipient countries. By 1997, the world's poorest ('least developed') countries alone owed $215 billion, up from $183 billion in 1990 and $55 billion in 1980.[5] As Table 6.1 indicates, this trend towards ever-higher levels of indebtedness also applied to more economically advanced countries in the South.

As a clear testament to the failure of this entire 'development' project, the UN reports that:

> In the past 15–20 years more than 100 developing and transition countries have suffered disastrous failures in growth and deeper and more prolonged cuts in living standards than anything experienced in the industrial countries during the Great Depression of the 1930s. As a result of these setbacks, the incomes of more than a billion people have fallen below levels first reached 10, 20, or sometimes 30 years ago.[6]

Undeterred by this lack of 'development' success, the foreign aid project continues, albeit at reduced levels since the end of the superpower rivalry. With the end of the bipolar Cold War order and the emergence of the United States as the global hegemon, discourse has also become ever more unabashed in its insistence that neo-liberal solutions hold the key to development. The rest of this chapter will look at how these profound changes have affected the ability of governments to govern and ends with a critical assessment of the policy prescriptions advocated by Northern aid programmes for the South.

Globalization and the Changing Role of Governments

For the first time in human history, people around the globe are able to communicate in real time, thus transcending limitations of time and space. Core markets for capital, goods and services are increasingly integrated in a global economy operating in real time and largely ignoring the traditional geography of national as well as physical boundaries. The main actors in this new age are transnational corporations (TNCs), huge organizations whose wealth and power far exceeds that of many nation-states. They operate in a global network of production and exchange, guided by financial gains to be made rather than by national or any other loyalties to be honoured. By the mid-1990s, the 350 largest corporations accounted for 40 per cent of world trade, and their total turnover exceeded the GDP of countries in both industrialized and developing countries.[7]

Much has been written about the impact of these developments on Northern governments and their ability to protect their populations from the hostile winds of global competition. What is interesting is that much of the helplessness and violation of sovereignty that now faces the governments of the advanced industrialized countries has been part and parcel of the experience of postcolonial governments since the early days of formal political independence. The governments in the advanced countries until recently were sovereign not only with regard to their ability to rule without foreign interference domestically, but also in the unfettered global pursuit of their national economic interests. The Cold War represented a collective response on the part of these governments to remove the one serious threat to their global economic interests: real socialism, with its (mainly rhetorical) challenge to the existing international economic order. In the old dependency and world-systems parlance, the advanced capitalist countries of the North constituted the 'core' of a global system established through colonialism and maintained through a variety of the neo-colonial mechanisms that shaped the profound asymmetry of power between continents, regions and individual states.

'Globalization' has significantly reduced the power of governments in the core to direct or control the workings of international capitalism. While there was clear collaboration and co-operation between corporations and these governments in earlier eras, the process of capital accumulation has now become so autonomous that individual states in North and South alike stand helpless in its unrelenting wake. The owners of capital now clearly think globally, and fall back on national governments only when it suits their particular needs at a particular moment in time. Suddenly, the position of governments in core and periphery *vis-à-vis* global capital is more similar than different: both seek to entice corporate investments through a variety of concessions, from tax breaks to lowering wage, social security and environmental standards, and both have to be keenly aware of the 'competitive' position of their respective country in the world economy. Europe's much vaunted welfare states are now among the prime targets of this process of globalization with its demand for sacrificing basic social security for the working majority at the altar of global capitalism.[8]

Helen Milner and Robert Koehane, two mainstream US political scientists writing largely about the advanced industrial societies, argue for example that: 'we can no longer understand politics within countries – what we still conventionally call "domestic" politics – without comprehending the nature of the linkages between national economies and the world economy, and changes in such linkages.'[9]

The power and influence of the international economy have increased to such an extent that these types of assessments have become rather commonplace. Curiously, however, few of these insights find their way into the 'development' prescriptions advanced by either individual donors or multilateral organizations such as the UNDP and the World Bank. While the growing power of global capital and its unrelenting forces of accumulation are readily acknowledged in assessing the diminishing power of governments in the core, such deliberations are considered largely irrelevant and leftist propaganda when it comes to the global periphery. Instead, the prevailing attitude about the failure of the development project is laid squarely in the lap of the governments and peoples in the South. As stated in a BMZ publication: 'Experiences over the past development decades have shown that successes or failures in development have been primarily due to the *internal* conditions in the respective countries.'[10]

The World Bank, for its part, devoted an entire issue of its annual development reports to 'The State in a Changing World', in which it argued: 'Development – economic, social, and sustainable – without an effective state is impossible. It is increasingly recognized that an effective state – not a minimal one – is central to economic and social development, but more as a partner and facilitator than as director. *States should work to complement markets, not replace them.*'[11] This insistence on blaming the state for the plight of the South leads to very inconsistent and contradictory policy prescriptions on the part of Northern 'donors' and 'benefactors'. Following is a brief analysis of assessments and prescriptions advanced by the German development aid ministry BMZ, as well as by the UNDP.

Policy Prescriptions for the South

During the Cold War era, both East and West approached the newly decolonized world with competing visions of development. Not surprisingly, the East's prescriptions were based on a statist model replete with suggestions for how to mobilize a (largely non-existing) proletariat under the guidance of a vanguard party.[12] The West, for its part, advocated pluralist political systems and a commitment to free markets. In the wake of statism's demise, the West's insistence that only neo-liberal solutions will lead to economic development has become even more emphatic. As expressed by the BMZ:

> The global transformations after the collapse of the former East Bloc have fundamentally changed the framework for development and development co-operation. Due to the failure of the dirigistic-socialistic model there has been a worldwide acceptance of the view that those societies whose economy is based on a social market order as well as participation in the political process have the best preconditions for a development that does justice to the people.[13]

Except for the insistence that there is now a 'worldwide acceptance' of neo-liberalism as the panacea for solving the problems of under-development, not much has changed in the German prescription for 'development'.[14] Bonn's 'five criteria' for granting ODA to any Third World country in the post-Cold War era were enunciated by Carl-Dieter Spranger, the 'development minister', in 1991. They are:

1. Respect for human rights.
2. Popular participation in the political process.
3. Democratic governmental structures and the rule of law.
4. A commitment to an economic order based on a social and free market.
5. A government committed to development.[15]

It is interesting that the worksheet that BMZ bureaucrats in Bonn must complete for each loan application under criterion no. 5 includes the question as to whether the recipient government is willing to accept 'reform programmes' mandated by the IMF and the World Bank.[16] This means that any country not willing to accept Structural Adjustment Programmes fails a key eligibility criterion.

The profound hypocrisy that characterizes the BMZ's approach to foreign aid is further reflected in its refusal to acknowledge the very real constraints that their particular type of integration into the global economy represents for developing countries. In a special informational brochure produced for the German public, for example, we find only one reference to issues such as the deterioration of the terms of trade. This reference is hidden in a section entitled 'Development can only occur from *within*' that even quotes Pope John Paul's encyclical *Populorum Progressio* in insisting that poor countries are the masters of their own fate. Almost as an after-thought, the text concludes with a quote from paragraph 2.2 of the UN's Agenda 21 which states emphatically that 'favourable *external* economic conditions are of decisive importance' and goes on to mention the debt burden and the deterioration of the terms of trade as key aspects of the external economic environment in which developing countries must oper-ate.[17] According to the UNDP:

> Since the early 1970s the least developed countries have suffered a cumu-lative decline of 50% in their terms of trade. For developing countries as a group the cumulative terms-of-trade losses amounted to $290 billion between 1980 and 1991. Much of this catastrophic fall was due to the decline in real commodity prices – in 1990 they were 45% lower than in 1980 and 10 per cent lower than the lowest prices during the Great Depression, in 1932. But poor prices were not confined to commodities. Developing countries' terms of trade for manufactured goods also fell – by 35% during 1970–91.[18]

The BMZ does not explain how exactly the government of a poor and highly indebted country can overcome these external constraints 'from within'. Governments in sub-Saharan Africa have to spend *four* times the amount they spend on public health for debt servicing. What does it mean to establish a criterion for foreign aid that calls for a commitment to 'development', but ignores the very real financial restraints imposed by a crushing debt burden and a very disadvantageous participation in the international division of labour?

Bonn does not hesitate, however, proudly to point to its own past ODA efforts, particularly in sub-Saharan Africa. For example, Minister Spranger mentioned in an article written in June 1998 entitled 'New Concepts for Co-operation with Africa'[19] that (West) Germany has provided sub-Saharan countries with roughly DM35 billion since 1956. The minister approvingly mentions two states, Ethiopia and Benin, that have carried out the type of reforms that warrant future assistance from Bonn. What the minister applauds is the abandonment of any type of socialist agenda and the embracing of neo-liberal prescriptions for economic growth. However, what about the countries to which most of the DM35 billion were disbursed in the past? What about the DM537.8 million that were sent to Zaire between 1960 and 1985, for example? What about Bonn's complicity in keeping African dictators and kleptocrats such as Mobuto Sese Seko in power?

In descending order, the following countries were the top ten recipients of West German financial aid between 1960 and 1985: Sudan, Kenya,

TABLE 6.2 Terms of trade of selected African countries, 1985–94 (1987=100)

Country	1985	1994
Kenya	124	80
Tanzania	126	83
Cameroon	113	79
Zaire/Congo	150	93
Mali	100	103
Ivory Coast	109	81
Ethiopia	119	74
Nigeria	167	86
Uganda	149	58

Source: IRBD, in Manuel Castells (1998) *End of Millennium*. Malden, MA: Blackwell, p. 88.

Tanzania, Ghana, Cameroon, Zaire, Zambia, Mali, Somalia, Ivory Coast.[20] One would have expected the minister to address the question as to what happened to the 'development' of most of these countries, given these massive infusions of German deutschmarks. As shown in Table 6.2, many of these countries experienced massive economic declines due to a severe deterioration in their terms of trade in the following decade (1985–94), while two (Somalia and Sudan) de facto disintegrated under the ravages of civil war.

The solution offered by Bonn and other western governments to these collapsing economies was to offer more aid rather than to begin to address some of the underlying causes. For example, the export earnings of these countries could have been significantly raised had the North not pursued a trade policy based on the heavy protection of its own agricultural producers. According to the UNDP, industrial countries spent $182 billion in 1995 alone on subsidies. And the OECD has calculated that 'the per capita transfer to US farmers amounted to $29,000 in 1995'. Given the predominance of US agriculture in global trade, these subsidies have a very serious impact on Southern export earnings. An example of how these subsidized farm products directly hurt Southern producers comes from Ugandan Vice President Specioza Wandira Kazibwe: 'after her country started trying to market significant maize surpluses in neighbouring Kenya, tonnes and tonnes of yellow maize, very cheap, were dumped into Kenya by the United States ... Where is the equity in this issue of global liberalization?'[21]

The Reality of Aid provides yet another example of this completely contradictory policy in the European governments' practice of dumping subsidized EU beef in Southern Africa while simultaneously supporting the development of communal cattle-farming in the region![22] According to one estimate, a reduction of only 30 per cent in subsidies paid to farmers in industrial countries would earn countries in the South an extra $45 billion a year. The UNDP concludes: 'In the real world, as distinct from the imaginary one inhabited by free traders, survival in agricultural markets depends less on comparative advantage than on comparative access to subsidies.'[23]

Given the valuable role played by the UN in pointing to the many inconsistencies of Northern policies *vis-à-vis* the South, UNDP's own policy recommendations for the South are surprising. For example, under the heading 'National policy in an era of globalization', the 1997 UNDP *Human Development Report* states: 'How to open more opportunities for the poorest countries? How to ensure that the benefits of global integration are more equally shared? The immediate responsibility lies with national governments, perhaps powerless to steer world markets, but able to minimize the damage and maximize the opportunities.'[24]

The authors continue by offering some 'key policy options':

1. *Manage trade and capital flows more carefully*. National governments can exercise more discretion when adopting policies of liberalization. A selective approach to the global market would follow the example of most East Asian economies.

Several objections can be raised to this 'option':

(a) The poorest countries are also the most indebted and thus most vulnerable to IMF-mandated SAPs. I am not familiar with one case in which SAPs gave national governments *more* discretion in opening up or, conversely, selectively closing their economies.

(b) East Asian development followed a very particular development path, taking advantage of several factors that presented themselves at a particular historical juncture, including carrying out land reforms and pursuing an export-oriented Kaldorian growth strategy. It is highly improbable that the poorest countries could successfully duplicate this export-oriented growth in the present world economy. Given the radically changed nature of post-Cold War geopolitics, the same import concessions would probably not be made by the advanced capitalist countries.

(c) As the 'Asian meltdown' has shown, even these newly industrializing countries are extremely vulnerable to the world economy. Even little tigers are unable to withstand an attack by big bad wolves.

(d) Contrary to prevailing views, the Asian tigers did not succeed economically under democratic conditions, including competitive and free elections, freedom of the press, etc. In fact, human rights in these countries were systematically violated, while civil society was ruthlessly suppressed.

(e) Private financial flows in form of FDIs are largely bypassing the world's poorest countries. For example, in 1996 'the top 12 out of 108 developing countries received 73% of private capital flows ... while countries in sub-Saharan Africa received only 4.8%'.[25] Only twenty-five of the developing countries even have a credit rating that thus enables them access to bonds, commercial bank loans, and portfolio equity. Pretending that this is an option generally available to governments in the South is simply disingenuous.

2. *Invest in poor people* ... The diffusion of new technology increases the payoff to higher levels of human capital and to more flexible sets of skills.

Again, there are several problems:

(a) Even in the advanced capitalist countries ever-larger numbers of workers are becoming economically marginalized in this information age. The poor are particularly vulnerable in this process. If the richest countries in the world have largely failed at finding a solution for overcoming the deindustrialization of their economies and the growing marginalization of their workforces, how can the poorest countries be expected to do this successfully?[26] Furthermore, as Manuel Castells has pointed out: 'The thesis of "skills mismatch," according to which inequality is a short-term phenomenon related to income premium for skills, which will even out over time as more are educated for current technology, has been empirically refuted by a number of experts.'[27]

(b) The poorest countries also have the lowest levels of material infrastructure (electricity, telephone lines, etc.) without which even the most highly trained human capital cannot participate in the new technologies. According to the UNDPs own figures in its 1997 *Human Development Report*, the least developed countries only have 0.3 telephone lines per 100 inhabitants, compared to 40.1 for the industrial countries and 11.5 for the world as a whole. Computer and internet use is so negligible that it does not even warrant an entry. Per capita electricity consumption further confirms this situation: while in 1994 each person in the industrial countries used 7,514 kilowatt-hours of electricity, in the developing countries as a whole that figure was 763 per capita. In the poorest countries, the figure was 74 kilowatt-hours per capita in 1994. Under such conditions of extreme material underdevelopment the UNDP's prescription seems cynical at best.

3. *Foster small enterprises* ... One of the most important ways for globalization to reduce poverty is through the incubators of microenterprises

and small and medium-size firms – they are more labour-intensive than large firms and will provide the bulk of new jobs for the poor for some time.

(a) Given the size and sheer preponderance of TNCs, organizations that stand at the core of the process of globalization, it is difficult to understand how small and medium-sized firms as well as micro-enterprises can succeed economically in the poorest countries, especially under the conditions of trade and investment liberalization that are part and parcel of the present package of reforms pushed on the South. This will become even more difficult should the OECD countries manage to get the Multi-lateral Agreement on Investment (MAI) ratified at some point in the future. As pointed out in *The Reality of Aid*:

> The agreement's key principles of 'national treatment' and 'non-discrimination' would require governments to give the same or better benefits to foreign investors as they give to national businesses. Protection of, for instance, small and medium sized enterprises of national origin against multinational foreign investors would be prohibited, as would some government initiatives to promote skills development in the workforce.[28]

(b) This 'option' is completely contradictory with no. 1 above, in which emulation of the Asian model is advocated. This model was quintessentially based on the development of large, export-oriented sectors of the economy. It is difficult to understand how UNDP can simultaneously argue for options 1 and 3.

4. *Improve governance.* Globalization usually weakens the state's in-fluence – but in many ways it demands a stronger state, to help people reap its benefits and mitigate its costs. Better governance is vital not just to ensure the rule of law and protect against international organized crime, but also to maintain and expand social and economic infrastructure.

(a) The poorest countries are also postcolonial societies in which governments continue to face the difficult task of state-building under simultaneous conditions of extreme poverty and lack of resources. If globalization weakens the sovereignty of governments in advanced industrial societies, how is it possible for governance to be strengthened in countries with immeasurably fewer resources? Globalization 'demanding' a stronger state does not mean that this is a realistic policy option, especially under conditions of underdevelopment.

(b) The 'good governance' issue again is a way of deflecting attention from the structure and constraints imposed by the world economy. The Asian meltdown is a good example of this approach: until the summer of

1997 the Asian NICs and their governments were showcased by the industrial countries in order to 'prove' that self-sustaining growth in the South was indeed possible and that dependency theorists were thus utterly wrong. Now that the miracle has turned into somewhat of a mirage, the same governments are being attacked for having pursued very faulty economic policies that predictably have led to the current disaster in the entire Asia Pacific region. Except, of course, that very few analysts predicted the meltdown before it began!

The Success of the Development Project in Poverty Alleviation

As should be clear by now, I do not believe that ODA, or 'foreign aid', has any prospect of helping in its professed objective of poverty alleviation and thus, at least implicitly, to help close the gap between rich and poor. That is why, as a start, I would advocate that terms such as 'aid' or 'development assistance' should henceforth no longer be used to describe the particular regime that emerged in the wake of decolonization in order to continue controlling the economic and political destinies of the former colonies. As Friedrich Nietzsche suggested long ago, language is: 'a moveable host of metaphors, metonymies, and anthropomorphisms; in short, a sum of human relations that have been poetically and rhetorically intensified, transferred, and embellished, and that, after a long usage, seem to people to be fixed, canonical, and binding'.[29]

Four decades of 'aid' have done little to help alleviate poverty, and have contributed much to the vicious cycle of indebtedness that has trapped most of the postcolonial countries in more poverty and despair. It is time that we acknowledge this fact by discontinuing the use of Orwellian terminology.

There are other problems. The aid regime has reduced entire regions, particularly in sub-Saharan Africa, to a 'political economy of begging'.[30] As Frantz Fanon predicted in *The Wretched of the Earth* before most of the continent had even gained political independence, the neo-colonial African elite would never rise to the historically progressive role played by the European bourgeoisie in the process of industrialization. Foreign aid became the mechanism of choice for paying off co-opted elites in order to maintain the economic and political status quo. Even in countries such as Tanzania where local elites consciously sought to build a different postcolonial society, aid had unintended negative consequences. In the end, Tanzania became as drawn into the vicious cycle of indebtedness and IMF conditionality as any other country that had accepted donor funds for development purposes.[31]

The governance issue now so favoured by Northern governments to explain the failure of economic development in the South is not completely misplaced and has been raised by radicals throughout the world for decades.[32] However, a linear relationship between successful economic development and a western-style democracy has not been empirically documented anywhere in the South. Insisting on such a link as a prerequisite for success is ahistorical even for the advanced industrial countries. It is difficult to see how better governance and transparency would alter existing patterns in the global economy in favour of the South. For example, although 37 per cent of total FDI flows in 1997 went to developing countries, more than 80 per cent went to twenty countries only, with China receiving the preponderant share. By contrast, 100 countries received less than $100 million a year, and nine countries had negative FDI flows.[33] If good governance, democracy and transparency were prime determinants of private capital flows, China would certainly not rank in first place!

Furthermore, the aid regime itself has directly contributed to the weakness of national governments. First, aid has filled public coffers without governments needing to establish proper mechanisms for the efficient administration of a state, from budgeting to taxation. Second, it has further divided the government from the masses by enriching the national political elites, whose lifestyles were more in line with those of their Northern counterparts than their own compatriots. Third, all states are territorially differentiated, with minorities having access to government mainly at the local/regional levels. This allows enough flexibility for the system as a whole to survive, while allowing the balancing of competing interests at local and regional levels. Since the aid regime has dealt primarily with national governments, it has upset this 'complex geometry', with dire consequences for national unity as well as civil society.[34] In the case of sub-Saharan Africa the absence of this 'complex geometry' is a significant factor in the breakdown of the state and the emergence of 'tribalism'.

This is not to argue that concern for good governance, with its insistence on the building of efficient governmental institutions and regularized and transparent rules of behaviour is irrelevant. Instead, what is argued here is that the main constraints for the realization of good governance in the South lie not in the personal or professional failings of Third World politicians, nor in the overly zealous policy prescriptions of development aid bureaucrats. Instead, the primary blame goes to the structure of the international economy that has retained most of its neo-colonial features of power and control. Until foreign aid donors are willing to address this issue squarely, and to end their complicity in this system, the governments and peoples of the South will be condemned to a perpetuation in a status quo that structurally condemns them to witness an ever-widening gap between the rich and the poor.

Notes

1. UNDP (1999) *Human Development Report 1999*. New York: Oxford University Press, p. 28.

2. Judith Randel and Tony German (eds) (1997) *The Reality of Aid: An Independent Review of Development Cooperation 1997–1998*, London: Earthscan, p. 6.

3. BMZ (October 1996) *Entwicklungspolitische Konzeption des BMZ*. Bonn: BMZ, p. 2.

4. Cited in David Horowitz (1967) *From Yalta to Vietnam: American Foreign Policy in the Cold War*. London: Penguin.

5. UNDP (1997), *Human Devleopment Report 1997*. New York: Oxford University Press, p. 11.

6. Ibid., p. 7.

7. Ibid. Various statistical tables and appendices.

8. See Brigitte H. Schulz (2000) 'Globalization, Unification and the Future of the German Welfare State', in *International Social Science Journal*, 163, February.

9. Robert O. Keohane and Helen V. Milner (eds) (1997) *Internationalization and Domestic Politics*. New York: Cambridge University Press.

10. BMZ (April 1998) *BMZ Jahresbericht 1997*. Bonn: BMZ, p. 7. (Author's translation and emphasis.)

11. World Bank (1997) *World Development Report 1997*. New York: Oxford University Press, p. 18. (My italics.)

12. For a detailed description of the East's model of Third World development, see Chapter 2 of Brigitte H. Schulz (1995) *Development Policy in the Cold War Era: The Two Germanies and Sub-Saharan Africa 1960–1985*. Munster: Lit Verlag. For a further elaboration of East–South relations, see Brigitte H. Schulz and William W. Hansen (eds) (1989) *The Soviet Bloc and the Third World: The Political Economy of East–South Relations*. Boulder, CO: Westview Press.

13. BMZ (October 1996), p. 1. (Author's translation.)

14. For a full elaboration of the genesis and execution of West German development aid, see Schulz, *Development Policy*, Ch. 3 and *passim*.

15. BMZ (January 1998) *Entwicklungspolitik im Schaubild*. Bonn: BMZ, pp. 32–3. (Author's translation.)

16. Ibid., p. 71.

17. Ibid., p. 38.

18. UNDP (1997), p. 84.

19. Carl-Dieter Spranger (1998) 'Neue Konzepte für die Zusammenarbeit mit Afrika', *Wirtschaftskurier*, June.

20. Schulz, *Development Policy*, p. 99.

21. Ernest Harsch (1997) 'Africa Strives to Revitalize Agriculture', *Africa Recovery*, 11, 2 (October), p. 10.

22. Randel and German, *The Reality of Aid*, p. 11.

23. UNDP (1997), pp. 86–7.

24. Ibid, p. 89.

25. Randel and German, *The Reality of Aid*, p. 14.

26. For an interesting discussion of growing polarization in the United States, see Manuel Castells (1998) *End of Millennium*. Malden, MA: Blackwell, pp. 128–49.

27. Ibid., p. 134.

28. Randel and German, *The Reality of Aid*, p. 14.

29. F. W. Nietzsche, 'On Truth and Falsity in their Ultramortal Sense', quoted in: Nelson W. Keith (1997) *Reframing International Development: Globalism, Postmodernity, and Difference*. Thousand Oaks, CA: Sage, p. 241.

30. Castells, *End of Millennium*, p. 114.

31. Severine M. Rugumamu (1997) *Lethal Aid: The Illusion of Socialism and Self Reliance in Tanzania*. Trenton, NJ: African World Press.

32. See, for example, the writings of André Gunder Frank, particularly *Lumpen-bourgeoisie, Lumpen-development*.

33. UNDP (1999), p. 31.

34. Castells, *End of Millennium*, pp. 270–1.

7

Poverty Reduction and Policy Dialogue: The World Bank and the State in Zimbabwe, Zambia and Malawi

Nazneen Kanji

This chapter examines the nature of the policy dialogue between the World Bank and the state in the formulation of poverty reduction strategies at the country level. The World Bank is an important actor in development policy and programming in sub-Saharan Africa and wields considerable power and influence. A key argument advanced in this chapter is that although the Bank has renewed its commitment to poverty reduction in the 1990s, it does not do enough to promote debate on the issues affecting poverty nor is it flexible enough in relation to its own policy prescriptions. Malawi, Zambia and Zimbabwe are discussed as case studies; they are all located within Southern Africa and all three are recipients of structural adjustment loans from the Bank. The case studies allow for a more 'bottom-up' assessment of how the Bank operationalizes its poverty reduction strategies and of its recent attempts to create a more demand-driven institution with a stronger country focus.[1]

I begin by assessing recent shifts in the Bank's poverty reduction policies and their operationalization at the country level. Although policy dialogue or the process of policy-making is the central issue, understanding the content of the Bank's own policies is important when assessing how flexible (or rigid) they are in the different political, institutional and social contexts of individual countries. I then move on to discuss the role of policy dialogue in the Bank's formulation of its country assistance strategies, questioning the extent to which the Bank focuses on poverty issues and the extent to which its own strategies are negotiable. The problems inherent in a discussion of poverty which does not address political and institutional issues is the subject of the next section. Finally, recent attempts by the Bank to involve civil society in policy dialogue are discussed and some reflections are offered for more productive and effective partnerships to address poverty.

The World Bank and Poverty Reduction: Assessing the Post-1990 Strategy

Poverty reduction has officially remained the first priority for the World Bank since the publication of the 1990 *World Development Report*. The Bank then renewed its commitment to reduce poverty through the formulation of what was later to become known as the 'three-pronged strategy'. This is based on three pillars: broad-based growth, 'human capital' development and safety-nets. It represents continuities as well as breaks with the past. At the level of development theory, the Bank has maintained a remarkably consistent approach to poverty reduction throughout its fifty-year history. Its assumption has always been to view development and poverty reduction as fundamentally an issue of economic growth. Poverty reduction was not originally a goal in itself, but rather an expected, albeit unarticulated, consequence of economic growth.

The current, more explicit concern with poverty emerged in the latter half of the 1980s. The severe disruptive social and political impacts of the early Structural Adjustment Programmes (SAPs) in Africa forced the Bank to pay more attention to the 'human dimensions' of the policies it advocated and supported. The current three-pronged strategy is outlined below in terms of its continuities with and departures from the Bank's historical orthodoxy.

The first part of the three-pronged strategy signalled a greater focus on broad-based economic growth, that is, a labour-demanding growth pattern that can provide increased employment and income. However, the main approach to achieve this objective has remained a formula from the neo-liberal agenda of the 1980s centred round a minimalist state, 'undistorted' markets and the public provision of infrastructure which, according to the Bank, stimulate and facilitate investment in the private sector. There does not seem to be a significant change in fundamental premises since the 1980s nor a clear conception of how the more recent strategy for labour-intensive growth might be advanced in an era of globalization. At least in the three countries that are the focus of this chapter, income poverty has increased overall in the 1990s with ongoing liberalization and adjustment policies, although this process has been uneven with some poor groups improving their position while others have found themselves worse off. There continues to be a heated debate about the actual impact of liberalization policies on poverty and income distribution, with many arguing both have worsened (see Killick 1995 for an excellent overview).

The second prong in the Bank's approach to poverty reduction is the development of human resources primarily through the provision of primary health-care and education but also through other basic services. The focus on these issues follows a decade of neglect in which the Bank's concerns with the issue of debt repayment and reductions in budget deficits contributed to a major decline in public spending. This decline in spending had a strong negative impact on the social sectors, especially health and education, reflected in declining social indicators. Considerable criticism on the part of some governments, many international non-governmental organizations (NGOs) and the UN agencies, notably UNICEF, prompted a new emphasis on investment in the social sectors in the Bank's policies, particularly in Africa. The Bank's rationale for this shift is couched in terms of 'human capital' rather than basic needs or basic rights. Developing the 'asset base of the poor' through improving their health and qualifications, it is argued, increases the ability of the poor to gain access to the labour market and employment. In other words, increasing access to services is seen instrumentally in that it promotes more efficient and effective development, rather than as basic needs or basic rights which was the way it was viewed by many governments in the post-independence period. Many would argue that human development and provision of social services should be seen as a justifiable goal in itself and would give greater emphasis to such issues compared to Bank priorities.

An example of the Bank's instrumentalist view of social services is the rationale for increasing girls' access to schooling. In Bank documents, this tends to be seen as an important cornerstone of education policy because of the high economic and social returns to such investment in terms of lower fertility rates, better health for children and increased labour and economic productivity. This is the primary rationale which dominates operational documents as contrasted with an argument for education as a basic right for girls, increasing choices and contributing to the empowerment of women and greater gender equality.

The Bank pursues its 'human capital development' agenda primarily through efforts to protect and increase a country's public spending on health and education, especially at the primary level. This has been pursued through policy dialogue, investment lending and technical advice but also increasingly through conditionalities attached to adjustment loans.

Cost sharing through the introduction or raising of user fees has been an important component in Bank prescriptions for policy reform since the 1980s, when resources became more constrained. In some case, user fees may have led to an expansion of primary services, but in most cases evidence seems to suggest that they reduced access to primary services for poor groups. Exemption systems are often difficult to manage and the actual cost recovery may be limited. This has led to some reassessment within the Bank which may suggest a more flexible attitude regarding cost recovery at the primary level (Adams and Hartnett 1996). The point being made here, though, is that even where primary services are protected to some extent, reductions in public expenditure coupled with cost-sharing may not in effect increase access by poor households.

The third and final prong in the Bank's approach to poverty reduction is the provision of safety-nets. Safety-nets are basically income maintenance programmes that protect a person or household against adverse outcomes such as chronic incapacity to work and earn, and a decline in this capacity caused by shocks through economic recession, very bad harvests or deaths of breadwinners. The safety-net concept is reminiscent of the residual model of social welfare of the 1950s and early 1960s, where 'modernization' or 'accelerated economic growth' was the dominant paradigm for development, except that in its 1980s guise it came to be specifically associated with compensatory measures in relation to the social costs of adjustment. Within the residual model, public intervention to meet social needs was restricted to the most vulnerable groups in society who would not benefit from the 'trickle-down' effect of wealth generated by growth in the formal or modern sector. The safety-net concept was originally applied in economies where the formal sector was predominant and where poverty was viewed as transitional, but has been diffused uncritically by the Bank to very different socio-economic contexts.

In sub-Saharan Africa, the Bank's efforts and lending in this area have been concentrated on what is termed 'social action programmes' and 'social funds'. These are multisectoral programmes, implemented parallel to economic reforms. In Africa, in recognition of widespread and structural poverty, they have a broader mandate than safety-nets to reduce poverty and reintegrate vulnerable groups into society (Marc et al. 1995).

Social funds are intended to be demand-driven mechanisms that channel resources to 'the poor' and support sub-projects that respond directly to their priority needs. The unit managing the social fund has a special autonomy outside government and the power to select or reject sub-projects formulated and implemented by Community-based Organizations (CBOs), NGOs, municipalities and private firms. In practice, the emphasis in terms of the content of the projects seems to be the improvement of economic infrastructure and social services which are usually the responsibility of line ministries.[2]

Two questions arise here. The first is whether the funds are creating parallel structures to the sectoral ministries responsible for these areas of infrastructure and services. In Malawi and Zambia, this seems to be case and, furthermore, there also seems to be little effort being made to integrate policy lessons from these sub-projects into sectoral policies and programmes.

The other question is whether the projects respond to the priority needs of the community and, if so, to which groups within communities. As the term 'demand responsiveness' implies, the funds respond to proposals from organized community groups which are usually required to make up-front financial as well as labour contributions to the projects. These contributions are substantial, for example in Zambia, they constitute 25 per cent of project costs. Furthermore, there are no explicit strategies to address inequalities within communities or households. The obvious danger is that less powerful groups and groups most in need are unable to gain access to social funds. For example, a Bank study of social funds (Narayan and Ebbe 1997) notes that the extent to which attempts are made to reach women is unclear.

This focus on poverty reduction, during the 1990s, through the three-pronged approach has led to changes in the Bank's lending profile in Africa. Most significant is a major expansion of lending to social sectors, especially primary services and the efforts to invest in social funds and safety-nets. Changes in the traditional 'growth investments' can also be recorded; mainly through a drop in lending to infrastructure and agriculture (Tjonneland et al. 1998). There are also some changes within those sectors with a stronger emphasis on small farmers, rural infra-structure, small- and medium-sized enterprises and the informal sector. The economic liberalization approach continues through the Bank's dominant structural adjustment operations. A recent study of the Bank's operational strategies for poverty reduction (Tjonneland et al. 1998) raises questions about the effectiveness of the three-pronged strategy in highly unequal societies in Africa, when little attention is paid to the distribution of assets. 'Assets' here refers to both material resources such as land and capital and non-material resources such as political power and social organization.

The Bank's Country Assistance Strategies (CAS) and Policy Dialogue

The shifts in the Bank's approach to poverty reduction in the 1990s are closely associated with changes in operational policies and institutional reforms, the most recent being the 'strategic compact' initiated by the current president, James Wolfensohn (World Bank 1997a). The intentions are to strengthen borrower orientation through an improved CASs, to build a more flexible Bank through decentralization of powers and functions to resident missions, to design new lending instruments and to create a more open and responsive Bank through dialogue and co-operation with other donors and NGOs. The Bank's formal system for generating poverty-focused policies and interventions is based first on research and assessment of poverty. This should feed into the Bank's CAS which is intended to provide the basis for the Bank's lending programme and non-lending services.

The three countries discussed in this chapter are often cited in Bank documents as examples of good practice in terms of the close links between poverty studies and the Bank's CAS. These strategies should be based on policy dialogue with governments and other stakeholders in borrower countries, including consultations with NGOs and bilateral and multilateral donors. CASs summarize the Bank's assessment of economic and social performance, the borrower country's development objectives and the Bank group's lending and non-lending assistance. The CAS document is increasingly viewed as the key policy document in the Bank's relation with the borrowing country. Although formally an internal Bank document, it is increasingly portrayed as a negotiated strategy between the Bank and the borrowing country.

The Bank influences national policies directly through a variety of conditionalities (mostly linked to the adjustment loans), sector policy prescriptions and technical advice. While the main pressure and conditionalities have been directed at economic reform, these have also, in the 1990s, included conditions on levels of public expenditure on primary social services and in some cases on social funds and safety-nets. More indirectly, the Bank wields power through the sheer size of its lending and through its influence on other donors.

The Bank clearly has significant financial resources and technical expertise to influence the government's understanding of its investment priorities, but it pays too little attention to its inordinate power and resources in the context of negotiations. This is particularly so in sub-Saharan Africa, given the dependency on aid in this region. Within the three country case studies, the weight of the Bank is variable with Zimbabwe being least dependent on aid and Malawi being most dependent. In addition to current conditions of aid dependency, historical and institutional factors also affect the weight of the Bank in influencing policy. This is notable in Zimbabwe where government is institutionally stronger and there is only a short and uneven history of dependence on the Bank's IDA loans.

Is the Bank's Three-pronged Strategy Negotiable?

In all three case study countries, the Bank supports investment in smallholder agriculture as an important strategy for poverty reduction. However, the policy advice is always to lift subsidies (sometimes in one go), liberalize prices and privatize, irrespective of the local context and of research which has shown the negative impact on food security and incomes for poorer farmers (see Wold 1997 for Zambia; Evans 1997 for Malawi).

While no conditionality may be directly linked to this, where the Bank is a large investor and the government is under pressure to cut public expenditure, governments are in practice forced to implement these policies.

Zambia is a case where structural adjustment in the 1990s – deregulation of agricultural marketing, commercialization of agricultural services and liberalization of financial services – dramatically altered the producer environment for small-scale farmers. These economic reforms were supposed to lead to increased food production and improve welfare. In fact, they have had severe and serious adverse impacts on household food security in all but the most central areas and those close to the main railways. This has resulted in rural-to-urban dislocation, losses in social capital and decreases in social welfare (Wold 1997).

In Malawi, the EU is of the opinion that the lifting of subsidies on fertilizers had resulted in undue hardship for small producers and had suggested a partial subsidy in the short term. However, various donors and government officials interviewed were aware that this policy approach did not meet the approval of the Bank and of USAID (another major funder in this sector) and that the programme might be dropped. Certainly, most bilateral donors tend to follow the Bank's lead on sectoral policies. Production of the staple food crop, maize, has fallen but there is no agreement on the main causes of the situation. A rapid assessment study in five sites in 1997 found that the decline in maize production had a significant negative impact on food security (Evans 1997).

The Bank-supported abolition of restrictions on the main export product, tobacco (under the Banda regime this was legally restricted to mostly the major farming estates) led to remarkable growth in tobacco production among small-scale farmers with an estimated 200,000 households entering production. This liberalization has been lauded by the Bank as a successful measure promoting poverty reduction. However, the impact has been uneven and some groups may be worse off than before. A recent study indicates that although tobacco-growers have increased their incomes, this has resulted in short-term rises in consumption followed by increased dependency on being hired as agricultural labourers to offset food deficits later in the season. Even more worrying are the findings that nutritional status has fallen among families of tobacco-growers and that women's workload has increased, leaving them less time for food preparation and the care of sick children.

In Zimbabwe, the influence of the Bank in agriculture and rural development is very different. Apart from an Emergency Drought Recovery project in 1992, the Bank's lending activities to agriculture and rural development have, during the first half of the 1990s, centred on agricultural credits for export promotion. This lending is directed to large commercial farmers and any benefits to smaller farmers, for example in horticultural and cotton research, has according to Bank officials been indirect and unintended. The Bank has supported the privatization of parastatals (for example, the dairy board) and cost recovery for agricultural services (e.g. livestock services) within broader policy reforms under the Economic Structural Adjustment Programme. The effects of these reforms on poverty reduction have not been examined directly, in that the costs and benefits for different groups of the population have not been adequately assessed.

Although the Ministry of Agriculture in Zimbabwe has not in the past viewed poverty reduction as its main concern, but rather the maximizing of yields, both Bank officials and the ministry say that there has been a shift towards a concern with smaller farmers (1–7 hectares of land). A current Agricultural Services Management Project includes beneficiary assessments and client satisfaction surveys which provide baseline information, and the project also aims to have a stakeholder advisory panel. There are, however, some doubts voiced by Bank officials as to whether the poorest farmers will benefit, particularly those in the poorest and dry regions.

The argument being made here is that in relation to the first prong of the Bank's strategy for poverty reduction, the Bank remains dogmatic on policies of privatization and trade liberalization. Although there have been shifts in emphasis in the 1990s towards smaller farmers and rural infrastructure, the liberalization formula is still the basic prescription. The full weight of the Bank, along with the IMF, serves to inhibit the exploration of alternatives which might be better rooted in the economic, political, social and cultural context of particular countries in sub-Saharan Africa.

To a great extent, the same argument holds for the other two components of the Bank's poverty reduction strategy in the social sectors. This is not to say that the Bank has not, in some instances, positively influenced government thinking on social sector programmes. A case in point is the expansion of primary education in Malawi where the Bank probably helped improve the design of programmes. However, in this case, it was the new government which came to power in 1994 that took a policy decision to make primary schooling free, resulting in the doubling of school enrolment rates. According to Bank officials, they would not have advised this policy shift but did support the government when it was taken.

Advice and even conditionality to maintain or increase public spending for primary services can only promote poverty reduction. However, as already discussed, the issue of user fees and cost sharing may work in the opposite direction. The doubling of school enrolment rates in Malawi with the abolition of school fees would suggest that access is constrained when parents have to pay. A study in Zambia found parents were bitter that their contributions were rising sharply, when government was providing fewer materials than in the past. The same study recommends that more attention is given to safety-nets and exemption systems for both health and education fees for the poor (Booth et al. 1995). In Zimbabwe, primary school fees were introduced in 1991 in urban areas but not in rural areas, with lower fees for low-income urban settlements and higher fees for high-income areas. Nevertheless, parents in poor urban areas found it difficult to find the fees at the beginning of term without cutting consumption or getting into debt (Kanji 1995). There are a number of studies in sub-Saharan Africa which show that girls' access to school is even more negatively affected than boys' access when parents have to make choices in the face of resource constraints (Odago and Heneveld 1995).

In Zambia, fees were introduced at all health facility levels across the country, with an observed decline in patterns of utilization at some health centres. A study on user fees in the health sector in four districts in Zambia illustrates how, even if the particular preventive services are free and if an exemption system is included, a number of factors result in a decline in utilization in a range of preventive and curative services (Kalyalya and Milimo 1996). These include lack of consultation with and information for user groups and staff, weak administrative capacity including the inability to identify vulnerable groups and the inability of some groups to pay cash. The government recently (1996–97) experimented with a pre-payment scheme which was not successful and has now been abandoned.

In Malawi, fees are not charged at health facilities. In Zimbabwe, the introduction of fees at health-centre level in the early 1990s is acknowledged to have caused problems for poor groups, and in 1995 they were abolished for rural centres. As one review points out, experimenting with various forms of user fees is not a substitute for the development of a health-financing policy which systematically examines different financing options, including higher charges for better-off groups, and uses operational research to test viability (Ministry of Health, Zambia 1997: 24).

Introducing or raising user fees for services is a contentious issue with political implications for the government in question. It runs counter to views of what used to be considered responsibilities of the state by many African governments in the post-independence period. However, these issues do not seem to be adequately discussed in policy dialogue.

Finally, on the issue of social funds, the way in which these are designed is also problematic and may actually undermine the role of the state in service provision. In Malawi and Zambia, improvement of health and education services and water supply constituted the overwhelming majority of projects which received funding (Tjonneland et al. 1998: 72). The issue that arises here is whether the projects are creating parallel structures to the sectoral ministries responsible for education, health and water. Although there is some co-ordination at the district level in terms of siting and staffing of social infrastructure, these initiatives cannot substitute for national policies and programming by the relevant ministries. It is argued in Bank documents that independent project management structures are essential to the success of the projects in terms of community responsiveness and quick disbursement of funds. Although in some cases institutional capacity building and reform of the social sectors is underway, there do not seem to be any efforts to integrate policy lessons from these sub-projects into sectoral policies and programmes. Thus, although social infrastructure is being improved, the integration of these initiatives and the lessons learnt around partnerships and community involvement are not shared sufficiently with existing government structures responsible for social services. Certainly, this does not seem to be a planning focus from the inception stage.[3]

Does the Bank Emphasize Poverty Issues Enough in Policy Dialogue?

The country cases shed some light on how the Bank has addressed poverty reduction in policy dialogue. It is clear that that Bank has put poverty on the agenda in its relations with these three countries. The issue of poverty reduction has featured prominently in the series of workshops and meetings that the Bank now conducts as part of the CAS process with government and stakeholders in all three countries. The Bank has also attempted to raise the issue in situations where the government, or some parts of government, has been reluctant or unwilling to address poverty. For example, the sections on implications for poverty inserted into Zimbabwe's original Economic Structural Adjustment Programme, primarily negotiated with the Ministry of Finance, were largely a result of Bank pressure.

The question which arises is whether the Bank, as a powerful (albeit external) agency, fully exploits opportunities to promote debate on poverty reduction and remains open to solutions that do not conform to its three-pronged strategy. To make progress it is crucial both to be able to respond quickly and flexibly and to be able to assist political processes to further poverty reduction without unduly interfering in domestic politics and decision-making. While this is by no means an easy task, development agencies with far less aid funds at their disposal have often proved to be more effective here. UNDP, for example, is widely seen as playing a far more important role in promoting poverty reduction policies in Zimbabwe, although it has limited funds for programmes. Certainly, the UN agencies tend to use a framework which emphasizes the multidimensional aspects of poverty and vulnerability as opposed to the more 'money-metric' indicators used by the Bank.

Bilateral donors active in Zimbabwe have had some success in pursuing poverty reducing objectives at the sectoral level working through line ministries even when the national government has been less receptive to donor calls for poverty reducing programmes and projects. The Bank does say that borrower commitment to poverty reduction is important in deciding on volume and composition of lending. In practice, it has not (yet) acted on this beyond stating this in CAS documents and saying that it may have implications for future lending.

There are a number of organizational factors which act as constraints within the Bank. One is the centralized structure and weak residential missions which have made it more difficult for the Bank to interact with local authorities and political processes. A related problem has been the limited capacity to work closely with other donors pursuing poverty reducing aid. Interviews in all three countries conveyed a fairly uniform picture: donors, NGOs and to a lesser extent governments complained that the Bank did not properly interact, consult and liaise with domestic stakeholders (government and non-governmental) and donors. They are seen as relying far too heavily on visiting missions flying in and out of the country. This is confirmed by recent Bank-commissioned client feedback surveys (see for example, Kadoole 1997) which indicate that the Bank should be more flexible, devolve greater decision-making powers to resident missions and be more responsive to local needs. They should listen more and lecture less during consultations.

On the positive side, the feedback surveys do record improvements in local perceptions of the Bank. There is improvement in consultations with stakeholders and donor partners, there are ongoing attempts to decentralize authority to resident missions and, more recently, new lending instruments intended to be more flexible and adaptable have been introduced. The 'strategic compact' involves a series of further institutional changes to renew 'the Bank's effectiveness to fight poverty' (World Bank 1997a) and although it is too early to assess its effectiveness, initiatives such as the relocation of country directors from Washington to the field will be welcome.

Are Political and Institutional Issues Discussed in Policy Dialogue?

This section examines the Bank's Country Assistance Strategies as the products of policy dialogue, with reference to the three country case studies. In particular, the focus is on the limitations of these documents in discussing context-specific, political and institutional factors which contribute to poverty and have a bearing on poverty reduction strategies.

First, these CAS documents lack a thorough discussion of the impact of regional developments and external relations on policies for sustainable poverty reduction. Debt issues, world prices and trade issues have strong implications for poverty trends, but these implications are barely touched upon in these documents. Even more noticeable, given the geographical location of the countries, is the absence of an appropriate assessment of regional relations. Southern Africa was undergoing tremendous changes in the mid-1990s with major implications for the development of the region, but the CAS documents have little if anything to say about the constraints and opportunities for poverty reduction emerging out of the end of the war in Mozambique or the change to democracy in South Africa. At best, these documents mention economic sectors which may benefit from liberalization and the lifting of restrictions on trade.

Second, a neglected issue in all three documents is the domestic political and institutional framework for poverty reduction. The CAS documents list, or sometimes discuss, the government's formal policy statements, action plans and public commitments to poverty reduction, but beyond that these are issues avoided in the CAS documents. Typically, they give little emphasis to the underlying social forces that drive and sustain pro-poor development, nor do they examine in any depth the winners and losers in past and future policies. Implementation capacity is not properly assessed and the social and political background of the polices and programmes are not examined. The CAS documents are particularly weak in their focus on gender. There is hardly any discussion of gender issues and strategies to address gender inequalities.

Some, but not all, of these shortcomings are addressed in ongoing economic and sector work and other analytical studies which the Bank carries out. In general, however, the strategy documents tend to be technocratic, descriptive and prescriptive and do not yet reflect the institutional focus of the strategic compact. Ambitious reform objectives are delineated without due attention to institutional capacity and political will. A case in point is the Agricultural Sector Investment Program (ASIP) in Zambia which was launched in 1995 as a major programme to assist poor farmers and promote rural development. It is supported by fourteen donors, with the Bank playing a major role in its conception and funding. ASIP is widely regarded as a failure both within the Bank and with donor agencies interviewed in Zambia. Institutional reforms in the ministry have taken much longer than expected; only the upper layers have been involved to date and decentralization has not taken effect. According to one NGO working in twenty-seven districts at the end of 1997, ASIP has generated considerable uncertainty about the future among district and extension workers and further weakened the state system. A review of ASIP carried out in 1997 by the University of Zambia's Institute of Economic and Social Research confirms this view, stating that staff at lower levels believe that restructuring is only about retrenchments, pointing to a lack of information and communication from central levels of the Ministry (University of Zambia 1997). The main problem, according to Bank officials, is the weak institutional capacity of Zambia's Ministry of Agriculture and lack of commitment to ASIP. However, in policy dialogue and in the two-year preparation period, these issues were not adequately addressed.

The problems of addressing sensitive political and institutional issues by an external development agency such as the Bank are not to be underestimated. However, it has to be recognized more clearly that poverty reduction is not simply a technical question; it involves broader political issues of redistribution and it often challenges existing power relations, at an international and national level, embedded in inequalities based on class, gender and ethnicity. Policies which address asset inequalities are particularly sensitive. The Bank has been reluctant to engage with these although there are some shifts and exceptions. An example of this is the land issue in Zimbabwe which surfaces periodically in national political fora. The skewed distribution of land is widely accepted to be an important constraint for poverty reduction but redistribution is a highly politically charged issue. The Bank's view is that land reform is important for the generation of employment and for poverty reduction but that such land reform will have to be undertaken in a transparent manner and without undermining commercial farming. The Bank has offered the government support to look into and learn from land reform in other countries.

Finally, a major constraint to effective policy dialogue may be related to the Bank's image, negotiating style and legitimacy in Africa. Trust is an important aspect of dialogue, and the Bank and the IMF have been highly unpopular agencies in Africa. Unpopular adjustment policies, the ideological edge to the Bank's pronouncements and its perceived arrogance in dealing with African governments all affect the quality of policy dialogue. While there may be improvements in Bank–government dialogue since the hostile relations which characterized the 1980s, Bank relations with NGOs and other organizations of civil society are still tense. However, the Bank has made increasing efforts to involve such organizations in policy dialogue and a discussion of these developments is the subject of the next section.

What is the Role of Civil Society in Policy Dialogue?

In Zimbabwe, the Bank's involvement with the Economic Structural Adjustment Programme (ESAP), initiated in 1991, has been much criticized for its negative impact on poverty by some parts of government and local and international NGOs. The Bank acknowledges that there has been much criticism (see for example World Bank 1997b) and has responded with initiatives to promote more open dialogue in order to create a broader consensus for future reforms. Zimbabwe is one of the countries participating in the Structural Adjustment Participatory Review Initiative (SAPRI).[4] In Zimbabwe, the aim of SAPRI is to bring together the government, NGOs and the Bank in order to obtain a wide range of viewpoints to evaluate the first phase of reforms and formulate the next phase.

There are very mixed views about SAPRI and it is too early to judge whether it will have an impact on pro-poor policy-making. Some NGOs see SAPRI as a Bank initiative to persuade NGOs that the Bank has a human face and is concerned about poverty, without any follow-through, accountability mechanisms or active partnerships. Others see it as an opportunity to try and influence policy-making, although they are wary of the extent to which the Bank and even Washington-based NGOs control the resources and the agenda.

ZIMPREST, the Zimbabwe Programme for Economic and Social Transformation, was drawn up by government in 1997. Consultations with civil society were carried out although there were still questions in 1999 about how the document was actually going to be operationalized. The dialogue between government and NGOs has been weak and conflict-ridden and many NGOs voice the view that poverty reduction does not have the commitment of government at the highest levels. A recent assessment of the policy environment for poverty reduction in Zimbabwe comes to rather negative conclusions (Killick et al. 1997). Through case studies and interviews, the report illustrates that poverty reduction is not high on the government's list of priorities. The government tends to deal with donors individually and there is little dialogue on policies affecting poverty at a general, as opposed to sector-specific, level. The report also concludes that donors, including the Bank, have not pressed strongly enough for policy dialogue on poverty reduction.

In Malawi, the Bank has stated that it is working with a government which seeks the participation of its people in determining development priorities (World Bank 1996a). It states that the government has encouraged the Bank to seek inputs from various segments of society in developing its assistance strategy. Since 1995, the Bank has engaged in a series of consultations and feedback exercises. Some officials in the Bank expressed concern about the commitment of the government to pursue poverty reduction actively and see the dialogue with a variety of stakeholders to prepare the Bank's CAS as a way of influencing the government to be more pro-active.

There are definite shifts in the Bank towards wider consultations with organizations of civil society and more open processes of formulating CASs with clearer poverty reduction objectives. Much depends on the strength and coherence of advocacy organizations of civil society and these are not very well developed in any of the three country case studies. In Malawi in particular, NGOs are a relatively new phenomenon given the policies of the last government. In Zimbabwe, too, a view voiced by some academics and activists is that the majority of NGOs are still welfare-oriented and lack the capacity to have an effective dialogue with powerful institutions such as the Bank. NGOs in all three countries expressed concern that the Bank and government have convergent interests which do not allow them to question and change policies, at both international and national levels, so that they can focus seriously on poverty reduction.

Although the Bank has made increasing efforts to consult more widely in the formulation of Country Assistance Strategies, some local organizations voiced the view that inputs from local dialogue 'disappear' when Bank teams return to Washington and documents are streamlined in internal processes. Such perceptions are reinforced by the fact that many documents remain classified and are not formally accessible to organizations outside the borrowing governments.

If addressing the causes of poverty is acknowledged to be a political issue, the absence of an active debate within national political structures on what policies are required to address poverty is a critical constraint. Political and institutional constraints to poverty reduction are raised in many independent studies and in national political fora, both formal and informal, but rarely constitute the agenda for policy dialogue between the Bank and governments in Africa. Until these more sensitive but fundamental issues are placed on the agenda, it is hard to see how more 'active' partnerships (Lewis 1998) to reduce poverty can be developed between the Bank, the state and civil society.

Implications for the Role of the State in Poverty Reduction

The study on which this chapter is based points out the limitations and constraints that the Bank, governments and indeed organizations of civil society all face in engaging effectively in policy dialogue for poverty reduction. The role of the state in Africa, in particular, has been progressively weakened through the 1980s and early 1990s, at least in part by the neoliberal agenda so aggressively pursued by powerful institutions including the Bank. While the importance of 'strengthening' civil society has been much emphasized in achieving more transparent and accountable government, the weakness of many states and the emphasis on the market to provide economic growth and social welfare mean that, in some contexts, such organizations have nowhere meaningful to direct their demands.

Although the 1997 *World Development Report* signals a welcome shift back to recognizing that the state has an important role to play in poverty reduction, strengthening the capacity of fragile states in difficult political and economic circumstances in most of sub-Saharan Africa is an extremely complex process. The focus of many aid agencies, including the Bank, on decentralization and strengthening the capacity of local governments has been criticized for not acknowledging that, in many cases, both strong central and local governments are required for effective poverty reduction (Tendler 1997). Tendler argues in her study on Brazil that improvements in local government were less a result of decentralization per se than they were of a three-way dynamic among local government, civil society and an active central government.

Supporting local government in a situation where local and central governments are competing for resources from aid agencies can be problematic. In Zimbabwe, for example, decentralization and the strengthening of rural district councils is seen by the Bank as an important vehicle for rural development and poverty reduction. In 1997, the Bank approved a rural district council pilot capital development project, the RDC Pilot. It will lend USD12 million over two years for this component which is part of a five-year rural district council capacity building programme. The programme is intended to strengthen the country's fifty-seven rural district councils through funding for institutional development, human resources development and capital development (service and infrastructure provision). According to the Bank, rural women will benefit from the capital development component's top priority to water and sanitation; and rural poverty will be reduced through provision of basic services and community participation (World Bank 1997c). This is a new project and it is too early to draw any conclusions about its impact on poverty reduction. There is, however, concern in the Ministry of Local Government, Rural and Urban Development (the implementing agency) that there is no real consensus about what decentralization means and that central government is being deprived of resources (by donors) while district councils are weak and could constitute an additional level of bureaucracy in getting things done. The Association of Rural District Councils, an independent body representing district councils, is less concerned with capacity constraints and more concerned that decentralization of functions and responsibility may take place without devolution of power and resources. These 'difficult' issues, however, have not been part of the policy dialogue between the Bank and government although individuals were ready to discuss them with independent researchers.

The emphasis on the poor performance of governments, especially in Africa, has also tended to imply that they are monolithic and that there is nothing to be learnt from their experiences. Within particular countries, some government agencies may perform well while others do not. The decentralization process in the health sector in Zambia is a case in point and provides a strong contrast to the above example from Zimbabwe. There is some consensus that the Sector Investment Programme is proceeding well and that its success is due to the strong leadership shown by the Ministry of Health, good donor co-ordination as well as attention to staff morale and community representation at health-centre level. Furthermore, interviews with staff in ministries in all three countries discussed in this chapter indicated that there are (still) committed individuals who struggle to do their jobs well in difficult environments. Tendler's study (1997) suggests that government workers' dedication to their work was an important factor in successful health and rural development initiatives and that more attention should be paid to strengthening worker commitment in the public sector.

Conclusions

Although the Bank has broadened its poverty reduction strategy since the 1980s, to include a greater role for the state, the 'liberalization' agenda still dominates, despite concerns that it has negative implications for poverty in highly unequal societies in Africa. Although there are positive shifts, the Bank could do more to place poverty reduction, rather than efficient, economic performance, at the centre of policy dialogue. This is implicitly acknowledged in a recent speech by the current president of the Bank when he says: 'Too often, we have focused on the economics, without sufficient understanding of the social, political, the environmental and the cultural aspects of society' (Wolfensohn 1998). The argument put forward here is that political and institutional issues, at both national and international levels, which affect poverty have to be discussed and addressed. At the present time, the Bank's 'three-pronged strategy' for poverty reduction is not sufficiently flexible, nor open enough to negotiation, while governments are not actively encouraged and supported in orienting poverty reduction to the economic, political, social and cultural realities of their countries.

While the process of institutional change that Wolfensohn has instigated within the Bank, with its greater poverty and country focus, is very positive, it appears to be slow and rather weak when viewed from the country level, at least in Zimbabwe, Zambia and Malawi. Changing the Bank's practice in the *process* of arriving at a Country Assistance Strategy to include the voices of local experts and of people affected by development policies, is a critical step in allowing changes to the *content* of policy. However, if more genuine policy dialogue is to take place, involving active partnerships between governments, the Bank and civil society, the Bank's negotiating style has to change and it has to be acknowledged that no institution can currently claim the technical or moral high ground with regard to poverty reduction.

Notes

1. This chapter is based on an assessment of the World Bank's operational strategies for poverty reduction in Africa, carried out in 1997/98 by the Chr. Michelsen Institute (CMI) and the Comparative Research Programme on Poverty (CROP). The study was commissioned by the Norwegian Ministry of Foreign Affairs and included three country case studies: Zimbabwe, Zambia and Malawi.

2. The World Bank's study of social funds by Narayan and Ebbe, based on a review of these fifty-one projects using project reports and interviews with task managers, provides substantial information to assess these funds. A breakdown of projects by components shows that most (89 per cent) support the creation of economic infrastructure (roads, civil works, irrigation, land reclamation and natural resource management). Other most common activities were the creation of social service infrastructure (59 per cent) and development of social service programmes (65 per cent). Twenty-three per cent of projects mentioned credit and enterprise. Only 27 per cent talked about community development and organization at a grass-roots level and 16 per cent institutional strengthening of private firms, NGOs or municipalities.

3. In Zimbabwe, although it is too early to judge success, the implementation of CAP by the Ministry of Public Services, Labour and Social Welfare has the potential to increase existing institutional capacity, encouraging the ministry to change to a more participatory approach in its programming. However, the indications from the ministry are that this programme will also focus on social infrastructure, which belongs to the core activities of other ministries.

4. This is a global project of the Bank, governments and NGOs to improve the understanding of the impact of adjustment policies and to seek ways of incorporating the participation of civil society in future policy formulation. Seven other countries have agreed to participate. See Structural Adjustment Participatory Review Initiative (SAPRI), First Global Forum Proceedings, World Bank Headquarters, July 1997.

References

Adams, A. van and T. Hartnett (1996) *Cost-Sharing in the Social Sectors of Sub-Saharan Africa: Impact on the Poor*, World Bank Discussion Paper no. 338. Washington, DC: World Bank.

Booth, D. et al (1995) *Coping with Cost Recovery: A Study of the Social Impact of and Responses to Cost Recovery in Basic Services (Health and Education) in Poor Communities in Zambia*. Report to SIDA.

Evans, J. E. (1997) *Growth Prospects Study: Rapid Assessment of the Impact of Policy Changes on Rural Livelihoods in Malawi*. Report prepared for the World Bank and financed by UNDP, Lilongwe.

Kadoole, B. F. (1997) *Malawi Client Feedback Survey*. Lilongwe: Malawi Institute of Management.

Kalyalya, D. H. and J. T. Milimo (1996) *User Fees in the Health Sector: Policy, Practice and Perceptions*. Study Fund, Social Recovery Project, Zambia.

Kanji, N. (1995) 'Gender, Poverty and Economic Adjustment in Harare, Zimbabwe', *Environment and Urbanisation*, 7, 1.

Killick, T. (1995) 'Structural Adjustment and Poverty Alleviation: An Interpretive Survey', *Development and Change*, 26, 2, pp. 305–31.

Killick, T., J. Carlsson and A. Kierkegaard (1997) *European Aid and the Reduction of Poverty in Zimbabwe*. Draft Report.

Lewis, D. (1998) *From Dependent to Active Partnership: Some Thoughts on Partnership as Process*. Social Development Newsletter, Department of International Development.

Marc, A., C. Graham, M. Schacter and M. Schimdt (1995) *Social Action Programs and Social Funds: A Review of Design and Implementation in Sub-Saharan Africa*. World Bank Discussion Paper no. 274. Washington, DC: World Bank.

Ministry of Health, Zambia (1997) *Comprehensive Review of the Zambian Health Reforms*, Vol. I, Main Report.

Narayan, D. and K. Ebbe (1997) *Design of Social Funds: Participation, Demand Orientation and Local Organizational Capacity*, World Bank Discussion Paper no. 375. Washington, DC: World Bank.

Odago, A. and W. Heneveld (1995) *Girls and Schools in Sub-Saharan Africa: From Analysis to Action*. Technical Paper no. 298, Washington, DC: World Bank.

Tendler, J. (1997) *Good Government in the Tropics*. Baltimore and London: Johns Hopkins University Press.

Tjonneland, E. N., H. Harboe, A. M. Jerve and N. Kanji (1998) *The World Bank and Poverty in Africa: A Critical Assessment of the Bank's Operational Strategies for Poverty Reduction*. Report submitted to the Norwegian Ministry of Foreign Affairs by the Chr. Michelsen Institute and the Comparative Research Programme on Poverty (CROP).

University of Zambia (1997) *Zambia: Agricultural Sector Performance Analysis and a Review of the Implementation of the Agricultural Sector Investment Program*, Institute of Economic and Social Research, University of Zambia, Lusaka.

Wold, B. K. (ed.) (1997) *Supply Response in a Gender Perspective: The Case of Structural Adjustment in Zambia*. Oslo: Statistics Norway.

Wolfensohn, J. D. (October 1998) *The Other Crisis*. Address to the Board of Governors, Washington, DC.

World Bank (1996a) *Malawi Country Assistance Strategy*. Washington, DC: World Bank.

— (1996b) *Staff Appraisal Report*. Washington, DC: Malawi Social Action Fund.

— (1997a) *The Strategic Compact: Renewing the Bank's Effectiveness to Fight Poverty*. Planning and Budgeting Department. Washington, DC: World Bank.

— (1997b) *Zimbabwe Country Assistance Strategy*. Washington, DC: World Bank.

— (1997c) *Staff Appraisal Report Zimbabwe Rural District Council Pilot*. Washington, DC: Development Project.

8

Poverty, Discourse and State Power: A Case Study of Morocco

Blandine Destremau

This chapter attempts to relate approaches to poverty with the system in which they are embedded, taking Morocco as a case study. Poverty definitions and approaches will be considered as socially constructed discourses, and the perspective developed has been (unpretentiously) borrowed from Foucault's illuminating work, that of 'trying to define how, to what extent, at what level discourses, particularly scientific discourse, can be objects of a political practice, and in what system of dependence they can exist in relation to it' (Burchell et al. 1991: 69).

Among the constitutive elements of this system, this chapter will focus mainly on definitions and measurements, explanations of the existence and reproduction of poverty, poverty alleviation and management policies, as well as ideological and political hypotheses and implications linked to these approaches. This analysis is centred on the state, in its role in producing definitions and discourses that are partly translated into policies, and as a political actor. The chapter tries to show that each definition or approach of poverty commands a set of stakes that are directly linked to the political arena, poverty being perceived as an issue which threatens 'the political establishment and the very fabric of society', especially in contexts where it is suspected of ties with political movements (Geneletti 1996: 51). The issue of power, in its diverse manifestations, is therefore crucial for any analysis that would not take a positivist definition of poverty for granted, but would strive to discover by which processes poverty discourses are socially constructed, whom they serve and for what purposes poverty is discussed. Finally, it is important to examine how poverty discourses (definitions and approaches) contribute to support the defence of interests and power structures.

A brief presentation of the three main families of poverty approaches – income poverty, social/human poverty and social exclusion – will set the framework for the examination of the Moroccan case that follows.

Three Approaches to Poverty

Approaches in terms of income poverty Income poverty is usually expressed by means of a ratio of declared poor to the total population. It is a fundamentally numerical approach. Individuals or households whose income or consumption is found to be below that of a set poverty line are defined as poor.[1] In poor countries, the poverty line represents the income equivalent of a basket of goods and services deemed to be the minimum necessary for life. It is therefore an absolute threshold, although some choices have to be made as to which items are considered necessary or superfluous, to what proportion the non-food items are included, the extent to which the socio-economic environment should be considered and so on. The level of the poverty line varies, mainly depending on which goods and services are included in the basket, their relative weight and the price chosen for them.[2] The higher the line, the higher the assessment of the incidence of poverty, and the reverse.

In developed countries, income poverty line is expressed as a percentage (40, 50 or 60 per cent) of average income. It is relative, it evolves according to the general trend of income. The assumption is thus that a 'decent' standard of living can be defined only in a general context of well-being, and that each country possesses its poverty line. Poverty, as administratively defined, generally corresponds to a lower level of deprivation in industrialized countries than it does in poor countries.

Income poverty approaches have been considered as unidimensional, as they seem to take into consideration only income or consumption. It is true only to an extent, as the value of the poverty line is often obtained after having converted a certain number of items into an income measure, when part of these goods and services may be obtained through non-market channels (barter, solidarity or other transfers, self-production, government supply). It remains that the unspecified nature of an income expression implies that the individuals are supposed to have access to a basket of goods at a price expressed in income units. Furthermore, it is assumed that the disposal of an income automatically translates into the satisfaction of the corresponding basic needs, that the income will not be spent otherwise, that the goods and services concerned are in fact available and accessible. The main means of access to the necessary resources is therefore employment, which commands access to revenue and, depending on the context, the right to health insurance, the right to a retirement.

The fundamental assumption is therefore that needs are supposed to be satisfied in the first place on a private basis (individuals or households), and mainly through markets of labour, goods and services. Social transfers are organized on a public, private or associative basis, for those unable to acquire their means of subsistence on these markets. The insistence upon individual responsibility and the virtues of market functioning justifies a process of sorting out the poor, only the ones acknowledged as 'incapable' being entitled to cash transfers.

Income approaches to poverty are the simplest to set up, since they rest on variables that are relatively easy to quantify. Their main protagonist in the Third World is the World Bank, along with other international and national institutions.

Approaches in terms of social or human poverty Included in this category are all approaches focusing primarily on the satisfaction of basic needs, and include not only food and shelter, but health, education, sanitation, as well. These approaches include goods and services satisfied on a collective basis and consider the satisfaction of needs deemed basic at the level of their access (implies existence) and impact on people's lives (i.e. using social indicators such as longevity, mortality, schooling) and not at the level of their income potentialities (i.e. revenue). The UNDP Human Poverty Index (HPI), developed in the past years, is probably one of the most elaborated within this approach. It rests upon three indicators, each with its own criterion, threshold and scales: the chances of dying before the age of forty years, the illiteracy rate among adults, and the deficit in terms of living conditions, measured by a combination of access to health services, access to potable water and undernutrition among children under five (UNDP 1997: 19).

The UNDP definition of human poverty in industrialized countries is adapted to their specific context. It is based on the same three aspects of human existence used in the 'poor country HPI', but uses measures that better reflect the social and economic conditions of these countries. It also adds a fourth aspect, which is meant to express the degree of social exclusion/integration in society, measured by the rate of long-term unemployment. Revenue is explicitly taken into account, as a means of access not only to basic goods, but also to 'social' goods, coherent with the general ways of life. The approach of human poverty in industrialized countries therefore widens the scope of what is being considered as basic necessities.

The Human Poverty Index, as other complex poverty indicators based on a set of data varying in nature, is said to be pluridimensional. However, as soon as we wish to express this heterogeneous set into a single index that could build a unique ranking of the countries concerned, and constitute a means to follow their progress, then we need to synthesize these indices into one only. This is the case for the HDI and HPI indices. The pluridimensionality of the initial measures is then partially lost, and the result does not match any concrete reality: for example, both the HDI and the HPI are abstract, in the sense that they do not designate a specific group of people, and have a relative meaning only. This type of indicator is only partly numerical, since each sub-indicator sets a line and a specific head-count index, but not the synthetic index.

The UNDP approach differs from most other basic needs definitions in the sense that these needs are considered not only as an end in themselves, but as means to fulfil other necessities of life. It is the essence of Sen's theory of capabilities, which largely inspired UNDP. For the UN programme, the basic necessities of life should be considered as a universal right, and include not only material goods but also all resources necessary for personal fulfilment, going as far as political freedom, personal security and sharing in community life (UNDP 1997: 18). More important, perhaps, they should be satisfied in a way that ensures everyone is able to choose the way they want to conduct their lives.

The UNDP approach postulates that the necessary goods and services cannot be obtained through entry into the labour market and procurement of income revenue only, but that some of the services should necessarily be socialized, in the sense that their fulfilment for all should be covered not by the individual capacity to pay for oneself, but by a socialization of revenues and risks. Access by the poor to wages through working cannot constitute a sufficient means for poverty to be eradicated, considering the extent of vulnerability of poor families and individuals. Although NGOs can play an important role in the fulfilment of basic needs, state institutions are generally considered the most responsible body to 'provide economic support to vulnerable individuals (or families) when they fail to get that support from the regular economic system itself' (Sen 1988: 9).

A 'soft revolution' should take place through improvement of public social services, of their accessibility (physical, financial, social) and of their gender, regional, ethnic distribution. Rationalization of public expenses occurs through increasing the taxes on the highest income categories and reducing military expenses for the benefit of education and health. Social welfare is based on social justice and equity in the distribution of all types of resources. The role devoted to the state, as well as the link established between the basic needs and rights of individual human beings and groups, involves an explicit consideration of the politics of poverty and poverty alleviation.

Sen's capability approach to poverty adopts a radical shift from utilitarian and welfarist perspectives, deeply deliberating on the question of 'equality of what' (Gore 1995: 8). It has been found, however, that 'it remains wedded to an excessively individualist, and insufficiently social, view'. The shift is taken further by approaches in terms of social exclusion, which focus on relational issues and attempt to develop the main question, 'equality among whom?', in relation with that of the nature of social justice (pp. 8–9).

Approaches in terms of social exclusion Notions and analyses of social exclusion are built on the basic hypothesis that social and economic well-being constitute rights, as the UNDP approach does. Far from being equated with poverty, social exclusion refers to 'a process of social dis-integration', grounded on different inter-related dimensions, and has been linked by the European Commission 'with the idea that it is the inadequate realisation of social rights' (Gore 1995: 2). However, having been developed in the industrialized countries, they rest on specific premises that widen their scope.[3]

Social exclusion is a notion that was developed in frameworks where basic survival rights are more or less satisfied, where starvation, epidemics and child mortality have been drastically reduced and no longer constitute a major problem (even though some are now surfacing again), and where access to basic sanitation, drinking water and schooling is almost universal. These approaches have been developed in a context of intense urbanization rates, with a weakening of family relationships, parallel to the reinforcement of labour as the main vector of social linkages and social identity, as well as the main medium of access to means of survival. Social exclusion from formal wage labour therefore commands a whole trickle-down of other types of social problems, the basic safety-net being part of the role devoted to public institutions (state or mutualized, corporatist organizations).

The protection role of the state is a product of the political development of these 'First World' countries, in terms of citizenship rights. Democracy means that the citizens can exert pressure on political authorities for their rights to be satisfied. Democratic citizenship further implies that some kind of a 'social debt' exists that links people together in a sort of com-munity of destiny. The state is the guarantor of this balance, and uses redistributive machinery to this purpose. The construction of formal wage labour into a social and political status goes along with the development of institutions such as the mutualization of wages as a form of insurance against a certain number of risks. Economically, it represents a guarantee against a drastic – and political in nature – reduction of social budgets. Politically, these rights are therefore to an extent defended against the fluctuations of power interests. The discourses on social exclusion thus appear as defensive, against the withdrawal of the state from some of its post-war welfare functions, while labour can no longer play the same role both of integration and protection.

Approaches in terms of social exclusion are not quantitative; they do not attempt to measure poverty, but rather to understand how it represents a dynamic process, how it is produced and reproduced, how people fall into or get out of a state of deprivation and social marginalization, and which are the institutions that regulate exclusion. They are thus not submitted to the necessity of choosing measurable criteria, and to synthesize diverse dimensions into a single indicator. They usually take very subjective data into consideration: representations, feelings, psychological symptoms. However, more and more, social exclusion is associated with a set of symptoms that are close to those of absolute poverty: material deprivation, housing problems, vulnerability to diseases and even undernourishment. On the other hand, budgetary restrictions in a context of economic crisis, in a dominant neo-liberal ideological framework tend to reduce state responsibility in poverty alleviation, reduction of inequalities and social integration.

Social exclusion paradigms have very rarely been used for Third World countries, the major problem being that some of their major conceptual foundations and assumptions often present a different profile in these environments: citizenship rights, based on equality of citizens and democratic participation, often do not cover a range beyond civic rights, or concern only a fraction of total population; wage labour does not constitute the matrix of integration, not only in consumption, but in social protection; social security is seldom extensive and institutionalized, but limited to a 'privileged' nucleus, while for most of the population it rests largely upon family solidarity and religious charities. However, the use of social exclusion paradigms in poor countries responds to a felt need not to assign the poor of poor countries to a poverty of rights,[4] and not to draw a comfortable divide between economics (including poverty concerns) and political issues.

The book edited by Rodgers and et al. (1995), a contribution to the World Summit for Social Development, successfully attempts to adapt the concept of social exclusion to contexts other than European countries, while remaining conscious of the risk of falling into the trap of 'exporting concepts from the North to the South', in contexts where 'poverty and deprivation are *not* associated with "lack of integration" as the European literature implies' (Gore 1995: 4–5). The main findings suggested by this book's contributions are:

- processes of social exclusion need to incorporate various international relations […] and the nature and design of international regimes which underpin them;
- in the context of developing countries and countries in transition the focus needs to include other factor [than labour] markets, as well as the processes through which these markets are developing;
- it is important that work in developing countries does not simply focus

on social rights as the western European literature has done, but on civil and political rights;
- it is important to focus on various social institutions in which rules governing exclusionary and inclusionary practices are negotiated, including households and national states which are focal in European debates, but going beyond them. (Gore 1995: 4–10)

Restoring the political dimension of poverty The preceding sections have briefly shown the basic focus of each of the three main approaches to poverty. Clearly, all these three definitions/approaches revolve round the satisfaction of basic needs, the main difference between them in this regard being what is encompassed within basic needs. The issue of income poverty is mainly related to two spheres: that of the capitalist markets of goods, services and labour, on one hand; that of moral ideologies that advocate work as a remedy for the poor's body and soul and as a social value, and pity the 'incapable' poor only, who can benefit from humanitarian support. Its definition of basic needs is minimalist for Third World countries; it rests on the implicit assumption that 'the persistence of widespread and chronic deprivation of basic needs nowadays makes absolute poverty the obvious priority in terms of definition, measurement and political action from the international point of view' (Rocha 1997: 1), basic needs being understood as food, shelter and essential manufactured goods.

The issue of human poverty takes into consideration both needs whose satisfaction depends upon private resources and needs that call on the state's function of redistribution and social service provision. For UNDP, basic needs should be considered only in respect of the degree of well-being they confer to the persons concerned, well-being being defined according to a value system that grants limited value to the benefits of material consumption. Basic needs therefore include opportunities to make the most essential choices for human development: longevity, health, creativity, the ability to have decent conditions of life, freedom, dignity, self-respect and respect of others (UNDP 1997: 4). The ideological background of this approach is that of capabilities that should allow individuals and groups to lead a satisfactory life, exert their freedom of choice and be protected in their human rights.

As for the scope of social exclusion, it rests mainly upon the consideration of needs that should be fulfilled for an individual to be integrated in the society in which he or she lives, and to perform the basic activities that have become standards. Basic needs are immediately considered in a context of rights. Their ideological framework is that of citizenship, understood as a set of civic, political and socio-economic rights that determine social integration and are guaranteed by a set of social conventions and institutions that place solidarity at the centre of social cohesion. Building an inclusive citizenship requires the establishment of a redistributive machinery, along with insurance-type mechanisms, that takes into consideration the inter-relationships between the different dimensions of exclusion and articulate markets, states and civil societies. But these pragmatic measures necessarily rest on political will, and the capacity to impose it on the part of the state, so that redistribution does not operate on charitable lines but rather is based on a paradigm of social integration rooted in a system of rights.

Discourses on poverty have recently tended to use notions from all three approaches that have been delineated, and which have all gained some degree of legitimacy among policy-makers and researchers. To an extent, the discourses and approaches on poverty have been globalized, after the end of the Cold War, with the unification of the world under the dominating banner of neo-liberal economic ideologies. The state is called upon as an intermediary, a mediating body for this ideology, just as it had been the mediating body for the penetration of capitalism, or the ideology of development and progress. However, whereas in the preceding period the role of the state was that of a major entrepreneur of development and growth of productive forces, in the present time the state is supposed to withdraw partially, and leave space for the play of market forces and the intervention of NGOs and international agencies.

Each of these approaches is linked to different stakes, as far as the state function is concerned: the income view on poverty favours a state that establishes and maintains conditions favourable to the functioning of markets, avoiding distortions, and establishes conditions for the exercise of individual freedom, that is formal democracy and institutional account-ability. The state should be involved in human capital upgrading as far as it constitutes an investment for economic growth, will allow 'the poor' to find employment and thus not to depend on social assistance. The state called upon by the UNDP is involved in inequality reduction, redis-tribution based on taxation of the highest revenues, investment in and management of social infrastructure, as well as setting a legal framework guaranteeing equality of rights. It can be defined as a welfare state, although perhaps rather in a functional sense. The state that acts in the context of social exclusion discourses is political in essence. The findings of the book edited by Rodgers et al. on the topic of social exclusion (1995) suggest the contours of a non-exclusionary state in its Introduction (Gore 1995): it possesses the capacity to take decisions and act according to the national interest, within international relations, in particular in so far as 'the relative role of the State and markets as allocation and accumulation mechanisms; the policies for growth, poverty reduction and structural transformation are concerned' (p. 30); it mediates the relationships between markets and individuals, in terms of access to economic, political and cultural assets (e.g. access to land, to credit, to employment); it exists through social and political structures that manage the balance of powers in a way that grants social groups a status and a set of (civil, political and social) rights, determining a paradigm of social integration.

The main stake today appears to be not so much the formal definition given to poverty, but rather the political content embodied in these approaches, knowing that technocratic policies or economic technology can easily pretend to confront material problems, without questioning the fundamental distribution of power, and of political, economic, cultural and symbolic assets (or capital, as Bourdieu would say), that lie at the heart of poverty, in all its dimensions. I will attempt to tackle this issue in the case of Morocco, considering in turn each of the three approaches I presented above.

The Issue of Income Poverty in Morocco

Poverty has become a major issue in Morocco in recent years, which means both that the objective facts of poverty have been given a dramatic profile, that these facts have been measured and made known to various audiences (national, international), and that a consciousness has developed in the country about it, so that it has become a question that the Moroccan authorities can no longer avoid.

Income poverty indicators Tables 8.1 to 8.3 show to what extent income poverty estimates vary greatly in the Moroccan case: the World Bank indicator is amazingly low in the 1990s, whereas UNDP indicators point to a catastrophic situation. National estimates are situated in between:

TABLE 8.1 Assessments of income poverty rate according to the World Bank poverty line (1 US$ PPP 1985 per person per day)

	Morocco	MENA[1]
1984–85	6.06	
1985	7.11	6.06
1990	2.49	5.59
1991	1.64	
1994	1.58	5.01

Sources: Van Eeghen 1995 and World Bank 1995b

Note: 1. Middle East and North Africa.

TABLE 8.2 Official assessments of income poverty rate according to national poverty lines

	Morocco	MENA
1984–85	21.1 (total)	
	32.6 (rural; line 525 $ 1985 PPP/year)	
	17.3 (urban; line 541 $ 1985 PPP/year)	
1990	13.1 (total)	
1990–94	13 (total)	15.4[1]
	18 (rural; line 535 US$ 1985 PPP/year)	
	7.6 (urban; line 552 US$ 1985 PPP/year)	

Source: Van Eeghen 1995

Note: 1. 1990; line set at 50 US$ per month on average

TABLE 8.3 Assessments of income poverty rate according to UNDP poverty line

1980–90	28 (urban)
	45 (rural)
	37 (total)
1990	28 (urban)
	32 (rural)

Sources: UNDP 1994 for 1980–90 and UNDP 1995 for 1990

According to the World Bank, Morocco is among the countries whose income poverty rate is the lowest (1.6 per cent in 1994 against a regional average of 5.01 per cent). Furthermore, it is also the country in which this poverty rate has decreased the most drastically in the decade 1984–94. Some years after the start of the Structural Adjustment Programme (1983), 'poverty was nearly cut in half between 1985 and 1990, an exceptional performance. [Morocco and Tunisia] started economic reform earlier [than Jordan], and with a new trade orientation [Morocco] generated many jobs of the type most relevant to the poor. Well-targeted public spending cuts were also achieved without hurting the poor' (World Bank 1995b: 5). This optimistic opinion is seriously challenged by other sources. According to the World Bank, these very positive performances are mainly due to the implementation of structural adjustment reforms, which boosted an essentially labour-intensive growth, and to the creation of low-wage employment opportunities, which led to an increase of the participation rate of low-qualified, temporary labour power and of women (World Bank 1995a: 57).

However, as El-Ghonemy (1998: 189) puts it: 'This politicization of poverty gives the impression that poverty levels were substantially reduced.' As a matter of fact, the UNDP assessments of poverty disagree with the optimistic views of the World Bank: according to the programme, within the MENA region, Morocco has the third worst ranking for real GDP per inhabitant (in 1995 PPP), income poverty rate is among the highest, and tends to decrease only in rural areas. According to a national family survey led by CERED (Centre for Demographic Studies and Research from the Moroccan Ministry of Population) in 1990/91, partly updated by additional surveys in 1995, 13.1 per cent of the Moroccan population live under a very low poverty line, which means they do not have enough to eat, while 47.3 per cent are deprived (51.3 per cent in rural areas, 43.7 per cent in urban areas; CERED 1997). For Abdel Gadir Ali, who has done quantitative analysis of data presented by Chen, Datt and Ravalion,[5] whichever of two assessments is chosen, '[b]oth rates of increase of poverty are higher than the population growth rates in the countries of the sample [which includes Morocco], implying that the absolute number of the poor has increased by more than the growth of the population' (Abdel Gadir Ali 1996: 73).

As far as relative income poverty is concerned, as no relative poverty line officially exists in Morocco, we can refer only to the scarce data concerning income distribution. According to the World Bank (1995c), in 1990–91 the lowest quintile was getting 6.6 per cent of the total income, while the uppermost one received 46.3 per cent, a picture close to that of France, for instance. Income was more concentrated in the top 10 per cent, which were getting 31.84 per cent of total revenue, while the bottom 10 per cent received only 2.66 per cent of total income (Abdel Gadir Ali 1996: 70). However, distribution inequalities are, by far, not as drastic as in many Latin American or African countries, at least from what official figures show. Wage gaps in the public service, to take only one example, are of one to seventy, when they do not exceed one to nine in France.[6] The Gini index (usually called the 'coefficient') has increased from 39.1 in 1985 to 39.57 in 1991, without reaching alarming levels either (World Bank 1995a), and would even have declined during the 1980s, at an average rate of 0.25 per cent a year, according to Abdel Gadir Ali (1996: 74).

Nevertheless, El-Ghonemy[7] stresses the fact that, parallel to a substantial reduction of poverty, there has been a slight worsening of income distribution in the years following the launching of structural adjustment reforms: inequality would have increased in urban areas and decreased in rural areas (El-Ghonemy 1998: 189). It has also been pointed out by one of the World Bank economists that, in Morocco, income redistribution was actually negative and tended to work contrary to the growth effect. In other words, changes in income distribution contributed to increases in poverty, and 'the decline in poverty would have been larger if income redistribution had not occurred' (Van Eeghen 1995: 25).

Measuring poverty represents the cornerstone of income approaches. Clearly, differences in estimates can be mechanically related to the level of the poverty line. The choices made to establish this line are, however, almost never explained, while the result in terms of a head-count index are widely used and advertised. Positions are then taken as a result of the gravity of the problem diagnosed, as though the number of poor was a 'natural' piece of data and not a direct function of the definition given to it. It appears that the more important the stakes behind different assessments of poverty, the more decisive the battle over figures, and the more adamant the pretension of scientific assessments and analyses. The wide legitimacy of income poverty approaches precisely rests on this appearance of 'objectivity', which is deeply rooted in the nineteenth century, hiding the process of its emergence, functioning and transformation.

Putting the poor to work In the Moroccan Social Development Programme, the issue of income poverty is essentially dealt with in the fashion of creating employment for the poor. Unemployment in Morocco was established at 22 per cent in 1999, compared to around 16 per cent at the beginning of the 1990s, after a significant increase since the beginning of the 1980s (9 per cent in 1980–84). Significantly, almost half of the Moroccan unemployed are first-time job-seekers, and a quarter of them have secondary education (World Bank 1995b). Structural unemployment would also burden 30 per cent of the poor active population, and 47 per cent of the younger among them (fifteen to twenty-four years old), a higher ratio than in other socio-economic categories (UNDP 1997b). Although the size of government employment is rather low in Morocco compared to other Arab countries, it reaches about 30 per cent of total in 1992, and distributes higher wages than the private sector at all skill levels, so that the wage bill reaches 15 per cent of GDP (World Bank 1995b: 20). Following the implementation of structural adjustment reforms, public job-creating investment has fallen from 27.5 per cent of national income before adjustment to 23 per cent in 1989–93 (El-Ghonemy 1998: 189). Public hiring has stopped, but people, especially graduates and first-time job-seekers, continue to look to the state as the employer of last resort. Unemployment of secondary school and university graduates constitutes a specific problem since, as in many Arab countries, they represent a rather strong pressure group with the means to voice their discontent, and they have particular expectations of the state. In 1993, their number was estimated at 50,000, and they have been leading demonstrations in recent years. The main response to these movements was a budget provision in 1993 to create 15,000 positions in the public service, and a programme to support self-employment.

The equivalence asserted between unemployment and poverty implies the creation of jobs in the private sector as a solution to poverty, over-looking the fact that low wages represent a factor of reproduction of poverty, the argument being the necessity for international competition. Following evidence on the positive effect of structural reforms on macro-economic indicators, and even more after the king gave signs of his will to favour political opening, which was interpreted as a guarantee for social stability, foreign investment has been soaring in Morocco. The new employ-ment generated as an effect of macro-economic and structural reform 'consisted essentially of temporary and of low-skilled, low-wage jobs in export oriented manufacturing sectors such as textiles, leather and agro-industries', which reflects a 'rational use of surplus labour and sharp increases in employment and labor participation' (Van Eeghen 1995: 24), especially of women. This may explain why the unemployment rate seems not to come down, in spite of job creation.

The World Bank quotes studies showing that the minimum wage, set at 60 per cent of the average urban wage, was relatively high by international standards; that non-wage costs imposed on employers were high (20 to 35 per cent of wages); that the minimum wage had risen by 25 per cent during 1984–94, while average wages stagnated; that firing regulations were very restrictive for workers in permanent positions; and that, according to empirical studies, these regulations tended to reduce the demand for young skilled workers, to discourage hiring in permanent positions and to en-courage hiring of young unskilled workers at less than the minimum wage, their share in permanent employment having fallen from 75 per cent in 1984 to 42 per cent in 1990. Informal employment is particularly high, and rising, in Morocco, reaching 57 per cent of all non-agriculture employment in 1982, and 63 per cent in 1991. The recommendations drawn from these assertions are to reduce the cost of labour to employers by cutting payroll taxes, in order to eliminate the bias against formal employment (World Bank 1995b: 16), and to make labour laws more flexible, as was recently done, in order to adapt them to new market conditions and to the re-quirements of foreign investors. In assembly sub-contracting activities in particular, the nature of the work performed, the structure of investments, the weakness of training and credit programmes and the instability of demand led to a high degree of labour informalization, in the fashion of petty workshops, home labour, family occasional helps, as shown by several surveys (e.g. Mejjati Alaoui 1994). This tendency drives labour market dynamics away from the development of contractual and institutionalized frameworks, while reinforcing paternalistic tendencies and the role of the family in the logic of redistribution.

While employment expanded by 25 per cent in export-oriented sectors between 1984 and 1989, that is the five years following the initiating of structural adjustment, real wages dropped by 2.6 per cent a year over the same period, which is considered good news for the country's export performance, but is bad news for the workers' purchasing power. The RCA (Revealed Comparative Advantage) of Morocco, measured as the ratio between the share of Moroccan clothing exports to total Moroccan exports, on the one hand, and the share of world clothing exports to total world exports, on the other, has tripled between 1981–83 and 1994–96, which is a sign of a quite good competitive level on the world market (ERF 1998: 98). Available studies show that, although the minimum wage tended to increase until 1996, it has lagged behind the growth of national income and has remained constant in nominal terms between 1996 and 1999, which implies a loss of purchasing power. The real public wages index (in government sectors), beginning from 100 in 1975, reached 80 in 1990, and 77 in 1993 (Said 1995; Shaban et al. 1994). Manufacturing wages went down as well, decreasing in real terms by 2.5 per cent a year on average between 1980 and 1992 (World Bank 1995c). At a high of 113 in 1980 (1970 = 100), the manufacturing wage index went down to 86 in 1990, then slightly increased again, to reach 93 in 1993, thus below its 1970 level (World Bank 1995b). The interpretation put forward by the World Bank is that the drop in real wages, which is paralleled by a drop in labour productivity of about 2.5 per cent a year, is 'essentially a reflection of increased participation of low skilled labor and temporary workers in the production process', therefore a proof that the poor benefit from the expansion of total output (Van Eeghen 1995: 39). However, contradictory evidence is forwarded by the Economic Research Forum (ERF 1998: 118): between 1970 and 1995, the share of wages in value-added has dropped from 44.8 to 36.7 per cent; the wage rate from US$1,313 (1970) to 1,055; unit labour cost from $15 (1970) to 12; while productivity remained stable in terms of average compound growth rate, at $8,628 (1970) and $8,551 (1970) in 1995.

In the absence of unemployment compensation schemes, wages for most of the least qualified jobs in the production, services and building sectors are actually well below the poverty line, especially when they take place in informal contexts. Added to the fact that a lot of these activities are unstable and irregular, it comes out clearly that they do not allow participants to escape poverty and to achieve dignity, even if they take place in a formal context (Salahdine 1991: 25; La Nouvelle Tribune 1999). More recently, Guecioueur (1996: 167) stated that, in Morocco, 'in urban areas the poor are basically self-employed or wage earners; [t]he typical poor wage earner earns around one-third of the average wage and about half the legislated minimum wage'. UNDP (1997b) adds that, although women represent 25 per cent of all wage labourers, they constitute one-third of poor wage labourers. Furthermore, average yearly length of employment is shorter for the limited-income urban households than the urban average (eight months against ten). A drastic curtailment of food subsidies (divided by 9 as a share of GDP between 1981 and 1993) contributed significantly to the decrease of wages' purchasing power, particularly for the lower incomes. The cost of living index grew from 42.4 in 1975–79 to 124.8 in 1990–93. Popular reactions, notably in the form of food riots as occurred repeatedly in the last two decades, show the social impact of these restrictions.

Informal income transfers to the poor The non-working poor are expected and supposed to depend in the first place upon intra-family, primary networks and associative solidarity,[8] even though, as a literature survey has shown, '[t]he traditional system of social assistance [in the Arab world] appears unable to meet the demands of a growing population, but no alternative is evident, particularly in the conditions of financial crisis' (Geneletti 1996: 59).

Data tend to show that private transfers represent a very significant source of income for the poor in Morocco; for Van Eeghen (1995: 35), '180,000 more people (5 per cent of the total) would be added to the number of poor were it not for private transfers from relatives working abroad'. According to the CERED study, a very large share of the lowest revenue category (group 4, socially marginalized) received financial transfers: 90.3 per cent, against slightly less for groups 2 (86.9 per cent) and 3 (76.1 per cent) (CERED 1997: 280 ff.). In 80 per cent of the cases, the source of income of the 'socially marginalized persons' almost exclusively depends on informal transfers, family solidarity and grants (p. 44). However, the CERED study also shows that the higher the socio-economic level of the family, the greater the benefit drawn from intra-family solidarity. The families of group 4 are more or less as numerous as the ones from other groups using their money transfers for current consumption (around 80 per cent of them do). They are a bit more in proportion in using this money for children's schooling expenses (57.5 per cent) but less than groups 1 and 3 in using it for health expenses, and much less for housing construction.

In other words, since redistribution operates horizontally, mainly within the same groups, there is no evidence that intra-family solidarity, if it may soften the plight of the poorer of the poor, would contribute to reduce inequalities between families. This is all the more true since migrants' incomes and remittances are generally submitted to dynamics and factors favouring family accumulation of various types of assets, and reinforcing rather than weakening inter-family inequalities. Furthermore, studies tend to show that, in the Arab world, '[u]rbanization and the growth of the individualistic morality that accompanies economic growth have weakened family ties and social obligations' (Geneletti 1996: 58).

Another kind of informal income transfer to the poor operates through begging, which is widely discussed in Morocco at present. Although, to my knowledge, no precise data exist on the increase of begging, it is often presented as a growing 'problem', against which the government is expected to fight more actively. Begging would constitute a frequent way of subsistence of the group 4 of the CERED study quoted above, among which 0 per cent work, and would partly justify their label of 'socially marginalized'.[9] In fact, the struggle against begging has intensified in Morocco, parallel to the apparent increase of the number of beggars in the street of the large cities. According to Zouiten (1998: 33), this endeavour mobilizes several types of argument, not very different from those used in similar contexts in other countries and in earlier times. Begging is presented as an immoral activity, in the sense that the beggars do not work, or make a profession of using honest citizens' (or honest Muslims') guilt feelings in order to extract their subsistence from them without work. It should be noted that begging is systematically opposed to 'honest labour' even though the 'professionalization' of beggars is just as often mentioned. The 'bad beggars' are the ones who make a living out of it, or are beggars by profession, with the suspicion that they are not as poor as they make out to be. Bad beggars are therefore also the ones who cheat, who are not really poor or, paradoxically, who actually escape poverty by begging.

Begging makes poverty visible in a fashion which disturbs public order in the street, or an intended image of public order. The terminology used in the struggle against begging is that of prophylaxis: 'cleansing', in the name of restoring the beggars' lost dignity. Cleansing will be implemented in two ways: put the beggars to work ('real work'), and repress those who refuse their own salvation. Begging is against the law, which criminalizes begging and wandering (Articles 326 to 333). This law allows the jailing of beggars and hoodlums who are considered to have other means of subsistence, or as being able to work. Punishment is more drastic against beggars who falsely pretend to be wounded or invalid, and/or are accompanied by young children. Finally, in Morocco, begging would supposedly deter tourists and hurt Morocco's image as a peaceful, safe and comfortable holiday destination. This last argument points to the sharp contrast which exists between, on one hand, the international image of Morocco as a rather 'modern' and 'well-to-do' country and, on the other hand, the appalling human poverty indicators which associate it with Yemen and Iraq.

The Issue of Human Poverty in Morocco

Human poverty profile   Following structural adjustment reforms, public spending tended to decline in real terms:

> Because budget cuts were conditional for disbursement of loans by the World Bank and the IMF, the government found it politically easier to reduce public capital expenditure than to cut military spending [...]. The cuts have adversely affected physical capital expenditure on the construction of, and the provision of, equipment for schools, hospitals and the purification of drinking water in rural areas. The World Bank's own analysis found that both total and per capita government spending on all social services have declined in real terms. (El-Ghonemy 1998: 189)

Development and poverty indicators, although in marked progress since the first years after independence, have been affected by these measures and demonstrate a high level of deprivation of basic capabilities, as shown in Table 8.4.

Morocco ranks 125th out of 174 countries taken into consideration by UNDP's HDI scale in 1998[10] (it was ranked 123rd in 1996), and third to last on a regional MENA scale, just before Iraq and Yemen. It performs badly compared to the rest of the MENA region in most of the areas taken into consideration in the Human Development Index. For the years in which data are available, it ranks in the three or four last countries in terms of child mortality, medical birth assistance, literacy rate, access to sewerage, and second to last (just before Yemen) for access to health services. It ranks last for access to potable water, women's literacy, and for crude enrolment rate of schooling, knowing that the region as a whole performs badly for education indicators.

The case of Morocco illustrates the considerable stakes behind the various ways of measuring poverty, which produce very different assessments. It also shows the relevance of comparing the various indicators used, in terms of socialization of revenues and social progress in a country. Its HDI/GDP per head (1994 PPP) ranking gap was -26 in 1997, which means that its performances in terms of human development are much less satisfactory than those in terms of income per capita, or than those in terms of income poverty. This large discrepancy is a sign of low socialization of the various types of resources and revenues in the country.

In the 1998 UNDP report, Morocco ranks fifty-third at world level according to HPI (among a group of seventy-seven countries only); the higher the ranking, the worse the level of human poverty. Among the eleven Arab countries that were included in the HPI calculation, Morocco is the second to last, just before Yemen. Among this reduced group of

TABLE 8.4 Development and poverty indicators

		Morocco	Arabic countries
Real GDP/inhabitant (US$ 1985 PPP)	1995	3,477	4,454
Human Development Index (HDI)	1995	0.557	0.636
Human Poverty Index (HPI)	1995	40.2	...
Life expectancy at birth (years)	1960	46.7	45.5
	1995	65.7	63.5
Population exposed to die before 40 (%)	1995	12	14
Child mortality (for 1,000 live births)	1960	163	166
	1995	64	55[1]
Child weight deficiency under 5 (%)	1990–96	9	16
Population deprived of access to drinking water (%)	1990–96	35	23
Population deprived of access to health services (%)	1990–95	30	13
Population deprived of access to sewerage (%)	1990–96	42	30
Adult literacy rate (%)	1970	22	31
	1995	43.7	56
men	1995	56.6	67.2
women	1995	31	44.2
Raw rate of schooling, all levels (%)	1980	38	47
	1995	48	58
boys	1995	50.7	59.9
girls	1995	40.6	52.7
Children dropping out of primary school (%)	1995	22	7

Source: UNDP 1997
Note: 1. 1996

countries, the HPI/HDI ranking gap is 16 for Morocco, which means that the performance in terms of human poverty is less satisfactory than that for human development. This large discrepancy points to the fact that the average level of social indicators hides deep inequalities between the sexes, and between regions and social groups, as well as the existence of large pockets of unsatisfied basic needs, and a relatively poor distribution of human development benefits, particularly in the rural areas. Typical portraits of Moroccan deprived populations can be found in a special report issued by a national daily on the occasion of the signature of the agreement between the UNDP and the Moroccan Ministry of Population:[11] poor agricultural workers finding themselves without protection and without the jobs they had had for years in a rural neighbourhood of Casablanca, faced with expulsion from their now-illegal settlement; inhabitants of a fishing harbour condemned to growing misery and illegal trafficking by the reduction of the catches; large numbers of children abandoned to street violence, sexual abuse and cheap drug consumption by the poverty of their parents; men submitting to a mafia-type organization to gain the privilege of sorting out garbage in a public dump.

The image of the Moroccan 'social poor', as drawn by the CERED study, matches classical definitions of idle, dependent, illiterate large families, in a rather stereotyped fashion. The typical poor in Morocco are rural: seven poor out of ten live in a rural *douar*, against only 50 per cent of the general population. On the basis of the national poverty line, the share of the rural population who are poor – 18 per cent on average – is therefore higher than the share of the urban population – 7.6 per cent – on average (CERED 1997: 51 ff.). The Moroccan poor would make 'the deliberate choice of illiteracy and procreation' (p. 88). The fertility rate is higher among poorer women, but the discrepancy is much higher according to the place of residence – rural households having a significantly higher fertility than urban ones – than it is according to the socio-economic level of the household (pp. 152 ff.). It was calculated that 'the risk of poverty increases by 10 per cent each time an extra child reaches schooling age'. The Moroccan poor are illiterate: two-thirds of the poor families' head of household cannot read or write, a figure which goes up to 80 per cent in rural areas, and 90 per cent for women (both rural and urban) (p. 124). The Moroccan poor do not work: none of the persons of the lower group examined by the CERED study (socially marginalized) works, and 15 per cent of them are considered unemployed (p. 180). Without questioning the excellence of the CERED surveying work and the precision of the data collected, we may however wonder about the interference of the representations associating poverty and backwardness expressed in the commentary made in this study.

Launching a struggle against human poverty The official discourse states that social marginalization, as expressed in restricted access to social services and basic infrastructure, occurred following the SAP started in 1983, thus freeing the state from part of its responsibility (CERED 1997: 5). This assertion can be criticized, if only for the fact that low literacy and schooling rates, especially for women, date back many more than fifteen years and show an imbalance in the distribution of social progress, and a deficit in social investment.

However, there is no doubt that structural adjustment reforms have had dramatic effects on social welfare. In 1980, central government expenditures on health represented 3 per cent of the total, education 16.6 per cent, housing and social security expenses 5.6 per cent, whereas defence was using 17.9 per cent. In 1991, health had remained stable at 3 per cent of total public expenditures, education had increased to 17.9 per cent and military spending had been reduced to 13 per cent (UNDP 1997). In a context of strictly controlled budget spending, the state thus concentrated its efforts on education, which absorbed six to seven times more resources than health. However, if we look at the social expenditures as a ratio of GNP, then we notice that education as well as health have been relatively restricted during the 1980s: health from 1.1 per cent of GNP in 1980 to 0.9 per cent in 1991, education from 7 to 5.5 per cent in the same years (UNDP 1995). As for the ratio of military spending to health and education combined, it has gone down from a high of 76 per cent in 1980 to 72 per cent in 1991 (from 49 per cent in 1960) (UNDP 1995).

Cuts in government capital expenditures in the social sectors have had adverse effects on all kinds of social infrastructure and facilities (the number of hospital beds per 1,000 inhabitants decreased between 1975–77 and 1985–90, for instance). In the education sector, the trend of expenditures is 'misleading' (El-Ghonemy 1998: 201):

> between 1980 and 1991 allocations within public spending on education were switched from primary to higher education (to secondary schools in Morocco [...]). The ugly result of this budgetary meddling during adjustment has been acute deterioration in the quality of primary schooling. This is well exhibited in crowded classrooms, the falling real value of teachers' salaries, rising levels of dropout rates among pupils, and increasing child labor among school-leavers to support their poor parents during the economic hardship. (El-Ghonemy 1998: 201)

Taking into consideration the risks involved by such degradation (e.g. massive cost-of-living riots in 1981 and 1984), a Social Priority Plan was elaborated in 1986. Social assistance measures mainly consist of (Van Eeghen 1995: 33 ff.):

- health-care, in principle available to all, but highly skewed in effect: 'the richest 20 per cent of the population appropriates 40 per cent of public spending in health, while the bottom 40 per cent receive less than 20 per cent'; certificates for health-care, 'aimed, in principle, at giving free access to basic services to the poor, fail to meet their objectives'
- activities of mutual aid, which represent 0.7 per cent of total central government budget expenditures and 'target needy population through nutritional assistance, pre-school education, vocational training and aid'
- food support and nutrition programmes, which cost 0.5 per cent of GDP at the beginning of the 1990s, and involved 2.5 million people; although 875,000 children get food at school, 'poor children are less likely to benefit since they are more likely to reside in rural areas and do not attend school'

- public works programme, initiated in 1961, which employs 50,000 persons annually, and appears to reach the poor
- women's programmes, which serve 56,000 poor and illiterate women.

As for basic food subsidies, even though they amounted to 5 per cent of GDP in the mid-1980s, their benefit was skewed towards the rather well-to-do: 'only 16 per cent of the food subsidies went to the poorest 30 per cent of households, while nearly half went to the richest 30 per cent' (El-Ghonemy 1998: 190).

The data on human poverty included in UNDP reports, widely echoed in the press, could not be concealed but were incompatible with the image the country wanted to present both to foreign investors and to tourists. The Moroccan government thereupon engaged in an intensification of its initiative against poverty. In 1993, a Social Development Strategy for the 1990s was elaborated, articulated around three axes (Ibrahimi 1998: 19–20):

1. Widening the access of deprived groups to basic social services, particularly the improvement of access to potable water and sewerage; access to basic health services; an increase in schooling rates at primary level; and the development of social housing programmes.
2. The increase of employment opportunities and of the population's income through maintaining an appropriate macro-economic framework, the suppression of institutional and regulatory obstacles to job creation and the reinforcement of mechanisms of intermediation and insertion into the labour market.
3. The reinforcement of assistance and social protection programmes, by means of good targeting on the vulnerable categories, the allocation of 'protected' resources to these programmes and an efficient management of social safety-net services.

The implementation of the Social Development Strategy started with the setting up of the first social priority programme (BAJ I), in the 1996/97 budgetary year. It included a basic education project, a basic health project and a project of follow-up of living and employment conditions. Two other programmes are planned within a framework of co-operation between the Moroccan government and the World Bank. In parallel, an agreement was signed in September 1996 between the Moroccan government and UNDP, bearing on the implementation of a 'Programme for Sustainable Human Development and Struggle against Poverty'. A social development fund is also planned, on the basis of various countries' experiences.

New actors of social development Some of the main organizations in charge of social development belong to the Moroccan government institutions. The main body in charge of the protection of socially vulnerable groups and of the support and framing of civil society actions and voluntary organizations is the Ministry of Employment and Social Affairs, recently integrated into a single structure, so as to promote better integration of its programmes as well as better co-ordination between local administrations and NGOs. However, in spite of measures promoting the professionalism of its employees and enhancing its operational capacities, this ministry remains limited by the weakness of its budgetary allocation: only 0.28 per cent of the general public budget (UNDP 1997b).

The National Solidarity Programme, which constitutes the most consistent social safety-net in towns, manages four kinds of structures: socio-educative centres for poor mothers of young children; education and work centres, which provide vocational initiatives for poor girls; Muslim charity associations, which care for poor orphans or abandoned children; and day-care centres for poor children. This essential programme suffers, however, from the weakness of its budget, depending upon state subsidies, and that of the qualification of its personnel. The Ministry of Finance is narrowly involved in employment promotion in the public and the private sectors, while the Ministry of Population has horizontal competencies and represents the focal point in the government for everything that concerns co-ordination of the various actions in terms of struggle against poverty. Other ministries and departments have sectoral competencies, such as the Ministry of Interior, in charge of local administrations (which saw its responsibilities increased in the framework of the decentralization laws), the Ministry of Public Health, the Ministry of Habitat, the Youth Department, the High Commissariat for Handicapped Persons, and the National Promotion Programme, which mainly seeks to promote rural development and employment-generating projects. All these official bodies, however, saw their effective role constrained by the budgetary and financial restrictions induced by the SAP.

On the other hand, making poverty data public, and reinforcing national plans of struggle against human poverty, were done with a marked contribution from international agencies. According to the World Bank (1995c), net official development assistance to Morocco increased from 448 million dollars in 1987 to 1,233 million dollars in 1991, but tended to decrease from then on, to 751 million dollars in 1993. It therefore seems that international aid agencies partly take over responsibilities that the state, tending to an essentially economic role, assumes less and less. Their local partners are mainly NGOs, involved in the implementation of human poverty alleviation projects.

As a matter of fact, it appears that NGOs fulfilling economic and social functions of a rather technical character, have clearly benefited from the tolerance, and even the encouragement, of the regime in the past ten years (Denoeux and Gateau 1995; UNDP 1997b). Their extension took place parallel to the implementation of liberalization reforms and the withdrawal of the state from certain social functions, such as health. Technical NGOs have dedicated themselves in particular to social action in favour of deprived and vulnerable populations and women, as well as to the promotion of small and medium-size enterprises and self-employment, essentially by means of micro-credit (UNDP 1997b), notably in the framework of the self-employment job creation for unemployed graduates. According to Korany (1998: 174), one of the objectives of the government, underlying its encouragement of NGOs, is 'to relieve the state of some of its responsibilities, given its declining resources'. Their existence is requested by the donors in order to grant their support to programmes aimed at the improvement of the population's capabilities. They thus represent the only means to capture foreign assistance, while benefiting the image of the regime, credited for its tolerance: '[i]t is also the state's way of capitalizing on available foreign resources (from the United Nations Development Program; the World Health Organization; the United Nations Educational, Scientific, and Cultural Organization; and the US Agency for International Development) that are virtually all channelled through NGOs' (Korany 1998: 174). Public discourse is also insisting on the benefits of volunteer and associative action over state action, in the name of better proximity and popular participation (Denoeux and Gateau 1995). However, the tight control to which they are submitted implies that their scope in terms of deep social and political changes is severely limited, as will be shown below.

It furthermore appears that NGOs are the main elements in the regime's strategy of avoiding a politicization of Islam at a time when it could benefit from the partial withdrawal of the state, from the rising poverty and from the increasing pauperization of the middle classes, all of which discredit the state (Korany 1998: 177). Islamic institutions tend to develop social services in deprived city quarters, as they do in other Muslim countries (Leveau 1998), and social justice is on the agenda of most of the numerous Islamist associations found in Morocco, which tend to 'concentrate their work on civil society per se' (Korany 1998: 163), eventually using it as a means to reinforce their political clientele. In 1998, it was proposed that the *zakat*, a Muslim alm, be included in the fiscal role; in others words, that it change from being a voluntary contribution to religiously managed charitable assistance according to an individual's conscience, to become a compulsory payment at a set rate. This can certainly be interpreted in terms of increasing the public funds available for social services, and channelling the *zakat* through a unified plan of priorities. At the same time it indicates a will to control the use of these alms, and to make them enhance state legitimacy rather than Islam's popularity.

The Issue of Social Exclusion and the Challenge of Citizenship in Morocco

The issue of social exclusion needs to be tackled at two levels. One is that of the social fabric and relies on micro-level studies; it will not be dealt with in this chapter. The second – beyond evidence of deep inequalities in revenue, and its counterpart, income poverty; of wide discrepancy in access to social services and well-being, measured by the various human poverty indicators – needs to be related to the framework of the Moroccan political system and correlated to the nature of citizenship and its content in terms of rights.

Political changes and the debate on poverty Until very recently, governing institutions were under the direct control of the king, in a fluctuating alliance with the army and notable families. The wide majority of the population has been to a large extent kept out of any decision-making process, excluded from the power structure, subject to a monopoly of political and economic control. This situation, whereby popular masses have little means to voice their demands, weigh little in policy orientations, and are kept silent by the use of repression and a powerful ideological apparatus, is typical of non-democratic states. It can account for some choices which, made during the decade following structural adjustment agreement, contributed to worsen the poverty situation:

> The sacrifice in human welfare manifested in a widespread illiteracy of 56 per cent and under-5 mortality of 50 per 1,000 in 1993 could have been mitigated if the government had given priority to social services over non-essentials (military spending and the rapid repayment of foreign debt costs). Moreover, the hardship due to adjustment could have been reduced had the dirham not been abruptly and severely devalued when there was a wage freeze, rising unemployment and prolonged drought. Lastly, sudden and large profits (windfall profits) earned by entrepreneurs from trade liberalization have not been taxed for the benefit of the poor, which has contributed to greater inequality. (El-Ghonemy 1998: 190)

The elections of November 1997 opened a new phase in which the monarchy remains the central actor of the political system, but is no longer able to impose its will without taking into consideration the existence and interests of the prime minister, of the coalition of centre-left opposition forces as well as of new elites negotiating their incorporation into the political system (Leveau 1998). New challenges are gaining public legitimacy and tend to be taken up by the traditional ruling groups to prevent them from becoming issues that might support a reinforcement of the leftist camp; among them, the question of social inequalities and poverty. Ignored and avoided until recent years, poverty has become a widely debated issue since the birth of a pluralist political scene in Morocco, and even more so since the formation of the centre-left government in 1998. Official policies and discourses show a fear of the risk posed by a rising consciousness of standard-of-living discrepancies, by social instability and urban riots; however, they also demonstrate the strength of the resistance to an in-depth transformation of the modes of resource distribution.

In the various programme documents I consulted, no mention is made of a change in the distribution of assets in favour of the poorer segments of the population except for a decade-long land reform movement that took place in the first decade of the structural adjustment reforms:

> the redistribution of 327,000 hectares of fertile land with rich water resources lying near the Mediterranean and Atlantic coasts, to 23,600 poor peasants between 1974 and 1984. By a series of royal decrees, a total of 0.7 million hectares recovered from former French settlers was redistributed into units, each yielding an annual income per family that was above the established poverty line.

This land distribution would explain part of the rural poverty reduction in the years thereafter. In total, three land reform laws were issued in Morocco (1956, 1963 and 1973), distributing private land representing 4 per cent of total arable land to 2 per cent of total agricultural households (El-Ghonemy 1998: 190 and 155).

The use of income tax to reinforce the redistributive system and reduce income inequalities is not on the agenda, neo-liberal doctrines rather pushing towards a reduction of tax disbursement on the part of higher income groups. In 1980, taxes on income, profits and capital gains represented only 19.2 per cent of total central government current revenue, and social security 5.4 per cent, the bulk of it originating from taxes on goods and services and on international trade transactions (World Bank 1995c). In 1986, a tax on added value was introduced. In 1990, a general tax on income was created which suffered from three main ills: a low base line, so that even revenues hardly above subsistence level would be taxed; a strong progressive element for the first income brackets, which concentrate on most of the wage labour force; and a low progressive element for the highest incomes, the marginal tax rate having been reduced and exemptions multiplied (Akesbi 1993). For El-Ghonemy (1998: 256), 'despite the emphasis on structural tax reform and "ensuring social justice", tax on income and profit as a percentage of national income (GDP) remains almost unchanged from 4.8 per cent in 1981 to 4.6 per cent in 1985 and 5.3 per cent in 1990'.[12] In 1993, budget planning included income tax exemptions for the lowest revenues, but also a further reduction of the taxes imposed on the higher revenue categories and firms (Lecat 1993: 157; Berrada 1994: 14). These reforms have, to a large extent, failed to achieve either better equity or better efficiency. There are various reasons for this, among them the non-reassessment of tax brackets in parallel with inflation, and the narrowness of the categories targeted by taxes on salaries (because of the concentration of wage labour in the lowest deciles), while revenues from property (financial assets, land or real estate), profits and inherited wealth are taxed at a lower rate and/or can more easily escape taxation. Tax avoidance by firms is seemingly extremely widespread in Morocco and sanctions against evaders have become lighter. Globally, the Moroccan tax system is regressive, the pressure in favour of the protection of high revenue categories remains strong, supported by structural adjustment and economic efficiency *doxa*, and there is no political will to reform the tax system thoroughly, nor to guarantee bare *égalité devant l'impôt* (Akesbi 1993; Berrada 1994).

Interestingly, the issue of solidarity has recently been tackled within a charitable set-up, through the Mohammed V Foundation for Solidarity. The king has personally launched a 'campaign of solidarity with the most deprived', which aims at 'encouraging at the same time generosity, spontaneous gifts and the awareness that Morocco needs a greater involvement of the privileged ones in a necessary redistribution and a better distribution of wealth' (La Nouvelle Tribune 1999). In a recent article, the wealthiest are depicted as 'expatriates in their own country', 'turning their back on misery and aggravating the isolation of the excluded ones'. The campaign has met with wide success, gathering gifts in kind and in money. It is interesting to note that the money collected has been in large part transferred to Muslim charity associations in order to upgrade their premises and buy medicines.

More than ever since the leftist opposition has been incorporated into the ruling institutions, Islamism is seen as a viable alternative by dissatisfied popular masses and impoverished middle classes; it is recruiting on university campuses and developing palliative social services in deprived areas. Demonstrations led by unemployed graduates illustrate further the extent of the pressure placed on the government. These threats to public order are used to justify the continued surveillance of citizens which, while it contradicts the will for political liberalization, is acceptable to both the modernizing monarchy and the hard-pressed government. It is not clear whether the present period can be analysed as a simple renewal of elites which does not compromise the king's domination, or as a social-democratic project of transition towards democracy (Leveau 1998).

The measures taken to struggle against poverty, however publicized, remain rather superficial. They are hampered by the permanence of the control effected by the ruling elites and the king and by their various privileges; by the requested structural adjustment reforms that impose high social costs and fuel public dissatisfaction; and by the military tension that will persist as long as the problem of the Western Sahara is not resolved, justifying high and untouchable military spending.

The limits of the civil society There are signs of a change in the nature and content of citizenship in Morocco, or, rather, of a change from a population of subjects to one of citizens endowed with rights. One of these signs is the development of associative life, which may be considered as a testimony to the emergence of a popular will to mobilize and face the challenges confronting the country, and perhaps of civil society, presented by the regime as a proof of its will to favour democracy and consultation (Denoeux and Gateau 1995). Foreign donors' conditionality and concern for the development of civil society and social participation certainly play a role in this regard: UNDP, for example, tries to set up participatory approaches within the programme it is implementing, such as the institutional building of participation and consultation. However, the NGOs' effective scope tends to be limited to a formal function of satisfying donors' requests, and to a real function of containing internal dissatisfaction, while the challenge that they could represent for the established order is kept strictly limited.

Apart from the technical NGOs mentioned in an earlier section, some NGOs do deal with issues of clear political content and scope. They are of three kinds: those promoting human rights, those promoting an improvement in women's living conditions, and those advocating a larger space for Berber culture. Their development, and the tolerance the regime shows towards them, is mainly due to internal and external pressures, which tend to alter the strategy of legitimization of the monarchy both inside and outside the country. The recent freeing of political prisoners and the establishment of a list of 'disappeared' persons can be seen as a proof of this strategy. But the state keeps these political NGOs under tight control, and has used several strategies to neutralize them politically and turn their activities to the benefit of the monarchy. According to Korany, '[e]xternal rewards or pressures [...] do not seem to have guaranteed at present the autonomy of these associations – a prerequisite for an effective civil society and democratization process'. The second objective behind the government's encouragement of NGOs is 'to organize the political arena, rather than encouraging a political vacuum that could be occupied by uncontrollable social forces [...] the exclusion of alternative political forces, the co-optation of civil society, and the regulation of its demands. In order to avoid putting in question the bases of the political regime, the state worked to clientelize civil society' (Korany 1998: 174–6). Another element which would tend to reduce the political impact of NGOs in terms of the development of citizenship rights is the fact that their members are for the most part from the upper and middle classes, or they are Moroccan emigrants abroad, or members of international organizations (Denoeux and Gateau 1995). They tend to be another institutional form of charity and clientelization, while the participation of popular segments of society in NGOs is challenged by the strength of family and village solidarity networks.

The effect of the existence of numerous associations, and their recent tendency to occupy a wider social space, is not negligible in terms of social integration and communication, be it between the state and society, or between different social groups and power circles (Korany 1998: 175). They have helped to revitalize regional solidarities, to reconstitute and consolidate tribal networks on new bases, as well as allowing 'the integration of the most enterprising members in the circles of notables and secur[ing] the revitalization of state personnel'.[13] Social exclusion, presented as a set of symptoms, can be alleviated by various combined measures: employment, family and associative solidarity, foreign non-governmental support, defence of human rights. Its uprooting, though, would require the transformation of the fundamental framework of its reproduction and permanence: denial of civic, political, social and economic rights. The consolidation of a civil society can be considered only as a potential powerful lever for social and political change, but it is still doubtful that it can, as of today, be seen as a structural transformation of the nature and content of citizenship in Morocco.

Conclusion: Poverty Discourse and Issues of Power

Based on the Moroccan case, this chapter has attempted to show how various approaches and basic definitions of poverty constitute a discourse (or discourses) related to issues of state power. It has pointed to the fact that the international context, advocating ethical liberalism, constitutes a sort of hatchery for poverty discourses, and that the chronic dependency of an underdeveloped state such as Morocco has been a powerful medium for their emergence on the domestic scene (through structural adjustment, conditionality of money-lending, development assistance and so on). It has also shown how poverty discourses, once in existence, become embedded in political practice and function from within this practice, and that their potential for transformation – notably towards more radical advocacy – remains tightly controlled, as do their enunciators. Income poverty approaches, as well as the minimal (basic needs) version of social poverty approaches, constitute the ideal consensus basis for poverty discourse, in congruence with the global neo-liberal economic and moral *doxa*, with the form of integration of these countries in the international division of labour, and with the dominating domestic power structures. Poverty alleviation policies that give priority to the income approach to poverty tend to set the terms of the struggle against poverty in a technocratic field: liberalize market forces, take measures to favour growth, add a few social safety-nets in order to allow the poorest to catch the train of growth, and the economic machinery should, almost spontaneously, solve the problem of poverty. The discourse on human poverty itself can easily be stripped of its inherently political content, involving the role of the state, and made out to be a kit of social measures that promote human capital. Social exclusion approaches, on the other hand, along with a more political understanding of human poverty, constitute potential levers for a profound transformation of poverty discourses and, from there, of social and political orders.

I have tried to argue that poverty discourses of a highly ideological nature and content, and more widely the discursive field around poverty or, as Foucault has worded it, the system of dependence in which discourses can exist in relation to political practice (Burchell et al. 1991: 69), represent the cornerstone of poverty management. The chapter has outlined some of the stakes involved behind the emergence of a poverty discourse, and the content of this discourse in Morocco: the opening of an arena for debate; the acknowledgement of a 'problem'; the official circumscription of this problem in terms of measurements and causality; the relation between the problem as described and the policies being implemented; the justification of the existing economic, social and political order in relation to this problem. In countries where the space for public expression is, to a large extent, controlled by the state, official discourses have a dominant relative weight. The first relation between poverty definition and power is thus the implicit and explicit authorization to mention a fact, and the means by which the authorities define this fact as a problem, uncovering some of its aspects while concealing others. In the Moroccan case, as in numerous others, issues of inequality of assets distribution, and of imbalance in the allocation of public investment and expenditure in geographic and social spaces, are marginalized in public discourse on poverty.

On the other hand, moral values are being conveyed by the official discourse, as part of the neo-liberal 'package' of poverty alleviation. One of the most obvious concerns the virtues of work, not only in economic terms – to obtain a revenue and not depend upon public budgets – but also in terms of social 'hygiene'; the poor are encouraged to work, but not the wealthy who may well, as is the case in most of the world's countries, obtain the major part of their income from rents, not from labour. Begging is condemned largely in this framework, law then representing the formal aspect of the discourse, 'cheating' being socially stigmatized. If work is redeeming in itself, then less insistence is put on whether or not it actually constitutes a way out of poverty: in other words, poor inactive or unemployed persons are pressed to accept any kind of work, whatever the remuneration and the conditions proposed. In this context, obtaining a working position and benefiting from the respect of protective labour laws are not a right for the poor, but rather a duty and a favour, which contributes to the maintenance of paternalistic and domination/submission relations of labour. The integration of Morocco in the international division of labour, and its competitive performance are set on these bases, which also justify social and political control of the poor.

Another value which is stressed in this view is that of the family: whereas transfers to the poor are seen as encouragements to laziness and dependency, intra-family transfers are not only legitimate, but encouraged, no matter what the side effects may be, in terms of social control, weight of tradition, inequality of resource allocation between family members and reproduction of social inequalities. Family solidarity discourse may not only justify the weakness of other types of transfers and income support programmes to the poor, it conceivably also contributes to legitimate intra-family transfers of all kinds of assets, such as patrimonial items or power functions, among the highest income groups. It may also support the perception that the country is not affected by social exclusion, the family being the main integration cell. Furthermore, intra-family transfers are also presented as legitimate because, for large numbers of Moroccans, they originate from the labour proceeds of one of the family members, working abroad and contributing to his family's sustenance. In this regard, they may have an effect in presenting as 'normal' the dependence upon external labour markets, making up for the scarcity of jobs and the weakness of wages at home.

Poverty definitions and approaches are also related to power as far as the implementation of policies is concerned. For legitimacy and credibility purposes, policies need to be coherent with the diagnosis made of poverty, its extent and its causes, while managing the balance of power in society. In Morocco, considerable emotion was raised when human poverty figures became widely known, in particular in terms of health and education. It seems that this profile of poverty allowed a switching of attention from income issues – and specifically income and property distribution – to a renewed stake in modernization and social progress. As the inhabitants of remote under-developed places were suddenly 'discovered' to be living in conditions unworthy of the country's global image, the state became the new patron of human development promotion, notwithstanding its capacity to attract foreign assistance, which may also have distracted from close critical examination of the distribution of public expenses – in particular military expenses – and from the sources of public income – in particular the undertaxation of the highest incomes. Policy implementation can also remain rather superficial, or formal, without altering the factors of repro-duction of poverty. This is probably best exemplified by the process of democratization which, while representing a real step forward and a very significant transformation of the political system in Morocco, has not so far allowed for a wide popular voicing of demands, or for a more equitable distribution of economic, political, social and cultural assets.

It should not be overlooked that states such as Morocco are caught between their basis of legitimization (well-being of their population, modernization, employment) on the one hand; and on the other the inter-national pressure they are all the more subjected to since they depend on foreign military, budgetary, technical, commercial and political support, and are engaged in structural adjustment and debt negotiation processes. Their margin for action is therefore limited. However, their role is also strongly determined by their own social nature, and by the interests of their ruling families. Poverty has to be managed within these narrow borders, and can be understood only in the context of the exercise and the reproduction of state power, especially since it may constitute one of its most dangerous challenges. As surveys on historical processes of institutionalization of the protection of the poor in the developed world clearly show, 'conflict over the meaning of social rights and civil society also meant conflict over the role of the State [over] the *agenda* and the *non-agenda* of the State' (Gordon 1991: 29). It should be added that the conflict also concerns the political content of this agenda, technocratic measures often being proposed as part of the scientific and modern welfare machinery, in an attempt to disconnect it from acknowledged political interplay.

The paradigm of full citizenship, as developed by Marshall, should be carefully used in other contexts than the European one; it may be true that '[p]rojecting the European discourse of "social exclusion" onto developing countries [...] would [...] be a grotesque relabelling of long-standing approaches to problems, whose only rationale would be the supposed intellectual superiority of European concepts' (Gore 1995: 4–5). The fundamental challenge raised by poverty discourses ultimately appears to be that of the establishment of forms of integration and citizenship adapted to the specific context of the countries concerned, while respecting basic and universal human, civic, political, economic and social rights, inscribed in the UN charter.

Notes

1. Other derived measurements evaluate the poverty gap, that is the amount that would be necessary to bring all the poor at poverty-line level; and the dispersion of the poor.

2. It also depends on the factor of conversion into purchasing power parity and exchange rates chosen.

3. Two main sets of premises exist: those developed around the French tradition of republican solidarity, to which the elements presented below would belong; and those pertaining rather to the Anglo-Saxon liberal tradition.

4. See Genugten and Perez-Bustillo (eds) (forthcoming).

5. 'Is Poverty Increasing in the Developing World?', *Review of Income and Wealth*, 40, 4 (1994).

6. 'La face cachée du libéralisme', *L'opinion*, 3 March 1998.

7. Quoting C. Morrisson (1991) 'Adjustment, Incomes and Poverty in Morocco', *World Development*, 19, 11, pp. 1633–51.

8. According to my knowledge, there does not exist a public financial transfer scheme to the poor in Morocco. Charitable practices of support to the poor set up by associations, Islamic or not, will not be dealt with in this chapter.

9. *La Vie Economique*, 2 May 1997. The same article ironically headlines: 'First of all, we should not say poor, but "unfavoured". It is the term officially adopted by the CERED, and it concerns 47.3 per cent of the Moroccans.'

10. That is in the 1998 UNDP report, but based on 1995 data.

11. *La Vie Economique*, 2 May 1997.

12. Figures based on IMF (1995).

13. Ghazali, Ahmed (1989) 'Contribution à l'analyse du phénomène associatif au Maroc', *Annuaire de l'Afrique du Nord*, 28, p. 253. Quoted by Korany (1998: 184, note 97).

References

Abdel Gadir Ali, Ali (1996) 'The Behavior of Poverty in the Arab Countries', in UNDP and UNDDSMS, *Preventing and Eradicating Poverty*, Report on the experts' meeting on 'Poverty Alleviation and Sustainable Livelihoods in the Arab States', Damascus, Syrian Arab Republic, 28–29 February, pp. 61–80.

Akesbi, Najib, (1993) *L'impôt, l'état et l'Ajustement*. Collection Economie et Développement. Rabat: Editions Actes.

Bakir, Muhammad Hussein (1996) *Measures of Poverty in the Economic and Social Commission for Western Asia* (in Arabic). ESCWA, United Nations.

Benlachen Tlemcani, Mohammed (1993) 'Les leçons des élections législatives au Maroc', *Les Cahiers de l'Orient*, 31 (troisième trimestre), pp. 129–36.

Berrada, Abdelkader (1994) 'L'Etat et l'enjeu budgétaire au Maroc', *Annales Marocaines d'Economie*, Revue de l'Association des Economistes Marocains, 10, pp. 5–48.

Burchell, Graham, Colin Gordon and Peter Miller (eds) (1991) *The Foucault Effect, Studies in Governmentality*. Chicago: University of Chicago Press.

CERED (Centre d'Etudes et de Recherches Démographiques) (1997) *Populations vulnérables: profil socio-démographique et répartition spatiale*. Royaume du Maroc, Ministère chargé de la population.

Denoeux, Guilain and Laurent Gateau (1995) 'L'essor des associations au Maroc: à la recherche de la citoyenneté?', *Monde arabe Maghreb Machrek*, 150 (October–December), pp. 19–39.

Destremau, Blandine (1998a) 'Comment définir la pauvreté?', in Salama and Poulin (eds), *L'insoutenable misère du monde*, pp. 27–34.

— (1998b) 'Les indicateurs de pauvreté dans les approches de la Banque Mondiale et du PNUD: une analyse critique', in Salama and Poulin (eds), *L'insoutenable misère du monde*, pp. 65–90.

— (1998c) 'A la porte de Dieu?: Profil de la pauvreté et de l'appauvrissement en Afrique du Nord–Moyen–Orient', in Salama and Poulin (eds), *L'insoutenable misère du monde*, pp. 65–90.

— (1998d) 'Pauvreté et appauvrissement en Afrique du Nord–Moyen–Orient : quelques repères', in 'Crise et contestation au Maghreb et au Moyen-Orient. Algérie, Maroc, Egypte, Soudan, Jordanie, Iraq', *Les Cahiers du GREMAMO*, 15, Laboratoire Sociétés en Développement dans l'Espace et dans le Temps–Université Paris VII, pp. 55–69.

Destremau, Blandine and Pierre Salama (1999) *Les mesures de la pauvreté*. Collection 'Repères'. Paris: Edition La Découverte.

Destremau, Blandine and Pierre Signoles (1995) 'Le difficile ajustement d'économies différenciées en rapide mutation', in *Maghreb Moyen-Orient Mutations*, Dossiers et Images Economiques du Monde. Paris: SEDES, pp. 5–84.

Diwan, Ishac and Michael Walton (1996) 'Opening up and Distribution in the Middle East and North Africa: The Poor, the Unemployed and the Public Sector'. ERF Working Papers WP 9616. Cairo: ERF.

Economic and Social Commission for Western Asia (ESCWA) (1996) *Poverty in Western Asia: A Social Perspective*. Eradicating Poverty Studies Series 1. New York: United Nations.

Economic Research Forum for the Arab Countries, Iran and Turkey (ERF) (1998) *Economic Trends in the MENA Region*. Cairo: ERF Indicators.

El-Ghonemy, M. Riad (1998) *Affluence and Poverty in the Middle East*. London and New York: Routledge.

Geneletti, Carlo (1996) 'Poverty in the Arab Region: A Synthesis of the Main Issues in the Relevant Literature', in UNDP and UNDDSMS, *Preventing and Eradicating Poverty*, Report on the experts' meeting on 'Poverty Alleviation and Sustainable Livelihoods in the Arab States', Damascus, Syrian Arab Republic, 28–29 February, pp. 49–60.

Genugton, Willem van and Camilo Perez-Bustillo (eds) (forthcoming) *Transcending the Poverty of Rights: Latin America, Human Rights and the Eradication of Poverty*. London: Zed Books.

Ghalioun, Burhan (1991) *Le malaise arabe. l'Etat contre la Nation*. Paris: Editions la Découverte.

Gordon, Colin (1991) 'Governmental Rationality: An Introduction', in Burchell et al. (eds), *The Foucault Effect*, pp. 1–52.

Gore, Charles (with contributions from José B. Figueiredo and Gerry Rodgers) (1995) 'Introduction: Markets, Citizenship and Social Exclusion', in Rodgers et al. (eds), *Social Exclusion*, pp. 1–40.

Guecioueur, Adda (1996) 'Social Safety Nets: Experience of Arab Countries', in UNDP and UNDDSMS, *Preventing and Eradicating Poverty*. Report on the experts' meeting on 'Poverty Alleviation and Sustainable Livelihoods in the Arab States', Damascus, Syrian Arab Republic, 28–29 February, pp. 164–74.

Ibrahimi, Ahmed (1998) 'Les actions pilote en matière de lutte contre la pauvreté au Maroc', in *Les Politiques de Lutte contre la Pauvreté dans le Bassin Méditerranéen*. Rabat: INSEA, Synthèse des travaux, pp. 19–26.

IMF (1995) *Resilience and Growth Through Sustained Growth: The Moroccan Experience*. Occasional paper 117. Washington, DC: IMF.

Karshenas, Massoud (1994) 'Structural Adjustment and Employment in the Middle East and North Africa', ERF Working Papers WP 9420. Cairo: ERF.

— (1997) 'Economic Liberalization, Competitiveness and Women's Employment in the Middle East and North Africa', ERF Working Papers WP 9705. Cairo: ERF.

Korany, Bahgat (1998) 'Monarchical Islam with a Democratic Veneer: Morocco', in Bahgat Korany, Rex Brynen and Paul Noble (eds), *Political Liberalization and Democratization in the Arab World*, Comparative Experiences, vol. 2. Boulder, CO and London: Lynne Riener Publishers, pp. 157–84.

La Nouvelle Tribune (1999) Special issue: 'Pauvreté, la plaie purulente du pays', 183, (28 October–3 November), Casablanca, Morocco.

Lecat, Bernard (1993) 'L'ouverture marocaine', *Les Cahiers de l'Orient*, 31 (troisième trimestre), pp. 147–58.

Leveau, Rémy (1998) 'Réussir la transition démocratique au Maroc; la monarchie, acteur central du système politique', *Le Monde Diplomatique* (November), pp. 14–15.

Mejjati Alaoui, Rajaâ (1994) 'Dynamiques des activités informelles au Maroc: mode de développement, rationalité et réseaux (le cas de la petite confection à Fès)', *Annales Marocaines d'Economie*, Revue de l'Association des Economistes Marocains, 10, pp. 173–82.

Richards, Alan, and John Waterbury (1990) *A Political Economy of the Middle East. State, Class and Economic Development*. Cairo: The American University in Cairo Press.

Rocha, Sonia (1997) 'On Statistical Mapping of Poverty: Social Reality, Concepts and Measurements.' Background paper prepared for the expert group meeting on Poverty Statistics, Santiago, Chile.

Rodgers, Gerry, Charles Gore and José B. Figueiredo (eds) (1995) *Social Exclusion: Rhetoric, Reality, Responses*, International Institute for Labour Studies, UNDP (A contribution to the World Summit for Social Development).

Said, Mona (1995) 'Public Sector Employment and Labor Markets in Arab Countries: Recent Developments and Policy Implications', ERF Working Papers WP 9630. Cairo: ERF.

Salahdine, Mohamed (1991) 'Le marché du travail urbain au Maroc'. Institut International d'Etudes sociales, Discussion papers, Programme Marché du Travail, DP/33/1991, Geneva.

Salama, P. and R. Poulin (eds) (1998) *L'insoutenable misère du monde: le retour en force des inégalités et de la pauvreté*. Hull (Québec): Editions vents d'Quest, collection 'l'Alternative'.

Salih, Siddig A. (1996) 'Poverty alleviation and sustainable livelihoods in the region for Arab states', in UNDP and UNDDSMS: *Preventing and Eradicating Poverty*. Report on the experts' meeting on 'Poverty Alleviation and Sustainable Livelihoods in the Arab States', Damascus, Syrian Arab Republic, 28–29 February, pp. 175–88.

Sen, Amartya (1988) *Hunger and Entitlements.* Research for Action, World Institute for Development Economics Research, United Nations University.

Shaban, Radwan A., Ragui Assaad and Sulayman Al-Qudsi (1994) 'Employment Experience in the Middle East and North Africa', ERF Working Papers WP 9401. Cairo: ERF.

UNDP (1994, 1995, 1996, 1997, 1998) *Rapport Mondial sur le Développement Humain.* Paris: Economica.

— (1996b) *Développement Humain et Lutte contre la pauvreté.* Programme du Gouvernement du Royaume du Maroc, MOR/96/002.

— (1997b) *Programme sectoriel national 1er volet: lutte contre la pauvreté urbaine,* Coopération Maroc – UNDP, 1997–2001.

Van Eeghen, Willem (1995) *Poverty in the Middle East and North Africa.* First draft of a background paper prepared as part of the 1995 World Bank study on the MENA region.

— (1996) 'Poverty in the Middle East and North Africa', in UNDP and UNDDSMS: *Preventing and Eradicating Poverty.* Report on the experts' meeting on 'Poverty Alleviation and Sustainable Livelihoods in the Arab States', Damascus, Syrian Arab Republic, 28–29 February, pp. 211–26.

World Bank (1995a) *Claiming the Future. Choosing Prosperity in the Middle East and North Africa.* Washington, DC: World Bank.

— (1995b) *Will Arab Workers Prosper or be Left Out in the Twenty-First Century?* Regional Perspectives on World Development Report. Washington, DC: World Bank.

— (1995c) *Workers in an Integrated World.* World Development Reports. New York: Oxford University Press.

Zouiten, Mounir (1998) 'Quelques mesures de lutte contre la mendicité au Maroc', in *Les politiques de lutte contre la pauvreté dans le bassin méditerranéen.* INSEA. Rabat Synthèse des travaux, pp. 33–40.

9

Trade Policy, Poverty and Inequality in Namibia

Dirk Hansohm, Klaus Schade and Arne Wiig

Introduction: The Namibian Economy and Poverty

Namibia gained its independence in 1990. Its per capita income of US $2,220 per year (1997; World Bank 1999) is more than four times higher than the sub-Saharan African (SSA) average. Although Namibia's growth record since independence has been favourable, compared both with its past and the SSA average, it has, on average, not been higher than population growth, so that per capita average incomes have stagnated. Furthermore, statistical averages conceal the reality in Namibia. The local economy and society in general are characterized by a dual nature that emanates from both its mineral-based enclave economy and from the past policy of racial segregation, apartheid, which restricted many of the benefits of education and other social services to a privileged minority.

The Namibian economy is essentially driven by a large non-tradable sector (government services) and an export-oriented primary sector (fisheries, agriculture and mining). The fisheries and mining sectors are mature and relatively capital-intensive, and thus not able to improve the unemployment situation in the country. Moreover, the fisheries and diamond-mining sectors are quota-driven, while the remaining mining sub-sectors are demand-driven, indicating that growth is mainly influenced by external factors. Growth in the supply-driven agricultural sector has been low as a result of drought-related shocks.

Fewer people are being employed in agriculture (although it remains by far the most important sector in terms of employment) and in the mining sector, while government (included in 'services') and finance/real estate are the most important growth sectors in terms of employment. Although visualized as the main engine of growth, the manufacturing sector has in fact grown only slowly.

Namibia's labour market consists of an informal and a formal sector. The scarce evidence on wages suggests that the incomes of informal sector workers are largely market-determined and probably stagnating, while formal sector workers, highly organized in various trade unions, have seen real wage increases, especially at the higher levels. According to the Labour Force Survey of 1997 (MoL 1998), unemployment has grown steadily since independence, from 19 per cent (1991) to 33 per cent (1997). The combined un- and underemployment rate is estimated to be as high as 60 per cent.

Namibia has one of the highest income inequalities world-wide. Its Gini-coefficient of 0.70 (UNDP 1998: 9) is higher than any recorded in the latest World Development Report (World Bank 1999: 198–9). The income disparity between the poorest and highest income groups is vast (CSO 1996a): the household income of the highest quarter (N$52,672) is twenty-six times that of the lowest (N$2,067). In the official statistics (CSO 1996b), 38 per cent of households are regarded as poor (spending 60 per cent or more on food), while 9 per cent are very poor (spending 80 per cent or more on food). The income disparities are substantiated by relative figures. Since households of the lower income group consist of greater numbers, the income inequalities per capita will be even higher than the inequalities between households.

Thirty-four per cent of households are based in urban areas, earning more than three times the amount of those in rural areas (CSO 1996b). Namibia is also characterized by huge regional income disparities. The northern communal areas, where the majority of Namibia's population lives, are worse off (average household income of the poorest region, Ohangwena: N$6,439) than the affluent commercial agricultural regions of, say, Karas (N$26,991), Hardap, Omaheke and Otjozondjupa. However, the high average income of these regions mask intra-regional income differences, since poor communal farmers exist alongside affluent commercial farmers. The commercial and political centre of Windhoek in the Khomas region has by far the highest average household income (N$47,409).

The Namibian government has set itself four key development objectives to address these challenges: economic growth, employment, and the alleviation of poverty and inequality. In 1998 it adopted a Poverty Strategy (RoN 1998). As in other countries, policy-makers focus on policies aimed directly at alleviating poverty (e.g. transfers, income-generating schemes), and on investment in social sectors (education, health) which promise both a direct contribution to welfare enhancement and long-term benefits. However, the important impact which other government policies have on growth, income distribution and poverty are barely acknowledged.

The aim of this chapter is to illustrate the influence which a wide range of policies, designed with completely different objectives, have on poverty (Lipton and Ravallion 1995). This illustration is made to strengthen the argument that in order to reduce poverty in a significant and sustainable way, the entire range of government policies must be scrutinized for their conformity with the aim of poverty alleviation (Hansohm and Presland 1997).

One policy area is selected here: trade policy. This is because trade policy is currently of particular relevance to Namibia, as different options with regard to membership of regional integration schemes are under consideration and controversial (although the implications for poverty are rarely recognized), and little is known of the impact of the Uruguay Round on Namibia.

Until 1990, Namibia was under South African rule and thus part of its economy. Together with Botswana, Lesotho and Swaziland (BLS), Namibia continues to be closely integrated with South Africa, notably as a member of the Southern African Customs Union (SACU) with BLS, and of the Common Monetary Area (CMA) with all except Botswana.

Furthermore, Namibia is a member of the Southern African Development Community (SADC), and the Common Market of Eastern and Southern Africa (COMESA). It is also part of the Cross-border Initiative (CBI), a grouping of Southern African countries which aim to reduce barriers to trade and investment on the basis of single country commitments, based on the disillusionment with the slow pace of integration of the regional agreements (COMESA, SADC). There are, moreover, a number of bilateral trade agreements planned. In existence is a scheme with Zimbabwe. The large number of partially overlapping and competing agreements in itself can be regarded as a barrier to trade and investment (Sharer 1998).

The old integration schemes of SACU and CMA are regarded with suspicion in Namibia because of their colonial origin. While the impact of SACU is in fact double-edged, the benefits of CMA are clearer. SADC is viewed more positively, although it still has a long way to go before it is an integrated economic region – a free trade area (FTA) is planned within eight years. International integration is seen by many as a threat, rather than as an opportunity. Economic welfare in the future is often equated with independence (from South Africa) rather than with further integration. For this reason, notions of 'self-sufficiency' are popular.

This contrasts with the international academic discussion which is currently dominated by powerful arguments that 'open', 'outward-oriented' economies have a better record both in terms of growth and poverty alleviation; a lesson which is believed to be especially relevant for Africa (e.g. Ng and Yeats 1997; Sachs and Warner 1997). However, this position is not undisputed (e.g. Wood and Berge 1997). This chapter intends to contribute to this discussion by examining the case of Namibia. It analyses the impact of a change within the trade regime on Namibia's poverty and inequality: unilateral trade liberalization – if Namibia were to leave SACU and set external tariffs to zero and the quantitative restrictions on agricultural products were to be abolished.

This chapter is organized into three further sections. The next section provides an introduction to the structure of Namibia's foreign trade and its trade regime. The main section analyses the impact of current trade policy and of trade liberalization on poverty and inequality. The final section relates to the international discussion and offers some policy conclusions.

Namibia's Foreign Trade and Trade Regime

Namibia conforms to the classical picture of an African raw-material producer (see Figure 9.1). The traditional resource exports (diamonds and other minerals, fish, beef, fruit) continue to dominate. Manufactured exports increased from 13.1 per cent in 1981 to 27.5 per cent in 1997, down from a high of more than 30 per cent in 1992–94. With manufacturing exports, there is no sustainable trend towards diversification and deepening. Rather, the relative importance of raw-material processing has increased from 63 per cent (1981) to 76 per cent (1997).

In real terms, exports have remained stagnant, while imports have grown, leading to increasing trade deficits. The import structure has changed little. The most significant categories are services (around 25 per cent), intermediate goods (21–24 per cent), food (15–18 per cent), and capital goods (12–13 per cent).

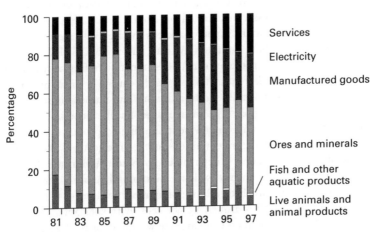

FIGURE 9.1 Namibia's export structure (% of major groups), 1981–97
Source: CSS (1998)

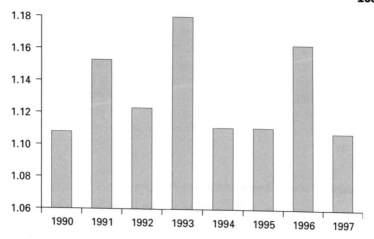

FIGURE 9.2 Trade openness – ratio of imports plus exports to GDP in %,
1990–92 *Source*: BoN (1999)

Namibia's integration into the world economy, as far as foreign trade is concerned, remains volatile and is not increasing (see Figure 9.2). Other means of global integration (foreign direct investment [FDI], aid) do not counter this trend: FDI has picked up somewhat since independence, but remains small (6.9 per cent of GDP in 1997; BoN 1999). Foreign aid shows a declining trend, as in other SSA countries.

The origin of Namibia's imports remains highly concentrated on SACU (imports from South Africa amounted to 86.3 per cent of the total in 1993). Exports are less concentrated on South Africa (27.4 per cent in 1993). The most important export market is the EU, with more than half. Trade within the whole Southern African sub-region (SADC) remains insignificant. Only 1.8 per cent of SACU's imports are from other SADC countries (World Bank 1998). This is partly due to a great number of remaining tariff and no-tariff (both traditional and non-traditional)[1] trade barriers within the region. The main reason for the poor intra-regional trade is the similar resource endowment and limited production structure of all countries (with the exception of South Africa; World Bank 1993).

Namibia's trade regime is determined by South Africa, the dominant partner in SACU. Although it is slowly becoming liberalized, this system is protectionist in nature. Presently, the simple average level of the Common External Tariff (CET) is around 15 per cent, with substantial dispersion (WTO 1998: 29), amounting to an average weighted tariff of 24.4 per cent (Ng and Yeats 1999: 28). In addition, there are numerous non-tariff barriers. A study on trade policy and governance in Africa accordingly assesses

TABLE 9.1 SACU import tariff rates by sector (%), 1996

Sector	Trade w'ted ave. rate	Collection rate	Simple ave. rate	Maximum rate	Minimum rate	Share of tariffs collected
All	6.1	4.5	8.3	61	0	100.0
Consumer goods, primary	1.1	0.7	6.4	35	0	0.3
Consumer goods, manufactured	11.1	10.8	14.0	55	0	28.2
Intermediate goods, primary	2.2	0.2	2.5	26	0	0.2
Intermediate goods, manufactured	5.7	4.5	7.1	61	0	41.8
Capital goods	1.6	2.6	6.2	61	0	14.0
Textiles and garments	27.4	14.5	13.0	52	0	9.4
Passenger motor cars	60.7	26.4	34.9	61	0	4.0
Petroleum and power	0.0	0.0	3.5	15	0	0.1
Other	37.4	5.8	17.3	46	0	2.0

Source: World Bank (1999)

Namibia's trade policy as 'very poor', i.e. rather restrictive (Ng and Yeats 1999: 28). This implies a strong importance of SACU income in total revenue.

The system of tariff and non-tariff barriers is highly complex, with some 7,800 lines, and a maximum rate of 61 per cent. With the exception of the low taxation of capital goods, it is a system of cascading rates (lowest on raw materials, highest on consumer goods), and serves primarily to protect South Africa's industry (see Table 9.1). Most important in terms of revenue collection are taxes on intermediate goods, which amounted to 42 per cent of all tariffs collected in 1996 (they have a simple average rate of 7.1 per cent). Taxes on manufactured consumer goods come second with a share of 28.2 per cent (average rate of 14.0 per cent). These figures indicate the assembly-type nature of South Africa's industries. The system establishes a bias towards import substitution, and therefore an anti-export bias.

Namibia has established a number of export incentives in order to overcome the anti-export bias of the SACU system, including tax reductions, training allowances and export promotion allowances. However, the success of these schemes has remained limited on account of bureaucratic procedures (MTI 1999a).

Impacts of Trade Policy on Poverty and Inequality in Namibia

One can distinguish three main effects of a liberalized trade regime. It may influence growth, the government budget, and income distribution. This section is structured along these dimensions.

Growth impacts The effect of trade policy on economic growth is a controversial issue. A number of authors such as Sachs and Warner (1997, 1995), Edwards (1997), Ng and Yeats (1999) find empirical evidence for a statistical and significant relationship between openness and growth. Sachs and Warner (1997) estimate that African countries would have grown 1.4 per cent higher had they implemented the same trade policy as in South-East Asia, with the same adverse geographic and structural conditions (climate, landlocked and transport). Applying this scenario to Namibia, its growth rate may double. Another argument is that there is a spurious relationship between trade policy and growth, since growth may vary during periods when trade policies stay the same. It is, according to Wood and Berge (1997: 54), wrong to expect that an open trade policy would lead to an outcome similar to that of South-East Asia, when the country in question has a low skill/land ratio as is the case in Namibia. Countries will trade according to their resource endowments. Only when they have high skill/

land ratios will they export manufacturing products. Such products are assumed to have higher potential growth effects than primary products. An interesting contribution to this debate is that of Rodrik (1995), who identifies investment, not trade, as the engine of growth in South-East Asia. On the other hand, Rodrik argues that investments generated demand for imported input, supporting the idea that trade and economic growth are interlinked.

Even though the theoretical foundation for such a relationship is yet not clear, some mechanisms of open trade policy stimulate economic growth. Openness to trade may affect the level of the steady state income through learning effects from the use of imported goods or through technology spill-overs. Increased competition may enhance total factor productivity and therefore economic growth. Trade may also facilitate the mobility of factors, and therefore promote the convergence of income across counties.

Leaving this controversial growth issue aside, few dispute the fact that trade liberalization has static income effects (one-off increase in income level). Different estimates are given in the relevant literature, but they are generally assumed to be in the range of between 2 and 10 per cent of GDP. Trade liberalization will also influence the distribution of income, and thereby the poverty situation. The scarcest factor of production loses, while the abundant factor gains. We assume that similar mechanisms occur in the Namibian case.

Fiscal impacts One key concern with trade liberalization is the negative impact it may have on social spending through the negative impact on taxes on foreign trade; in general, developing countries are highly dependent on taxes on trade, and Namibia is a case in point. However, to assess the fiscal impact on the poor and on income distribution in general, a more comprehensive analysis is necessary:

1. The poor are concerned as tax payers:
- the overall tax burden (tax revenue as percentage of GDP) is important; a high tax burden will stifle economic activity and thus hurt the poor
- the distribution of taxes will affect income distribution

2. The poor are concerned as beneficiaries of expenditure:
- less expenditure means in general less expenditure for social spending
- however, the distribution of expenditure in general, as well as of social expenditure, is relevant
- the efficiency of public spending is important

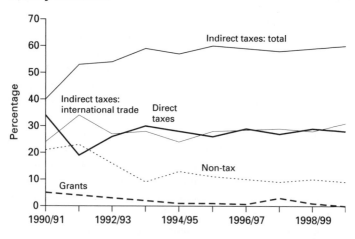

FIGURE 9.3 Composition of government revenues in %, 1992/2000
Source: RoN (1999)

3. If expenditure is financed through increasing debt, the poor are negatively affected, as an increasing share of expenditure will have to be devoted to debt service.

Namibia's tax burden has increased significantly over the last few years, from 29.5 per cent in 1994 to 33.7 per cent in 1999. Only a few high-income countries surpass this rate. This has an anti-poor impact by stifling business activity and thus employment.

The most important tax source is indirect taxes, notably General Sales Duty (GST) and Additional Sales Tax (ASD). Presently, there is less than perfect compliance with GST. Particularly in the North, where most of the poor live, tax enforcement is weak.

About 30 per cent of tax income comes from SACU. As this is a tax on imported consumer goods, the impact on consumers is dependent on the import-intensity of their consumption basket. In a developing country, one would expect a lower import intensity for poorer and for rural households. However, this difference is not great, because few consumer goods are produced in Namibia, and the import intensity of poor and rural household consumption is high. As far as production inputs are taxed, the impact depends on the import-intensity of the production process of the enterprises.

Direct taxes amount to less than 30 per cent of total tax income. The poor are less affected by direct taxes. Thus, a higher contribution of direct taxes could be expected to be pro-poor. However, experience shows that the higher taxation of labour incomes increases the price of labour and

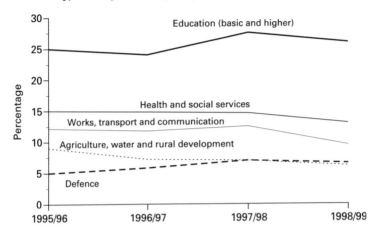

FIGURE 9.4 Expenditure structure by area, % of total budget, 1995/96–1998/99
Source: RoN (1999)

thus reduces employment growth. In general, high direct taxation is not advisable because it results in a reduction of entrepreneurship and investment, and thus higher unemployment for low-income households. It is expected that any gain to these households from the redistribution of higher taxation would be less than the gain to them from maintaining the growth of income and employment. Namibia's over-complex system of company taxation, including a myriad of exemptions to promote specific sectors, cheapens the cost of capital relative to that of labour in many sectors. This contradicts the policy of employment creation and poverty reduction (World Bank 1995: 139).

Trade liberalization leads to a lower income from trade taxes. This leads to pressure to reduce spending on wages, salaries and social services among others. A reduction of public wages would mainly affect the non-poor, while a reduction of social spending would rather have an anti-poor bias. Figure 9.4 shows the high importance of spending on health and social services, and education.

Of concern is the increasing share of personnel costs (see Figure 9.5), which squeezes capital expenditure, thereby reducing the productivity of the publicly employed. Public employment in itself is not a pro-poor policy, as it is not primarily the poor who are publicly employed (see Figure 9.6). Furthermore, the increasing public employment contributes to the bloated size of the public sector, both from a revenue and expenditure perspective.

Namibia affords an exceptionally high share of public expenditure on education (9.4 per cent of GNP) – more than double the average of

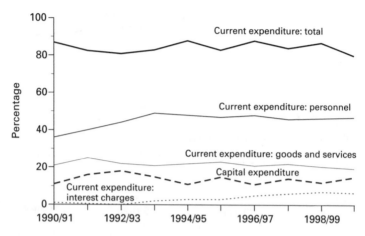

FIGURE 9.5 Government expenditure by item (%), 1990/91–1999/2000
Source: RoN (1999)

countries with comparable incomes. This seems appropriate in the light of an increasing acknowledgement of the importance of skills, and thus education, as a powerful explanatory factor for growth. Expenditure on education is also directly pro-poor, as education is an important way out of poverty. However, the efficiency of the expenditure on education remains limited, as shown by the high rates of drop-out and repetition of students (Schade et al. 1998: 39–45). Areas limiting poverty alleviation include:

- the high subsidization of tertiary education (which has higher private than social returns)
- persistent regional inequities (to the detriment of the poorest regions)
- limited attention to needs of the labour market (e.g. emphasis on vocational training, entrepreneurship)

Namibia's health expenditure is also exceptionally high (more than double the SSA average). This is principally pro-poor, both directly by improving the living standard of the poor, and indirectly by improving the quality of the labour force. Health indicators (e.g. infant mortality) are already showing improvement. Limitations of poverty orientation are continuing regional inequities (bias against the poorest regions) and the limited accessibility of health services.

Namibia inherited a non-contributory pension scheme. Every elderly, blind or disabled person is eligible to a monthly pension of N$160. This system plays an important role in poverty alleviation, as it is a major income source for the poor, reaching via the extended family beyond the beneficiaries. Drawbacks in terms of poverty alleviation are the fact that it is not targeted (the non-poor also benefit), and that not all eligible persons actually receive their benefit: it is estimated that only 79 per cent of the elderly and 27 per cent of the disabled receive their pension (UNDP 1996: 70).

In the Namibian agricultural context, subsidies have often proved to have detrimental effects and have not always reached the target group. A drought scheme aimed at helping communal farmers to market their cattle, implemented in 1995, actually led to an increase in heads of cattle. Obviously, money obtained from the marketing scheme was used to purchase more cattle, putting more pressure on already overgrazed land (Mupotola-Sibongo 1997: 54). Subsidies for the hiring of tractors, ploughs, for other inputs and credit have had some shortcomings concerning the target group. A study in the northern communal areas found that not only did very few farmers receive subsidies – some 3,500 out of 159,000 communal farmers (2.2 per cent) – but that in particular it was not the poorest farmers who benefited from these schemes, but rather farmers who were easily accessible and more vocal (NEPRU 1995). This example indicates that a cut in government expenditures will not necessarily hurt the poor.

In summary, Namibia can afford high social expenditures. Such expenditures are important to enable the poor to benefit from market integration and trade liberalization. However, there are problems of inefficiency and of targeting of the poor. In general, the poor have less access to such facilities as primary schools and clinics/hospitals. Other countries achieve more with lower levels of social expenditure.

Budget deficits have remained at around 5 per cent of GDP over the years, and public debt has increased steadily to around N$4.5 billion in 1999 (equal to 23.5 per cent of GDP). This increasingly limits the freedom of government to spend on poverty alleviation.

The Namibian experience is in line with international experience. There is no *a priori* relationship between fiscal discipline and level of social expenditure. One could even argue that countries which have been able to reduce their fiscal deficits, bring down inflation and achieve macroeconomic stability did not reduce their allocations to social expenditures, while countries with unsustainable fiscal deficits had to cut social expenditure more heavily than others. Political commitment seems to be the decisive determinant of social expenditure (Husain 1996).

Distributional impacts Key channels of the impact of trade liberalization on the poor are their participation in the production process on the one hand, and their consumption structure on the other. There is evidence

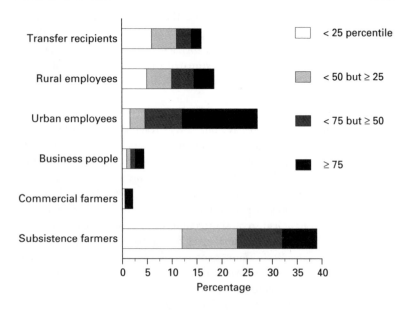

FIGURE 9.6 Percentage of functional groups belonging to certain income
percentiles   *Source*: CSO (1996a)

that the impact of trade liberalization on income depends more on the
household's sector of activity than on the income interval to which it
belongs (Khan 1997). Therefore, functional groups were constructed for
the purposes of this study, based on the 'main source of income' that was
indicated in the NHIES survey. The information available is restricted to
the main sources. This is unsatisfactory in so far as the poor in particular
tend to rely on more than one income source.

We have made a distinction between six functional groups: subsistence
farmers, commercial farmers, business people (urban and rural), urban
employees, rural employees, and recipients of transfers.

Poverty is concentrated among subsistence farmers, who also have the
lowest average income. The other two main pockets of the poor are among
rural employees and transfer recipients. On the other hand, urban employees benefit overwhelmingly from high wages and salaries in the formal
sector, their average income being almost as high as that of business.
Interesting to note is that the percentiles are almost equally represented
within the functional group of rural employees, indicating that poor and
affluent people are similarly represented. The non-poor rural workers are
predominantly formal sector workers, particularly in the mining sector.

TABLE 9.2 Spending of functional groups on different items (%)

	Sub-sistence	Com-mercial	Busi-ness	Urban	Rural	Trans-fer	Total
Education	1.9	5.2	3.0	2.8	2.6	2.3	2.4
Food	57.5	35.6	40.9	35.7	52.8	51.8	49.1
Housing	24.4	22.7	28.5	31.9	20.0	31.1	26.8
Transport and communication	2.6	18.7	9.6	8.8	5.8	3.2	5.4
Clothing	5.4	1.0	6.2	6.3	6.0	3.2	5.4
Other	8.1	16.8	11.8	14.4	12.9	8.4	10.9
Total	100.0	100.0	100.0	100.0	100.0	100.0	100.0

Source: CSO (1996a)

The stark urban–rural differences are exemplified by the fact that urban employees receive wages and salaries that are almost two and a half times higher than those for rural employees. As importantly, there are few urban employees in the poorest quartile, while more than half of them are in the richest.

Households are also affected through their consumption patterns. Table 9.2 shows that rural groups (subsistence farmers and rural employees) spend the most on food in relative terms. These groups will be most affected by price changes in food, unless they are net producers, i.e. they produce more than they consume. In absolute terms, recipients of transfers spend the least (N$274) followed surprisingly by commercial farmers (N$414)[2] and subsistence farmers (N$485), whereas urban employees spend the most (N$1,191). Households dependent on transfers (pensions, cash remittances) will also be hard hit unless they are involved in subsistence farming and are net producers. Net consumers will lose. As expected, urban employees allocate the highest share of all groups on housing, whereas commercial farmers have to spend a good deal of money on transport and communication.

A more detailed breakdown into percentile sub-groups reveals that the lowest percentile group within each functional group always spends the least on education, transport and communication, and clothing, but the most on housing. This indicates that it is income rather than the functional group itself which determines the consumption patterns.

Different population groups are affected in their capacity as participants in the production system as well as consumers. Our presentation will concentrate on the distributional effect of trade liberalization on farmers, but we will also cover business people and urban employees. The reasons for this emphasis on farmers are as follows:

1. Agriculture includes two production sectors that correspond to two functional groups; subsistence farmers and commercial farmers.[3] Subsistence farming is the most important income source for 35 per cent of households in Namibia, and the relative importance of this sector is increasing.
2. For agriculture in particular, it is the functional group to which a household belongs that influences whether it is poor or not. In the poorest 25 per cent of households (lowest quartile), subsistence farming is the main income source for 46 per cent of them. On the other hand, 54 per cent of commercial farmers belong to the richest quartile of the households.

FARMERS According to Table 9.1 above it can be seen that SACU's CETs are higher for manufacturing products than for agricultural products. In a general equilibrium model, one would expect that the removal of all tariffs would lead to a *relative* price increase of agricultural products – as the prices of imported manufactured goods fall more than those of imported agricultural goods – which in the longer run may stimulate the production and growth of agricultural products. This is also what was expected as a result of the Uruguay Round. Industrialized countries such as the USA and members of the EU are committed to reducing their subsidies on food products. One therefore expects an increase in the border (import parity) prices of these goods (Goldin et al. 1993; 1995; FAO 1995; Ingco 1997, 1995).

It is, however, difficult to assess general equilibrium effects without a proper general equilibrium model. Let us rather look more closely at one particular market, the agricultural sector, by applying a partial analysis similar to the approach taken in the rest of the chapter. The unilateral removal of tariffs on agricultural products will lead to a reduction in (absolute) prices (see Table 9.3). Assuming world market prices are given for Namibia, the reduction in domestic prices depends on the size of the trade barriers. Based on a particular formula, SACU imposes an external tariff on white maize and wheat when the US price of yellow maize is lower than a certain level. Currently the tariff is zero.

Article 12 of SACU gives individual member countries a right to protect their agricultural products. Namibia has since the mid-1980s imposed quantitative restrictions on imports of maize and maize products and wheat and wheat products from *all* sources. Imports of white maize and wheat

TABLE 9.3 SACU's current import tariffs and WTO–cereal

Products	Current SACU rates (%)	WTO (bound rate) 2000 (%)
Maize	0 (Formula)	50
Maize flour	5	99
Wheat	0 (Formula)	72
Wheat flour	50	99
Millet	25	43
Sorghum	3	33
Agriculture	8	–

Source: MAWRD (1997)

are not permitted until the entire marketable domestic harvest has been acquired by millers. The factual quantitative restrictions on imports of white maize have only been imposed for a short period, but the potential threats of such restrictions and protections in the milling industry have raised the domestic price of cereals.

The price of white maize is approximately 20 per cent higher than if Namibia has no import controls (and also liberalizes its milling industry), while the price of wheat is between 10 and 23 per cent higher (Division of Agricultural Planning 1997).

Namibia has during the current SACU negotiations suggested a tariffication of its quantitative restrictions. The tariff rates proposed for white maize and maize products are 20 per cent and 30 per cent respectively. Based on the price effect described above and Namibia's position in the SADC negotiations, we therefore assume that the tariff-equivalent of the current quantitative restrictions are in the range between 10 and 30 per cent.[4] Removing these barriers will therefore lead to a similar reduction in producer prices, assuming world market prices are given.[5]

To assess the distributional effects of trade liberalization on the agricultural sector, we analyse the supply responsiveness of farmers in this section. We expect that trade liberalization will result in increases or decreases in the prices of agricultural products. These price effects may create windfall gains or losses respectively. Based on historical data, this section intends to shed some light on how the producers respond to changes in prices (we are unable to control other variables determining farmers' responses). If producers were non-responsive in the past, we may assume the same for the future. Unless farmers respond to price changes through a change in their production, the main effect of trade liberalization

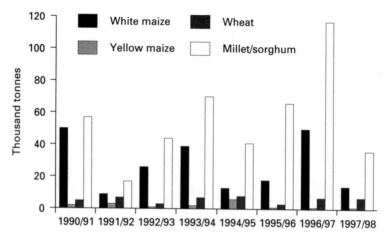

FIGURE 9.7 Cereal production (in tonnes), 1990/91–1997/98
Source: MAWRD (1998)

on the farmers is a distributive one only: this distributive effect depends on whether the farmer is a net producer or a net consumer. Deficit producers will gain (lose) if prices decrease (increase), while surplus producers will lose (gain).

Crops Namibia is a net importer of cereal, which constitutes almost 50 per cent of the total calorie intake in Namibia. On average each person consumes 132kg of cereal per year. For the 1998/99 season, FAO (1999) estimates the import requirement at 155,000 tonnes (mainly maize), or 65 per cent of domestic consumption (estimated at 240,000 tonnes). Removing trade barriers in this sector will reduce the prices of imports of cereal, and thus lead to a reduction in domestic prices. Consumers will gain. At the same time it may influence production. Figure 9.7 gives an overview of total cereal production (in tonnes).

Millet (Mahangu)/sorghum is the most important cereal produced. During the last few years its share of total domestic production of cereal has varied between 60 and 75 per cent. In terms of area planted, its importance is even greater (80–90 per cent). In the communal areas in the north, millet covers 77 per cent of total grain production (CSO 1998). Millet is approximately four or five times more important than sorghum. It is produced only in the northern communal areas, and mainly consumed in rural areas, especially in the north. Millet is preferred by the majority of rural households to maize meal (Keyler 1994). No imports of millet are

TABLE 9.4 Structure of grain production in Namibia: net producers

Production units (hectares)	Number	Grain area
Communal 0–5	89,867	206,944
Communal 6–10	11,490	73,365
Communal 11 +	847	11,704
Emerging commercial	139	11,120
NDC farms (irrigated)	4	1,064
Private dryland	86	12,900
Private irrigated	35	2,800
Sum	102,468	319,897

Source: Division of Agricultural Planning (1997)

registered, but some millet is imported from Angola. Since there are few farms with surplus production of millet, and millet is the common staple food, millet production is generally not traded. According to Keyler (1994), less than 10 per cent of millet production is commercially traded.

The large increase in the price index for sorghum and millet, without any corresponding changes in production and trade of millet (MAWRD 1998: Table 3.2), indicates that the production is inelastic to prices of millet, at least in the short run. But is the production influenced by the prices of other crops?

Liberalization will lead to a lower price of millet, but an even higher reduction in the price of maize since the external tariff of maize is higher than for millet. Since the price of millet reflects the price of maize, an additional second round price effect on millet will occur. One may assume that the cross-price elasticity of supply is non-positive, while the demand cross-price elasticity is positive. If the demand effect is greater than the supply effect, the second order effect is positive and will counterbalance the first order effect of a price reduction. But since these second order effects generally are lower than the first order effects, it is reasonable to assume that the price of millet will decrease. Since only a small portion of millet is traded and production seems to be inelastic to price, at least in the short run, we expect that the effects on producers are minimal.

White maize is the second most important cereal. According to MAWRD (1998: Table 4.7.1), in 1997 72 per cent of white maize production was grown by the commercial sector. The rest was grown by the communal sector in Caprivi and Kavango. Imports of white maize have during the last few years varied between 40,000 and 90,000 tonnes.

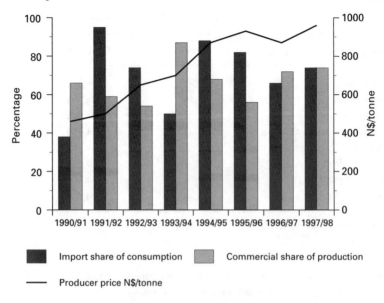

FIGURE 9.8 Sectoral composition and price changes for white maize
Source: MAWRD (1998)

From Figure 9.7 and Figure 9.8 it can also be seen that production, consumption and imports have fluctuated for all the individual categories of cereal, but mainly for millet and white maize. Total consumption or supply (imports and production) of grain also fluctuates.

Table 9.4 illustrates the grain production sector in Namibia. It comprises around 103,000 units. Most grain farmers are very small. Surplus producers constitute only 1 per cent of the farmers, and their grain area constitutes around 10 per cent of the total grain area in Namibia. Except for a small group of large communal farmers (Communal +11 in Table 9.4), deficit producers correspond to communal farmers (or subsistence farmers), while surplus producers correspond to commercial farmers.

By disaggregation between commercial and communal farmers, an indication of the relative responsiveness of the commercial sector to price changes is given in Figure 9.8. The figure indicates absolute price increases, but it appears that no correlation between price and domestic commercial share of production exists. Thus, the commercial sector is neither more nor less price-elastic than the communal sector as far as white maize is concerned. In fact, both sectors' supply is price inelastic (see Figure 9.9). The import share is not determined by price, since it is a residual variable depending on the domestic production.

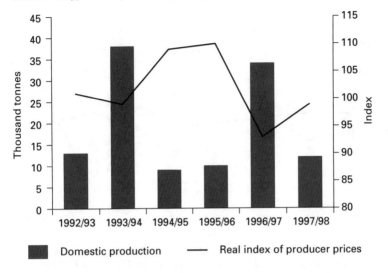

FIGURE 9.9 Correlation between production and real output price indices
for white maize: commercial farmers   *Source*: Namibia Agricultural Union
(1998: Tables 18 and 20)

Although nominal producer prices increased significantly from 1990 to
1997, the real prices do not differ much from the 1992/93 level. Since
farmers have no practicable option other than to sell all their grain on the
domestic market while millers must buy the full domestic marketed harvest
before getting a permit to import, supply is perfectly inelastic. This indicates that commercial farmers do not respond to price changes, at least
in the short run. Since we found that communal and commercial farmers
responded similarly to price changes (see Figure 9.8) and face similar
rules concerning the marketing of the product, this indicates that neither
communal farmers nor commercial farmers seem to respond to price
changes.

Because subsistence farmers are net consumers and do not respond to
price changes, the overall conclusion with respect to cereal is that they will
gain from trade liberalization.[6] The opposite is the case for commercial
farmers.

Livestock Cattle are the most important livestock in Namibia and constitute around 40 per cent of agricultural output. In 1997 the cattle herd
was about 2.1 million, of which 61 per cent was communal. Each year
around 20 per cent of the herd is marketed. Eighty per cent of the
marketed production is exported, mainly to the RSA. The importance of

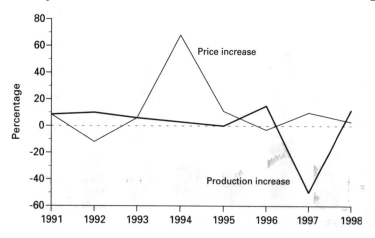

FIGURE 9.10 Growth rates of beef production and producer prices (carcass) in the commercial sector *Source*: Namibia Agricultural Union (1998: Table 4)

the RSA as an export market can be illustrated by the fact that 150,000 live animals are exported annually to the RSA, of which 60 per cent stems from eastern and northern communal areas. In addition 27,000 tonnes of beef is exported to the RSA, both from commercial and communal areas. Namibia has a quota of 13,000 tonnes of beef to the EU, produced solely by commercial farmers.

Beef constitutes around 80 per cent of meat production and is therefore of vital importance to farmers' income. SACU has currently a CET tax on beef of 40 per cent. If Namibia liberalizes, and thereby withdraws from SACU, it may risk South African retaliation with a tariff of 40 per cent. Should this be the case, it would definitely harm all livestock farmers (except the poorest of the poor with few livestock) unless they are able to sell on other markets, increase their production or switch to other activities. However, this does not appear to be a realistic scenario. First of all, if Namibia intends to withdraw from SACU, it has to request temporary adjustment measures in the livestock sector. South Africa on its side will not accept preferential treatment of Namibia without being sure that imported goods are produced in Namibia. If not, there is a risk that Namibia will act as a transit country for goods produced in other countries in order to eliminate tariffs. Namibia must therefore implement strict rules on country of origin. Given such rules, retaliation may undermine SACU's legitimacy towards WTO, and we therefore assume that the external conditions facing livestock producers are the same as under the current trade regime. They may even improve since the relative price of cereal to beef is decreasing, and farmers are net consumers of cereal but net producers of beef. In the following we assume that beef prices *do not decrease.*[7]

Figure 9.10 and Figure 9.11 give an indication of the extent to which beef and mutton producers respond to price changes. If producers are responding to changing prices, we would expect to find a positive relationship between prices and production, indicating an upward-sloping supply curve. Figure 9.10 illustrates the growth rates in beef production and the corresponding growth rates in the average producer price.

Figure 9.10 indicates (1) that no relationship seems to exist between the prices of beef and production, even when we adjust for a time-lag between the two variables. This result was also confirmed by undertaking a regression analysis and conforms to results of other studies (Von Bach et al. 1992). And (2) that there are explanations other than strictly economic reasons for the variation in production (such as drought and the inflexible agricultural system).

An increase in prices of beef and live animals would therefore be most likely to lead to an increase in income for both subsistence and commercial farmers, but would hardly have any effect on production. As opposed to the case of cereal, both groups of farmers may gain from trade liberalization, since one can assume that subsistence farmers are generally surplus producers of livestock.

An extension of cattle farming cannot be expected because land is often already overgrazed and could not cope with a further increase in the number of cattle. The extent of exports of cattle on-the-hoof to the RSA, weaners in particular, underscores the poor soil quality and the difficulties of feeding them in Namibia. Trade liberalization will hardly have any effect on these feeding possibilities. The scarcity of water adds to the limitation. Thus, the supply responsiveness of commercial farmers, although market-oriented and well informed about prices for different kinds of agricultural products, is restricted by natural conditions. Apart from prices and natural conditions, the accessibility of slaughtering facilities influences supply responsiveness, as a study conducted by von Bach et al. (1992) revealed.

Mutton constitutes around 19 per cent of meat production. Figure 9.11 illustrates the growth rates in mutton production and the corresponding growth rates in average producer prices. It is hard to find any particular pattern between prices and production. This indicates an inelastic supply curve, and the conclusions for mutton producers are similar to those derived for beef producers.

In sum, we find little support for the conclusion that trade liberalization through its effects on prices of agricultural products has a substantial

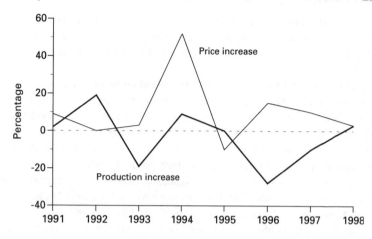

FIGURE 9.11 Growth rates for mutton production and producer prices
Source: Namibia Agricultural Union (1998: Table 4)

impact on agricultural supply. This is also in line with results obtained from other countries (e.g. Wold 1997).

The market does not function; supply is determined by other factors than prices. The responsiveness of farmers is limited by a number of factors. Farmers are able to increase production of agricultural goods or switch from one agricultural activity to another only if the soil and rainfall allow it. Namibia is characterized by arid or semi-arid geographical conditions, rainfall is low and unreliable and the carrying capacity of the soil is poor. Cattle farming is possible in the northern and central regions, while sheep farming is predominant in the south. Since water subsidies will gradually be phased out, the viability of irrigation schemes as an alternative is limited (Auty 1996: 26; NPC 1997). Communal ownership of land implies that the potential for extending plots for crop production or increasing the number of cattle is limited. Furthermore, access to markets, credit and inputs is also restricted (see also Presland and Pomuti 1998: 17). Von Bach et al. (1992: 429) further found that 'none of the trend, climatological or economic variables has a significant effect on cattle numbers and stocking rates in the traditional communal areas'. Thus, it can be assumed that price incentives do not have a major influence on decisions concerning what kind and what quantity of crop to plant.

Since structural rigidities are limiting the potential change in production and the switching to new activities, trade liberalization has minor effects on farmers' efficiency. Changes in prices, however, lead to distributional effects. The effect of decreasing prices of cereal and increasing or stable prices on livestock depend on whether farmers are net producers or not, and on their expenditure pattern on different commodities. The discussion above shows that most farmers are net producers of livestock, and therefore the net effect is positive. Subsistence farmers are, however, net consumers of cereal. Also, in this case trade liberalization will have a positive effect on the poor.

BUSINESS PEOPLE AND URBAN EMPLOYEES   The two functional groups 'business people' and 'urban employees' are discussed together, since distributional impacts are supposed to be similar. However, a distinction has to be made between business and employees in the urban formal sector on the one hand, and business in the small-scale/informal sector and its employees on the other. While the former are sheltered by the CET, the latter operate more closely to market conditions.

In the formal sector, the public sector is large and growing, despite an official freeze in recruiting. Present public employment is estimated at over 78,000 (NEPRU 1999), while the employed labour force amounts to 357,000 (Ministry of Labour 1998: Table 4.2). The parastatal sector, taken over from the pre-independence administration, is also growing. The parastatals have a dominant position in many of the markets in which they operate (Abdel Rahim 1996).

In the private formal sector, manufacturing remains small. Due to the small and dispersed population, the market is dominated by South African firms. The number of companies in most sectors is small and competition is limited. The state of low competition and widespread inefficiency can be explained by the shelter provided by the CET. The market structure can be classified as somewhat oligopolistic, or even monopolistic, ensuring rents for companies cushioned in a sheltered environment. For example, an analysis of the Namibian banking sector shows that profitability is very high compared to the ratios achieved in South Africa (returns on assets and equity being twice as high), and also relatively high in comparison with Botswana. This can be explained by risk-adverse attitudes in a protected environment, higher charges and lower expenditures. Indicators point to a lack of competition in the banking sector (NEPRU and Trendline 1998).

As shown in Figure 9.6, urban employees are the second most important functional group, with a quarter of households (business people amount to only 4 per cent). It is significant that more than half of the urban employees are in the highest quarter of incomes. These two indicators show both the large size of the formal sector and its high average income level. Both are atypical of SSA countries.

Also distinguishing it from other countries, Namibia's economy is highly formalized and highly integrated into the South African economy. The informal, small enterprise sector remains small and trade-oriented: 70–90 per cent provide services. While in other SSA countries small enterprises (with fewer than ten workers) consistently provide more than half of industrial employment, in Namibia this share is 12 per cent (Hansohm 1996: 9). Informal sector workers often combine this work with other activities. Those who do so are often not classified as 'urban employees' (but under their major activity).

Figures on wages in Namibia are incomplete. They seem to indicate that incomes in the public sector are slightly lower than those in the private sector, but those in parastatals surpass all by far (74 per cent more than those of private limited companies, and 5.8 times as high as incomes in agriculture; MLHRD 1994: 99). Incomes in the informal sector vary greatly, but are generally lower than those in the 'formal sector'. This is corroborated by the view of most small entrepreneurs that they are rather 'pushed' to self-employment by a lack of alternatives, and prefer wage employment (Hansohm 1996: 14–15; MTI 1999b). Workers in the informal sector are not strongly organized as an interest group, and their wages are largely market-determined and probably stagnating.

Since independence, income disparities both between informal and formal sector participants and within the formal sector have probably widened, as most wage agreements provided for percentage increases. Figures on recent wage agreements suggest that the labour costs in the formal sector in Namibia, at least in the higher echelons, are increasing faster than the inflation rate, and higher than the opportunity cost of labour.

As the labour market is not unduly regulated (there is no minimum wage, although this has been discussed), a main factor determining high labour costs is the strong influence of the trade unions in the formal sector (public and private). Half of the labour force in mining, 40 per cent in public administration, and more than half in education and health provision are unionized (Ministry of Labour 1998). The trade unions are very vocal and influential, not least because of their close link to the ruling party. As they largely represent the relatively highly-paid employees of the public sector and large private firms, Namibia conforms to the picture of a 'labour aristocracy' (Arrighi 1973), rather than that of an 'informalization' of the labour market. The dualism is enforced by the highly different rates of participation in the social security system. While overall half of the labour force is registered, only 20 per cent of subsistence farmers (without paid employees) are registered, compared with 84 per cent of urban employees (Ministry of Labour 1998).

TABLE 9.5 Wages in Southern African countries

	Semi-skilled	Skilled	Managers
Botswana	100	600	1,000
Lesotho	97	–	–
Kenya	40	90	160
Malawi	33	–	–
South Africa	350	–	–
Zimbabwe	65	500	1,000
Namibia	277	1,111	1,944

Source: Ministry of Trade and Industry (1994)

The shaky figures on regional comparisons of labour costs (see Table 9.5) suggest that wages may be uncompetitively high in Namibia. This can partly be explained by the shelter provided by trade barriers, and partly by the character of the capital-intensive mature mining sector. The effects amount to a bias against labour and towards capital, and to a redistribution from those working under little protection to those who are highly protected. Trade liberalization will threaten these rents through more international competition, owing to lower tariffs resulting in pressure on wages and salaries, or even in retrenchments. Furthermore, the limited flexibility of the formal labour market and skills shortages will limit the responsiveness of employees to trade liberalisation.

On the other hand, companies already confronted with world-wide competition will be better off when it comes to their adaptability to changing environments. They could even benefit from new markets opening up due to trade liberalization. However, international competition will steadily force companies to increase productivity and effectiveness with impacts on the number of employees and their remuneration.

On the positive side, imported inputs for industries (either directed at the domestic or the world market) will become cheaper. Because of the import intensity of industries this is an important impact. Food and other consumption goods will become cheaper (under the present system the poor do not benefit from subsidized food), which is also an important impact with respect to poverty alleviation. Again, because of the import intensity of the consumption basket of even the poor, this impact is considerable.

Conclusion

The analysis shows that trade liberalization can be expected to lead to higher growth. Namibia conforms to the typical SSA picture of low growth and high trade barriers, which are claimed to be causally linked (Sachs and Warner 1997; Ng and Yeats 1997, 1999). The key channel is cheaper imports which stimulate exports and boost incomes of consumers. As in many other African countries, trade liberalization would contribute to a more equal income distribution, as the main losers on the income side are those in the formal urban sector (business and employees in these firms and in the public sector), who generally do not belong to the poor.

On the downside, the evidence shows that the distributional impact is significant as compared to the efficiency and growth gains. This goes some way towards explaining the seeming paradox of the resistance to trade liberalization in the presence of both low growth and high barriers (a point emphasized by Rodrik 1998).

A major impact of trade liberalization would be fiscal; 30 per cent of Namibia's taxes are on foreign trade. The loss of these taxes puts pressure on the high social expenditure, and is thus anti-poor. However, the negative impact is qualified by the overly high level of present taxation (which implies that one should not aim to replace current taxes fully), and the exceptionally high social expenditure with limited efficiency. Examples indicate possibilities of both streamlining the budget and increasing the impact of social expenditure on poverty (Husain 1996).

The gains from trade liberalization are not as clearly positive as in other countries. On the positive side, many of the rural poor (the subsistence farmers) will gain from lower grain prices, as they are net consumers of grain. At the same time, the commercial grain farmers will lose (this will have some anti-poor impact, as far as the agricultural workers are concerned). Concerning beef, the most important agricultural product, both subsistence and commercial farmers will gain as net producers from prices increasing relative to cereals.

However, on the production side, the analysis has shown that the agricultural sector, which has the largest number of poor, faces severe obstacles to gaining from trade liberalization. First, strong supporting measures are necessary in order to enable the poor to benefit (e.g. marketing, extension services). Second, even in the presence of such measures, the limits to growth in agricultural output and productivity are narrow because of inherent constraints (rainfall, soil). For this reason, a key measure to alleviate poverty in Namibia would be a bundle of measures to assist the rural poor to switch their activities to non-agricultural areas.

Last, though not least, one conclusion is obvious from this analysis: the need for a system of comprehensive and timely economic statistics as a basis for a more detailed policy analysis and subsequent appropriate economic policy.

Notes

Contributions of Lesley Blaauw and Daniel Motinga to the initial draft are acknowledged. We thank the participants of the workshops 'The Role of the State in Poverty Alleviation II' (18–22 September 1998, Cape Town), 'Policy, Poverty and Inequality in Namibia. The Cases of Trade Policy and Land Policy' (12 August 1999, Windhoek) and 'Poverty and Migration in Namibia' (19–20 August 1999, Bergen) for constructive comments, especially the discussants Camilo Perez-Bustillo, Neil McCulloch and Stefan de Vylder, as well as Hildegunn Nordas, Robin Sherbourne, Inge Tvedten, Wolfgang Werner, Francis Wilson and colleagues at NEPRU.

1. Traditional non-tariff barriers are defined as barriers to trade which can be addressed by means of changes in government legislation, regulations and procedures. Non-traditional non-tariff barriers are, for example, the perception of traders; the capacity of trade promotion agencies; limited information on trade opportunities, etcetera.

2. This figure could be explained by the small number of households belonging to this group. Extremely low figures given by a few respondents influence the mean value markedly.

3. Agricultural workers are included in rural workers.

4. Low (1994a) refers to pre-Uruguay Round tariff equivalents of 120 per cent and 68 per cent for wheat and maize respectively, indicating that our estimates are biased downwards.

5. Low (1994b) assumes that prices of maize will reduce by 30 per cent if Namibia deregulates its maize sector.

6. Currently the protection of domestic white maize production is mainly politically motivated: the potential for riots among producers in Caprivi. The government is not as concerned about what could happen in the commercial sector. It may, for instance, be the case that farm workers would be sacked.

7. We analyse the case in which they increase, because this is the most interesting.

Abbreviations

ASD	Additional Sales Duty
BLS	Botswana, Lesotho and Swaziland
BoN	Bank of Namibia
CBI	Cross-border Initiative
CBS	Central Bureau of Statistics
CET	Common External Tariff
CMA	Common Monetary Area
COMESA	Common Market for Eastern and Southern Africa
CROP	Comparative Research on Poverty
CSO	Central Statistics Office

EU	European Union
FAO	Food and Agriculture Organization
FDI	Foreign Direct Investment
FTA	Free Trade Area
GDP	Gross Domestic Product
GNP	Gross National Product
GST	General Sales Tax
IMF	International Monetary Fund
MAWRD	Ministry of Agriculture, Water and Rural Development
MLHRD	Ministry of Labour and Human Resources Development
MoL	Ministry of Labour
MTI	Ministry of Trade and Industry
NAMAC	Macro-economic model for Namibia
NDP1	National Development Plan 1
NEPRU	Namibia Economic Policy Research Unit
NHIES	National Household Income and Expenditure Survey
NPC	National Planning Commission
RoN	Republic of Namibia
RSA	Republic of South Africa
SACU	Southern African Customs Union
SADC	Southern African Development Community
SSA	Sub-Saharan Africa
UNDP	United Nations Development Programme
WTO	World Trade Organization

References

Abdel Rahim, Aisha (1996) *Review of Public Enterprises and Parastatal Bodies in Namibia* Research Report 14 (September) Windhoek: NEPRU.

Arrighi, Giovanni (1973) 'International Corporations, Labour Aristocracies, and Economic Development in Tropical Africa', in Giovanni Arrighi and John S. Saul (eds), *Essays on the Political Economy of Africa*, New York: Monthly Press Review, pp. 105–51.

Auty, Richard M. (1996) *Namibia: Achieving Sustainable Development.* Draft (January).

Bank of Namibia (BoN), various Annual Reports.

Central Bureau of Statistics (CBS) (1998) *National Accounts 1982–1997.* Windhoek: CBS.

Central Statistics Office (CSO) (1996a) *Data Set of the 1993/94 Namibia Household Income and Expenditure Survey.* Windhoek: CSO.

— (1996b) *Living Conditions in Namibia. The 1993/94 Namibia Household Income and Expenditure Survey.* Main report. Windhoek: CSO.

— (1998) *1996/97 Annual Agricultural Survey, Basic Analysis of Communal Agriculture.* Windhoek: CSO.

Division of Agricultural Planning (1997) *Food Security or Food Self-sufficiency for Namibia? The Background and a Review of the Economic Policy Implications.* Discussion Paper 1. Windhoek: MAWRD.

Edwards, S. (1997) *Openness, Productivity and Growth: What do We Really Know?*, NBER Working Paper no. 5978.

FAO (1995) *Impact of the Uruguay Round on Agriculture*. Rome: FAO.

— (1999) *Food Supply Situation and Crop Prospects in Sub-Saharan Africa*, 1 (April).

Goldin, Ian and D. Van der Mensbrugghe (1995) 'The Uruguay Round: An Assessment of Economy-wide and Agricultural Reforms', in W. M Martin and L. A. Winters (eds), *The Uruguay Round and the Developing Economies*. World Bank Discussion Paper no. 307. Washington, DC: World Bank.

Goldin, Ian, O. Knudsen and D. Van der Mensbrugghe (1993) *Trade Liberalisation: Global Economic Implications*. Paris and Washington, DC: OECD and World Bank.

Hansohm, Dirk (1996) *The State of the Informal Sector in Namibia: Role, Characteristics and Prospects*. Working Paper no. 49 (May), Windhoek: NEPRU.

Hansohm, Dirk and C. Presland (1997) 'Poverty, Inequality and Policy in Namibia. The State of Knowledge and the Way Ahead in Poverty Research', in *In Search of Research. Approaches to Socio-Economic Issues in Contemporary Namibia*. Windhoek: NEPRU, pp. 51–102.

Husain, Ishrat (1996) 'Globalization and Liberalization: An Opportunity to Reduce Poverty', in *Globalization and Liberalization: Effects of International Economic Relations on Poverty*. New York and Geneva: UNCTAD, pp. 129–48.

Ingco, Merlinda D. (1995) *Agricultural Trade Liberalization in the Uruguay Round. One Step Forward, One Step Back?* Policy Research Working Paper 1500. Washington, DC: World Bank.

— (1997) *Has Agricultural Trade Liberalization Improved Welfare in the Least-Developed Countries? Yes*. Policy Research Working Paper 1748 (April). Washington, DC: World Bank.

Keyler, S. (1994) 'Informal and Commercial Millet Marketing in Ovambo and Kavango', in *Second National Pearl Millet Workshop: Proceedings of a Workshop 7–8 November 1994*. Bulawayo: ICRISAT.

Khan, Farida C. (1997) 'Household Disaggregation', in Joseph F. Francois and Kenneth A. Reinert (eds), *Applied Methods for Trade Policy Analysis: A Handbook*. Cambridge and New York: Cambridge University Press, pp. 300–27.

Lipton, Michael and Martin Ravallion (1995) 'Poverty and Policy', in J. Behrman and T. N. Srinivasan (eds), *Handbook of Development Economics*, Vol. 3. Amsterdam: Elsevier, pp. 2551–657.

Low, Allan (1994a) *GATT: Effects and Consequences for Namibia*. Paper presented at Bank Windhoek/AGRECONA Agricultural Outlook Conference, 10 March 1994.

— (1994b) 'Linkages between Maize Marketing Margins, Household Food Security and Mahangu Production', in *Second National Pearl Millet Workshop: Proceedings of a Workshop, 7–8 November 1994*. Bulawayo: ICRISAT.

Ministry of Agriculture, Water and Rural Development (MAWRD) (1997) *Grain Production Models and Policy Support Impact Analysis*. Mimeo: Directorate of Planning,

— (1998) *Agricultural Statistics Bulletin* (August). Windhoek: MAWRD.

Ministry of Labour and Human Resource Development (MLHRD) (1994) *Employment Structure and Wage Levels in Namibia. A Report Based on Establishment Survey 1992/93* (August). Windhoek: MLHRD.

Ministry of Labour (MoL) (1998) *The Namibia Labour Force Survey 1997: An Interim Report of Analysis*. (October). Windhoek: MoL and the Central Bureau of Statistics of the National Planning Commission.

Ministry of Trade and Industry (1994) *Trade Policy Reform Study*. Windhoek: unpublished (June).

— (1999a) *Review of the White Paper on Industrial Development of 1992* (March). Windhoek: MTI.

— (1999b) *The 1999 Small Business Baseline Survey, Erongo and Otjozondjupa*. Final draft report (May). Windhoek: MTI.

Mupotola-Sibongo, Moono (1997) *Effects of Liberalisation on Beef and Maize Sectors in Five SADC Countries*. NEPRU Working Paper no. 57 (April).

Namibia Agricultural Union (1998) *Agricultural Statistics – March 1998 Financial Position of Farmers*. Windhoek: NAU.

Namibian Economic Policy Research Unit (NEPRU) (1995) *Commercialisation of Agricultural Services in Communal Areas* (May). Windhoek: NEPRU.

— (1999) *Namibia: Economic Review and Prospects 1998/99*. Windhoek: NEPRU.

Namibian Economic Policy Research Unit (NEPRU) and Trendline (1998) *Namibia: Financial Services and the GATS*. Paper prepared for the Co-ordinated African Programme of Assistance on Services (CAPAS), July.

National Planning Commission (NPC) (1997) *Poverty Reduction Strategy*. Windhoek: NPC.

Ng, Francis and Alexander Yeats (1997) 'Open Economies Work Better! Did Africa's Protectionist Policies Cause Its Marginalization in World Trade?', *World Development*, 25, 6, pp. 889–904.

— (1999) *Good Governance and Trade Policy. Are They the Keys to Africa's Global Integration and Growth?* Policy Research Working Paper 2038 (January). Washington, DC: World Bank.

Oyejide, Ademola (1998) 'Trade Policy and Regional Integration in the Development Context: Emerging Patterns Issues and Lessons for Sub-Saharan Africa', *Journal of African Economies*, 7, 1, pp. 108–45.

Presland, Cathy and Akiser Pomuti (1998) *The Market for Millet and Millet Products*. NEPRU Working Paper no. 63 (September).

Republic of Namibia (RoN) (1998) *Poverty Reduction Strategy for Namibia*. Windhoek: Ministry of Finance.

— (1999) *Budget Statement For the 1999/00 Financial Year*, 7 (April).

Rodrik, Dani (1995) 'Getting Interventions Right: How South Korea and Taiwan Grew Rich', *Economic Policy: A European Forum*, pp. 53–97.

— (1998) 'Why is Trade Reform so Difficult in Africa?' *Journal of African Studies*, 7, 1, pp. 43–69.

Sachs, Jeffrey D. and Andrew M. Warner (1995) 'Economic Reform and the Process of Global Integration', *Brooking Papers on Economic Activity*, 1 (August), pp. 1–118.

— (1997) 'Sources of Slow Growth in African Economies', *Journal of African Economies*, 6, 3, pp. 335–76.

Schade, Klaus, Mary Hansen, Dirk Hansohm, Daniel Motinga and Anna Erastus Sacharia (1998) *Overview of Poverty in Namibia*. Namibia: NEPRU.

Sharer, Robert (1998) *Africa, Regionalism and Globalism*. Paper presented to the Seminar on Regional Integration and Globalization, Windhoek, 10–13 June.

Stolper, Wolfgang F. and Paul A. Samuelson (1941) 'Protection and Real Wages', *Review of Economic Studies*, 9, pp. 58–73.

Taylor, L., E. Bacha, E. A. Cardoso, and F. J. Lysy (1980) *Models of Growth and Distribution for Brazil*. Oxford: Oxford University Press.

UNCTAD (1996) *Globalization and Liberalization: Effects of International Economic Relations on Poverty*. New York and Geneva: UNCTAD.

UNDP (1996) *Namibia. Human Development Report 1996*. Windhoek: UNDP.

— (1997) *Namibia. Human Development Report 1997*. Windhoek: UNDP.

— (1998) *Namibia. Human Development Report 1998*. Windhoek: UNDP.

von Bach, Helmke Sartorius, Johan van Zyl and Nick Vink (1992) 'Empirical Information on Beef Production in Regions of Namibia as an Aid to Restructuring the Livestock Farming Industry Along Equitable Lines', *Development Southern Africa*, 9, 4 (November).

Wold, Bjorn K. (ed.) (1997) *Supply Response in a Gender-Perspective. The Case of Structural Adjustment in Zambia*. Oslo: Statistics Norway.

Wood, Adrian and Kersti Berge (1997) 'Exporting Manufactures: Human Resources, Natural Resources, and Trade Policy', *Journal of Development Studies*, 34, 1, pp. 35–59.

World Bank (1993) *Namibia. Reassessing Namibia's Membership of the Southern Africa Customs Union*. 16 August. Washington, DC: World Bank.

— (1995) *Namibia. Public Expenditure Review*. Report no. 13558–NAM, July.

— (1998) *Trade and Trade Regimes in the SADC Region*. Progress report. 19 June.

— (1999) *World Development Report 1998/99*. Washington, DC: World Bank.

World Trade Organization (WTO) (1998) *Trade Policy Review Namibia*. Report by the Secretariat. Geneva: WTO.

10

The State and Poverty Reduction Policies in Zimbabwe, 1980–97

Brian Raftopoulos

As it has become increasingly clear that Structural Adjustment Programmes (SAPs) in Africa have further marginalized large sections of urban and rural producers, 'Poverty Alleviation' has re-emerged as a buzz-word in international development discourse. The 1997 UNDP *Human Development Report* has noted that sub-Saharan Africa has the highest proportion of people, and the fastest growth, in human poverty, with some 200 million people considered income poor. Furthermore, the report predicts that by the year 2000 'half the people in Sub-Saharan Africa will be in income poverty'. Globally the rate of income inequality has also seen a marked increase, with the share of the poorest 20 per cent of the world's population in global income declining from 2.3 per cent in 1960, to 1.4 per cent in 1991, and reaching 1.1 per cent in 1997.[1]

Under such conditions both national governments and international financial institutions have become concerned with both the economic and political implications of the SAPs. As Mkandawire has written:

> Whatever theoretical conclusions on the impact of SAP on equity and social being are reached, the politically most important issues are the lived experiences of the main stakeholders – the majority of Africans. These have witnessed deteriorating living standards both before and after SAPS and they have lived under conditions where the end of shortages due to trade liberalisation has been accompanied by even greater polarisation of consumption styles.[2]

This chapter seeks to trace the record of the postcolonial state in Zimbabwe on poverty reduction issues, given the background of the rhetoric of the liberation movement, and the 'socialist' pronouncements of the 1980s. The chapter also seeks to understand the responses of urban and rural producers to state policies in this area over the period 1980 to 1997. Out of such an analysis it is our intention to develop an overview of the current balance of social and political forces in Zimbabwe in the face of the increasing impoverishment of the working majority. At the outset it should be noted that this chapter will not deal with the Indigenization Debate in Zimbabwe as this has been examined elsewhere.[3]

The Place of Poverty Reduction Policies in the Politics of the Zimbabwean State: 1980–90

By the late 1970s, on the eve of the independence settlement, the discourse of the liberation movements was often punctuated by a general, populist and imprecise commitment to redistributive policies. Such pronouncements were often couched in a vague socialist rhetoric that had more to do with perceptions of international alliances and tactical political gains, than with hegemonically related party structures geared to such radical outcomes.[4]

With the establishment of political independence in 1980, the government developed the policy of 'national reconciliation', which in economic terms sought to ensure a continuity of production structures, while improving the conditions of the majority of blacks neglected during the colonial period. Confronted with the dilemma of a highly expectant mass support base eagerly in search of a more equitable share of the national cake, the new Zimbabwean state sought high economic growth rates, increased incomes and social expenditures and the promotion of rural development. The first economic policy document of the new government, *Growth with Equity*, was published in February 1981.

In this document the rationale for equity concerns was made clear:

> economic exploitation of the majority by the few, the grossly uneven infrastructure and productive development of the rural and urban and distribution sectors, the imbalanced levels of development within and among sectors and the consequent grossly inequitable pattern of income distribution and of benefits to the overwhelming majority of this country, stand as a serious indictment of our society.[5]

Moreover, the first Minister of Economic Planning and Development stated that: 'our development strategy goes beyond the mere increase in the material wealth of society. Equity in the distribution of wealth and income is one of the cornerstones of our economic policy.'[6]

The broad objectives of *Growth with Equity* were defined as follows:

a) The establishment of a socialist society.
b) Rapid economic growth.
c) Balanced development and equitable distribution of income and productive resources.

d) Economic restructuring.
e) Development of human resources.
f) Rural development.
g) Worker participation.
h) Development of economic infrastructure and social services.
i) Fiscal and monetary reform.

Following the *Growth with Equity* document, the government launched the Transitional National Development Plan (TNDP), which was supposed to achieve the objectives set out in the former document. The TNDP 'was intended to provide a programme for transition from the war economy to a normal situation, and to allow the development of an appropriate planning infrastructure'.[7]

The TNDP was based on an economic growth rate of 8.2 per cent per annum, for the period from 1982 to 1985. The revenues from this high growth were to be used for redistribution in the form of a reoriented public sector expenditure. The first decade of independence indeed witnessed a rapid growth of social services for the neglected majority in Zimbabwe. Real per capita state recurrent expenditure for the Ministry of Health and Child Welfare rose from Z$10.25 million in 1980 to a peak of Z$14.78 million in 1990. In the area of education, real per capita government recurrent expenditure rose from Z$29.55 million in 1980 to Z$38.91 million 1989.[8] In the primary school sector the number of schools rose from 3,161 in 1980 to 4,530 in 1990, an increase of 43.3 per cent. The number of pupils enrolled increased from 1,235,994 in 1980 to 2,294,934 in 1991.[9] At the secondary level the number of schools rose from 197 in 1980 to 1,512 in 1990, with enrolment figures increasing from 73,105 in 1980 to 710,619 in 1990.[10]

This impressive expansion in social services thus underlined the state's commitment to the following: support for policies that identified equity and the need to develop human resources; allocation of substantial budgetary resources towards social sectors; and the utilization of aid funds for the development of key social sectors.[11]

In terms of the land question, by the end of the 1980s, the state had acquired over 3 million hectares of land for distribution, with over 44 per cent of this land in the dry and infertile Natural Regions IV and V. As a percentage of its overall expenditure, government expenditure on agriculture increased until 1987/88, after which there was a decline.[12] During this period the government land policy has been described as 'cautious and conservative', avoiding laws on farm sub-divisions and a land tax as a stimulant for the break-up of large-scale commercial farmers, which would have made available more land for redistribution. However, even where land was purchased, it was not fully utilized, with over 235,000 hectares of land acquired for resettlement not being used by 1990.[13] By the end of the 1980s the land policy in Zimbabwe was described as follows:

> Little emphasis was given to the need to address the land question within the context of developing national democracy and national reconciliation, in the early nation-building agendas in Zimbabwe. Rather land reforms were generally perceived to be an invidious 'political balancing act' played by the Zimbabwe state under Mugabe, in an attempt to address what tended to be received as 'irrational' political demands, which it was thought were subsidiary to the need to promote development.[14]

Indeed, for much of the 1980s while the Zimbabwean state proceeded cautiously on the land question, there was little autonomous organizational pressure from the rural poor and landless for more substantive land reforms. The National Farmers Association in Zimbabwe (NFAZ), established in 1980 to represent communal farmers, proved a weak force in the 1980s. The Zimbabwe National Farmers Union (ZNFU) established in 1980, represented the more successful, small-scale farming elite. Prior to 1980, the ZNFU was known as the African Farmers Union and represented the 9,500 African Purchase Area farmers who had been allowed to purchase freehold title during the settler-colonial regime. The ZNFU and the NFAZ amalgamated in 1991 to form the Zimbabwe Farmers Union (ZFU). While the ZNFU had more lobbying impact than the NFAZ in the 1980s, both were largely subordinated to the lobbying dominance of the white-led Commercial Farmers Union (CFU). The formal representation of the rural poor, the landless and the small-scale farmer was largely organized through the constituency politics of ZANU PF. Moreover, policy demands were also pursued at an informal level, by the marginalized constituencies, through strategies such as 'squatting', national resource poaching, and pressures on Members of Parliament.[15]

Pressures exerted through decentralization of local government structures have also been limited. In 1984 and 1985, the *Prime Minister's Directive on Decentralisation* provided for the establishment of representation at village, ward, district and provincial levels. These various levels were to be represented as follows. Village development committees (VIDCOs) were to be elected bodies, given the responsibility of identifying needs at a local level. Decisions made at this level were then to be passed on to ward development committees consisting of VIDCO representatives from six villages, which would then pass on local needs to the district council and then to the more powerful provincial councils. This attempt at providing a focus for more localized decision-making has proved problematic for several reasons. These include the continued domination of central government, particularly at provincial level; the proclivity of small elites to 'represent' local interests; poor planning skills at local levels; the continued influence of traditional leaders; and the ever present role of the ruling party.[16]

In terms of urban labour, the 1980s also provided both opportunities and constraints, in terms of poverty issues. During the first five years of the postcolonial period, the state developed a state corporatist strategy which took the form of a loose pact between the state, the national labour centre and capital, mainly on the issue of the repression of strikes. However, this pact did not necessarily include individual unions.[17] During this period the state co-opted the labour movement leadership and intervened in the formation of the Zimbabwe Congress of Trade Unions (ZCTU), because of the absence of a central labour body to control the widespread activity during the years 1980–82. Sachikonye observes that the corporatist arrangement which emerged during this period was fragile and 'not the result of a consensus between the state and industrial union leadership and employer interest'.[18] He also notes that the state was compelled to intervene in the manner that it did 'because the bourgeoisie lacked the organisational cohesion and political strength to negotiate with organised labour'.[19]

However, the strategy towards labour on the part of the state was not only based on control but, as with even a loose corporatist arrangement, on some measure of protection. This took the form of several forms of legislation. First, the Minimum Wages Act 1980, which was a political response to the strike activity during the period 1980–82, but which also involved the state in the setting of wage levels for low-income workers. Second, the Employment Act of 1980 which attempted to restrain dismissals in the private sector. Complementing this was the Employment (Conditions of Service) Regulations 1981, which prohibited the retrenchment of workers from employment without the approval of the Minister of Labour. The organizational rights of unions, workers' committees, works councils, national employment councils and national employment boards were also spelt out in the Labour Relations Act 1985. However, this Act also severely restricted the right of trade unions to strike, emphasizing the state's major objectives of control.

In terms of the incomes of labour, the lack of a coherent incomes policy has resulted in the lack of growth of real incomes for the labour sector. Shadur shows that while real wages increased in mining, industry and commerce up to 1982, they then declined to below the 1980 level by 1987. In the lowest wage sectors of agricultural and domestic workers, wages increased above 1980 levels for most of the 1980s, but did not reach the Poverty Datum line set by the Riddell Commission (1981). Shadur

TABLE 10.1 Trends in average real annual consumption earnings, 1980–94 (indices)

Sector	1980	1982	1984	1986	1988	1990	1992	1994
Agriculture	100.0	160.3	138.6	130.4	130.3	130.1	69.7	76.0
Mining	100.0	127.2	108.5	110.0	112.5	116.6	97.3	89.4
Manufacturing	100.0	113.7	98.2	97.4	101.2	102.9	82.8	89.6
Electricity	100.0	104.5	95.6	95.3	97.1	95.2	82.8	89.6
Construction	100.0	114.5	104.1	93.4	83.6	77.0	56.2	47.5
Finance	100.0	101.7	83.9	88.0	92.9	94.5	92.2	80.1
Distribution	100.0	116.6	89.3	88.7	88.0	84.1	70.0	57.6
Transport	100.0	107.4	77.6	77.8	81.1	91.2	66.7	61.2
Pub. admin.	100.0	87.4	64.1	60.3	62.1	60.5	41.2	34.9
Education	100.0	85.8	66.8	69.9	76.9	81.8	64.2	48.5
Health	100.0	100.2	77.0	81.3	80.8	89.8	67.8	55.7
Domestics	100.0	111.8	79.7	94.8	91.6	81.6	48.2	30.9
Other services	100.0	104.5	82.9	76.9	75.7	80.0	61.5	55.0
Total	100.0	119.7	97.5	97.4	100.8	102.9	78.0	67.4

Source: G. Kanyenze (1996), *Labour Markets and Employment During ESAP*, Harare.

concludes that statutory minimum wage adjustments for much of the 1980s did not result in the increase of real wages of all low-income workers nor did it result in the narrowing of the income gap.[20] Kanyenze[21] also shows (see Table 10.1) that in almost all sectors of the economy, real average consumption earnings declined substantively between 1990 and 1994. As a result of decreasing incomes, the growth of a more autonomous labour movement and the move towards Structural Adjustment Policies in the late 1980s, the fragile corporatist pact between the state and labour broke down from the mid-1980s to the early 1990s.

To summarize this section on the 1980s, the following observations can be made. For much of the 1980s the state attempted to address poverty issues through a number of strategies, including a welfarist social expenditure programme, increased expenditure in the agricultural sector and limited land reforms, and attempts at minimum wage regulation. By the end of the 1980s all these strategies had began to show their limitations. With regard to the welfarist strategy, as Jenkins has concluded, constraints on growth meant that living standards would not rise, and additionally any hope of a trickle-down effect for the poorest, could not be achieved.[22]

For the marginalized groups in the rural and urban areas, the end of the 1980s found them still on the periphery of the policy-making process, with a limited organizational capacity to press their demands on poverty issues. In the rural sector the ruling party tended to dominate constituency issues, leaving little room for autonomous organizational interventions. In the urban sector, the labour movement found itself on a collision course with the state, and on the borders of the policy-making process. Opposition of the labour movement to the move towards the one-party state, its critique of the intended Structural Adjustment Programme, and the general attempt by the movement to develop an autonomous, critical presence, found little favour with the authoritarian style of the ruling party.

The 1990s: The Period of Structural Adjustment

The introduction of the Economic Structural Adjustment Programme (ESAP) in 1990 was intended to shift the balance of forces in the economy, from a significant degree of state intervention to a greater reliance on market forces. The strategy sought to establish a more balanced macroeconomic framework, to achieve more efficiency in relative prices and resource allocation, and to curtail declining terms of trade and inflationary pressures. The major targets set by ESAP included:

- an increased average economic growth rate of 5 per cent per annum
- a rise in investment levels to 25 per cent of GDP
- An increase in savings to a level of 25 per cent of GDP
- an export growth rate of 9 per cent per annum
- a reduction of the budget deficit from 10.4 per cent to 5 per cent of GDP
- reduced rate of inflation from 17.7 per cent in 1990 to 10 per cent over the ESAP period
- reduction of the civil service by 25 per cent
- removal of direct subsidies from Z$629 million in 1990/91 to Z$60 million over the adjustment period
- liberalization of trade
- establishment of the Social Development Fund (SDF)[23]

For the marginalized working groups the experience of ESAP has, according to available indications, increased levels of poverty, as we discuss below.

The changing conditions of labour and the response of the labour movement An ILO study has noted that the Structural Adjustment Programme has affected urban households most severely in Zimbabwe, as a result of declining real wages, declining formal sector employment levels, the decreasing investment in education and health coupled with cost

TABLE 10.2 Trends in rates of growth in employment for before and during economic reforms, 1981–94

Sector	1981–84	1985–90	1991–94
Tradables *of which:*	-2.9	1.5	1.7
agriculture	-4.5	1.2	2.8
mining	-4.6	-0.9	0.7
manufacturing	1.2	2.9	0.4
Non-trades *of which:*	.0	4.0	2.1
electricity	2.2	3.0	-0.1
construction	2.1	9.2	3.2
finance	5.9	2.0	5.7
distribution	.4	.1	2.4
transport and communications	2.4	1.0	-0.2
Other sectors:			
public administration	7.1	0.8	-4.6
education	-2.4	4.3	1.1
health	6.0	3.9	0.9
domestics	0.7	0.7	0.0
other services	-2.9	5.1	5.8
Total	3.0	2.4	1.4

Source: G. Kanyenze (1996), *Labour Markets and Employment During ESAP*, Harare.

recovery measures in these areas.[24] The low-income consumer price index rose from 361.9 in 1990, to 453.6 in 1991 and 741.2 in 1992, while real average earnings decreased from Z$8,600 per annum in 1990 to Z$6,700 in 1992, with current levels equivalent to the 1970 standards.[25] The inflation rate rose from 16.1 per cent in 1990 to 23.3 per cent in 1991 and 42.1 per cent in 1992. The inflation rate for lower-income urban household was 47 per cent in 1992, while the figure for higher income households was 35.9 per cent.[26] In general, indicators for inflation, employment and real average earnings between 1991 and 1994 show signs of deterioration.[27]

For example, as Table 10.2 shows, total employment has decreased from an average growth rate of 2.7 per cent in the period 1981–90, to 1.4 per cent during the years 1991–94.

Declines in social service expenditure have also contributed to the deteriorating conditions of labour. From 1990/91 to 1995/96, spending on education declined by 30 per cent as a proportion of the government's total budget. Similarly, in health, expenditure declined from 18 per cent of the government's budget in 1990/91 to approximately 15 per cent in 1994/95.[28] In terms of expenditure on food, a study of a relatively well-off, middle-income site-and-service suburb in Harare carried out in 1992 indicated that such expenditure has declined by 5 per cent for the top 25 per cent income earners, and 23 per cent for the bottom 25 per cent wage-earners. Moreover, most households interviewed were eating fewer or cheaper cuts of meat, and reducing their intake of chicken, fruit and eggs. Predictably, women and children suffered most from the reduced consumption levels.[29] Research in this area has also shown a decline in the capacity of workers to save, and a worsening of food consumption levels, with 80 per cent of informal sector households reporting changes of diet, 68 per cent consuming less meat and 59 per cent less bread. The most recent study of urban poverty in two high-density suburbs in Harare has revealed the following results. In Dzivarasekwa it was found that the average household income of Z$935 was lower than both the National Food Poverty Datum Line of Z$1,511.77 and the Total Consumption Line of Z$2,554.89. Findings also indicated 'food shortages, inadequate clothing, poor accommodation, failure to pay school fees and poor health services'. Similar findings were reported in the area of Tafara, where average monthly household income was Z$359.[30] Both studies indicate an increasingly impoverished urban workforce, especially among women. In Gibbon's words, the 'picture emerging ... is of a working class, formal and informal, generally on the verge of destitution'.[31]

Along with the retrogression in the conditions of social reproduction of labour, the SAP has also witnessed the disciplining of labour in the area of industrial relations and a growing pattern of retrenchment, intensification of work and job enlargement. In 1992 the Labour Relations Act was amended to streamline hiring and firing procedures, thereby reducing delays in retrenchment. Moreover, granting plant-based works councils the power to negotiate collective bargaining agreements and codes of conduct provided the potential for undermining agreements negotiated by unions at national level. Such problems were compounded by labour's vulnerability during the 1991/92 drought, which provided conditions conducive to the spread of company-based arrangements to help ease the plight of desperate workers. The paternalist style of such interventions, when combined with the extension of casual labour in industry, has added to the debilitation of union activities.[32] The proliferation of the informal sector has in turn presented new challenges for labour organization. A 1991 study of this sector estimated that there were approximately 1.04 million micro- and small-scale enterprises in Zimbabwe.[33] However, despite the expansion of this sector, its capacity substantively to expand employment, output, and income has been exaggerated. As Mhone has written: 'The sector has not demonstrated a tendency to expand efficiently by increasing productivity and real incomes, nor by up-grading its production

into previous formal sector activities or by subsuming activities downgraded
by the formal sector. The sector has also failed to develop efficient forward
and backward linkages with the formal industrial sector.'[34]

Nevertheless, there is a growing trend for formal sector workers also to
engage in informal sector activities. Sachikonye's survey of textile and
clothing workers showed that 24 per cent of such workers participated in
the informal sector, largely though knitting and vending clothes and
blankets.[35] A ZCTU study carried out in 1993 also indicated that about 36
per cent of the 673 workers interviewed were engaged in supplementing
their wage income.[36] Such supplementary activities ranged from selling
clothes, cross-border shopping and security guard work, to sending out the
women and children of their household to engage in various informal
sector vending activities. In much of these types of informal sector activities,
it is the older women who bore the brunt of increased work and family
responsibilities.

Given the erosion of the security of the wage sector, there are a number
of other strategies that workers have used to survive, many of which are
an intensification of labour initiatives and structural relationships developed
during the settler-colonial period. Most workers maintain a 'straddling'
structural relationship with their families in the rural areas. A survey of
trade unions in 1991/92 indicated that 64.1 per cent of those sampled had
permanent rural homes, while 34 per cent stated that their permanent
homes were in urban areas. Moreover, 85 per cent of the respondents noted
that the permanent homes of their parents were in rural areas. In terms
of diversifying their incomes from rural sources, 90 per cent indicated that
their earnings were supplemented through agricultural activities such as
growing maize, vegetables and fruits or rearing cattle goats and chickens.
Over 50 per cent of the wives of these workers lived permanently in the
rural area, forming a regular source of food supplement.[37] Workers also
form savings clubs at the workplace, from which they can make low-
interest loans. Such savings are occasionally used, if they accumulate
sufficiently, to form the basis of housing co-operatives.[38] However, these
savings clubs have many limitations such as 'the limited capacity of the
savers to handle credit matters, erratic member participation and excessive
absenteeism'.[39] Moreover as Bond writes: 'the transition from savings club
to formal credit oriented institutions is an immensely difficult one when
temporal and spatial constraints are added to the general difficulties of
mere survival in the Zimbabwean countrywide.'[39]

A more enduring survival strategy for workers has been the use of
burial societies which developed from about 1908[40] among migrant workers
largely to provide burial assistance, social support and recreational facilities.
Membership of the societies was largely based on certain ethnic or regional

TABLE 10.3 Organizational involvement of Kambuzuma residents

	Women		Men	
	1991 (n=99)	1992 (n=98)	1991 (n=86)	1992 (n=86)
Religious groups	25	28	7	8
Burial society	18	19	18	8
Social/sport	3	3	1	2
Political	4	4	0	1
Trade union	1	3	5	6
Professional group	2	2	2	1
Co-operative	2	1	0	0
Total	55	60	33	37

Source: N. Kanji and N. Jazdowska (1993), *The Gender Specific Effects of ESAP on Households in Kambuzuma*. Harare.

groupings. A study carried out in 1985 revealed that 41 per cent of the burial societies formed maintained restrictions on membership varying from district grouping (e.g. Gutu District) to ethnic groups (e.g. Karanga) to national groupings (e.g. Malawians).[41] Moreover, the study revealed that even though financial security was the first reason given for joining a burial society, the 'maintenance of tribal/regional links' was the second most popular reason given by respondents.[42]

A later study in 1993 showed that involvement in burial societies, whose social welfare function has grown even more important in the era of the SAP, remains strong, as shown in Table 10.3. For trade unions, this complexity of the labour force presents major problems of mobilization and organization. A variety of layers of involvement in the economy, accompanied by a complex interplay of identities, both complementary and contradictory, presents important strategic problems. Incentives for involvement at shopfloor level are sometimes faced with countervailing pressures from ethnic organizations and national politics. As Mihyo and Schiphorst have observed:

> To make up for the loss in the modern sector, trade unions will have to open up towards workers in the informal sector and in the rural areas, which will involve different strategies and tactics. Not only will trade unions also have to address different kinds of workers than those who formed their traditional constituency, but they will also have to address issues of a broader nature in

order to attract the non-waged worker while remaining meaningful to the wage-worker who now has to survive on a multiplicity of income sources each with its specific problems.[43]

The above obstacles facing Zimbabwean trade unions can already be seen in the problems currently facing union organization. Many workers show 'very scanty knowledge about the functioning of their unions'.[44] Moreover, many workers are not aware of the institutional achievements of their unions through the collective bargaining process, even though workers' committees are fairly widespread.[45] The male dominance of union structures also reflects the problems of mobilization, for even though women can be found in increasing numbers in the agricultural, municipal, commercial, food processing, textile and clothing sectors, they are not well represented in either workers' committee or trade union structures.[46] Such developments may be indicative of the declining capacity of institutions, such as unions and other labour relations structures, to form identities at the workplace. This in turn could have major implications for the maintenance of 'regulatory regimes, codes of behaviour and the nurturing of institutional loyalties'.[47] All these issues are further complicated by the attitude of workers to the state with regard to the SAP. As Sachikonye's survey of textile and clothing industry workers has shown, while two-thirds of the sampled workers blamed the government for the economic problems in the country, approximately 50 per cent of the workers believed that the government was doing its best to ease the problems of the SAP.[48] Such an ambivalence on the part of workers stems from rural–urban linkages in the lives of workers and the capacity of the state to retain legitimacy in the rural sector of a worker's life through interventions such as drought relief, while antagonizing that same worker through more authoritarian labour relations structures. This capacity of the state to exploit the diversity of workers' experiences and to speak to them in different political accents, are formidable weapons in the arsenal of the ruling party.

At a central organizational level, the Zimbabwe Congress of Trade Unions (ZCTU) has struggled against the increased economic marginalization of its membership. In the development of the ESAP programme in Zimbabwe, the labour movement was largely peripheral to the consultation process preceding the launching of the new economic strategy. The business organizations in industry, agriculture and mining were, on the other hand, an important part of the process, seeing in the new programme the prospect of less state involvement, access to more foreign exchange, more export openings and increased investment. The ZCTU strongly criticized the state for its lack of consultation, and the design of the ESAP programme which, it claimed, would further impoverish labour. This acrimony between the state and the labour movement lasted from the latter half of the 1980s until 1992, when the ZCTU adopted a more proactive strategy. Largely accepting the 'necessity' of adjustment, the ZCTU sought to make space for itself in the consultations on the second phase of the adjustment programme by presenting the state with an alternative framework for the programme design. In its document entitled *Beyond ESAP*, the ZCTU sought to stress to the government of Zimbabwe that it should adopt a process of economic development that 'entails a move from a situation of underdevelopment in which the majority of the population are steeped in endemic and structural poverty, to that where this majority's socio-economic welfare and well-being is progressively improved over time'.[49]

This ZCTU strategy has attempted to build a more solid corporatist agreement between the state, capital and labour. To carry out this objective, the ZCTU has recommended the establishment of the Zimbabwe Economic Development Council (ZEDC), which would serve as a body in which relevant interest groups and stakeholders could participate in policy formulation, decision-making and implementation. Speaking through a broad nationalist voice, the ZCTU has been concerned to develop a 'truly national compromise' on economic and political strategy.[50]

The future of such a strategy still hangs in the balance, given the government's wavering commitment to a strong corporatist arrangement. The ZCTU recently expressed misgivings about the state's continued reticence towards broad participatory structures. Commenting that although the state has made some effort to establish national dialogue, the secretary general of the ZCTU has observed that: 'This dialogue has been on an ad hoc basis, and most unfortunately the government goes on to implement policies without taking the dialogue seriously.'[51]

Social relations on the land and the differential responses to state policy The fundamental problem of the land question has far-reaching consequences for the future of the struggle against poverty in Zimbabwe. The nature and extent of land reforms, or lack of them, in the future, will be a determining factor in the process of class formation on the land, changes in the regime of accumulation and the possibilities of alliances between rural and urban classes in the pursuit of various policies. It should be remembered that it was only with the intensification of land alienation in the 1950s and the more intensive migration of indigenous workers into the cities from this period, that a national movement both in terms of geographical spread and a unifying ideology began to emerge. Radical shifts in social relations in the land, therefore, could cause seismic shifts

in Zimbabwean politics. This may be one factor in the cautious approach
of the state to land reform.

The iniquitous state of the land problem is beyond question. About
4,660 large-scale commercial farms, largely owned by white farmers, occupy
11.2 million ha. with 34.6 per cent of this land in natural regions I and
II, 21.5 per cent in region III and 43.9 per cent in regions IV and V. The
communal areas, with a population of approximately 6 million blacks, is
made up of 16.4 million ha., or 42 per cent of land in the country, with
74.2 per cent of this land situated in the poorest agro-ecological zones,
namely natural regions IV and V.[52] The post-1980 period has seen increasing differentiation on the land. With regard to regional difference, of the
170 smallholder areas, eighteen accounted for 75 per cent of marketed
surplus in certain periods. A recent summary of regional differences in
rural incomes in communal areas has noted the following:

> remittances make up a large share of poorer households total incomes;
> unskilled labour income is important in areas where there are large scale
> commercial farmers nearby; crops are a negligible income source in Natural
> Regions IV and V and even for better off households; the more food-secure
> households attain this status not through on-farm production but due to
> skilled labour income ... agricultural income makes up at most 50 per cent
> (more usually only ⅓) total cash income in any social group, rural house-
> holds diversifying their income sources including urban wage income.[53]

With approximately 30 per cent of householders practically landless,
and particular groups such as young men, and single, separated and de
facto women heads of households, most in need of land, there are clearly
heterogeneous experiences of land shortage.[54] Not surprisingly, these
different experiences of the land problem have resulted in different forms
of land struggle including 'squatting', trespassing on large-scale commercial
farms for access to better national resources, and migration across communal areas.[55] The major black farmers' organization, the Zimbabwe
Farmers Union, itself represents a variety of interest and policy demands,
ranging from the demand for more community land in small quantities by
peasants short of land, to the call for increased freehold tenure for productive purposes, by the more elite black farmers who dominate the ZFU
leadership. In the process the demands of the elite tend to dominate policy
demands.[56]

At the local level, land struggles have taken on forms that have raised
difficult problems about the relationship between state and party structures
and traditional authorities. The 1994 Land Commission concluded on this
problem that:

Local level institutions administering tenure have been characterised by conflicts particularly between the traditional authority and 'elected' leadership. The intractable nature of these land administration disputes has, however, been further complicated by the subsequent superimposition of local ruling party structures and later, of government village and ward development committees. This profusion of overlapping and incongruent local organisational structures, each with its own boundaries and drawing in different sources of legitimacy, has thus created weak and disparate local institutions.[57]

The commission notes that the dissolution of traditional authority at independence was premature and that 'over time people in communal areas have gravitated towards traditional leaders on issues of land and natural resource management'.[58] In fact, even during the period of the liberation struggle, the role of traditional leaders was not as discredited as was once supposed. Many such leaders were supportive of the liberation movement, co-operating with both guerrillas and spirit mediums. In the post-independence period, the demobilization of party structures and the 'authoritarian and modernisation ethic of the development bureaucracies'[59] has breathed new life into the popularity of traditional authorities. This development has also been observed in Tandon's study of the Zambezi Valley in which he observes the growing importance of what he calls 'traditional grassroots democracy', which is 'strongly guided by a spiritual bond between the dead, the living and the unborn', and through which rural households attempt to find solutions to the lived experiences of their postcolonial land struggles.[60]

Thus, the differentiated struggles and varied layers of interest involved in the Land Question in Zimbabwe have produced a complex set of power relations. The state, with its limited policy on land redistribution, has attempted to offset this limitation with a policy of increasing the access of black farmers to inputs and market outlets. As a strategy against poverty this has had, for the most part, a limited effect on the majority of rural producers. In response, the differentiated rural population has responded not only through limited organizational lobbying and pressure on the ruling party structures in the rural area but also through opposition to a centralized modernizing bureaucracy, via a 'traditional' idiom of opposition. The result of these struggles has been a persisting rural poverty. The results of a Poverty Assessment Study Survey carried out in 1995 by the Ministry of Public Service, Labour and Social Welfare are revealing. Poverty ratios were calculated on the basis of two poverty lines. The first was a Food Poverty Line (FPL), defined as the amount of income required to purchase a basket of basic food needs by an average person per annum. The second was a Total Consumption Poverty Line (TCPL) which established the amount of income required to purchase a basket of food and non-food needs by an average person per annum. Having set a national FPL of Z$1,331.87, and a TCPL of Z$2,213.28 per person per annum, the survey found that 62 per cent of all Zimbabweans were living in households with income per person 'below a level sufficient to provide basic needs'; and were therefore considered poor. In addition, 46 per cent of households were living below the FPL and were considered 'very poor'. As expected, rural poverty was more prevalent, with 72 per cent of rural poor in the combined poor and very poor categories; as opposed to 46 per cent of urban households.[61] The World Bank has also indicated deteriorating trends with regard to poverty in Zimbabwe. These trends include: falling incomes from formal employment over the period of the 1990s; an increase of income inequality; and negative impact of 'stagnant or declining provision of social services' on the poor.[62]

The response of the state to increasing poverty levels In the face of a clearly deteriorating situation, what interventions has the state undertaken? In 1991 the Social Development Fund (SDF) was established as part of the broader SAP in Zimbabwe. The major thrust of the fund was to 'cushion vulnerable groups and poor communities against the negative effects of the reform programme', through specifically targeted interventions.[63] Under this fund, two programmes were developed. First, the Social Welfare Programme (SWP) attempted to compensate the poor for new or increased user charges in education and health, and deregulated maize prices. These payments were aimed at covering exemptions from school fees and examination fees for households with incomes below Z$400 per month; exemptions from health fees for households with incomes below Z$400 per month; a per capita cash food benefit of Z$4 per month for urban households earning less than Z$200 per month, with the intention of assisting households in the face of a deregulated increased price for maize. The second programme under the SDF was the Employment and Training Programme (ETP). This intervention had a two-pronged approach, namely, an introductory one-week training course in starting up a new business, and loans for small enterprise startups.

In the event, both programmes have had serious limitations. Overall there have been serious limitations in the financing of the SDF. After increasing the budget from Z$20 million in the fiscal year 1992/93 to Z$150 million in 1993/94, expenditure declined to Z$100 million and Z$50 million in the years 1994/95 and 1995/96 respectively. Expected donor assistance has been slow. More specifically, in the case of the SWP the following problems have arisen:

- the majority of qualifying households remained outside the scheme
- in the case of school and examination fee exemptions, there was evidence of a gender bias against girls
- the administrative procedures involved were slow, cumbersome and over-centralized
- insufficient staffing at central and provincial levels

With regard to the small-enterprise loan scheme the problems included:

- a slow delivery system
- a bias towards retrenchees from the public sector in the distribution of loans
- a gender bias against women, with only 9 per cent of beneficiaries being women
- a strong urban bias

The problems faced by the ETP were:

- training programmes were too short
- retrenchees have had limited options, namely participation in the micro-enterprise scheme; many retrenchees have had neither the skills nor the motivation to succeed in such schemes[64]

In addition to the SDF, the government introduced the Poverty Alleviation Action Plan (PAAP) in 1993. The PAAP sought to build on to the programmes of the SDF as well as to provide a broader framework for poverty alleviation activities. The major aspects of the PAAP strategy included:

- targeting of social expenditures
- decentralization of programme implementation
- a participatory approach to poverty alleviation
- a partnership approach to address distortions in social provisions and poverty alleviation[65]

It is envisaged that a central aspect of the PAAP will be the Community Development Project (CDP) which will finance small grants and technical assistance for investments in social and economic infrastructure, improve natural resource management, as well as other small-scale activities identified by communities. This intervention is being proposed in order to strengthen local structures, in the context of the redefined responsibilities between the state and civil society that have taken place under the SAP. The local power structures in which it is intended to build up the CDP are described as follows:

local leaders, both male and female, are often among the wealthier members of their communities and thus tend to represent vested interest with direct personal concerns about how additional resources enter their community. This situation has often created a barrier or distortionary impact on pro-poor oriented activities. In such cases, participation and involvement of local communities often turns out to mean co-option of local elites and leadership. Furthermore, one of the characteristics of Zimbabwe is the tight integration of the various sectors of the economy through the very mobile labour force – making the urban-rural modern–informal sector dichotomies less glaring than in other African countries. At the same time, however, traditional leaders and values remain very strong and real influences on the lives of ordinary people.[66]

Quite how the CDPs are meant to increase the level of empowerment of local communities in the absence of more substantive local government reforms is not made clear at this stage. Indeed, it is precisely on the issue of increased decentralization that there remains a good deal of uncertainty on the part of the Zimbabwean state. The Ministry of Local Government, Rural and Urban Planning sees decentralization as its domain, and has been reluctant to develop a co-ordinated decentralized strategy with other central ministries, especially the Ministry of Finance.[67] As a deputy secretary in the Ministry of Finance admitted: 'It is clear … that the institutional structures which were put in place to spearhead the development of the human factor through decentralisation, have not made it.'[68] Thus, financial decentralization remains a distant prospect particularly because of the central state's reluctance to entertain such an inroad into its powers.

In addition to the SDF and the PAAP, the state has also made some broad policy statements on poverty in two documents currently under discussion: namely, the Zimbabwe Programme for Economic and Social Transformation (ZIMPREST), and the Zimbabwe Vision 2020. Discussion in both documents does not go much beyond the positions developed in the PAAP.

From the discussion in this section, it is clear that poverty reduction remains a marginal part of the policy direction of the state. Programmes such as the SDF are unlikely to make serious inroads into the poverty problem in Zimbabwe, especially during a time of falling aid budgets. The weekly paper of the ruling party itself recently admitted to 'the dismal failure of the Party and Government in sustaining the SDF, the health delivery system, road and dam construction programmes, housing programme, as well as containing the situation whereby numerous factories are being liquidated, unemployment is ever rising, and the solution to the land question not taking off the ground'.[69]

Conclusion

Given the state's limited strategy on poverty reduction, particularly its lack of substantive land reform, and given the increasing impoverishment of large numbers of rural and urban producers during the structural adjustment period, what has been particularly striking is the ruling party's ability to maintain political support and marginalize opposition politics. One view, vehemently expressed by opposition parties, is that this state of affairs is the result of the largely coercive politics of the state. There is truth to this assertion. However, a more comprehensive explanation is required to understand the continued domination of the ruling party in the face of increasing poverty levels.

Much of the critique on democratization and interest groups in Zimbabwe has had an urban focus.[70] Analysis has focused on the capacity of the African middle class, workers' organizations, students and formal business organizations to influence government policy. There has been little attempt to link such urban interventions and their limitations to a broader analysis of the state's continued hegemony in the rural areas. Yet such an overall view of state power is necessary to understand the strengths and limitations of particular classes and groups in society to intervene in the policy debate on poverty.

From the foregoing analysis it is clear that the state has managed to maintain relative peace in the largely poor rural areas because of a number of factors. First, the state's welfarist policies of the 1980s impacted largely on the rural areas, and such policies resulted in the accumulation of ideological capital that is still available to the ruling party. Second, because of the strong existence of 'traditional' structures in the rural areas, a good deal of the state's dealings with the rural producers has been through an appropriation of and accommodation with such structures.

The appropriation of such customary and traditional cultural forms for legitimacy and in the formation of national identity was an integral part of the liberation war and has continued in the postcolonial period. The nature of this disjuncture between traditional structures and the civic sphere in the urban areas has meant that the state has been able to maintain a reservoir of legitimacy in the rural sphere, even as it saw such legitimacy eroded among the marginalized urban population. The complex and uneven relations between rural and urban structures have also resulted in difficulties in urban social movements articulating their demands with marginalized rural producers. Third, among rural producers themselves, social differentiation has resulted in different policy demands which at an organizational level tend to be dominated by the rural elite, best able to lobby the state.

Under such conditions, developing structures and organizational capacity for dealing with poverty issues has proved extremely difficult. Such a political and institutional environment has largely maintained marginalized groups on the edges of policy debates, weakening local initiatives and the capacity for growth. Against such structural limitations, policies on poverty reduction remain largely determined by the interface between the imperatives of donor logic at a particular time, and the announcements of policies of 'national interest' by a state whose record on policy dialogue remains poor.

Notes

Paper presented at the Economic History Conference, University of Zimbabwe, 4–7 August 1997.

1. UNDP (1997) *Human Development Report*. Oxford: Oxford University Press.

2. Thandika Mkandawire (1996) 'Economic Policy Making and the Consolidation of Democratic Institutions in Africa', in K. Havnevik and B. Von Arkadie (eds), *Domination or Dialogue – Prospects for African Development Cooperation*. Uppsala, Sweden: Nordiska Afrikainstitutet, pp. 31–2.

3. B. Raftopoulos (1995) 'Fighting for Control: The Indigenisation Debate in Zimbabwe', *Southern Africa Report*, 11, 4 (July); B. Raftopoulos and S. Moyo (1995) 'The Politics of Indigenisation in Zimbabwe', *East African Social Science Review*, 1, 2 (June).

4. See the growing historiography on the liberation struggle in Zimbabwe by N. Bhebe and T. O. Ranger (1995) *Soldiers in the Liberation War*, Vol. 1. Harare: University of Zimbabwe Publications; and N. Bhebe and T. O. Ranger (1995) *Society in Zimbabwe's Liberation War*, Vol. 2. Harare: University of Zimbabwe Publications.

5. Zimbabwe Government (1981) *Growth with Equity: An Economic Policy Statement*. Harare: Government Printers, p. 1.

6. Bernard Chidzero (1981) 'Development Overview', in *Report on Conference Proceedings, Zimbabwe Conference of Reconstruction and Development*. Harare: Government Printers, p. 53.

7. Government of Zimbabwe (1986) *Socio-Economic Review 1980–1985*. Harare: Government Printers, p. 11.

8. Munhamo Chisvo and Lauchlan Munro (1994) *A Review of the Social Dimensions of Adjustment in Zimbabwe 1990–94*. Harare: UNICEF.

9. L. N. Nyangura and A. C. Mupawaenda (1994) *A Study of the Factors Affecting the Education of Women and Girls in Commercial Farmland Areas of Zimbabwe*. Harare: Ministry of Education and Culture, Government of Zimbabwe.

10. Secretary for Education (1993) *Annual Report 1991*. Harare: Government of Zimbabwe.

11. R. Loewensen and M. Chisvo (1994) *Transforming Social Development: The Experience of Zimbabwe*. Harare: UNICEF.

12. ZCTU (1996) *Beyond ESAP*. Harare: ZCTU, p. 30.

13. Ibid., p. 28.

14. S. Moyo (1996) *Land and Democracy in Zimbabwe*. Harare: unpublished mimeo.

15. Ibid.

16. F. Stewart, J. Klugman and A. H. Helmsing (1994) *Decentralisation in Zimbabwe*. Harare: Department of Rural and Urban Planning, University of Zimbabwe.

17. L. Sachikonye (1997) *The State and the Union Movement in Zimbabwe: Cooptation, Conflict and Accommodation*. Unpublished mimeo.

18. Ibid.

19. Ibid.

20. M. Shadur (1994) *Labour Relations in a Developing Country: A Case Study on Zimbabwe*. Aldershot: Avebury, pp. 125–6.

21. G. Kanyenze (1996) *Labour Markets and Employment During ESAP*. Unpublished mimeo.

22. C. Jenkins (1995) *Economic Policy and Investment in Zimbabwe 1980–1900*. Oxford: Centre for the Study of African Economies, University of Oxford.

23. Government of Zimbabwe (1991) *Framework for Economic Reform, 1991–95*. Harare: Government Printers.

24. ILO (1993) *Structural Adjustment and Change*. Geneva: ILO, p. 43.

25. P. Gibbon (1995) 'Introduction', in P. Gibbon (ed.) *Structural Adjustment and the Working Poor in Zimbabwe*. Uppsala, Sweden: Nordiska Afrikainstitutet, p. 16.

26. ILO (1993) *Structural Adjustment and Change*, p. 39.

27. ZCTU (1996) *Beyond ESAP: Framework for Long-term Development Strategy in Zimbabwe*. Harare: ZCTU, p. 29.

28. World Bank (1996) *Understanding Poverty and Human Resources in Zimbabwe*. Washington, DC: World Bank, pp. 62–5.

29. Nazneen Kanji and Niki Jazdowska (1993) *The Gender-Specific Effects of E.S.A.P. on Households in Kambuzuma*. February. Harare: unpublished mimeo.

30. N. R. Matshalaga (1997) *The Gender Dimensions of Urban Poverty: The Case of Dzivaresekwa* Harare: Institute of Development Studies, University of Zimbabwe; N. R. Matshalaga (997) *The Gender Dimensions of Urban Poverty: The Case of Tafara*. Harare: Institute of Development Studies, University of Zimbabwe.

31. Gibbon (ed.), *Structural Adjustment*, p. 30.

32. Lloyd Sachikonye (1995) 'Industrial Restructuring and Labour Relations Under ESAP in Zimbabwe', in Gibbon (ed.), *Structural Adjustment*.

33. Michael McPherson (1992) *Micro and Small Scale Enterprises in Zimbabwe*. Maryland: Gemini, p. 7.

34. Guy C. Z. Mhone (1993) *The Impact of Structural Adjustment on the Urban Informal Sector in Zimbabwe*. Geneva: ILO.

35. Sachikonye, *The State and the Union Movement*.

36. ZCTU (1993a) *Structural Adjustment and Its Impact on Workers*. Harare: ZCTU.

37. ZCTU (1993b) *Workers Participation Development Programme*, Report on Research Findings from the 1991/92 Educational Seminars. Harare: ZCTU.

38. Sachikonye, 'Industrial Restructuring'.

39. Patrick Bond (N.D.) *The Geography of Rural Financial Markets in Zimbabwe*. Unpublished mimeo.

40. Ibid.

41. Louis Masuko Masuko (1990) *Social Movements in Southern Africa: A Case Study of the Zimbabwean Burial Society*, Harare: Institute of Development Studies. Unpublished mimeo.

42. School of Social Work (1985) *Burial Societies in Harare*. Harare.

43. Paschal Mihyo and Freek Schiphorst (1995) *Trade Unions in Development: Africa*. Unpublished mimeo.

44. ZCTU (1993b) *Workers Participation Development Programme*.

45. ZCTU (1993c) *Workers Participation Development Programme*, Second Report on Research Findings from the 1991/92 Educational Seminars. Harare: ZCTU.

46. ZCTU (1993d) *Workers Participation Development Programme*, Some Notes Regarding Women's Participation. Harare: ZCTU.

47. Yusuf Bangura (1994) 'Economic Restructuring, Coping Strategies and Social Change: Implications for Institutional Development in Africa', *Development and Change*, 25, p. 815.

48. Sachikonye, 'Industrial Restructuring'.

49. ZCTU (1996) *Beyond ESAP*, p. 9.

50. Ibid., p. 90.

51. *Zimbabwe Independent*, 7 February 1997.

52. Sam Moyo (1995) *The Land Question in Zimbabwe*. Harare: SAPES, pp. 83–4.

53. World Bank, *Understanding Poverty*, pp. 63–6.

54. Moyo, *The Land Question*, p. 165.

55. Ibid., p. 166.

56. Ibid.

57. *Commission of Enquiry into Appropriate Agricultural and Land Tenure Systems* (1944), Vol. 1, Harare, p. 26.

58. Ibid., p. 24.

59. Jocelyn Alexander (1993) 'Things Fall Apart, the Centre Can Hold: Processes of Post-war Political Change in Zimbabwe's Rural Areas', in Laurids S. Lauridsen (ed.), *Bringing Institutions Back in – The Role of Institutions in Civil Society, State and Economy*. Roskilde University Press.

60. Yash Tandon (1994) *Emerging Grass Roots Democracy in Zimbabwe*. Unpublished mimeo.

61. Ministry of Public Service, Labour and Social Welfare (1996) *Poverty Assessment Study Survey Preliminary Report*. Harare, p. 23.

62. World Bank, *Understanding Poverty*, p. 68.

63. Social Development Fund (1995) *Annual Report for the Year 1995*. Harare: Ministry of Labour, Manpower Planning and Social Welfare, Government of Zimbabwe, p. 1.

64. All the information on the SDF was taken from R. Moorsom, J. Matanga and L. Sachikonye (1996) *Evaluation of the S.D.F. in Zimbabwe: A Pilot Study*. Norway: CHR Michelsen Institute.

65. Government of Zimbabwe (1994) *Poverty Alleviation Action Plan*, p. 5.

66. Government of Zimbabwe (1997) *Zimbabwe: Community Development Project Terms of Reference*, p. 4.

67. Interview with Mr J. Chigudu, senior official in the National Economic Planning Commission, April 1997.

68. F. Pamacheche (1996) 'Economic Policy Development and Policy Alleviation', in *Institute of Development Studies Policy Dialogue Series no. 1, The Political Economy of Poverty in Zimbabwe: Fiscal Management Review*, p. 22.

69. Comment, *The People's Voice*, 30 March–6 April 1997.

70. See for example J. Moyo (1993) *Voting for Democracy*, UZ Publications; and I. Mandaza and L. Sachikonye (eds) (1991) *The One Party State and Democracy*. Harare: SAPES Books.

11

Poverty and Democratization: The Case of Botswana

Charity K. Kerapeletswe and Tsholofelo Moremi

This chapter provides an analysis of issues of popular participation and strategies for poverty reduction in Botswana. We argue that poverty reduction requires participation and organization of people in decision-making, mobilization of social energy, and development of capacities at all levels in society. Although the government of Botswana has expanded people's access to social services through stepping up social spending, the high incidence of poverty in Botswana may represent a failure to address a number of institutional and structural constraints for poverty reduction. Acknowledgements are made of a recent reduction in the level of poverty and of the existence of democratic institutions which facilitate popular participation. Still, the chapter points to a number of critical challenges and constraints related to the low level of participation by the poor in taking advantage of the opportunities presented. Participation of the poor represents both a means to and an end of poverty reduction. In this chapter we discuss the Botswana poverty alleviation strategy in a conceptual framework that depicts the interaction between government expansion of access to social services, and people's participation in taking advantage of the opportunities presented.

Background of Botswana

Botswana covers approximately 582,000 square kilometres, is landlocked, and shares borders with South Africa, Namibia, Zimbabwe and Zambia. In the west is the Kgalagadi Desert, which accounts for about 70 per cent of the area of Botswana. The country is characterized by semi-arid climatic conditions. The average annual rainfall ranges from 650mm in the north-east to 250mm in the south-west.

Botswana has a de facto population of 1.5 million (National Development Plan [NDP 8]), with a growth rate of 2.5 per cent (US Department

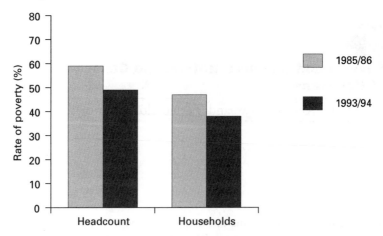

FIGURE 11.1 National poverty by headcount and household
Source: BIDPA 1997

of Commerce 1998). Since 1966 (when 95 per cent of the population was rural), there has been a rapid change in the settlement pattern, from a largely rural population towards an urban population. By 1991, about 48 per cent of the population were urban and 52 per cent rural (CSO 1995a).

When Botswana gained independence in 1966, it was classified among the poorest nations. Economic development has been rapid since the 1970s following the discovery of rich diamond deposits. By 1997, Botswana had a GDP per capita of US $3,210 (ADB 1998; ECA 1998). The annual rate of economic growth was especially high (13 per cent) during the 1980s, but has now levelled off to about 7 per cent (ADB 1998). Botswana has been a major recipient of donor funds due to the poor economic situation pre-independence and the responsibility of the government in handling donor funds. This has enabled the government to devote considerable resources to social and economic development, which led to significant improvements in social indicators. Donor funds began drying up in 1996– 97, when the country was designated a lower- to middle-income country. Some donors have terminated their country programmes giving priority to countries that fit their low-income criteria.

Botswana is one of Africa's oldest multi-party democracies, with a constitution that affords the citizens a non-racial democracy with freedom of speech, press, association and equal rights (Government of Botswana 1997a). General elections are held every five years. Botswana also offers an environment that has proven very supportive for local democratic governance.

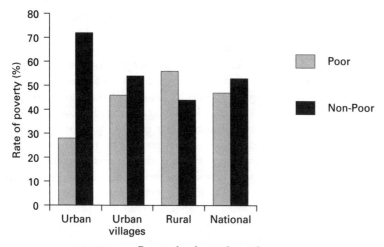

FIGURE 11.2 Poverty headcount by settlement type
Source: BIDPA 1997

The foundation for democracy in Botswana is the traditional self-rule system, with a village equivalent of a parliament called the *kgotla*, which is headed by a chief. The chief is responsible for settling customary disputes and co-ordination of community matters. Every member of the community has the right to participate in the discussions at the *kgotla*. To maintain traditional norms and values, a central tribal administration legislature presided over by the House of Chiefs was established. Various community institutions such as the Village Development Committee (VDC), the Village Health Committee (VHC), and the Village Extension Team (VET) contribute to decision-making and the implementation of programmes at community level. At district level, the tribal authority, District Administration and the Council play a co-ordination role. These structures widen the scope for popular participation in development.

Extent and Causes of Poverty in Botswana

In spite of Botswana's rapid mineral-led growth, in 1993–94, almost half its population (47 per cent) or about 38 per cent of households were estimated to be living in income poverty (BIDPA 1997). However, this represents a sharp decline in the percentage of Batswana living in poverty in 1985–86, when 59 per cent of persons or 49 per cent of households were living in income poverty (see Figure 11.1).

There are considerable income disparities and regional differences in poverty. Overall, 62 per cent of the poor are estimated to live in rural areas, where 55 per cent of the population was estimated to be living below the poverty line, as compared with 46 per cent in urban villages and 29 per cent in urban areas (see Figure 11.2).

Female-headed households experience greater poverty than male-headed ones, with 50 per cent of people living in female-headed households classified as poor compared with only 44 per cent of those living in male-headed households (CSO 1995a). Geographically, the rural south-west has a higher incidence of poverty, with 71 per cent of the population being poor and 59 per cent classified as very poor.[1] The region has a large percentage of ethnic minorities, especially the Basarwa (Bushmen). The major causes of income poverty is skewed income distribution and limited economic base (CSO 1995a). The limited income earning potential of the agriculture and manufacturing sectors exacerbate this problem. Poverty among rural people is influenced by poor access to and control of resources; limited economic opportunities; large families and poor coping skills for modern society. Social barriers and discriminatory social attitudes towards some ethnic groups such as Basarwa restrict their social and economic participation. Alcoholism is also a growing serious factor of poverty among the remote area dwellers, especially Basarwa. It has implications for inter-generational persistence of poverty, and may itself be resulting, in part, from several of the above other causes (BIDPA 1997).

Popular Participation and Poverty Reduction in Botswana

Botswana's national principles and objectives of democracy, development, self-reliance and unity, which are intended to lead to social harmony, have many similarities with the notion of popular participation. Emphasizing social harmony reflects the importance attached to ensuring that all people should share equitably in the country's economic progress. Botswana's success story is a result of its traditions of democracy, political stability and prudent economic management (Duncan et al. 1994; Perrings 1996). The framework below depicts the multidimensional interplay between the government's provision and people's participation. Government provision refers to all roles and activities of government that affect the people, viz. policies, legislation, justice system, social services, etc. The general outcomes of popular participation and provision are mainly democracy; equity and justice; people's health and survival; literacy and education; gender equality; and employment and incomes (see Figure 11.3). These outcomes are determined by the interaction of the state provision and people's participation. The extent of poverty reduction depends on government provision as well as people's ability and willingness to use the services. State provision and people's participation are affected by under-

MORE CHOICES THROUGH PROVISION AND PARTICIPATION

Outcomes of popular participation and state provision

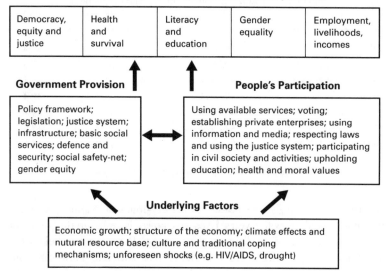

Democracy, equity and justice	Health and survival	Literacy and education	Gender equality	Employment, livelihoods, incomes

Government Provision   **People's Participation**

Policy framework; legislation; justice system; infrastructure; basic social services; defence and security; social safety-net; gender equity	Using available services; voting; establishing private enterprises; using information and media; respecting laws and using the justice system; participating in civil society and activities; upholding education; health and moral values

Underlying Factors

Economic growth; structure of the economy; climate effects and nutural resource base; culture and traditional coping mechanisms; unforeseen shocks (e.g. HIV/AIDS, drought)

FIGURE 11.3 Conceptual framework for government provision and people's participation *Source*: Adapted from UNDP 1997a

lying factors which include the natural resource base, social and cultural norms, climate, international market and external political situation.

This chapter examines the effect of the government of Botswana's provision and people's participation in selected areas: political participation; economic participation; participation in education, knowledge and skills; and participation in health and housing.

Political participation Taking any political action requires three decisions: first, whether or not to act; second, if you decide to act, what are you going to do; and third, how you are going to do it (Dwyer 1989). The standard socio-economic model of participation suggests that people with more education and income are more likely to participate in politics while the poor and less educated are less likely to be active in politics (Stanley 1985; Lijphart 1997). However, despite the significant improvement in educational attainment in the USA, there is a gradual decline of voter turnout, which suggests that there are other important underlying factors that determine political participation (IIDEA 1997).

PARTICIPATION IN PARLIAMENTARY ELECTIONS IN BOTSWANA The

TABLE 11.1 Participation in parliamentary elections

Year	Population	Voting age population (VAP)	Voter registration (%)	Vote/VAP (%)
1965	520,000	202,800	–	69.4
1969	570,000	205,200	54.7	37.5
1974	660,000	244,200	31.2	26.2
1979	783,872	290,033	55.2	46.4
1984	1,051,000	420,400	77.6	54.2
1989	1,245,000	522,900	68.2	47.9
1994	1,443,000	634,920	76.6	44.6

Source: Report on General Elections 1969, 1974, 1984, 1989, 1994

constitution vests legislative power in the forty-four-seat National Assembly which is elected every five years. Executive power is vested in the president, who is a member of parliament. Since 1965, Botswana has held parliamentary elections that were considered free and fair. However, voter turnout has not been outstanding. The highest voter turnout is 69.4 per cent, registered during the country's first elections (see Table 11.1). Low

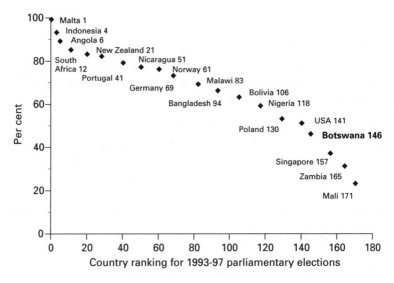

FIGURE 11.4 Ranking of countries by voter turnout in parliamentary elections
Source: International Institute for Democracy and Electoral Assistance

levels of participation may indicate that people are happy with the system the way it is, or that the voting and registration processes may be cumbersome to some, or simply voter apathy. The right to vote as of the age of eighteen was conferred upon on all Botswana citizens in 1997; before then the voting age had been twenty-one.

Compared with other countries, the Institute for Democracy and Electoral Assistance (IDEA) ranked Botswana 146 out of 171 countries for VAP turnout for the most recent parliamentary elections (1992–97). This shows that, by international standards, Batswana's participation in elections is quite low (see Figure 11.4).

PARTICIPATION IN POLITICAL PARTIES While there are several active political parties in Botswana, the country's politics have been dominated by the governing Botswana Democratic Party (BDP) which has held power since independence. The BDP won twenty-seven of the forty contested National Assembly seats in the October, 1994 elections. With the addition of four members the ruling party is authorized to appoint, the BDP held thirty-one seats in the Assembly. The remaining thirteen seats, won by the opposition Botswana National Front (BNF), represented an unprecedented challenge to the BDP and a substantial increase from its previous representation of only three seats. The BDP won 67.5 per cent of the popular vote compared to the BNF's 32.5 per cent (see Table 11.2). The National Assembly has forty-seven members, forty members elected for a five-year term in single-seat constituencies, four members co-opted by the elected members and two members ex officio and the Speaker (if elected from outside parliament). The BNF's strengths continue to be among urban voters and the economically marginalized, particularly youth, who respond favourably to BNF calls for increased government spending on human services. A change in the political landscape may be in the offing given the split in BNF. In June 1998, some members of the BNF formed a new party, the Botswana Congress Party (BCP). Eleven of thirteen MPs have crossed over to the BCP, along with many of the BNF's rank and file. The BCP now represents the official opposition in parliament, but it remains to be seen whether it will strengthen the opposition in the National Assembly. Voters have been drawn to the BDP for over thirty years, largely because its conservative fiscal programmes have contributed to Botswana's marked progress. However, some Batswana would prefer to see the government save less and spend more to spread the country's wealth more equitably (Good 1996).

The weak parliamentary opposition in Botswana could be due to the following factors: failure by opposition parties to mobilize voters due to weak group–party linkages, the small size of individual parties as well as

TABLE 11.2 Representation of political parties in the National Assembly in 1994

National Assembly: October 1994 (elected members)		100%	40
Botswana Democratic Party	BDP	67.5 %	27
Botswana National Front	BNF	32.5 %	13
Botswana People's Party	BPP	—	—

Source: Wilfried Derksen (1999) Elections around the World

internal party decisions and fragmentation. Opposition parties have increased from three to fifteen in 1998. However, no more than five of these parties have any considerable following. Few of the opposition parties have a country-wide organizational structure. In most parties, the party leader, who is not subject to competitive elections and holds the position for life, controls decision-making process. Merging of political parties to form a strong opposition has failed in the past.

The participation of women in Botswana's political parties is substantial even though they are underrepresented in leadership and decision-making positions. There has never been a female head of state in Botswana, and women have always been underrepresented in parliament. In 1998, there were three female ministers out of a total of fifteen ministers. At subministerial level (permanent secretary, executive director, etc.), women accounted for only 15 per cent of the positions (*Botswana Human Development Report* [BHDR] 1997).

LOCAL DEMOCRATIC GOVERNANCE Local government is a crucial institution in democratization. It is at the local level that people can best define their priority problems and organize to deal with them. Local government has a long history in Botswana, with a working administrative structure in place, and is filled with competent personnel. The Ministry of Local Government Land and Housing (MLGLH) is the *parent* ministry of local government in Botswana. Given that Botswana is a unitary state, local government has no constitutional status and is purely a statutory creation (Wusch 1998). In the governance of city, town and district and council affairs, this structure has been able to prepare and execute budgets dealing with personnel, supplies, and maintenance of several departments (SIDA 1993; Peter-Berries 1995).

There is a high flow of resources from central to local governments given the limited capacity of districts to raise funds (Good 1996). Rural districts raise funds through service fees, small business licences, and rents from council-owned housing. Urban districts have additional funds through property rates. A serious problem is the limited authority that local government has in setting fees, as MLGLH and other central agencies control fee levies for most local services. On the positive side, local governments already control their budgeting. Each locality has a development officer and engages in grass-roots development processes. In this way, local priorities are incorporated via a matrix planning system of the overall national plan (Wusch 1998).

The local political process is far more developed in Botswana than in neighbouring countries such as South Africa (Dahlgren 1995). Municipal (urban) councils are the most developed institutions involved in the local political process. Councillors employ several strategies to keep attuned to their constituents. They hold meetings in wards to exchange information with constituents, and are members of civic organizations. The fact that citizens do not have a direct stake in local government may force councillors to develop innovative means of engaging constituents.

OTHER FORMS OF POLITICAL PARTICIPATION Newspapers, radio and television could influence the way people vote. Observers of the political scene in Botswana will have noted a considerable measure of freedom of speech, particularly in the press. However, there is only one radio station, which is owned and controlled by the government. In most cases it presents the government's point of view on major political issues. Until quite recently, newspaper circulation in rural areas was poor. The availability of national newspapers per 1,000 persons was 412.3 in 1995. Political party newspapers are almost non-existent. There is no national television except for a private television station, which is limited to Gaborone and surrounding areas. Even then, not all people in the capital can afford a television set. Until 1998, parts of Gaborone (population 180,000), had no electricity, in particular the areas designated for low-income households. This situation in itself limited political participation as it limited the use of electronic information transmission devices. Recent political developments in Botswana with to respect to the media include the Mass Media Communications bill, introduced in 1997. The bill mandates that 80 per cent of the shares in the private press must be owned locally. This requirement may meet fierce criticism from international groups, arguing it threatens the freedom of the press (Southern Africa Research Consortium Consulting Services Press Releases 1998).

Political participation through trade unions, ranging from mining to banking and agricultural workers' unions, takes place in Botswana. However, these are small groupings and have limited effectiveness compared to the ones in neighbouring South Africa. Botswana has a large number of interest groups, especially women's pressure groups. Presently, there are three prominent women's groups: Metlhaetsile, Emang Basadi and Women and Law in Southern Africa. The participation of rural women is limited by various factors including education and accessibility. Women in urban areas are educated and thus are more informed about their socio-political environment. The outreach of some of the women's organizations is limited to urban areas.

Non-Governmental Organizations' (NGOs) influence on political participation in Botswana has been limited. This is because the government has been able to accept aid on its own terms, thus limiting the influence of NGOs and the ideas that they transmit. One reason for this is that the government has effectively serviced communities, obviating the gap-filling role played by NGOs in other countries (Burman 1996). The *kgotla* system, which provides a forum for community meetings, together with cultural norms have often made NGOs superfluous to the political and policy-making process in Botswana.

Despite a great deal of voter apathy in Botswana, democracy continues to flourish as a popular concept. The important point is that people must have access to the system and have the opportunity to participate if they wish to. The low voter turnout may due to lack of supporting institutions, false expectations or a reflection of poor people's inability to participate in politics. Low voter turnout is a serious democratic and poverty reduction problem. It means unequal turnout that is systematically biased against the poor. Unequal turnout spells unequal political influence. The inequality problem can be solved by institutional mechanisms that maximize turnout. One option is the combination of voter-friendly registration rules, proportional representation, infrequent elections, weekend voting, and holding less salient elections concurrently with the most important national elections. The other option which can maximize turnout is compulsory voting, despite the normative and practical objections to it. Encouraging research on important aspects of popular participation, particularly to identify the underlying causes for the lack of motivation to participate in elections, is essential. Approaches that are responsive to public wishes and demands should be adopted. These are enhanced when leaders are accountable to their followers (UNDP 1997b). An independent body responsible for supervising elections in Botswana was established in early 1998. Its effects are yet to be seen.

Economic participation People's participation in economic and social life is essential for building capacities, sustainable growth and achieving sustainable livelihoods. A stable and growing economy such as Botswana should give people the confidence to participate voluntarily and willingly in social and economic life. People participate in the market as producers,

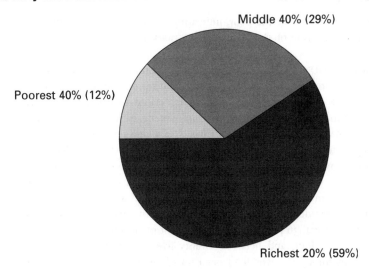

FIGURE 11.5 Income distribution in Botswana
Source: CSO 1995a

consumers and employees. This section discusses the extent of people's economic participation and the government's provision of social services.

DISTRIBUTIVE INEQUALITIES Botswana has a highly skewed income distribution, with the richest 20 per cent enjoying 59 per cent of the total income (see Figure 11.5). Income shares in Botswana are similar to those of South Africa, but fall short of the early 1980s income shares of countries such as United States and Japan (World Development Report 1997).

The Gini Coefficient for total household income in Botswana is 0.54 for urban areas, 0.45 for urban villages, and 0.41 for rural areas, indicating quite pronounced inequality in the urban areas. In the rural areas people are more or less equally poor. National-level Gini Coefficient is 0.54, slightly down from 0.56 in 1985–86, indicating a modest reduction in income disparities (CSO 1995a).

In traditional agriculture, ownership of cattle (a major source of wealth) is also skewed with 47 per cent of farmers having no cattle. In total, the poorest 71 per cent of the traditional farmers own some 8 per cent of the total traditional herd while the richest 2.5 per cent own 40 per cent. Disparities with respect to gender are such that approximately 66 per cent of female farmers have no cattle compared to 33 per cent for male farmers. The average number of cattle owned by female farmers is six versus twenty for male farmers (CSO 1995a). Clearly, the free market mechanism has not worked in favour of the poor, indicating a need to strike a healthy balance between the role of the state and the market.

PARTICIPATION IN THE LABOUR MARKET Employment is a form of economic participation that has a direct bearing on poverty reduction. The incidence of poverty in Botswana is associated with limited employment opportunities. The issue of unemployment is likely to persist, given Botswana's population which grows at 2.5 per cent, while the economy appears to have entered a phase of moderate growth rates (Jefferis 1995). Unemployment was 21 per cent in 1997, which implies that a fifth of Batswana have constrained economic participation. Unemployment is prevalent among young people, people in rural areas and women, hence the high incidence of poverty associated with these groups (O'Laughlin 1997). In 1994, 36 per cent and 27 per cent of people aged between twenty and twenty-four, and between twenty-five and twenty-nine respectively were unemployed. Overall 14 per cent of urban males were unemployed, compared to 22 per cent of urban females. In rural areas, 19 per cent of males were unemployed compared to 20 per cent of females. Labour force participation rate was approximately 50 per cent in 1993, with a participation rate of 60 per cent for males and 40 per cent for females (CSO 1995a). The need to reduce the high unemployment rate is a central concern of the government and measures to create sustainable employment growth will continue to dominate economic policies regarding investment. Programmes such as the Financial Assistance Policy (FAP) which awards grants to manufacturing enterprises and some agricultural projects on the basis of employment created are likely to be retained. The manufacturing sector, largely seen as the main sector of the economy holding the most potential for job creation, remains small and heavily dependent on government grants under FAP.

The economic recession in the early 1990s caused a decline in two very important sectors to the poor, manufacturing and construction, which generally employ blue-collar workers, the majority of whom are from poor households. The employment level in the construction sector fell from 15 per cent of total employment in 1991 to about 7 per cent in 1996. This has serious implications for poverty reduction, as income from employment accounts for more than 40 per cent of total household income (O'Laughlin 1997; CSO 1995a).

PARTICIPATION IN PRODUCTIVE ACTIVITIES: HELPING PEOPLE HELP THEMSELVES Botswana has pursued the long-term objective of enabling people to achieve sustainable livelihoods. The strategy adopted allowed policies to address issues of development, sustainable resource management and poverty alleviation. Specifically, the strategy was to reduce poverty through a process of targeting resources and services directly to identified target areas or households. This took the form of programmes such as self-targeting (e.g. public labour works programmes), household targeting (such as small farmer development programmes), and gender targeting (e.g. production credit for women entrepreneurs).

Institutionally, there were two sets of actors involved in this task: the government and donors. Various bilateral and multilateral donors have provided resources for the general development of the country and for poverty alleviation. Some of these donors have also been involved in providing resources for the directly targeted poverty alleviation programmes. For example, IFAD provided loans for expanding the small farmer development programme called the Arable Lands Development Programme (ALDEP). The effectiveness of the donor assistance for poverty alleviation is always contingent on the government policies under which these resources are mobilized. Due to prudent management of financial resources, most donor resources were effectively used. One of the government's strategies to promote economic participation was to implement programmes designed to help people help themselves. Among such programmes, there were ones designed for enterprise development, such as FAP, and ones for traditional agriculture, such as ALDEP.

FAP was introduced in 1982 with the objective of stimulating sustainable growth and productive employment. It provided non-repayable grants for establishing small (up to P75,000 total investment), medium (P75,000 to P1 million total investment) and large (more than P1 million total investment) enterprises. Though FAP was not targeted to the poor, it provided credit for job creation, some of which benefited the poor. The major barrier to direct participation in FAP by the poor was the fact that entrepreneurs had to make a contribution towards the investment from their own funds. Small-scale FAP was targeted to citizen entrepreneurs, a considerable number of whom are low-income earners. FAP compensated such beneficiaries for their lack of access to credit institutions. Small-scale FAP was also gender sensitive as it provided extra grants for projects operated by women. Between 1982 and 1993, small scale FAP had 14,279 projected jobs (BIDPA 1997). Given the unsustainable nature of the small-scale FAP enterprises (survival rate of 52 per cent after five years of operation), created jobs may not lead to any sustainable increases in economic participation, except that employees get a few months of income before the enterprise fails. Provision of credit alone may not increase economic participation and reduce poverty without addressing other issues such as capacity building, and market dynamics such as inputs availability and infrastructure. Rural labour market dynamics are characterized by migration

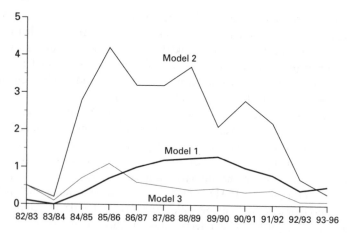

FIGURE 11.6 Participation in ALDEP (in '000s), 1982–96
Source: BIDPA 1997

of the young and able-bodied to urban areas for better paying jobs, thus reducing labour capacity in rural areas.

ALDEP was designed for poverty reduction, with the ultimate goal of enhancing rural development and welfare by raising arable incomes through improved agricultural productivity and income distribution by targeting smallholders. The target group was farmers with up to forty cattle, divided into three groups with regard to their assistance needs. Model 1 farmers were the poorest without cattle, Model 2 those who owned up to twenty head of cattle, and the not so poor Model 3 comprised farmers who owned between twenty-one and forty head of cattle. Participation of the very poor was limited by failure to raise the required own contribution. The not so poor thus benefited more from ALDEP as they could raise the required contribution (see Figure 11.6). Between 1982 and 1996, 21 per cent of the subsidy went to Model 1, 66 per cent went to Model 2 and 13 per cent to Model 3 (BIDPA 1997).

The limited participation of the very poor underscores the importance of targeting and capacity building. Participation in ALDEP also shows some pronounced gender disparities. Female farmers account for 44 per cent of total packages distributed to farmers. With the exception of Model 1 farmers – 56 per cent of packages were distributed to women in this category – more male farmers participated in ALDEP than female ones. Among Model 2, female farmers obtained 45 per cent of packages compared to 55 per cent for male farmers. For Model 3 farmers, there are more pronounced disparities, with female farmers obtaining 32 per cent of packages as compared to 68 per cent for male farmers. In order to encourage participation of women in ALDEP, a gender factor which favours female farmers was introduced in 1996. The high level of model female farmers may be indicative of the high proportion of poor female-headed households in the Model 1 category. The programme design should have taken into consideration the capacity of Model 1 type and female farmers to participate in the programme.

The other major underlying factor for the failure of ALDEP in poverty reduction is the persistent droughts Botswana experienced throughout the 1980s and early 1990s. ALDEP was not designed to work under conditions of perennial drought, but its implementation coincided with the drought period making it difficult to utilize the farm implements obtained through ALDEP. The majority of animals obtained through ALDEP for purposes of draught power were also lost during the drought. In the light of the experience of FAP and ALDEP, there is a need to employ new initiatives that encourage the participation of beneficiaries in the design of projects. Economic participation should be promoted through job creation, provision of market infrastructure, credit and citizen capacity building.

SOCIAL SAFETY-NETS   The government of Botswana made a deliberate effort to redistribute the benefits of growth and incomes by establishing social safety-nets. These include supplementary feeding for the school-children, pregnant mothers and children under five; destitute programmes and labour-based public works programmes (LBPWP). The latter is a large-scale drought-related employment scheme, which offers economic participation to those who would otherwise be engaged in agriculture. Social security has also been extended to the elderly (sixty-five years and above) who receive a monthly pension.

The LBPWP plays a safety-net role by conferring transfer and stabilization benefits to the poor during the time of drought. Given that the poor's most abundant asset is their labour, increasing demand for their labour in building rural infrastructure enhanced their incomes. The LBPWP reached a larger number of poor people than most of the government intervention programmes (see Table 11.3).

In 1992, drought conditions were more severe and resulted in crop failure. In order to mitigate the effects of the drought on farmers, district were issued with employment quotas to create in total 156,400 jobs for a budget of P50 million. Several district councils did not fulfil these quotas. Kweneng met 76 per cent of the quota and spent 59 per cent of the allocated funds (see Table 11.3). Most of the districts experienced problems of co-ordination and management (BIDPA 1997). However, LBPWP played a major role in drought relief. Its low wages primarily

TABLE 11.3 District LBPWP for 1992 – financial allocations (P 000s)

	Emp. quota	Projects #	Jobs created	Funds alloc.	Funds spent
Kweneng	25,650	216	21,185	5.84	3.48
Kgatleng	8,600	115	2,700	3.30	3.0
South-east	6,600	29	2,444	2.34	0.68
North-east	6,600	77	5,247	2.61	2.61
Kgalagadi	4,600	104	1,600	3.60	0.91
Southern	22,000	331	13,303	6.10	5.54
Ngami land	15,160	257	8,820	6.37	4.51
Chobe	1,240	31	464	0.79	0.25
Ghanzi	3,800	47	1,000	3.69	0.79
Central[1]	62,200	1,324	32,377	15.9	11.25

Source: BIDPA, 1997

Note: 1. Comprises five districts: Serowe/Palapye, Mahalapye, Boteti, Tutume and Bobirwa.

attract the poor, providing a self-targeting feature to the programme. This programme can have a long-term impact on the rural economy through infrastructure building, thus opening up remote areas for trade and commerce.

The delivery mechanisms of social safety-nets is highly decentralized, with central government, local government and the communities themselves participating in decision-making, including project choice. The Botswana case demonstrates that options to fight poverty such as targeting of transfer programmes and greater local self-governance have far more potential as long as there is participation by all stakeholders.

Participation in education Education enables participation in all aspects of life. In this regard, education has been called the great leveller, since it provides a means by which disadvantaged groups can improve their socio-economic condition. The more educated a person is, the easier it is to make use of health and other social services which enhance personal productivity. Empirical studies confirm that high levels of education are associated with higher standards of living, higher rates of technical progress, and lower fertility and mortality rates (UNDP 1997b; Dwyer 1989). In Botswana, households whose heads have higher education contain an average of 2.87 persons and higher monthly mean disposable incomes of more than P4,000 or US $1,000. Those with no education or lower education have average

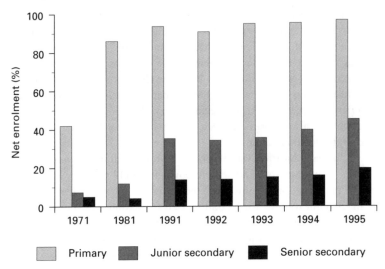

FIGURE 11.7 Participation in education   *Source*: National Development Plans,
Projest Reviews, Central Statistics Office (1990–97)

households consisting of 6.16 persons and lower monthly mean disposable
incomes of P724 or US $181 (CSO 1995a). Furthermore, true democratic
progress can take place only in an educated environment. Communication,
an active press and freedom of expression are all necessary for democracy,
and all require an educated public.

PARTICIPATION IN BASIC EDUCATION   The majority of the poor participate in basic education. The government of Botswana's mid-1980s
expansion of access to education by abolishing school fees for basic
education and providing more schools resulted in increased participation
of the poor and the improvement of education indicators. Primary school
enrolment increased from 42 per cent in 1970 to 97 per cent in 1997. This
dramatic increase shows that cost is one of the major barriers to participation in education. By 1995, the objective of providing universal access
to the nine-year basic education was almost achieved, only 3 per cent of
children of school age were not enrolled in schools (CSO 1995b). Reasons
for missing children include poverty, disability, dropouts, cultural beliefs
and remoteness of certain communities. Progression from primary school
to secondary school also increased from 22,671 in 1990 to 38,118 in 1996
(see Figure 11.7). The adult literacy rate increased from 41 per cent in
1970 to about 70 per cent in 1993. Most illiteracy occurs among older
people unable to participate in the expanded education system (UNDP

1997a). Female adult literacy increased to 70.3 per cent compared to the male literacy rate of 66.9 per cent. The higher literacy rate for women should not be interpreted to mean that women are likely to have higher incomes than men. In the past, few female students progressed beyond junior secondary school. Botswana has none the less done well compared to the rest of sub-Saharan Africa, which had a female adult literacy rate of 30 per cent in 1990 (Africa Region 1993). Participation in non-formal education was also impressive, even though it has not been characterized by accurate documentation.

Non-formal education was expanded beyond reading and numeracy to include training for work and self-employment (NDP 7 1991). In terms of parental participation in education, the majority of parents play a passive role in the education of their children. This situation is manifest in their low turnout at parent teacher association (PTA) meetings. PTAs are the monitoring systems of the school performance. Parents' involvement in PTAs provides checks and balance to make teachers accountable.

Evidently, the government has done well in providing access to education. This was made possible by the increase in basic social spending from less than 10 per cent to about 30 per cent of annual government expenditure between 1988 and 1995 (NDP 7 1991; NDP 8 1997). However, the general view is that this success has been limited to basic education. As the economy moves up the technological ladder, school-leavers and adults with only a basic education are likely to have diminishing prospects of finding work in high technological and higher-wage sectors. On average, about 50 per cent of the graduates of basic education find places in senior secondary and technical education institutions (UNDP 1997a; Government of Botswana 1997a). Already there is evidence of a mismatch between basic education and the job market, signified by high unemployment among those with only basic education. Schools should have an expanded role of training students for entering the labour market, and in teaching coping and socialization skills that they may not receive at home. Parents should be encouraged to contribute what they can, even if it is in the form of contributing services to the school-feeding programme, and the maintenance of school premises.

Participation in health-care People's participation in health has for some time been seen by many as a goal in itself. One of the first elements of the World Health Organization's (WHO) vision in primary health is that 'The people have the right and duty to participate individually and collectively in the planning and implementation of their health care' (WHO 1978). Participation is also one of the mechanisms used to achieve other specific goals, for example public accountability (Kearney 1993). The rationale for promoting people's participation is to improve services and decisions; to gain people's compliance; or as a means of bringing about social change with the redistribution of power or resources. The mechanisms and systems for achieving these should be open, participatory, and indeed enabling and empowering for the poor. In line with this, Botswana's health policy objective is to ensure health for all by the year 2000.

PEOPLE'S PARTICIPATION IN HEALTH SERVICE UPTAKE In order to improve people's participation in health-care, the government has created a link between the public health system and the communities through the Village Health Committees (VHCs). Their role is to create health awareness and mobilize people to participate in health. Improvement in health infrastructure and the quality of services, together with people's uptake of health services, led to significant improvements in health indicators. Life expectancy at birth increased from forty-two years in the 1970s to seventy years in 1997. By 1995, 94 per cent of people had access to safe potable water and 88 per cent were within 15 kilometres of a health facility. People's participation in the immunization of children aged less than two years has increased over time, from 65 per cent in 1981 to 82 per cent in 1995. This has resulted in the fall of the under-fives' mortality rate from 109 per 1,000 live births in 1981 to 56 in 1996. There was a sharp decline in under-fives' malnutrition from 25 per cent in 1981 to 12.8 per cent in 1995. The prevalence of malnutrition is associated with poverty and childhood diseases (BIDPA 1997). However, the percentage of sexually active people who are HIV free seems to be falling over time (see Figure 11.8). This implies that people are not fully participating in the avoidance of sexually transmitted diseases.

Low levels of participation in the prevention of diseases have serious implications for the government's ability to cope with future health demands. Already there is increasing pressure on the health budget given the scourge of HIV/AIDS. Botswana is ranked the highest country with respect to HIV/AIDS incidence, with 23 per cent of those aged between fifteen and forty-nine being HIV positive in 1995. This calls for people's participation in disease prevention (e.g. using condoms or reducing the number of sexual partners) as well as caring for the sick (home-based care). HIV/AIDS is likely to increase the number of deaths per household, and in most cases those who die are breadwinners. Thus, households' incomes are reduced and in many cases drive presently non-poor into poverty. People's participation in curbing the spread of HIV/AIDS is vital as there is little that the government can do without their involvement. The government has a programme of education which says fighting AIDS is easy as ABC: A-abstain; B-be faithful; and C-condomize. However, most

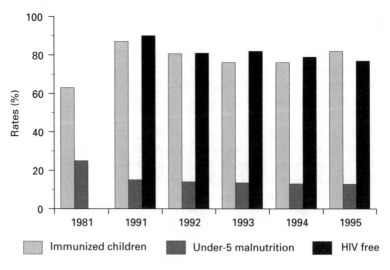

FIGURE 11.8 Participation in health and survival *Source*: UNDP 1997b;
World Development 1995, MOH and CSO 1981–95

of the focus falls on condoms as many think it is impossible seriously to consider A and B. As a result, condom distribution is very high but usage is doubtful given the increasing rate of HIV/AIDS cases in the country (Figure 11.8).

The level of consultation fee, and the quality and location of health services may serve as major barriers to participation by the poor. In the western part of the country, for some communities, the nearest health facility can be around 15 kilometres away. Although provision of health for destitutes is free, some still do not participate fully due to such long distances. There is also a general perception that staff in public health facilities are rude. This situation does not encourage the poor to participate in health activities. On the staff side, poor morale is acknowledged to be a serious problem, one that is familiar across much of the developing world (UNDP 1997b; WHO 1978).

Botswana has a relatively well established network of health facilities both in rural and urban areas. Integration of services through the community-based strategy may lead to improvement in the overall provision of health services in the country. There is need to facilitate competition from the private sector to provide incentives to curtail costs and enhance quality in competing for patient enrolment. As the wealthy continue to shift their consumption of health services to the private sector, there may be scope for improving equity. Health expenditure could be targeted towards improving health services for the poor.

TABLE 11.4 Government of Botswana financial support for housing development, up to 1996 (P million)

	Expenditure	Share of expenditure (%)	Housed (1990) (%)
SHHA	7.6	0.8	52
BHC	818.8	85.8	18
BBS	128.3	13.4	12 (18)[1]
Total	954.7	100	100

Source: Government of Botswana 1997a

Note: 1. Figures in brackets for those housed by government and mines

Participation in provision of shelter Shelter provision is generally on individuals' initiatives, especially in rural areas and low-income urban centres. In rural areas, people get free tribal land for residential purposes. In urban areas, the government's provision is in the form of serviced land and construction finance. The Botswana Housing Corporation (BHC) builds and manages urban housing for both the public and private sectors for rental or sale. The government also provides finance to district councils to build houses for council employees, as well as financial support to the Botswana Building Society (BBS), which in turn provides mortgage finance to individuals (see Table 11.4). The government also provides public servants with house mortgage schemes for property development.

Provision of shelter to the urban poor is on the basis of the principle of self-help. In the early 1970s the government introduced a housing subsidy programme called the Self-Help Housing Agency (SHHA) in order to assist the poor in urban areas to build houses. The government provides basic services such as earth engineered roads, communal water standpipes, and a pit-latrine to each plot. Tenurial security was through a Certificate of Rights (COR) which has now been upgraded regular title deeds. Plot holders also could obtain a building material loan (BML) of P1,200 (about US $400).

People's participation in shelter provision in urban areas is impressive, as demonstrated by SHHA which accounts for 52 per cent of the total housing provision. It accommodates 62 per cent of urban households. Although BHC gets the lion's share of government financial allocation for housing, it so far accounts for 18 per cent of urban housing. SHHA is participatory and quite successful, and thus the meagre allocation of government expenditure to the scheme suggests a mismatch between allocation and needs.

Effects of Underlying Factors

Promoting popular participation of the poor is now conventional wisdom in the delivery of poverty reduction interventions. Generally, there is a complementary relationship between what government should provide for the people, and what the people need to do for themselves to improve their welfare. Government provision and people's participation are in turn influenced by underlying factors, which include economic growth, structure of the economy, climate, culture and social norms and unforeseen shocks.

Economic growth Rapid economic growth, social justice and sustainable development have been the key ingredients in ensuring favourable human outcomes in Botswana. Economic growth created opportunities, generated employment, provided access to essential goods and services and financed social services and safety-nets. Botswana has had economic growth averaging 8 per cent per annum during the entire post-independence period. However, the national rate of income poverty is considered relatively high for a country of Botswana's economic growth record. This is mainly linked to the relatively high-income inequality in the distribution of income.

Structure of the economy Just as in many mineral-led economies, Botswana's economy is relatively undiversified, with limited employment opportunities in the highly capital-intensive mineral sector and the small manufacturing sector. This accounts for only a moderate reduction in poverty despite the continued growth over the past two decades. The physical size of the country coupled with the low population density (2.6 persons per square kilometre) make it expensive to ensure coverage in terms of access to basic social services and infrastructure. It undermines the viability of agriculture through long distances to markets. Therefore, the structure of the economy is a serious limiting factor for both the government's provision and people's participation in improving sustainable livelihoods and reduction of poverty.

Climatic effects Over much of Botswana, the climate and soils are poorly suited to arable agriculture. During the past three decades, drought conditions have become more persistent and severe. This limits the capacity of the government to alleviate poverty through the development of agriculture and growth in agricultural incomes. The case of the ALDEP demonstrates that despite the government's good intentions of helping people help themselves, there are limits to poverty reduction given the endemic nature of drought in Botswana. The gradual climatic change to a more arid environment has led to a fall in agricultural productivity (OED 1997).

Agricultural contribution to GDP dropped from 40 per cent in 1966 to less than 4 per cent in 1998. Own produce also contributes less than 20 per cent to household income (CSO 1991).

Low rainfall and poor soils imply that many who depend on arable agriculture are likely to be living in poverty (BIDPA 1997). The arable sector is characterized by low average incomes and yields, and high variability of incomes. Increasing population pressure also forces more and more arable farmers to move on to marginal lands, where there is little prospect of making an adequate living. In many cases, those households that rely on solely arable agriculture are not able to meet their basic household food requirements.

Culture and the erosion of traditional coping mechanisms Traditionally, there were support mechanisms in the past which enabled the poor to engage in production. Such mechanisms provided access to productive assets such as labour-sharing schemes and draught power through *mafisa*.[2] The transition from an agrarian to a cash economy has seen a societal change, moving people from extended family structures into nuclear families. There have been changes in attitudes towards self-reliance and self-help. During the first decade of independence, communities were more active in self-help projects, such as building schools, health facilities and water supplies. When the mineral revenues started flowing in, the government stepped up the pace of expanding social provision, gradually replacing the role of communities with that of government. In this respect, the development strategy has been for the people, and partly of the people, and in many instances by the state. This has created dependency syndromes killing the traditional spirit of self-help and self-reliance.

Certain customary and statutory practices undermine poverty reduction efforts. Gender relations put women in a subordinate position, which limits their access to productive resources. Traditionally, cattle are passed from father to son. This leaves most rural women resource poor and puts them in a weak position when bargaining for their rightful place as major participants in economic development (Kerapeletswe 1992). Despite having greater responsibilities for financing child-care, women also have inferior access to credit. Women married in community of property cannot acquire credit without the consent of their husbands, and this limits their economic participation as individuals. To ensure that women's chances of improving their welfare are not restricted by their husbands, these rules and regulations should be reviewed in favour of those which maximize the economic participation of women.

Conclusions

Government provision and people's participation are the major determinants of poverty alleviation. The examination of some of the key aspects of democratization and popular participation in Botswana shows that the government has over the years created an enabling environment for people's participation through expansion of social services. However, the level of economic participation remains low. Botswana seems to lack sufficient will fully to address the needs of the poor. The high incidence of poverty in the midst of plenty could indicate that the government appears not to fulfil the role of a caring entity and redistributor. The government's strong conviction that a sustainable way to poverty alleviation is to create a viable economy and generate sustainable employment has perhaps been a barrier to other, more direct, forms of poverty alleviation (e.g. the World Bank's broad-based three-pronged strategy). This may give the state the appearance of being a protector of the interests of the elite. The growth in capital-intensive mineral exploitation did not require the skills that the poor already possessed.

The reduction in poverty demonstrates that good social policies together with macro-economic policies are key ingredients to poverty reduction. Although economic growth is essential for poverty reduction, it is not sufficient on its own. The development policy must be pro-poor, expanding opportunities and life choices. The Botswana case demonstrates that the key to poverty alleviation is broad participation of people in social and economic development as well as government provision of social services. While macro-political reforms promoting shared government improve the enabling environment and allow for decentralization of political power, increased citizen participation achieves broader, better informed, voluntary participation in decisions that affect people's lives.

Because the benefits of growth were used to expand social services, Botswana thus powerfully demonstrates the positive linkages that can be established between growth and equity. However, the high unemployment rate in Botswana suggests that not many people return to basic education, particularly among the poor who cannot proceed to higher education. The basic education system of Botswana needs to be reviewed in order to match the skills required in the job market.

The health budget is coming under increasing pressure from the HIV/AIDS epidemic. This highlights the need for people to participate in the prevention of diseases, for example by changing their sexual attitudes and practices in order to reduce the spread of HIV/AIDS. The government should consult communities and come up with coping mechanisms for the AIDS orphans and those families incapacitated by the loss of breadwinners due to HIV/AIDS.

One remarkable characteristic of Botswana's democratic system is the existence of functioning local government. This recognizes the importance of local, participatory self-governance institutions. Despite the fact that some district councils lack the capacity to deliver social safety-nets, other grass-roots institutions such as VDCs play a major role in the identification of projects and the selection of beneficiaries. At national level, one remarkable feature of Botswana's democracy is the leadership transition which took place in 1998. After being in office for eighteen years, the former president His Exellency Sir Ketumile Masire voluntarily stepped down from power, paving the way for a new generation of leaders and broadening the scope for power-sharing and popular participation.

The government should improve on consultation and involve the intended beneficiaries of programmes in decision-making in order to ensure acceptance and commitment by all stakeholders. The Community-based Strategy for Rural Development (CBSRD), which is intended to adopt community-based approaches to rural development, may promote popular participation and strengthen local governance institutions. The CBSRD also specifically recognizes the need for a fundamental reorientation of national- and district-level structures to align development efforts with community needs and capabilities. This policy change is encouraging but it does not clearly specify the role of individual stakeholders. The poor should be able to have a fair influence in the programmes to be implemented under the CBSRD.

Notes

1. A household is considered very poor when its income is below that which will secure an acceptable food intake.

2. System of loaning cattle to others to use for production in order to manage risk.

References

African Development Bank (ADB) (1998) *African Development Bank Annual Report.* Abidjan: ADB.

Africa Region (1993) *Botswana Country Profile.* Nairobi: International Planned Parenthood Federation.

Beresford, P. (undated) 'Researching Citizen-Involvement: A Collaborative or Colonising Enterprise?', in M. Barnes and G. Wistow (eds), *Researching User Involvement.* Leeds: Nuffield Institute for Health Services Studies, University of Leeds, pp. 16–32.

Botswana Institute for Development Policy Analysis (BIDPA) (1997) *Study of Poverty and Poverty Alleviation in Botswana.* Gaborone: Ministry of Finance and Development Planning.

Burman, E. (1996) *Botswana's NGOs. Southern African Environment Page.* Ecodecision, Rhodes University.

Central Statistics Office (CSO) (1989) *A Poverty Datum Line for Botswana.* Gaborone: Government Printer.

— (1991) *Population and Housing Census*. Gaborone: Government Printer.

— (1995a) *Household Income and Expenditure Survey 1993/94*. Gaborone: Government Printer.

— (1995b, 1997) *Education Statistics*. Gaborone: Government Printer.

Cohen, M. J. and J. R. Wheeler (1994) *Improving Public Expenditure Planning: Introducing a Public Investment Program*. Cambridge, MA: Harvard University Press.

Dahlgren, S. (1995) cited in Wusch (1998) *Decentralisation*.

Davies, R., H. Goyder and W. Williamson (1998) *Participatory Impact Assessment*. Somerset, UK: Department for International Devepment-funded Action Aid Research Project.

Derksen, Wilfried (1999–2000) *Botswana Country Profile*. Elections around the World, URL: http://www.stm.it/elections/comment.htm

Duncan, T., K. Jefferis and P. Molutsi (1994) *Social Development in Botswana: a Retrospective Analysis*. Gaborone: Government of Botswana and UNICEF.

Dwyer, J. (1989) 'The Politics of Participation', *Community Health Studies* 13, pp. 59–65.

Economic Commission for Africa (ECA) (1998) *Economic and Social Indicators in Southern Africa: 1996–97*. Addis Ababa: ECA Southern African Sub-regional Development Centre.

Good, Kenneth (1996) 'Towards Popular Participation in Botswana', *Journal of Government of Botswana* (Estimates of Expenditure from the Consolidated and Development Funds, Gaborone, 1983–95).

Government of Botswana (1983–1995) *National Development Plan, Project Reviews*. Gaborone: Ministry of Finance and Development Planning.

— (1997a) *National Development Plan 8* (NDP 8). Gaborone: Government printer.

— (1997b) *Review of National Policy on Housing*. Gaborone: Ministry of Local Government Lands and Housing.

International Institute for Democracy and Electoral Assistance (IIDEA) (1997) *Voter Turnout from 1945 to 1997: A Global Report on Political Participation*. Vaberg: IIDEA.

International Monetary Fund (1994) *Government Finance Statistics*. Washington, DC: IMF.

Jefferis, K. R. (1995) *Economic Review: New Sources of Growth*. Gaborone: University of Botswana.

Kearney, J. (1993) *Healthy Participation: Achieving Greater Public Participation and Accountability in the Australian Health Care System*. Background Paper no. 12, National Health Strategy, Canberra.

Kerapeletswe, C. K. (1992) *Model 1 Female Headed Household Study*. Gaborone: Ministry of Agriculture.

Lijphart, A. (1997) 'Unequal Participation: Democracy's Unresolved Dilemma', *Modern African Studies*, 34, 1.

Ministry of Health (MOH) (1981–95) *Health Statistics*. Central Statistics Office (CSO), Gaborone: Government Printer.

Molutsi, P. (1988) *The Ruling Class and Democracy in Botswana*. Proceedings of a Symposium Held in Gaborone, 1–5 August. Botswana: Macmillan.

Mugerwa S. K. and C. L. Lufumpa (1995) *Poverty Alleviation in Africa: Putting the Challenge in Perspective*. African Environmental Working Paper Series no. 25, African Development Bank, Abidjan.

O'Laughlin, B. (1997) *Missing Men? The Debate Over Rural Poverty and Women-Headed Households in Southern Africa*. The Hague: Institute of Social Sciences.

Olsen, Clara (1993) *The Role of Non-Government Organizations in Promoting Democracy in Botswana*. Proceedings of a Symposium Organized by the Botswana Society, Gaborone.

Operations Evaluation Department (OED) (1997) *Livestock Management in Botswana: The Value of Previous Lessons*. Washington, DC: World Bank.

Oxfam International (1997) *Growth with Equity: An Agenda for Poverty*. Oxford: Oxfam.

Perrings, C. (1996) *Sustainable Development and Poverty Alleviation in Sub-Saharan Africa, the Case of Botswana*. Basingstoke: Macmillan.

Peter-Berries, C. (1995) *Aspects of Local Government Finance in Botswana*. Gaborone: Friedrich Ebert Stiftung.

Premchand, A. (1996) *Issues and New Directions in Public Expenditure Management*. Washington, DC: IMF.

Presidential Task Force (1997) *Towards Prosperity for All, Long Term Vision for Botswana*, Gaborone.

Somolekae, Gloria (1992) *Mobilising Public Opinion and the Role of Nongovernmental Organizations in Which Way Botswana's Environment?* Proceedings of a Symposium Organized by the Kalahari Conservation Society, Gaborone, 13–14 November.

Southern Africa Research Consortium Consulting Services Press Releases (1998) *Botswana Country Profile*. New York: World Press Review.

Stanley, H. L. (1985) *An Evaluation of Citizen Participation in the Planning Process in Hillhurst-Sunnyside*. PhD Thesis, University of Calgary, Alberta, Canada.

Swedish International Development Agency (SIDA) (1993) *Decentralisation in Botswana: Policy Paper and Action Plan*. Gaborone: SIDA.

Thomas, Alan (1995) *Does Democracy Matter? Pointers from a Comparison of NGOs' Influence on Environmental Policies in Zimbabwe and Botswana*. DPP Working Paper no. 31/GECOU Working Paper no. 4, GECOU Research Group, Open University, Milton Keynes.

UN Children's Fund (1996) *Public Expenditure on Basic Social Services*. Staff paper. New York: UN.

UNDP (1993) *Human Development Report 1993*. New York: Oxford University Press.

— (1995) *Egypt Human Development Report*. New York: UNDP.

— (1997a) *Botswana Human Development Report, Challenges for Sustainable Human Development – A Longer Term Perspective*. New York: UNDP.

— (1997b) *Human Development Report 1997*. New York: UNDP.

US Department of Commerce, National Trade Data Bank (1998) *Botswana Economic Trends and Outlook*. Gaborone: US Embassy.

Van de Walle, D. and K. Head (eds) (1995) *Public Spending and the Poor*. Baltimore, MD: Johns Hopkins University Press.

World Development Report (1995) *Workers in an Integrating World*. Oxford: Oxford University Press.

World Development Report (1997) *The State in a Changing World*. Oxford: Oxford University Press.

World Health Organization (WHO) (1978) *Declaration of Alma Ata: Report of the International Conference on Primary Health Care*. Geneva: WHO.

Wusch, S. (1998) *Decentralisation, Local Government and the Democratic Transition in Southern Africa: A Comparative Analysis*. Boulder, CO: Westview Press.

12

Providing So Little for So Few: Botswana's Social Assistance Scheme

Arnon Bar-On

Social policy, both as a practical activity and as a field of study, can be approached from two perspectives. On the one hand, it is a value framework, orienting the systems responsible for equity and social justice in the allocation of societal resources. On the other hand, social policy is an ongoing process of changing public programmes, with a view of readapting them to new patterns of socio-political organization through efficient and effective technical solutions (Morales-Gómez and Torres 1999). Sometimes these two perspectives complement each other, but more often the process approach is regarded merely as instrumental to the 'bigger', value framework that is best left to experts, typically behind-the-scenes bureaucrats. Consequently, many 'technical' dimensions of policy are given too little public debate, thus overlooking their critical role in shaping the 'who' and 'what' of policy.

This chapter examines some of the 'technical' issues involved in defining poverty and establishing social assistance schemes to help the needy, as formulated in Botswana. In part, this is because the options chosen in these regards in Botswana are similar to those in other developing countries. The primary reason, however, is to illustrate the importance of the details that make up policy and how cultural legacy and ideology may determine these details more than the state of the economy. The chapter begins with a review of the world-wide resurgence in social assistance schemes and some of the policy issues they involve. A brief introduction to Botswana follows because social policies are the product of specific historical experiences and Botswana is little reported on internationally. The main text then highlights the determinants of the country's Poverty Data Line and of its social assistance scheme. Finally, several explanations are offered for why so few of Botswana's poor benefit from the scheme and so meagrely.

The Revival of Social Assistance

Throughout the ages, people have been willing to help others less fortunate than themselves. Indeed, while the reasons for this propensity vary – ranging from personal feelings of pity, through the (partial) expediency of Confucius's benevolence, to the socialist notion of altruism – no society coheres without some imperative to assist the needy. Notable examples of this policy are the biblical law to allocate the poor a tenth of all personal and communal produce, Africa's and Asia's obligation systems of the extended family, and the Christian teaching of 'love thy neighbour' that, in theory, extends to one's enemies (Chow 1996).

For a long time, however, systematic discussion of this help, generally known as 'social assistance', was largely dormant. There are several explanations for this. For one, social assistance is envisaged mainly as emergency relief – an explicitly residual, short-term undertaking for the few. It was regarded, therefore, as a minor appendage to more institutionalized forms of welfare, and received attention accordingly (Silburn 1983). Second, many analysts believed that as the welfare state developed, the need for social assistance would decline or even dissipate, and so studying it was not warranted. This is because the dominant policies of the welfare state – involving, in the main, the expansion of social insurance on the one hand and the rehabilitation of the economically inactive on the other – were expected either to incorporate the poor or to facilitate their absorption by the labour market (Buhr and Leibfried 1995; Gilbert 1995). Third, because receiving social assistance often subjects its beneficiaries '[to be] habituated to the constraints inherent in their predicament such that their frustrations become less explicit' (Walker 1995: 115), their voices remained unheard. Consequently, agencies that served the destitute operated at the fringes of public concern, corresponding to the inferior social position mainstream society confers on their users (Doron 1997a). Finally, although many social assistance schemes have been updated and 'humanized' over the years, the field as a whole still retains its association with the infamous Elizabethan Poor Laws, whose mean-spiritness decreases their attractiveness for research for all but the radically minded who, by their nature, are few.

Yet, all this changed in the 1980s. The reasons for this change are well rehearsed so can be mentioned only briefly. First, beginning in the mid-1970s, social assistance did not contract but expanded. This reflected a growth both in the customary beneficiaries of the scheme, such as single women with child-raising commitments and people with chronic illnesses, and in the emergence of new populations in need, such as the long-term unemployed. Also increasing was the duration for which these people required help, with corresponding financial outlays (Eardley 1996). Second, and as a result of these changing numbers and compositions, the voice of the recipients could no longer be ignored, especially as the delivery mechanisms of many social assistance schemes were becoming increasingly legalistic and therefore opened to public scrutiny (Donnison 1977). Lastly, but perhaps more important, social assistance was elevated to the political limelight by the resurgence of neo-liberal discourse, as the Right accused many of its claimants of being scroungers (for example, Marsland 1996) and the Left rebutted by complaining of the institution's parsimony (for example, Squires 1990).

The upshot of these developments is that social assistance is gaining the stage in the provision of personal welfare, and therefore in the fight for poverty alleviation, only now it comes under the guise-term of 'targeting'. In current discourse, targeting restricts public help to the 'truly needy' in order to reduce the 'waste' of 'undeserved' subsidies, which translates to persons whose resources are deemed as insufficient to live on adequately (where 'resources', at least in most western societies, refer chiefly to capital and to income-generating labour in spite of some resurgence in intra-family responsibility). At first glance, this formulation reads as non-prob-lematical, which probably accounts for the popularity targeting now receives from across the political spectrum (Becker 1997, Doron 1997b). Yet, this simplicity is deceptive because choices, typically complex, have to be made regarding exactly who is eligible for help, what these persons will receive, and how this help will be delivered and financed. For social assistance, the answers to these questions hinge mainly on what is meant by 'adequate' living and which resources are believed sufficient for this purpose. Other concerns are what a particular society can afford to support its indigent members, and the presumed need to maintain in the recipients of social assistance an incentive to work.

Botswana: A Cattle-herding Society Transformed

Botswana is a landlocked country, larger than France and slightly smaller than the North American state of Texas, situated immediately to the north of South Africa. The Kalahari Desert covers 70 per cent of the land, and although the average annual precipitation is fairly healthy, droughts, often severe, are more the norm than the exception. Consequently, most of the people reside on the country's eastern rim, where the environment is more hospitable. In 2000, this population was estimated to number 1.6 million, which makes Botswana one of the world's most sparsely populated nations.

The harsh climate and poor soils have fully determined Botswana's historical legacy. In 1885, with no known opportunities for investment, Britain reluctantly declared the territory a protectorate (Bechuanaland), largely to offset German expansion from South-West Africa (today's Namibia) and South Africa's annexation aspirations. From this date, and for the next eighty years, life went on virtually undisturbed, with the routine being regulated by a handful of colonial officials who were made extraordinarily lethargic by the country's inability to cover even their salaries. Indeed, Botswana was regarded as a backwater that an ironically named 'resident' governor administered it from outside its borders until 1964.

In 1966, when Botswana gained independence, it was still unable to sustain itself economically or, for that matter, on almost any other front. Officially, the average annual per capita income was US $30. However, even this amount derived mainly from the remittance of relatives working abroad, with the remainder being earned primarily from small-scale cattle herding. In fact, so underdeveloped and impoverished was the country that there were only three kilometres of tarred road and the government had to rely for half its recurrent and for all its development budget on foreign aid (Harvey and Lewis 1990). As to human capital, the situation was even worse. For example, the establishment of the Cabinet denuded the entire school system of its only university graduates (Parsons et al. 1995).

By the mid-1970s, however, all this had altered. In 1968 extensive diamond pipes were found, whose proceeds accrued to the state, and within five years, helped by renegotiations of the Southern African Customs Union Agreement (that favoured its smaller signatories at the expense of South Africa), Botswana achieved a balanced recurrent budget from internal sources. After this, and throughout the 1980s, the economy grew in real terms at an annual average rate of 12 per cent, which enabled the state to expand considerable budgets to formal social provision, with which most its people practically had no experience. From 1976 to 1993 this investment increased on average by 13.5 per cent a year in real terms (outstripping the growth of the population fourfold), of which basic social spending accounted for over half (Duncan et al. 1994). This large social investment reflected a public effort to ensure that virtually everyone had access to basic education, health-care and clean water, and the need to educate people 'to welcome and benefit from [these institutions]' (Government of Botswana 1968: 63). Consequently, facilitated by a stable democratic regime and sound economic planning – remarkably uncharacteristic of Africa – rapid social gains accompanied Botswana's economic growth. For example, between 1970 and 1990 both the adult literacy and the primary school enrolment rates more than doubled (in an equal proportion of males and females), and life expectancy rose from forty-six to sixty-three years of age after the infant and the under-five mortality rates were cut by half.

Riches below Ground, Poverty above Ground

However, despite these social gains, which mainly infrastructure-led development achieved, economic growth has so far eluded as much as half the population, which continues to live at subsistence level. This disparity in income poses at least two questions that justify using Botswana to learn about social assistance schemes elsewhere. One question relates to the challenge mineral-based rentier states face in distributing their wealth, or what is commonly referred to as 'jobless growth' (UNDP 1993). This derives from the fact that mining has a narrow employment base and so can improve the income of only a few people directly (Duncan et al. 1994). The second question is whether successful infrastructure-led development can decrease the suffering of the poor and its associated phenomenon of social and economic inequalities.

Poverty has always been part of Botswana's socio-cultural experience. In the pre-colonial period, people were largely self-sufficient, although all apart from the ruling class lived at subsistence level. Most people made a living by small-scale stock rearing and arable farming, which they supplemented by harvesting a variety of veldt products, such as melons and Mopane worms. A sense of community being very real at the time, nuclear families that lacked these means of production benefited through indigenous institutions like *mafisa* (a system of social patronage in which the better-off loaned animals to the less fortunate in return for tending to the rest of their stock), or *majako* (farm employment paid in kind, usually with the harvest).

With the advent of colonialism, this system remained largely intact apart for two significant changes. One change was the introduction of money that, with increased trading, reduced the attractiveness of *majako*, as it was paid in kind. It also undermined the *mafisa* system because money transformed cattle from a source of domestic wealth into an object of trade (Mugabe 1997). The second change was a head-tax levied on all adult males, which forced many men into paid work. In the absence of local employment opportunities outside the family-based agricultural sector, this usually meant moving to surrounding counties, particularly South Africa, such that, by the mid-1940s, nearly half the male population of fifteen years of age and above was away from the territory (Parsons 1984). One consequence of this situation was that agricultural productivity plummeted because, customarily, it is men who look after the cattle and only they who plough. In addition, this vast migration of men contributed to a rising rate of single female-headed households, with a consequent feminization of poverty.[1]

It was in the long term, however, that the changing economy had its greatest effect. On returning home, many men bought cattle and associated agricultural equipment, largely because, traditionally, men without cattle were not considered 'real' men. This mode of investment was also driven, however, by the colonial regime regarding livestock as the only growth-pole of the economy and so subsidizing it heavily (Fidzani 1997). Yet, with successive droughts, now exacerbated by a fast degrading environment due to overgrazing, much of this capital eroded or vanished altogether, with a resulting spiralling in poverty. The last dry season shows this well. In the span of three years, half the country's cattle died, and the remaining stock was too weak to be used for ploughing. Consequently, less land was tilled and fewer farm labourers were required. Also, the demand for mechanized agricultural equipment went up, as a replacement for the weakened cattle, which only the rich could afford or possessed. Thus, income disparities increased,[2] and poverty, hitherto by and large confined to the rural areas, was transferred to the towns and cities through increased rural–urban migration.[3]

The government's primary response to these natural and socially induced economic difficulties was to cushion their effect by giving direct blanket relief to the residents in rural areas, which out of political expediency continued well into the post-recovery years. Chiefly, this help consisted of feeding programmes that, first in the late 1960s and again in the mid-1980s, served half the population (with special attention being given to expectant mothers and to children under five years of age). In addition, policies were established to provide subsidized farm inputs and wage-earning opportunities in public labour-intensive employment schemes. The latter programme, consisting mainly of small-scale construction projects, has now become virtually institutionalized under the title 'community development' though, in practice, it is little more than a money transfer scheme for the needy.

The principal purpose of the above policies is to augment personal economic activity, mainly agricultural, and thus relieve rural residents from immediate poverty. For people who are unable to support themselves even in part, however, social assistance is on offer, which until recently was also the only regular state-funded social security benefit available outside the formal employment sector.[4] However, before examining this policy it is necessary to see how poverty is defined in Botswana.

Poverty and the Poverty Data Line

In daily discourse, Batswana allude to the very poor as people who own nothing but head-lice because these insects cannot be used productively. An indirect consequence of this analogy is that poverty is strongly associated with malnutrition, as head-lice live off their host, and is indicated in the sustained inability of the poor to have at least a meal a day (BIDPA 1997).

Much of this thinking also pervades public policy on poverty, as defined by the local Poverty Data Line (PDL) that the Botswana's Central Statistics Office constructs. The PDL measures the lowest cost of a basket of goods a household requires to maintain the most minimal, but presumably sufficient, standard of living by local criteria, and so follows the budget standards approach to defining poverty. The basket of goods that is used for this purpose consists of five groups of items, most of which are specific to individuals, such as food and clothing, and some of which are required by the household as an entity, such as cooking utensils and housing. In addition, a sixth group of items lists articles that although they may be deemed 'desirable' to have, such as an overcoat and an umbrella, exceed the minimum and so are specifically excluded from the basket. All told, thirteen such baskets were constructed to typify most household compositions in the country (for example, a single male between twenty and fifty-four years of age, or two women, one of whom is elderly, with three girls and two boys). Also, as Botswana is large, with significant differences between cities and towns and between the rural east and the drier west, the PDL takes account of regional and urbanization differences in the cost of living. Consequently, rather than there being a uniform, nation-wide PDL, there are seventy-eight PDLs that relate to different household compositions in six locations.

Methodologically, the PDL costs the same basket in each locality, taking the lowest price at which each of its items is readily available in the area in small amounts. In other words, it presumes there is always a lower price for a given item in the area, and that the poor invariably go for this price but are unable to enjoy price discounts on bulk purchasing. Another assumption is that the poor utilize their resources as efficiently and effectively as possible, that is, that, economically, they are optimal housekeepers. Of course, neither of these assumptions is necessarily true.

The first PDL was constructed in 1974 for the rural areas and recalculated in 1976 for the country's then four peri-urban and urban centres, although these latter calculations were never used in the formulation of policy. The PDL that served the country in the 1990s was calculated in 1989, and is expected to remain intact well beyond 2000 (Central Statistics Office 1991, hereafter called CSO). The following paragraphs delineate this latest PDL in some detail. Although somewhat tedious to read, this method of writing is adopted in order to underscore how standard budget approaches define poverty in general and, in particular, to highlight the train of thought of Botswana's PDL authors. This latter objective also underlies the concluding description of the PDL, which compares it with its predecessors.

Food The quantity of food allowed an individual who is classed poor is the minimum required to maintain physical health in different age groups. In keeping with the local diet and the nutritional standards set by the Ministry of Health, most of this food consists of cereals, various vegetables and milk.[5] 'A person on this diet', as the authors of the PDL remark, 'will not be overweight, nor will their [sic] diet be interesting, but he or she will have enough energy to work every day and keep up a *fairly* active lifestyle' (CSO 1991: 4, emphasis added). For this reason, the authors reduced, for example, the food allowance for the elderly by 15 per cent, as compared with younger adults, 'to reflect [their] decline in mobility', and allocated to infants the extra food their mothers need to breast-feed. In contrast, other stipulations, such as the reduction of the nutritional needs of school-age children by the contents of school meals (which are provided free of charge), were probably introduced to lower the PDL.

Personal items This section contains eight items that together attend to toiletries and to health-care. The latter category consists of two annual visits to a medical clinic and one to a customary doctor, cough mixture, aspirin and Vaseline. These items are allowed all household members equally. For infants, however, poor parents can substitute the toothbrush and toothpaste that are also allowed with baby powder and extra soap, and women can also have sanitary towels and contraceptives (but only in a limited amount and only after reaching eighteen years of age). Poor men, on the hand, are not allowed contraceptives despite Botswana's horrific AIDS epidemic which, reputedly, is spreading faster than in any other country. Also included under personal items, but as a separate category, are eating utensils: one mug, one bowl and one spoon per person.

Clothing Itemizing the clothes people can have to be classed poor is usually one of the most difficult tasks in constructing a poverty basket because 'looking around, it is clear that everyone has a different idea of what [clothing] is necessary and what the minimum standard should be' (CSO 1991: 6). The Botswana PDL followed four allocation principles to this end: legality (because 'some clothing is needed for all people over a certain age'), decency (to allow people 'to take part in normal social life'), practicality (to enable an item of clothing to be washed), and protection (to keep warm). The product of these criteria, examples of which are reproduced in Table 12.1, also specifies the expected lifespan of each item, based on the assumption that the poor take greater care of their clothes than people who are better-off. Thus, trousers, for example, are expected to last for three years and underwear for two years, and to ensure that this is so, poor households are allowed to have a needle and some thread. In a

TABLE 12.1 PDL clothing budget and lifespan for children aged seven to seventeen

Boys item	Quantity	Lifespan (years)	Girls item	Quantity	Lifespan (years)
Leather shoes	1	2	Leather shoes	1	2
Canvas shoes	1	2	Canvas shoes	1	2
Trousers (14+)	1	2	School tunic*	1	2
Shorts	2	2	School blouse*	2	2
Shirts	2	2	T-shirt	2	2
T-shirts	2	2	Dresses	2	2
Jersey	2	4	Jersey	2	4
Underwear (14+)	2	2	Panties (14+)	4	2
School socks	2	1	Panties (7–13)	4	1
			Half slip (14+)	2	2
			Bra (14+)	2	2

Source: CSO 1991: 7

Note: * This item is not enumerated for boys because for boys, but not for girls, its price is similar to that of a non-school clothing item.

similar vein, no allowance is made for children growing out of their clothes because these items can be handed down, sold or exchanged.

Household goods For the household, the PDL provides items that are required nation-wide and others that are specific to rural or urban localities. The first category assumes that, where household goods are concerned, every poor household's standard of living, regardless of its location, should be the same. However, as the standard of living in rural areas is generally lower than in towns, the PDL uses the rural areas as its base-line. Excluded from the basket, therefore, is all furniture apart from a single suitcase for storing clothes and a single trunk for keeping food (the size of the household notwithstanding) and a bench for the head of the household to discharge his or her social obligations towards guests. Similarly, no lamps are included on the understanding 'that perfectly adequate home-made lanterns are available' (CSO 1991: 10). Consequently, allowances are made only for the cost of the fuel lighting requires.

Fuel also chiefly differentiates the residents of urban areas from their rural counterparts. In urban areas, it is assumed that people use paraffin, while in the rural areas it is assumed they use wood. The urban poor are therefore allowed a Primus and two saucepans for cooking, whereas in the rural areas a household is allowed a three-leg pot, which is heated by wood. For this reason the latter are also allowed to own an axe.

Lastly under this heading, the PDL includes blankets, which are meant to serve both their conventional purpose and as a substitute for mattresses. To be classed poor, a single person can have no more than three blankets for these purposes, but it is presumed that couples and every two children up to eighteen years of age, regardless of their sex, can share four blankets.

Shelter In rural Botswana, the typical dwelling is a mud or reed hut covered with thatch. The PDL assumes that the walls of these huts can be patched at no financial cost and allows, therefore, only for the cost of replacing the thatch. In towns, on the other hand, buildings are constructed from blocks and have tin roofs. These buildings, however, are relatively expensive. The PDL therefore takes the average rent in the cheapest areas as the urban equivalent of home ownership, but assumes, quite implausibly, that its cost decreases the larger the household (BIDPA 1997: Vol. 1, 10).

Exclusions Finally, the PDL enumerates several items that are purposely excluded from the basket of goods people can have to be counted as poor. This is done to underscore its minimalist approach. Among the articles specifically excluded are sweets and soft drinks, socks (other than for the school uniform of boys, but not of girls), knives, forks and plates, all cosmetics (apart from Vaseline), a clock and a radio, and all toys, books and writing materials. Also excluded is secondary school education which, albeit free of charge, carries extra financial costs, and all travel expenses. This latter item is excluded on the grounds that 'all journeys [by the poor] are made on foot, or put another way, that no long distance journeys are made which would cost money' (CSO 1991: 12).

The 1974, 1976, and 1991 PDLs: a brief comparison The PDL has remained largely unchanged since it was first constructed in 1974, apart from two elements. First, a few articles were either added or deleted to reflect changing lifestyles. For example, in 1991 a hat was added to the list of clothing items elderly men can have in order to help them keep warm, and infants were allowed plastic pants 'with the increase of babies who have to lie indoors' (CSO 1991: 6). In the same vein, T-shirts were substituted for vests 'as being more up-to-date', and the composition of the food basket was marginally changed to account for an increased consumption of vegetables and wheat at the expense of maize. However, overshadowing this updating, of which little occurred in the first place, the major change was that the new PDL significantly belittled the total poverty basket. For example, whereas in 1974 individuals could have had a bed, a mattress and a pillow and still be classed as poor, now these articles were deleted because although they may be desirable, they do not represent 'minimum' perceptions of poverty. Similarly, knifes and forks were replaced by spoons, and the number of stools a household can possess was reduced by half. In comparison, new additions, such as sanitary towels for women, were minor. Further, and underscoring this belittlement, the expected durability of many of the basket's goods was much expanded. Thus, whereas in 1974, a suitcase was expected to last for ten years, now it is expected to last for fifteen years, and underwear and shoes that in 1976 were meant to last a year, now are expected to last two years. Similarly, the lifespan of a jacket quadrupled to eight years, and an iron, which was previously meant to last for ten years, now is expected to last for thirty years.

The overall effect of these changes in the composition of the poverty basket was to moderately raise the PDL for most rural residents by 3 to 13 per cent, but lower it by up to 20 per cent for the smaller households, especially for single men. In the urban areas, on the other hand, the PDL was lowered across the board. For example, in Gaborone, Botswana's largest city, the PDL was reduced by a staggering 55 per cent for single women with an infant and by 49 per cent for single men, to almost an equivalent drop of 43 to 46 per cent for all other household compositions.

It would appear, however, that the compilers of the PDL were themselves taken aback by their approach to gauging poverty, which they correctly identified as having been less a reformulation of the PDL basket than 'a change [in] the perceptions of the minimum standard of living' (CSO 1991: 43). Hence, in the final chapter of the document, the authors concluded that a 'humane living level' should be set at 150 per cent of the PDL. This level of income, they wrote, would take account of the fact that in present-day Botswana neither an umbrella nor toys are 'unreasonable things to want', nor are a table and chairs and a bed and a mattress 'usually thought of as luxury' (CSO 1991: 52).

Yet, despite these misgivings, the PDL remained unchanged, and when it was published in 1991 it was estimated that 55 per cent of the country's households lived below its specifications, with the average depth of poverty in the rural areas twice exceeding that in towns (33 per cent and 17 per cent, respectively). Indeed, these differences persisted despite the significant levelling out of the perceived minimum standard of living between rural and urban localities. It is likely, however, that these figures were inflated, as they were extrapolated from data collected at the tail-end of a severe drought. More recent figures, calculated, however, not by the budget standards approach but by an Engel curve (by which poverty is gauged by a household consuming at least 60 per cent of its budget on food), estimate the number of households below the poverty line at 28 per cent, with those in severe poverty (spending 80+ per cent of their budget on food) totalling a tenth of all households (ranging from 2.2 per cent in towns to

14.4 per cent in the rural areas) (CSO 1996: 22–3).[6] The remaining part of this chapter focuses on the members of this latter population group because it is they who are the focus of targeting and so the potential recipients of social assistance.

National Destitute Policy

State-funded social assistance in Botswana can be traced to 1946 when a government welfare officer was appointed. But with only two assistants, and 'cases of indigence' being but one of the department's duties, the scheme was restricted to urban residents, who, at the time, made up only 3 per cent of the country's population (Wass 1969).[7] In the 1960s, this situation was slightly rectified, but it was only after 1974, when responsibility for social welfare was given to local government, that social assistance expanded.

As with many administrative changes, the results of this devolution were unexpected. With a closer ear to the ground, and an outreach programme that increasingly relied on indigenous leaders to identify potential beneficiaries, the number of social assistance recipients rose dramatically, and would have been far higher had it not been for a lack of labour to register all the applicants. Consequently, and confronted by each council now setting its own level of help, which was often inadequate to an extreme, the government reallocated to itself the responsibility for establishing guidelines '[to] provide some minimal [national] assistance to the truly destitute to ensure their good health and welfare' (Government of Botswana 1980: 1).

The results of this exercise were published as the National Policy on Destitutes [sic] 1980, and remain unchanged to date, although as an administrative rather than a legal document some of its guidelines have been differently interpreted by different officers over the years. Written on only six, double-spaced pages, half of which are a preamble, the policy defines people as destitute if they are without assets (land, livestock and cash), and if they are incapable of working because of old age or a disability. Also eligible are unsupported minors and persons rendered helpless due to a natural disaster or a temporary hardship. Among the assets means-testing is supposed to cover are also close family members (children, parents, uncles and aunts on the father's side). It remains unclear, however, if people are eligible for assistance only if these relatives cannot help them or also if they are unwilling to help, as the document uses these two situations interchangeably.

The benefits the social assistance scheme provides for are all in kind. They include food, soap and 'other essential household goods', but of which only 'tea, matches and some firewood' are enumerated (but only in the preamble). The food consists of 400g cereal, 40g milk, 40g pulses and 30g meat per day and is meant to provide 1,750 calories. Also provided are shelter (if required), medical care, exemptions from service levies, tools for rehabilitation, occasional work-related travel fares, rehabilitation or repatriation, and funeral expenses. All these items are financed by local government and can be given either permanently or temporarily after 'thorough investigation', pending final approval by the council.

Four points stand out in this policy. One point is that the guidelines are so general that they allow the officers in charge almost unfettered discretion in deciding who is eligible for help and what they will receive. For example, the policy fails to spell out what constitutes 'old age' or 'a disability', or exactly how many assets and of what type applicants can have to be eligible. Similarly, little is written on what help will be given apart from food. In fact, the only specific detail is the uniform sum with which the monthly benefit is to be purchased for the beneficiaries. In 1980, this amount was set at P8.50, which was supposed to be adjusted periodically. However, since then, the amount was adjusted only four times, such that by 1998, when the rate stood at P82.80, it had lost 40 per cent of it value from its last updating alone.[8]

The second point is the extreme minimum of the help, even by the already low standards of the PDL. This is especially true of the food component, which provides 30 per cent less than the minimum local average calorie intake requirement, estimated at 2,300 calories a day (UNDP 1992: 152), and 66 per cent less than the standard average requirement (2,900 calories).[9] Moreover, other than shelter and medical care, no mention is made of *any* other living essentials, although, in practice, recipients are given a new blanket every two years and occasional pieces of (donated) second-hand clothing. Also, children can get a school uniform. In comparison, in prison, inmates receive four blankets in summer and five blankets in winter.[10]

A third distinction of the policy is that its benefits are entirely personalized. Only individuals are recognized as destitute, not households, and normally only one person per household is eligible for help. The only exception to this rule, introduced in 1995, is that when a household has eight members it can receive two sets of rations (MLGLH/MLHA 1995). Given that half the country's poor live in households of six members or more (CSO 1996: 50), this directive makes a mockery of the scheme as a whole, as it presumes that in a household of seven people, each member can have 'good health and welfare' with 250 calories a day!

Lastly, compared to most social assistance schemes, what the Botswana policy fails to contain distinguishes it equally from it contains. These 'oversights' concern both content and administration. First, no allowances are made for unique necessities, such as for special diets or for disabilities. Second, there are no income disregards for personal expenses or as incentives to work. In fact, if the text of the policy is read literally – which is the safest route field-level officers can take – then eligibility is predicated on people possessing no assets beyond the shirt on their back and a place to stay. Indeed, they cannot even have a single Thebe (o.2 of one US cent). Third, despite repeated references to 'providing programmes and opportunities which will enable persons to help themselves and not to call upon government subsidy' (p. 2), no guidelines exist on rehabilitation. One consequence of this omission is that two of the six benefits on offer – occasional travel fares and tools – are effectively denied the destitute, as they are tied to rehabilitation.

As to administrative arrangements, two gaps stand out. One gap is that eligibility is free of any local or national residency requirements. This is despite the high rate of rural–urban migration and the fact that Botswana attracts many foreigners who often run into financial difficulty, especially when they remain in the country in old age. A possible explanation for this lacuna is that policies of this nature, much like unemployment schemes, are *ipso facto* meant to relate to nationals alone. Another possibility is that at the time the policy was adopted both internal and external migration were low, and so residency requirements were not taken into consideration. The second gap is a total absence of concern for abuse of the system. This is perhaps because, as the level of support is so low, it is unlikely that the better off will pose as needy. An alternative explanation is that as the local council, usually in open chambers, must approve each application, it is likely, given the small size of the population, that a member will know the applicant or have heard of him or her, and so be able to ascertain his or her eligibility.

In 1999, roughly 16,000 people received regular social assistance which, even by the most conservative estimates of the number of persons considered 'truly needy' by the criteria of the PDL, constituted a 40 per cent shortfall in the take-up of benefits. Most of these recipients lived in remote rural areas, where there are few viable means of production. In the towns and cities, on the other hand, the number of beneficiaries was almost insignificant. For example, in Gaborone, which had an estimated population of 180,000 in this year, only thirty people received social assistance, whereas, again by the most conservative estimate, this number should have been at least a hundred times higher.

Why?

In much of sub-Saharan Africa, the economy has long been in shambles, unable to keep pace with the growing population and little helped by neo-patrimonial regimes where the elite treat all governmental authority and its economic benefits as their private domain (Hyden 1996). More recently, neo-liberal Structural Adjustment Programmes have added to the plight of the poor by reducing even more what little public welfare expenditure was available. Under these circumstances, policies like the above, which at best sustain only the barest of physical existence, can at least be understood, if not necessarily condoned. Yet, little of this applies to Botswana. With a thriving economy and a sound democratic regime, its people should be able to do much more for the poor. We must conclude, therefore, that factors other than economic underpin the reasons why Botswana's social assistance scheme provides so little to so few. Like most explanations of policy, the answer to this predicament is complex. Most likely, however, it centres on the inter-relatedness between Botswana's historical social legacy and its physical environment and on some of the scheme's administrative arrangements.

Traditional Tswana life was both inward-looking and atomistic. Mainly it was built on and around the family and its extended kinship relations, which the household agricultural economy reinforced because it required the co-operation of all its members. A second element of cohesion, also characteristic of land-based economies, was that the elderly, who held title to the land, enjoyed full authority over their juniors in return for looking after their welfare.

Two features of these living arrangements that bear on the poor followed. One factor was that with the family being the focus of loyalty, the idea of 'society' was weak or non-existent. Caring for others was structured, therefore, by family duties rather than by feelings of social solidarity, religion or 'humanity', which militated against a sense of empathy for the 'other', not to mention the 'stranger'.[11] Yet, even within the family, the help provided to the poor was small. Chiefly, this resulted from the prohibitive cost of all unilateral giving among a people whose foremost concern was ontological insecurity, a situation where 'the ordinary circumstances of everyday life constitute a continual threat' (Laing 1971: 171). As Botswana's foremost writer, Bessie Head, reminded the Gods after describing Bats-wanas' inexplicable ability to live on next to nothing, 'that in case they have overlooked "desert and semi-desert places ... there are people here too who need taking care of"' (Eilersen 1995: 81). Indeed, even today, the failure of out-of-school youth to procure a job 'translate[s] into a diminished share in the distribution of available household consumption resources [made available to them]' (BIDPA 1997: Vol. 2, 83), which challenges the commonly held assumption 'that sharing or aggregation of resources does take place within households' (Alcock 1997: 104). Another reason for giving little help to the poor, however, was that looking after them was as much a tool for extending patronage as a family duty in return for which the poor deferred to their benefactors regarding a range of decisions. People had a strong incentive, therefore, to give the poor only enough to survive on rather than to help them to establish themselves.

Social habits being slow to change, the attitudes and norms this legacy has bequeathed continue today, especially as only one generation has lapsed since many Batswana have improved their material lot. On the macro-level, the responsibility for helping family members remains with kin, and there is no expectation that the state should replace this extended family function. In fact, it is the role of policy to promote and support this interdependence. For example, one of the first questions social workers ask their clients, regardless of the issue at hand, is whether they have approached their relatives to resolve their predicament, and, if not, why they have not done so. Similarly, in carrying out the destitute policy, local authorities go to extraordinary lengths to locate relatives of beneficiaries who have passed away in order to get them to bury the deceased. Another example from the implementation of this policy is the practice urban councils have adopted of repatriating applicants for social assistance to their home villages (including, if non-nationals, abroad), which also goes a long way to explaining why so few people in urban areas receive material help.[12]

Similar attitudes, but ones that may better explain the amount of assistance provided, are found at the micro-level. One expression of these attitudes is the persistent lack of empathy for the non-relative other. A typical example was exhibited in 1996, when the entire cattle herd in one of the country's districts, numbering 260,000 animals, was slaughtered due to an uncontrollable outbreak of cattle lung disease. Yet, when the government appealed to the people in other districts to help restock the herd, two out of five of whom own cattle, they donated only ninety-eight (0.14 per cent) of the 69,000 cattle required (*Daily News*, 26 February 1997, p. 1). But perhaps more importantly, most people – significantly including the officers charged with the policy – believe the level of help the needy receive is sufficient, albeit not for very large families (Raletsatsi 1997). This is likely to be for two reasons. One is that most of these officers grew up in a similar a state of poverty and many of their relatives still live in this state. Hence, with such prevalence of poverty and its consequent 'normalization', there is little pressure for change either from within or from outside the system. For example, no intra-departmental review of the policy has ever questioned the generosity of its benefits. Instead, such discussions on the policy as have taken place have dealt only with its administrative logistics and with its escalating costs due to the increasing number of applicants for help (Molojwane and Chiliwa 1994; Chiliwa 1995). The second reason is that many, if not most, of the people who receive social assistance belong to a minority, previously by and large nomadic, ethnic group whose members were until recently serfs of the country's dominant groups. Although this situation has formally changed, many still believe these people can and even want to live on next to nothing in order to preserve their 'traditional' lifestyle, so no reason exists to give them more than the barest minimum. Thus, ingrained social structures, values and practices of the dominant social groups lead to policy choices that reinforce inequalities while protecting their class interests, and political expediency leads to more attention being placed on coverage than on quality.

Conclusions

For close to a century, policy-makers have been looking to bureaucrats and academics to devise 'objective' criteria to class persons in need of social assistance. In part, this is to avoid having to engage in the sensitive business of defining vulnerability and deservingness themselves, which would certainly prove to be a political liability. A second reason, however, is that once the principle of state help is accepted, 'the way [is] unblocked for incremental advance: for increasing amounts of money, to be paid to increasing numbers of people, in respect of an increasing range of pre-dicaments' (Jones 1990: 218). At least in western societies, history bears this out. What began in Rowntree's (1971) pioneering studies on poverty as a search for 'the minimum sum on which physical efficiency could be maintained' (Rowntree 1941: 102), evolved to defining 'an income adequate for subsistence' (Beveridge 1962: 121–2), and then to identifying the minimum financial and other requirements for 'social participation' (Doyal and Gough 1991). In other words, policy moved from a circumscribed or 'absolute' paradigm of poverty that concerned itself only with physical survival, to a paradigm that is more socially inclusive or 'relative'. The terms 'absolute' and 'relative' in this context must be used sparingly because they denote ideal type, not reality-based, models. Thus, even in Botswana, where policy clearly follows the physical efficiency approach, the PDL allows for clothing that enables the poor to partake in 'normal social life', and people who receive social assistance are given tea, which has no nutritional value. In a similar vein, 'relative' definitions of poverty still require some absolute core to distinguish them from broader inequalities

(Alcock 1997). Hence, when applied to poverty, terms like 'absolute' and 'relative' are best conceived as opposite poles of a continuum, rather than as independent concepts, with reality somewhere in between.

The distinguishing feature of social assistance in the 1990s is the reversal of these developments. That is, income and means-tested programmes are being restructured back to the minimal lines required for physical survival, largely as part of the political project 'of cutting state services in the interest of capital accumulation' (Leonard 1997: 80). Of course, the parameters of this process differ from country to country, reflecting the fact that 'the terrible ancient task of survival' (Lyotard 1989: 10) requires more income and opulence in richer societies than in poorer ones and is subject to cultural variations (Sen 1983). But the general trend is the same: the replacement of collective solidarity by the neo-liberal reassertion of individual responsibility, which policy seeks to achieve by reiterating the moral value of family cohesiveness and by compelling persons hitherto dependent on social assistance to enter waged work.

Notwithstanding these changes, it is doubtful if social assistance schemes that have grown beyond the remit of physical efficiency will revert entirely to their base-line, if only because the number of persons affected would reduce the political expediency of such moves. Still, it appears that to revive family responsibility for the indigent and to curtail public expenditure, policy-makers will increasingly use the budget standards approach to define poverty and so determine the base-line of social assistance benefits which, in turn, dictates their generosity. This is mainly because budget standards are assumed to be more 'scientific' as compared with other approaches to defining poverty, and because the contents of their 'baskets', as shown by Botswana's experience, can be more easily and subtly manipulated to suit the prevailing ideology. Recent examples of this renewed interest in budget standards can be seen, for example, in the work of Bradshaw (1993a; 1993b) and of Oldfield and Yu (1993) in the United Kingdom.

This chapter has looked at some of the implications of using this approach in Botswana, which, to the author's knowledge, is also the only country that significantly lowered its poverty data line by belittling the composition and expanding the lifespan of many of its components. Clearly, one reason for this move was political. No democratic and economically sound government can afford to admit to widespread chronic poverty, especially, as with Botswana, when it controls most of the country's wealth. However, other commonly cited pressures for narrowing the PDL, with its consequence for social assistance, are conspicuously absent in Botswana. First, unlike most industrialized societies, Tswana society does not pathologize the poor. For one, with a narrow formal employment base, relatively few people have regular incomes and so many people depend on their relatives for much of their income. Consequently, there is little, if any, stigma in dependency. For example, many women regard it as 'natural' to be supported by men and get married mainly to support their children and themselves. Also because no stigma attaches to dependency, there is no 'culture of poverty' ideology that holds the poor responsible for their plight or castigates them for reproducing practices and values that mainstream society condemns. Second, as the government's primary expenditure challenge is how to plough the country's mineral wealth back into society rather than find ways to extract resources from the people through taxation (Cooper 1997), the middle class shows little concern about a distributive system for which it pays very little.

Yet, despite these particularities, Botswana's social assistance scheme fails many of the very poor completely, and those who do benefit from it are receiving steadily less of the nation's increasing prosperity. In part, this can be attributed to poor administrative arrangements, such as the inadequate indexing of the benefit, but this does not explain *why* the indexing is inadequate.[13] This suggests that other reasons must be sought to explain the meagreness of the benefits, and especially that more attention be given to social determinants such as the above when trying to define poverty, as poverty is perceived differently in different societies and consequently the help that the poor receive is different. The alternative is to accept that, where the poor are concerned, giving meagrely is a human trait, which is to say that people are willing to help but only to keep the poor alive. In his classic analysis of the evolution of citizenship, Marshal (1965: 88) argued along similar lines that the English Poor Law treated the claims of the poor 'not as an integral part of the rights of citizenship, but as an alternative to them'. Leaving the 'details' of the 'who' and 'what' of social assistance schemes to experts may contribute to this dichotomy, no matter their ethical commitment to human development.

Notes

1. In the mid-1990s, it was estimated that, in rural areas, the earning power of male-headed households was eight times higher than that of female-headed households. Consequently, almost three-quarters of rural female-headed households were below the poverty line as compared with between a third and a half of male-headed households (CSO 1996).

2. By the early 1990s, Botswana was reputed to have one of the largest income disparities in the world, with a Gini Coefficient of 0.56. Thus, whereas 61 per cent of income accrued to the top quintile of the population, the poorest two quintiles received only 11 per cent of total income (Jefferis 1996).

3. Other frequently mentioned reasons for the spread of poverty in Botswana are

the growing number of men who fail to support their children (despite the small, uniform, amount they are required to pay for this purpose by law), and the high level of alcohol consumption. In 1993/94, the average expenditure on alcohol in male-headed households was 16 per cent of total household expenditure and 11 per cent in female-headed households (CSO 1996: 26).

4. In 1996, the government introduced an old-age demogrant for citizens sixty-five years of age and above. This arrangement, however, presumably is meant to help only those persons deemed no longer economically active.

5. In adopting this approach, the CSO by and large rejected an 'ideal', scientific-based diet in preference to what people actually eat. This, as the PDL authors explain, is because although it may be desirable to eat a certain commodity every day, if this commodity is not generally consumed, then a change in its price would not affect the household's standard of living. The only exception to this rule is beer, which is specifically excluded from the basket. This is chiefly due to the authors' moral beliefs ('*We* believe that the PDL should not include alcohol' [CSO, 1991: 6, emphasis added]), but also because beer 'unfortunately ... [is not] part of the recommended diet' (p. 21).

6. In comparison, most northern countries use 30 per cent of household expenditure on food as the cut-off point to indicate poverty. If this criterion were applied to Botswana, then probably 60 per cent or more of the population would have to be classed as poor.

7. The sums involved were also small. In 1955, £500 was available for the destitute, which increased to £1,000 in 1959 (Hedenquist 1992). However, from 1959 to 1961 the post of welfare officer remained vacant, with only an assistant remaining, showing that welfare was very low in the administration's priorities.

8. Unwritten into the policy, but beginning from 1993, the benefit was reduced in urban areas by a third in order to reflect the lower cost of living in cities. Thus, from this year, a person who had been receiving destitute rations now received less than before.

9. In 1999, the typical monthly ration consisted of 12.5kg corn meal, 5kg sugar, 1kg beans, 1kg salt, 1.5 litres milk, 300g soup mix, 250g tea, and 750ml cooking oil. It also contained two 500g bath soaps, 260g washing soap and three boxes of matches. The exact composition varied on the availability of the goods and on their price in the locality but, as a rule of thumb, fell short of the nutritional standards set by the policy, especially with regard to protein.

10. The low generosity of the benefit notwithstanding, it is a big improvement in comparison to when its level was set locally. For example, in one district in 1979, the benefit was P3.00 a month (Chiliwa, 1995). This meant that after the national policy was instituted, the benefit increased by more than 280 per cent.

11. A notable exception to this was death, when the entire community helped the bereaved. Today, this practice continues to be the country's largest mutual aid project.

12. This latter practice also stems, however, from central government transferring the costs of assisting the destitute to the councils, albeit paying for between 60 and 95 per cent of their recurrent budgets. As Mabbett and Bolderson (1996) explain, where finance is provided in earmarked grants, the implementing body must regulate claims to live with the fixed budget or else bear the cost of increased claims from its own resources. Consequently, since the councils cannot change the amount of assistance provided, they reduce access, claiming that the applicant is a resident of another locality although the policy does not provide for this argument.

13. In 1990, a government-sponsored commission proposed to increased the level of social assistance, but this was rejected on the grounds 'that destitute amounts should

always be lower than the lowest minimum wages so as to ensure that such welfare payments do not discourage work effort' (Republic of Botswana 1990: 36). However, given that people are eligible for social assistance only if they are *unable* to work, this reads more like an excuse than a genuine concern for the issue.

References

Alcock, P. (1997) *Understanding Poverty* (2nd edn). London: Macmillan.

Becker, S. (1997) *Responding to Poverty: The Politics of Cash and Care*. London: Longman.

Beveridge, W. (1962) *Social Insurance and Allied Services (1942)*, Cmnd 6404. London: HMSO.

Botswana Institute for Development Policy Analysis (BIDPA) (1997) *Study of Poverty and Poverty Alleviation in Botswana*, Phase One, Vol. 1 (Overall Poverty Assessment Report), Vol. 2 (Technical Reports). Gaborone: Ministry of Finance and Development Planning.

Bradshaw, J. (ed.) (1993a) *Household Budgets and Living Standards*. York: Joseph Rowntree Foundation.

— (ed.) (1993b) *Budget Standards for the United Kingdom*. Aldershot: Avebury.

Buhr, P. and S. Leibfried (1995) '"What a difference a day makes": The Significance for Social Policy of the Duration of Social Assistance Receipt', in G. Room (ed.), *Beyond the Threshold: The Measurement and Analysis of Social Exclusion*. Bristol: Policy Press.

Central Statistics Office (CSO) (1991) *A Poverty Datum Line for Botswana*. Gaborone: Government Printer.

— (1996) *Living Conditions in Botswana: 1986 to 1994*. Gaborone: Department of Printing and Publishing Services.

Chiliwa, S. (1995) 'The Effect of Destitution on Council Budgets'. Paper presented at the University of Botswana Department of Social Work Open Seminar Series, 20 March.

Chow, N. (1996) 'Social Work Education – East and West', *Asia Pacific Journal of Social Work*, 6, 2: pp. 5–15.

Cooper, D. K. (1997) 'Working Class or Just Workers?: Development and Politics in an African Rentier State'. Paper presented at the National Institute of Development Research and Documentation, University of Botswana 31 October.

Dahlgren, S., T. Duncan, A. Gustavsson and P. Molutsi (1993) *SIDA Development Assistance to Botswana, 1966–93: An Evaluation of 27 Years of Development Cooperation*. Stockholm: SIDA.

Donnison, D. (1977) 'Against Discretion', *New Society*, 15 September, pp. 534–6.

Doron, A. (1997a) 'The Contradictory Trends in the Israeli Welfare State: Poverty, Retrenchment and Marginalization'. Paper presented at the ISA Research Committee, 19th Meeting, Copenhagen (21–24 August).

— (1997b) 'National Insurance: Its Struggle for Universality', *Social Security*, 49 (April), pp. 25–39 (in Hebrew with English summary).

Doyal, L. and I. Gough (1991) *A Theory of Human Need*. London: Macmillan.

Duncan, T., K. Jefferis and P. Molutsi (1994) *Social Development in Botswana: A Retrospective Analysis*. Gaborone: Government of Botswana and UNICEF.

Eardley, T. (1996) 'From Safety Nets to Spring Boards? Social Assistance and Work Incentive in the OECD Countries', in M. May, E. Brunsdon and G. Craig (eds), *Social Policy Review 8*. Cambridge: Social Policy Association.

Eilersen, G. S. (1995) *Bessie Head: Thunder Behind Her Ears*. London: James Currey.

Fidzani, N. H. (1997) 'Wealth Accumulation and Distribution in Botswana', in D. Nteta and J. Hermans with P. Jeskova (eds) *Poverty and Plenty: The Botswana Experience*. Gaborone: Botswana Society.

Gilbert, N. (1995) *Welfare Justice: Restoring Social Equity*. New Haven, NJ: Yale University Press.

Government of Botswana (1968) *National Development Plan (NDP 1): 1968–1973*. Gaborone: Government Printer.

— (1980) *National Policy on Destitutes*. Gaborone: Government Printer.

Harvey, C. and S. R. Lewis (1990) *Policy Choice and Development Performance in Botswana*. London: Macmillan.

Hedenquist, J. A. (1992) *Introduction to Social and Community Development Work in Botswana*. Gaborone: Ministry of Local Government, Lands and Housing.

Hyden, G. (1996) 'The Challenges of Analysing and Building Civil Society', *Africa Insight*, 26, 2, pp. 92–106.

Jefferis, K. (1996) 'The Quality of Life: Concepts, Definitions and Measurement'. Background paper for the Botswana Society Symposium on Quality of Life in Botswana, Gaborone.

Jones, C. (1990) *Promoting Prosperity: The Hong Kong Way of Social Policy*. Hong Kong: Chinese University Press.

Laing, R. D. (1971) *The Divided Self: An Existential Study in Sanity and Madness*. London: Penguin Books.

Leonard, P. (1997) *Postmodern Welfare: Reconstructing an Emancipatory Project*. London: Sage Publications.

Lyotard, F. (1989) 'Defining the Postmodern', in L. Appignanesi (ed.) *Postmodernism*. London: Free Association Books.

Mabbett, D. and H. Bolderson (1996) 'Decentralisation and Devolution in the Governance of Cash Benefits in Five Countries'. Paper presented at the Annual Conference of the British Association of Social Policy Association, Sheffield, 16–18 July.

Marshall, T. H. (1965) *Social Policy*. London: Hutchinson University Library.

Marsland, D. (1996) *Welfare or Welfare State? Contradictions and Dilemmas in Social Policy*. London: Macmillan.

Ministry of Local Government Lands and Housing (MLGLH) and Ministry of Local Home Affairs (MLHA) (1995) *Guidelines for Group B Destitutes*. Gaborone.

Molojwane, M. B. and S. Chiliwa (1994) 'The Efficiencies of the Destitute Programme in Botswana'. Paper presented at the Inter-Ministerial Drought Meeting, Francistown, 13–15 April.

Morales-Gómez, D. and M. A. Torres (1999) 'What Type of Social-Policy Reform for What Kind of Society?' in D. Morales-Gómez (ed.), *Transnational Social Policies: The New Development Challenge of Globalization*. Ottawa: International Development Research Centre (IDRC).

Mugabe, M. (1997) 'Social Welfare Issues and the Quality of Life in Botswana', in D. Nteta and J. Hermans with P. Jeskova (eds), *Poverty and Plenty: The Botswana Experience*. Gaborone: Botswana Society.

Oldfield, N. and A. Yu (1993) *The Cost of a Child: Living Standards for the 1990s*. London: Child Poverty Action Group.

Parsons, J. (1984) *Botswana: Liberal Democracy and the Labour Reserve in Southern Africa*. Boulder, CO: Westview Press.

Parsons, N., W. Henderson and T. Tlou (1995) *Seretse Khama 1921–1980.* Braamfornten: Macmillan.

Raletsatsi, B. M. (1977) *The National Destitute Policy: What Really Happens? A Case Study of Gaborone City,* BSW Dissertation, Department of Social Work, University of Botswana.

Republic of Botswana (1990) *The Revised National Policy on Incomes Employment. Prices and Profits.* Gaborone.

Rowntree, B. S. (1971) *Poverty and Progress. A Second Social Survey of York.* London: Longman.

— (1971) *Poverty. A Study of Town Life* (1901). New York: Howard Fertig.

Sen, A. (1983) 'Poor, Relatively Speaking', *Oxford Economic Papers,* 35, 1.

Silburn, R. (1983) 'Social Assistance and Social Welfare: The Legacy of the Poor Law', in P. Bean and S. MacPherson (eds), *Approaches to Welfare.* London: Routledge and Kegan Paul.

Squires, P. (1990) *Anti-Social Policy: Welfare, Ideology and the Disciplinary State.* Hemel Hempstead: Harvester Wheatsheaf.

United Nations Development Programme (UNDP) (1992) *Human Development Report 1992.* New York: Oxford University Press.

— (1993) *Human Development Report 1993.* New York: Oxford University Press.

Walker, R. (1995) 'The Dynamics of Poverty and Social Exclusion', in G. Room (ed.), *Beyond the Threshold: The Measurement and Analysis of Social Exclusion.* Bristol: Policy Press.

Wass, P. (1969) 'The History of Community Development in Botswana in the 1960s', *International Review of Community Development,* 2, pp. 81–93.

13

Towards Pro-poor Governance? The Case of Mozambique

Einar Braathen and Alessandro Palmero

What makes Mozambique a particularly interesting case in the analysis of 'pro-poor' governance, besides its former socialist orientation and its achievements in social development in the first post-independence years of Frelimo rule,[1] is the fact that in the 1990s it underwent profound and simultaneous transformations: from planned to market economy, from an autocratic party-state system to pluralist democracy, and from civil war to peace and stability. These transformations have made Mozambique a 'laboratory' to some extent, where two traditions of technocratic social engineering and top-down managed changes have merged. On the one hand, the donor-driven and aid-dependent nature of transformations gave the World Bank and IMF an upper hand, although donors were counter-balanced, on the other hand, by a party-state with an amazing capacity for self-reform and survival.

This chapter first presents some benchmarks of what we would define as pro-poor governance, followed by a brief assessment of Mozambique's government in this respect. Although its performance is not bad, the lack of institutional arrangements conducive to people's participation is identi-fied as the main weakness, which is explained in historical–institutional terms. The particularities of nation-building in a 'late developing' country like Mozambique produced imitative rather than innovative and partici-patory capacities. Two recent reform processes pointing at the centrality of institutional arrangements for state–society interaction are presented: the new land law and municipal reform. Research was conducted both at central and local level. At central level, sixty-six persons – government officials, donor agency officials, academics, journalists and civil society activists – were interviewed. At the local level, ten cities and rural towns in all the three regions of the country were studied.[2]

Background

At the end of the civil war, in 1992, Mozambique was profoundly divided in both political and regional terms, it had the world lowest GDP per capita and an extreme aid dependence;[3] some of the world's worst social indicators, severely disrupted health, education and transportation networks; and around 3.5 million people were internally displaced or refugees in bordering countries.[4]

The post-war challenges for government were thus exceptionally demanding. The first of them was the maintenance of peace and stability – involving the respect of the 1992 Peace Agreement, the building of confidence between the former belligerent parties, the resettlement of refugees and internally displaced people, the reintegration of demobilized soldiers into civilian life and the definition of the new rules of the games of the political system. The second was the design and implementation of institutional and structural reform favouring long-term economic growth and development. For both objectives, the rebuilding of state structures and the reinstatement of the state presence in large areas of the country were essential preconditions. However, these objectives could not be pursued without workable state–society relations. This statement is supported theoretically by comparative studies on the reasons for state failures[5] applied to the specific context of Mozambique that presents a strong rural-based opposition party, Renamo, and an emerging urban-based civil society that is increasingly critical to the Frelimo state's performance under democratic conditions.

In tackling such profound governance issues, the government of Mozambique had the opportunity to introduce pro-poor institutional and policy reform and to create the conditions under which all social forces could coalesce in favour of poverty reduction. To the government's credit, the Mozambican peace and reconciliation process is generally considered a success and an example for Africa, and the implementation of a comprehensive economic reform programme – one of the adjustment programmes which has been 'on track' longest in the whole African continent – has been quite successful in fostering economic growth.[6] GDP growth was a two-digit figure in 1997 and 1998 and this same level is expected for the two following years. Inflation is down from 70 per cent in 1994 to -1.3 per cent in 1998 and foreign investment is growing, thus reflecting increased confidence among private investors.[7] Rigorous economic management and democratic stability have allowed the country to maintain an extremely high influx of foreign aid, and to benefit from a US$3.7 billion debt reduction under the HIPC programme,[8] a figure higher than the initially allocated 2.9 billion.

Government proclaims that poverty reduction and improving poor people's livelihoods is one of its main priorities (Government of Mozambique, 1995a, 1998, 1999), together with peace, stability and economic growth. The latter two are essential preconditions to poverty alleviation and poor people's livelihood improvement. Katz (1999) shows in a comparative analysis of twenty-six countries the negative impact of social instability on poverty. None disagrees with Kanbur and Squire when they say that 'poor people have little to gain from stagnation or contraction' (Kanbur and Squire 1999: 16). Nevertheless, there is a long way to go from 'generally' good governance to *specifically pro-poor* good governance.

The Agenda of Pro-poor Governance

The 1990s saw poverty alleviation and good governance as two dominant themes in development studies and co-operation. Both topics were introduced – reintroduced, in the case of poverty alleviation – in the debate by the World Bank at the end of the 1980s[9] and have run in parallel for several years, as underlined by Goetz and O'Brien (1995). Until recently, poverty was dealt with as a problem in itself, ignoring the fact that it results from the interaction of economic, social and political factors. Scholars and donors, on the other hand, examined and supported 'good governance' by focusing on legally sanctioned social institutions and relationships and thus on issues such as the judicial system, public administration reform, accountability, democratization, transparency, budget management capacity, collection of information (market functioning, crisis prevention, demographic statistics and so on). However, as Sobhan (1998) has argued, few attempts have been made concretely to link these concerns with development outcomes, and with poverty alleviation in particular.

More recently,[10] the two agendas of poverty alleviation and good governance have somewhat merged into a single approach that concentrates on how the quality of governance impacts on, and which of its aspects facilitates, effective pro-poor public action. The underlying assumption is that poverty is not a sectoral issue. It is not a problem to be addressed by separate efforts: it is a multidimensional phenomenon whose causes, definition, perpetuation and management have a political and institutional dimension arising from the combined action of economic, social, political, institutional and cultural factors.

The overarching objective of research in this area is to highlight governance mechanisms which potentially benefit the poor. In other words, the focus is on the elements which can generate an 'objective-driven' exercise of governance, where the objective is to benefit the poor and support them in livelihood improvement.

While acknowledging that governance can be exercised at different levels (constitutional, political, social, administrative, economic), a number of themes determine to what extent governance mechanisms in place are favourable to the poor. We suggest here that 'pro-poor' governance, besides ensuring economic growth and social stability, should abide, at least, by the following conditions:

1. Poverty definition. A good base of information on poor and vulnerable groups and their characteristics, and its unbiased interpretation. Poverty assessments should include the participation of the poor in order to complement top-down quantitative approaches and foster ownership of the poverty agenda by those more directly concerned.
2. Policy-making. The pattern of economic growth should be biased in favour of the poor; and redistributive policies, via adequate design of fiscal instruments, should be pursued through adequate allocation to social sectors, disadvantaged regions and groups.
3. State institutions in charge of poverty alleviation and their relationships with other non-institutional actors engaged in poverty alleviation. The government should be committed to, and have a national strategic vision for, poverty alleviation. Public institutions responsible for implementation of these strategies should be responsive, efficient and in such a position as to influence effectively other ministries' policies. They should co-ordinate effectively with civil society organizations and, particularly in countries where aid has a large weight on public spending, international donors and NGOs.
4. There should be institutional arrangements conducive to poor people's participation in the definition of public policy and resources allocation. The governance framework should provide mechanisms allowing the monitoring of how poor people's contributions are actually fed into the policy-making process, how much their needs are taken into account, and to what extent the public sector is responsive to them. Accountability, a word dear to most donors, plays a critical role, but in a pro-poor-driven governance the question we should ask is 'Accountability to whom?' and the answer should unequivocally include poor people themselves.

Here, we analyse specifically the fourth point, i.e. we look at the country-case through the lens of the established *arrangements for poor people's participation* in the public realm at both central and local levels. Throughout this chapter, our use of the term 'participation' is defined in relation to the intensity of state–society relations and to how much the policy-making process is open to external contributions.

Within this framework, it is hardly surprising that particular attention should be given to poor people's own perception of their conditions and their own solutions to the problems they face. Too often, and Mozambique is a case in point, anti-poverty policies are designed and implemented without taking into consideration the beneficiaries' point of view and their needs. The result is that solutions imposed from above are of little effectiveness in improving people's lives.

Moreover, as we are dealing with governance issues, taking poor people's needs into account is not sufficient. What matters is the institutionalization of beneficiaries' contribution in policy-making by legally sanctioned mechanisms of consultation and effective protection of this right, aiming to achieve consensus on decisions concerning resources allocation. These institutional mechanisms should:

1. Encourage people's or their representatives' involvement and commitment by providing what Schneider (1999) defines 'windows of opportunities'. The clear definition of 'entry points' at institutional level is crucial to bring the institutions close to the citizens.
2. Establish the 'rules of the game': the definition of when and how consultations should be carried out is essential in order to avoid the creation of unrealistic expectations and build consensus around the process.
3. Ensure that beneficiaries' contributions are effectively taken into account at policy formulation, implementation and monitoring stages and by setting the appropriate corrective measures whenever necessary. For poor people civic engagement might represent a costly investment of time, which must offer a return to be sustainable. This 'return on investment' should be represented by policies that concretely take into consideration people's inputs. Moreover, allowing all actors to participate in policy monitoring is probably the best possible solution to the issue of accountability to the intended beneficiaries.

Within development theory, there have been recent attempts to transcend the dichotomies of state vs civil society, or state vs market. Peter Evans offers an innovative example of how to identify the role of the state, or government action, in relation to a concept like social capital.[11] He holds that trust-based social networks, or social capital, are necessary in order to reduce poverty effectively. However, social capital is assumed to be a product of interaction between the state and society. Hence, the main problem in developing countries is not the lack of social capital, but its scale. Social capital – particularly in Africa – is small-scaled and dispersed. The role of government action is to help *scale it up*.[12]

It is from this perspective that we try to assess the Mozambican government's effectiveness in creating a 'pro-poor' governance framework.

A brief assessment of government's poverty reduction efforts The
country presents several positive characteristics, in terms of institutional
and administrative arrangements, contributing to poverty reduction.

Policy-making capacity at the central level is adequate. An agency
specifically in charge of influencing other ministries' activities in favour of
poverty alleviation, the Poverty Alleviation Unit (PAU), was created since
1990. The PAU produced a national Poverty Reduction Strategy (PRS;
Government of Mozambique 1995b). In 1997 it became the Department
for Population and Social Development (DPSD) and was strategically
placed under the Budget Directorate in the Ministry of Planning and
Finance, a key position for directing allocations in favour of the least
favoured segments of the population. Indeed, the DPSD has more than
proven its capacity to 'ring-fence' expenditure in the social sectors, where
expenditure has consistently increased since 1994, thanks to the 'peace-
dividend' of reduced allocations to defence.[13] More recently DPSD produced a Poverty Reduction Action Plan (PRAP), intended to operationalize
the PRS, by setting specific quantitative objectives and monitoring benchmarks for public anti-poverty action. During the last three years, qualitative
and quantitative research aiming at a comprehensive national poverty
assessment was carried out and good base-line data are now available.
Institutional mechanisms conducive to strengthening the link between
public expenditure and poverty alleviation and to reduce inequalities are
being introduced with the future adoption of a new three-year rolling
budget management instrument, the Medium Term Expenditure Framework (MTEF). Given DPSD's privileged position in the organizational
structure of the Mozambican public administration and its track record,
there are good reasons to believe that the MTEF will be an effective
instrument for directing allocations to social sectors and to reduce regional
imbalances. Moreover, a high level of co-ordination exists between the
government and foreign donors. The relationship between these partners
is on its way to become a dialogue among equals, and the government has
maintained a good level of autonomy from foreign influence: quite an
achievement considering the sheer weight of aid on GDP.

However, external recipes are often absorbed without being 'metabol-
ized', i.e. without being adapted to local circumstances and supported by
adequate information, as was the case with the PRS and the PRAP. The
first was produced when no comprehensive national data on poverty of
any kind were yet available, as the qualitative and quantitative research
exercises were started the following year. It also bears a striking resemblance
with the WB-introduced 'New Poverty Agenda', with its three main prongs
focusing on enhancing agricultural productivity, fostering people's productivity by investing in the social sectors and social safety-nets exclusively

targeted to the unproductive segments of the society, such as old people, indigent, pregnant or lactating women and handicapped people.

The Poverty Reduction Action Plan (PRAP) was produced under an IMF-imposed deadline for accession to the HIPC programme for debt relief. The introduction to this document recognizes that the PRAP is mostly based on sectoral plans and programmes already approved within the ongoing Sector Wide Approaches to Planning (SWAPs) exercises in Agriculture, Education, Health, Water and Transportation. The programmes more likely to contribute to poverty alleviation are selected, deadlines for implementation are attributed and monitoring mechanisms established.[14]

Economic growth, stability, reliable information, effective institutions, commitment, co-ordination and mechanisms for ring-fencing public expenditure in favour of the social sectors are all important elements of pro-poor governance. However, pro-poor governance also requires openness and transparency in the policy-making process and legally sanctioned mechanisms aimed at fostering participation of the poor (or their representatives) in the decision-making process, in order to produce consensus on resource allocation.

In Mozambique openness and tolerance of criticism have clearly increased in parallel with the deepening of the democratization process. In some cases, such as the 'Campanha Terra', which will be examined later, and the 'Grupo da Divida',[15] social movements have been able to profoundly influence policy-making. However, participation of local actors other than government in policy-making is limited and there are few mechanisms in place to favour or elicit it. This is often due less to the inexperience of civil society than to the lack of tradition of consensual policy-making at the government level, and the heritage of the vanguard party years must certainly bear some responsibility.[16]

The limited attention paid by the government to participatory practices is reflected first by the role public institutions play in the definition of poverty and of who is poor. The little attention received by the Participatory Poverty Assessment (PPA) is significant. Albeit started in 1995, it was never completed because, according to one of its authors,[17] its results were in conflict with the financing donor's development programme. As a result, the second phase never started and the PPA bears little weight on decisions concerning poverty alleviation. Indeed, there are inconsistencies between the indications provided by the PPA and the policy decisions taken with the PRAP.[18] During a three-week field trip in which sixty-six representatives of governmental bodies, donors, international and local NGOs, academics and journalists were interviewed, very few of them knew the results of the PPA. This process confirms, once more, that 'the nature and scope of the poverty problem tends to get defined externally and in a particular highly economistic way' and that the poor in Mozambique are considered by policy-makers as a 'stock' of people, rather than a 'flow'.[19]

Government attitude in terms of policy-making is well represented by the fact that the PRAP, in its introductory pages, invokes people's participation in the *implementation* of the plan, but not in *formulation* and *monitoring*.

Most local NGOs, while acknowledging the government's increasing openness to criticism since the beginning of the decade, complain about the existence of a 'stumbling block' in their dialogue with public institutions. According to one interviewee: 'There is a consensus on increasing the level of consultation with civil society organizations; what is missing are mechanisms to do that. A structured dialogue does not exist ... there is no definition of the entry point. Which Ministry is in charge of dialoguing with us, Cooperation, Finance or Interior? ... Our action, in these circumstances, is necessarily unco-ordinated.' In the words of another activist: '[t]he government does not trust us enough to open all doors ... our initiatives for public debates on specific issues receive little attention from the competent ministries.' Still, these same NGOs carry out strong advocacy activities on the most disparate issues like landmines, children's rights, debt, social reintegration of former combatants, land use and tenure. However, the prevailing feeling is that their valuable contributions are not considered during strategy formulation, while they are warmly welcome to play a role in implementation. All of them are dissatisfied with the public rhetoric on eliciting civil society's contributions and concretely advocate that participation must be decreed by law, together with a (consensual) definition of the limits within which advocacy can be exercised. However, even as recently as June 1999, the government refused to include representatives of civil society in the discussion about the 1999–2002 Policy Framework Paper, after the IMF had proposed an open-door meeting.

The government has not been more accommodating with international NGOs operating in Mozambique. These are more than 100 and more often than not act like donors' implementing agencies. However, a limited number of them have been extremely active in supporting local NGOs' advocacy campaigns. Several representatives of foreign NGOs fear that this kind of activity will possibly be banned, with the introduction of a recent law which regulates their operations in the national territory. The very process of approval of the law was, according to several foreign NGO representatives, undemocratic, as after a first attempt at public debate, the government declared that 'the law was a government's business and would not be open to consultation'.[20]

Criticism about the government's lack of participatory practice is well summarized by one interviewee, who said that: 'Most programmes against poverty have failed because we have a preconceived idea about what the poor need ... we should not force people to do things or adopt methods that we think are better for them.'[21]

The Legacy of State-centred Nation-building

The current Mozambican efforts towards poverty alleviation are constrained by the way the founding national elite has institutionalized perceptions of poverty, of the poor and of participation. An historical analysis of the post-independence years can help understand why.

The national liberation front, Frelimo, was formed in 1962 by an urban elite dominated by young students and professionals from the south of the country. Its socio-cultural origins in the Europeanized *assimilado*[22] elite helped make the mimeosis[23] of the European nation-state. Its main social model was Portugal, Europe's oldest nation-state, with frontiers hardly changed since the thirteenth century, particularly homogenous in linguistic and religious terms, and with a powerful universalism developed by Catholicism. As pointed out by Michel Cahen, the elite's project on gaining independence in 1975 was to create a European – if not necessarily Portuguese – nation-state in Africa.[24] Its founding members were inspired by the radical interpretations of modernization theory and its implications for the 'latecomers', and they were strongly influenced by revolutionary Jacobin ideology on how to use state power to create a modern nation.[25] Hence, it makes sense to assess the Mozambique's Popular Republic in terms of a theory on the development of nation-states in Europe. The theory points out four stages:[26]

1. State building and consolidation. The borders are created, a state building elite is consciously working to consolidate state power, a capital (centre) is singled out which simultaneously creates the periphery, and, finally, political and administrative authorities are defined.
2. Cultural standardization. The state, the state elite and other organizations develop the idea of the national community and try to diffuse these ideas into the population.
3. The creation of bodies for mobilization and mass participation. Organizations of group interests appear in order to voice their opinions in the national space (parties, syndicates and associations). Gradually, they become *institutions* in the national state.
4. The creation of institutions for welfare distribution. Various institutions and compromises between the organized interests evolve into the welfare state.

We might say that as the capital in Lourenço Marques/Maputo became a political and administrative centre and as the borders were drawn and secured, the first two aspects were already in the making at the time of independence. The latter two aspects are more crucial for our discussion on pro-poor governance and will be approached below. With an impeccable confidence in their own ability to create a nation from above – with the power of the state in their hands – Frelimo built its Popular Republic. In the Jacobin–Leninist idea of a vanguard party the elite found a comfortable cover for dirigisme in order to achieve rapid modernization.[27] In this context, the aspects of mass participation became the most difficult one to sustain in the long term.

The creation of bodies for mobilization and mass participation When the Portuguese left in 1975, huge amounts of capital were sabotaged and financial assets were exported. Most of the people with more than a primary education left the country and with them most of the country's technical competence, a fact that would later create great problems. A very low level of literacy and racist discrimination had impeded any development of civilian interest organizations. The Portuguese left behind no 'civil society', and there were very few African citizens mobilizing to create an autonomous space outside the state taken over by Frelimo. Nevertheless, Frelimo spread much rhetoric indicating that people were to be drawn into a development based on people's power. Dynamizing groups, *grupos dina-mizadores*, were set up immediately after independence in both rural and urban areas. These groups were intended to spread information about the (Frelimo) state's priorities and then, in turn, communicate to the party which issues concerned people the most. These organs were important in urban areas to give the ordinary man and woman a say, for the first time in Mozambique, in public decision-making. They were instrumental in food distribution and in controlling illegal immigration to the cities.

The communal villages were a different matter and were begun partly as a response to the security problems, partly as a way of resettling villages affected by the large floods in 1977, and partly for ideological reasons, the socialist model for penetration, or incorporation, of the countryside. Frelimo cadres and centrally appointed district administrators had the upper hand. Very often, these administrators had little connection with, or knowledge of, the local environment. Formally, the administrators were to be responsible to the organs of 'people's power'. In many areas they served to promote the self-organization and self-interests of the local population. In other districts they were often regarded as tools of the party or empty shells, and the administrators were profoundly distrusted (many of them moved into the old colonial administrators' mansions).

Frelimo had made itself the only legal party, resulting in a system where the state, party and the organs of 'people's power' which Frelimo itself had set up became virtually indistinguishable. Organizations such as the huge national women's league (OMM) and the youth league (OJM) were created from above and had to follow the party line. These organizations worked simultaneously to represent, administer, control and organize people. In sum, there were episodes and pockets of real popular participation, but these positive tendencies were never extended to the whole state and society.

In this climate of ambiguity, the further development of initiatives for popular participation were quite vulnerable. The one-party state of Frelimo was certainly not capable of mobilizing the population to act as *citizens* as time passed. This produced frictions and fissions in the elite, from which Renamo recruited enough cadres for its 'resistance' movement. This contributed to fuel and perpetuate the civil war.[28]

The creation of institutions for welfare distribution In the first years after independence, economic revival and the welfare of the population were actually priorities for the regime. However, as in the administrative and political sectors, economic priorities were set from above. The belief in large-scale projects, the command economy, and the 'command administration' (such as large-scale movements of the population), was not only learnt from East European advisers but also from the Portuguese. In 1980, a national plan to eradicate underdevelopment – the Plano Prospectivo Indicativo – within ten years was presented. It illustrated the unrealistic approach of the Frelimo state. Furthermore, South Africa and Renamo's war of destabilization efficiently eliminated those existing infrastructures of welfare that rendered Frelimo legitimate.[29]

In other words, the legacies of the past have shaped the current policies in the following way: first, poverty has been defined by the Frelimo state as an externally imposed problem, mainly a problem of underdevelopment caused by colonialism. On independence, the optimistic emphasis was on eradicating poverty through radical industrialization measures, chiefly by means of state socialism. Later, after 1990, market liberalism was thought to bring about poverty eradication. Economic institutions – whether state-owned enterprises or co-operatives, or market institutions – were expected to produce welfare services for the population. As the civil war evolved, the impoverishment was similarly explained as a result of the external South-African-financed destabilization campaign. Foreign aid – or foreign direct investment – was the logical remedy to compensate for externally imposed poverty.

Second, the poor have mainly been defined as people in the countryside – peasants who have not yet been incorporated into modern forms of life, represented by the state and the market. Social development – the synonym for providing basic social services to the population through the communal villages (*aldeias comunais*) – has also served the idea of incorporating the population into state-controlled institutions of health and education rather than developing the human capital.

Third, 'participation' has been utterly controlled from above and hence, above all among peasants, been associated with repression. Participation has mainly been an instrument to legitimize the Frelimo one-party state, and is linked to politics rather than to economic resource mobilization; hence, more recent efforts to link popular mobilization with socio-economic development in a liberal-pluralist society would pose profound challenges to a reformed state. Furthermore, another main legacy for the new democratic regime seemed to be the divide, deepened after the civil war, between urban and rural areas. Mozambique was a 'bifurcated'[30] state *par excellence*, and one could expect that the legacy of 'centralized despotism'[31] would constrain severely the attempts to bring poverty and/or poor people's concerns into public policy-making.

Contradictions of Participatory Governance

The transition from an autocratic one-party state to pluralist democracy took place between 1990 and 1994. As in the transition to independence in 1974–75, 'internal' civil society and urban-based movements of workers and students played no significant role. The transition from war to peace and representative democracy in Mozambique was therefore very different from similar changes in most other African countries.[32] The process was orderly, orchestrated from the top in a three-part arrangement consisting of the Frelimo government, the Renamo leadership and the donor community represented by the special representative of UN's Secretary General, Mr Ajello.

As indicated earlier, the Mozambican government is inclined towards a state-centred, top-down and non-consulting management (governance) of growth and 'poverty'. 'Industrial nation-building', or growth in the national economy, is the top priority. The lack of capacity to 'metabolize' a policy, for example of poverty alleviation, by translating it into viable local-level strategies, is conditioned by the absence of institutional arrangements for state/society interaction at the local level. However, after 1994 with the democratization process we can identify two reforms that particularly break with the ruling trend in the country: the Land Law, and the municipal reform. To what degree do they point in the direction of pro-poor participatory governance?

The Land Law: a show of mobilization from below! The consultative process that surrounded the approval of the Land Law was a turning point both in the government's attitude towards popular mobilization and demand and in the practice of policy-making. The process led, for the first time, to the institutionalization of participation of actors other than the government in policy-making, as two Mozambican civil society organizations became members of an inter-ministerial committee on land issues.[33] Agrarian reform offers significant poverty reduction advantages in relation to other policies, as Herring (1999) argues, and, according to some interviewees, the new Land Law of 1997 might have been the most important pro-poor reform put in place under the new government.

The mobilization of civil society organizations around the reform of the law governing land use and tenure system introduced radical changes in the law and proved both the government's increasing openness and tolerance to criticism and the importance of mass actions in pro-poor politics. Campanha Terra's[34] efforts to disseminate information on the law and other NGOs' commitment in defending rural people's rights provide a striking example of the richness and dynamism of Mozambican social forces.

THE LAND QUESTION IN MOZAMBIQUE Access to land in rural areas is crucial in a country like Mozambique, where 65 per cent of the population and 80 per cent of the poor live in rural areas.[35] Entitlements to use of natural resources, in which land has a prominent position, currently represent the main source of livelihood for the great majority of the population. Smallholder agriculture as a whole employs 63 per cent of men and 92 per cent of women in the labour force, and represents more than 80 per cent of agricultural production value, contributing approximately 25 per cent to GDP (Devereux and Palmero 1999).

In the immediate aftermath of independence, all land was nationalized. This was not followed by redistribution, as the most fertile land, until then occupied by colonial settlers, was allocated to large state farms. Many rural dwellers were relocated in communal villages that served the purpose both of easily providing social services and of controlling peasants, who were seen as a labour reservoir for state farms.[36] Small-scale producers, bearing the heritage of colonial times, could not fit into Frelimo 'modernization'[37] programme until 1983, by which time, due to the prevalence of the war, large areas of the country were inaccessible.[38] The benefits of Frelimo's agrarian policy – intended to modernize the sector via high investment in collective state farms – for the rural poor never went beyond the few thousands of jobs offered.

Thus, state policies, rather than expanding people's opportunities and choices, attempted radically to modify their traditional habits and practices, considered by the incumbent vanguard party as opposed to social progress and modernization.

With the consolidation of the peace process and the market-friendly economic reform steadily on its way, a number of foreign investors, from both overseas and bordering countries,[39] became interested in investing in Mozambique. Also, affluent Mozambicans started what Negrão (1999) calls 'land hoarding', as land could be used as their contribution in joint ventures with foreigners providing capital funds.[40] The competition for high economic potential land increased, particularly in border zones and on the coast. The most valuable land located near roads, in irrigated areas or close to South Africa and Zimbabwe, was registered earlier, but since the mid-1990s several localized conflicts between investors, often holding a title deed released by the state, and rural dwellers have occurred. Some of these involved war refugees returning to the areas they had earlier abandoned due to the prevailing security situation.

The demand for land was determined by different purposes (food and cash crop farming, cattle rearing, forestry, mining, beach or hunting tourism). Different land uses might entail different rights, as in the case of exclusive exploitation which requires a title deed, and a concession of exploitation rights which does not require one.[41] However, all uses require tenure security, which the former law was unable to ensure.

THE DRAFTING OF A NEW LAND LAW   The drafting of the new law began when it was realized that a legal instrument to regulate both land use and a tenure system adapted to the prevailing political, social and economic circumstances was necessary.

A national conference on land was followed by a draft law produced in 1996 by the Ministry of Agriculture and approved by an inter-ministerial Commission on Land Issues. All actors other than government and donors were excluded from consultation. The draft proposed land privatization and the recognition of tenure security for smallholders by demarcating already occupied land and awarding title deeds. In other words, as in many neighbouring countries, the proposed solution entailed the physical division of the territorial space between the rural household and large investors, perpetuating a dualistic conception of traditional and commercial agriculture as if there was no interaction between them (Negrão 1999). Local power-holders, investors and several donors welcomed this proposal, particularly those who had supported the Ministry of Agriculture in drafting the law by financing a team of expatriate experts.

The draft bill was submitted to public debate in Maputo with participation from government representatives, NGOs and community associations, as well as private individuals. From the beginning, dissenting voices emerged. According to Negrão (1999), although the debate was characterized by the clear consciousness that the proposal was inadequate, civil society representatives concentrated on negative aspects of the proposal without offering an alternative.

A coalition of NGOs and associations brought the debate to the grassroots level, starting a comprehensive process of consultation with urban and rural dwellers. Demonstrations and cultural events, press conferences and workshops for smallholders were organized and it emerged that several aspects of the draft legislation were particularly problematic for small farmers: they did not want privatization but registration of communal land and consultations. Women's organizations complained that the land did not take into account the rights of women, who, according to customary law, work the land but do not own and cannot inherit it.

When the results were made public and communicated to the government, the initial reaction was, according to one activist, mildly sceptical. Protests and public campaigns to change the law were organized and farmers even marched on parliament to protest and demand conflict resolution in rural areas as well as consideration of their proposed amendments. The government did not object to the mobilization, but initially was not actively engaged. Ultimately, it was forced to take popular feeling into consideration and an enlarged committee, now including two national NGOs, revised the land bill.

THE OUTCOME: A PRO-POOR LAND LAW   The new legislation[42] does take into account many of the farmers' concerns and recognizes that smallholders have rights to land simply by virtue of their traditional occupation of a land area. This provision protects smallholders against occupation of their land by investors and against the granting of concessions in areas already under cultivation. Before any right to exploit land is granted, local communities must be consulted about the investment proposal. Communities are also invited to participate in the resolution of disputes over land occupancy and rights. The revised Land Law also enshrines women's rights to own and inherit land, in line with the 1990 constitution that recognizes the equality of women and men.

The main achievements of the revised Land Law are:

- it strengthens security of tenure for smallholders and women, both of whom did not enjoy it before
- it involves communities in land conflict mediation
- it does not intend to discourage foreign investors, but it does ensure that smallholders are not disadvantaged because of a lack of title deeds to land their family might have been farming for generations

- land grabbing and land hoarding are minimized because oral testimony about land occupancy and use is considered as valid as written evidence.

The Land Law is clear about the basic rights and obligations that have to be respected by all, including the state. The right to access and benefit from the land is directly associated with the duty to use it and the state's duty to enforce it. Any person who is granted the right of land use following the presentation of a development plan has to implement it within two years, in the case of foreigners, and five years, in the case of nationals. The obligation to implement the development plan is the major legal guarantee against land hoarding, provided there is effective monitoring.

THE CIVIC CAMPAIGN TO PREPARE THE IMPLEMENTATION OF THE LAW A consensus emerged at societal level that the new bill represented an advance in relation to the former law and that it was urgent to spread the information about what had been achieved to small farmers all over the country. A group of national and foreign development NGOs, activists and academics founded a national committee and started the so-called Campanha Terra in order to join forces in the dissemination of information aimed, in particular, at rural families.[43]

Three objectives informed the activity of the campaign: (1) to divulge the new Land Law; (2) to promote its enforcement; and (3) to stimulate discussion between the smallholder and commercial sectors occupying the same area in order to find mutually beneficial institutional arrangements. The rights and responsibilities introduced by the new Land Law provide the opportunity to overcome the dualistic conception of traditional and commercial agriculture (Negrão 1999).

The campaign, financially supported by a number of 'progressive' donors and international NGOs, organized seminars at provincial and local level. They produced a manual targeted at professionals, civil servants and literate people in general. Theatre in local languages, audio-tapes in both Portuguese and local languages, a video, guidebooks and posters targeted illiterate rural people. The main messages disseminated concerned dispositions about traditional and customary rights and the access of women to land.

There are no doubts that the consultative process around the campaign contributed to the maintenance of peace and stability through building consensus around such a crucial issue: had the government maintained its original position, popular protest would not have ceased and would have probably generated greater unrest. The authorities seem to have fully realized the potential political dividend of involving civil society in policy-making, as, according to one activist, government is now 'proud of the new Land Law and of the consultative process that surrounded it'.

The municipal reform: a show of non-participation?[44] The preparations to introduce local self-government – or democratic decentralization – in terms of municipalities started in the last years of the one-party state. This had unfortunate consequences for the municipal reform which was designed in the non-consultative and non-participatory fashion characteristic of Frelimo's earlier regime. We shall here argue that:

- first, a pattern of *exclusion* was brought to its logical end with the participation of only 14.6 per cent of the eligible voters in Mozambique's first-ever local elections in 1998
- second, there was still a large untapped *social capital* in the municipalized urban areas, which should not be confounded with the widespread distrust of political structures – such as political parties and public decision-making bodies
- third, there were clear indicators of strong *social discontent*, which, however, could easily be reinterpreted as social concern and support for joint municipal/popular action to improve urban and social services, and to alleviate urban poverty
- fourth, the newly elected municipal governments swiftly showed their abilities to improve local communities' perceptions of, and relationship with, the new local authorities

A PATTERN OF EXCLUSION AND NON–PARTICIPATION The first-ever local government elections were held on 30 June 1998. While 85 per cent of the registered voters participated in the 1994 presidential and parliamentary elections, only 14.6 per cent of them bothered to take part four years later. Although local elections in most countries attract much less attention than general elections, the drop in participation in Mozambique was rather dramatic. These were 'elections without people'.[45] However, they were the logical result of a process of political exclusion.

The local government elections (*eleições autárquicas*) represented the legal procedure to set up local councils, or more correctly bodies of local self-government: municipalities (*municípios*). The elections contained two ballots: one for the municipal assembly (*Assembléia Municipal*), and one for direct election of the mayor (*Presidente do Conselho Municipal*). Originally scheduled for late 1995, the municipal elections were postponed four times.[46]

In sum, Frelimo's policies – as formulated by the government as well as by the old guard leading the Frelimo bench in parliament – contributed to a pattern of confrontation with Renamo and, more widely, to a logic of political exclusion:

1. Exclusion of large parts of the population from municipal self-

government. First the rural areas were excluded with the replacement of the 1994 Law of Municipal Districts by a new law giving the government powers to introduce, on a top-down 'gradualist' and hence discretionary basis, municipalities only in cities and towns. Then all but ten rural towns were excluded from taking part in the first municipal elections.

2. At the national level, exclusion of large parts of political society from the formulation of the decentralization policy. The new laws and rules of the game for the local elections and municipalities were adopted despite dissent from the large opposition party, from 112 of the 250 representatives in parliament, and from nearly all the smaller parties.[47]

3. At the local level, exclusion of the entire political and civil society in the administration of elections and in implementation of the reform. In the 1994 general elections, the national electoral commission (CNE) was also represented in each province and district with commissions recruited from the political parties locally.[48] The commissions joined with all the parties and any civic organization to solve educational and more administrative tasks.[49] In particular, the district commissions were instrumental in helping the electoral administration (STAE) to reduce friction in the polling station machinery.[50] The Ministry of State Administration first proposed this version of CNE, but the Frelimo bench in parliament rejected it. They ended up with a centralized model for the political body (CNE), and local bodies of a purely 'administrative' character (STAE).

This institutional-electoral design, whether a result of past legacies or of present politics, was mainly responsible for the alleged 'local election fiasco' in two ways. First, it stripped the local electoral machinery of the only potential sources of increased efficiency and legitimacy, namely participation from leaders of the local political and civil society. Second, and as consequence, this non-inclusive set-up gave legitimacy to the boycott campaign initiated by Renamo and nearly all the other opposition parties.

Elections took place in thirty-three towns and cities. Frelimo was contested in fourteen of the municipalities, mainly by local independent lists or splinter groups from Frelimo, and uncontested in the remaining nineteen. At the end of the day, Frelimo won everywhere. However, Frelimo received the votes of only 10 per cent of the eligible electorate.

A LARGE UNTAPPED SOCIAL CAPITAL IN THE MUNICIPALIZED URBAN AREAS After stating that 75.8 per cent had accurate knowledge about the forthcoming municipal elections, we found that 74.3 per cent wanted to take part in local elections.[51] Even more interesting, every third

TABLE 13.1 Forms and extent of political participation in the ten sample cities and villages

Form of participation	'Yes' (%)
Voted in 1994 general elections	72.8
Going to vote in the 1998 local elections	74.3
Want to take part in 1998 the local elections campaign	24.7
Participated in a meeting to discuss or take action on a public issue	25.0
Participated in a public protest or demonstration	12.2
Written a letter or spoken on radio on a local public issue	8.5
Taken part in association(s) created locally in recent years	7.4
Taken part in national association(s) in recent years	6.1

potential voter, and 24.7 per cent of the sample, wanted to take active part in the electoral campaign (Table 13.1). The other questions revealed similar indications of high '*civic virtue*'[52] and high interest in public/political affairs. There were no particular differences between men and women and old and young. However, the propensity for political participation was higher in cities than it was in rural towns. Hence, when we leave out the three rural towns that were not going to be municipalized our sample proves an even higher willingness to use the ballot. Here, people did not answer on a hypothetical basis as regards taking part in the local elections. As Table 13.1 indicates, based on our sample of 1,573 citizens in seven of the thirty-three cities and towns to be municipalized, 80.9 per cent said they were going to vote. This high voting preparedness some nine to six months before the actual elections is confirmed by another survey conducted in October 1997 on a nation-wide scale.[53] It included all the thirty-three cities and towns eligible for municipal elections, and showed that almost 90 per cent of the residents stated that they would participate in the local government polls.[54] Another research project carried out in six sample municipalities showed similar 'strong and affirmative in beliefs concerning participation in the ballot'.[55] The stunning drop in 'political participation' when the voters came to the ballot day cannot be interpreted as anything but a conscious protest against the electoral-institutional arrangements depicted earlier, with virtually no competition between parties and no real choice offered.

At the outset, the political parties could not rely on much public trust or legitimacy. Our data on trust patterns revealed the following: while 80.9 per cent of our sample in seven municipalities wished to vote and 53.2 per cent in late 1997 said they thought the local elections were going to be free

TABLE 13.2 Citizens' preferential trust, ten Mozambican cities and towns

	(%)
Trust in family	29.1
Trust in 'civil society' representatives (traditional or religious leaders)	25.6
Trust in social network (other citizens or people to whom one speaks daily)	20.0
Trust in one or more of the political parties (or their representatives)	14.9
Do not know/ do not want to answer	10.4
Total	100.0

and fair, only 32.6 per cent professed trust in one or more political parties. This distrust was confirmed by 39 per cent of the non-voters in our post-election one-city survey, supporting the proposition that 'politicians are all the same'. Asked to whom they would turn if they had a problem with the government or a public official locally, only 14.9 per cent conferred such preferential trust on to one or more of the political parties or their representatives.

Notwithstanding the low trust in political society (politicians and political parties), there was a big pool of trust in other social entities, even outside the extended family. Combined with indicators of high civic virtues, measured as willingness to participate in politics and reported participation in associational life, we can conclude that there is a considerable stock of social capital in Mozambique. However, it was mostly untapped. It has not yet been channelled into scaled-up interaction or co-operation between citizens for common purposes.

STRONG SOCIAL DISCONTENT AND SUPPORT FOR ACTION The absence of alternatives to Frelimo either in the assembly or in the mayoral ballot in nineteen of the thirty-three municipalities made the elections a plebiscitary exercise, where the options in terms of loyalty, voice and exit (Hirschmann 1970) were a Frelimo vote, a blank ballot or abstention, respectively. To what degree were the local elections a plebiscitary expression of exit from the Frelimo party?

There was disappointment among the 1994 Frelimo voters with the policies and/or results of the party's rule. Some critical supporters of the Frelimo party stick to this explanation: 'The abstentions signify a "yellow card" to the Frelimo Party and Government.'[56] The editor of the *Mozambique Peace Process Bulletin*, Joseph Hanlon, wrote: 'A commonly heard comment of people who did not vote was: "We voted in 1994 and it did not make any difference; our lives have not improved." Economic issues

TABLE 13.3 Level of discontent with public services

	Beira	Montepuez	Xai–Xai	Pemba	Chimoio	Total
Sanitary conditions	0.9	0.8	0.7	0.6	0.5	0.70
Water supply	0.7	0.8	0.6	0.6	0.5	0.64
Agricultur. assistance	0.8	0.6	0.7	0.5	0.6	0.64
Piped water	0.7	0.8	0.5	0.5	0.6	0.62
Water holes/wells	0.8	0.6	0.5	0.6	0.5	0.60
Health services	0.7	0.7	0.6	0.4	0.5	0.58
Trash collection	0.8	0.5	0.7	0.6	0.3	0.58
Road maintenance	0.8	0.6	0.5	0.5	0.4	0.56
Road construction	0.7	0.6	0.5	0.4	0.4	0.52
Means of transport	0.6	0.8	0.4	0.4	0.4	0.52
Market place	0.6	0.5	0.4	0.5	0.4	0.48
Secondary school	0.6	0.3	0.4	0.3	0.6	0.44
Primary school	0.5	0.2	0.3	0.2	0.4	0.32
Total mean	0.71	0.60	0.52	0.47	0.47	0.55

Note: 0.0 = all satisfied; 1.0 = all dissatisfied; excluding those who answered 'don't know'

and corruption were often cited: the elite has prospered but the people feel poorer.'[57]

We find this explanation to be in line with the theoretical contention that the relationship between the Frelimo party and its constituencies has been clientelist by nature: political support for material gains. It is an expression of frustration that redistributive policies are not pursued. It is also a sign that the historical and ideological sources of legitimacy of the ruling party have dwindled. Unquestionably, Frelimo enjoyed popular support after winning the liberation war and, as discussed earlier, there were some significant improvements in social service provision after independence. Once its reputation as a people's party that executes 'government for the masses' had been tarnished, national print media gave space to those intellectuals who criticized increased patrimonialization[58] of the party state. This was cited as the main reason for the high abstention rate:

- 'marginalization' of the electorate caused by 'the privatization of the Frelimo party'
- 'generalized poverty and unequal distribution of wealth'
- 'loss of contact of the party top with the base', 'lack of internal democracy' and of 'dialogue with the opposition'.[59]

In Table 13.3 we have omitted the two rural towns in our sample, operating only with the five city municipalities.[60] On average, 55 per cent of our sample are discontented with any public service mentioned. There are two areas of discontent that stand out:

1.   Discontent with *agricultural assistance* rendered by the local state structures, in particular the local delegations of the Ministry of Agriculture. This area has the third highest single score of discontent, in spite of the context being cities. There may be two reasons for this: first, a surprisingly high percentage of the city population depends on subsistence agriculture. '*Machambas*' (agricultural plots) are visible everywhere, even in the city centres. This mainly indicates a very low income level – the high incidence of absolute poverty – in Mozambican cities; people depend on the informal economy and self-subsistence activities to survive. Second, public services provided in the cities are not at all adapted to this situation; there is a huge under-supply of agricultural assistance. This is in itself a sign of two structural features of Mozambican local government: low social responsiveness and very little adaptation to local conditions. It supports the arguments for increased local democratic control of public resources.

2.   Particularly high discontent with services related to the maintenance and improvement of *public health*, ranging from improvement of sanitary conditions (70 per cent are discontented) to garbage collection (58 per cent), to the demand for improved water supplies (60–64 per cent) and public health services (58 per cent). Interestingly, education has the lowest score of discontent.[61]

These figures indicate that food and public health are the most important issues for the electorate in the cities.

These data should not be read only as a vote of discontent, but also as an expression of social concern and support for joint municipal/popular action to improve urban and social services, to promote human development and to reduce urban poverty. To what degree have the new democratic municipalities been able to transform people's anxieties into public action?

THE CAPABILITIES OF DEMOCRATIC MUNICIPALITIES The seven municipalities in our study (first visited in 1997) were visited for the third time one year after the local elections, in July 1999. These were our findings:

First, local service provision has improved in all the municipalities visited, mainly in the following fields:

*   garbage collection
*   sweeping of public spaces, gardens, squares etcetera
*   painting and maintenance of municipal buildings and constructions

- maintenance of the transport network (mainly filling in potholes in non-tarred main roads)

However, the main challenge to the municipal service provision lies ahead, in the total rehabilitation and expansion of the infrastructure for basic 'urban services':

- water supply, e.g. the network of piped water and opening and maintenance of public water taps
- '*Saneamento*' (sanitation), e.g. the sewerage network and effective supply of improved latrines
- local road network, e.g. construction of roads with a proper system of drainage to new townships and between urban centres and main locations of land plots

This is actually an agenda for transcending palliative measures to obtain real poverty reduction. Although dependent on financing from central government and donor agents, such help has been subject to the condition that local governance improves, and that local financial sources of income exist. In this, the consciousness that the support and mobilization of its own citizens represent the main assets of the municipality will be critically tested in the future.

Second, the municipalities enjoy the participation of civil society in terms of injection of skills and knowledge into local government bodies. This has expanded their managerial and planning capacity. The fact that the new executive councils (*conselhos municipais*) consist of some of the most capable professionals available locally, handpicked and supervised by an equally competent mayor, represents a many-fold increase in such capacity of the local administrations. Besides, the new councillors' assemblies also tend to include representatives who can contribute to the development of sound visions and manageable plans to satisfy people's demands. However, the municipalities will be arenas for healthy confrontation between, on the one hand, bias towards belief in technical expertise and professionalism as seen in the composition of the executive councils, and, on the other, an appreciation of people's knowledge and an emphasis on popular participation.

Third, some municipalities already show signs of greater civic participation in local government. All the municipalities seem to initiate consultations with civil society,[62] and communication with the whole population, at the township (*bairro*) level. However, large differences appear in the regularity of meetings with civil society; in the inclusiveness of this consultation with regard to political opposition, traditional authorities, religious minorities, people with weak socio-economic position such as the youth, women, the sick, the elderly and socially marginalized groups; and in the channels for continuous and non-discriminating influence and participation of the citizens, that is, the inclusive democracy at the township level.

In some municipalities, good practices of voluntary work in the neighbourhoods and other forms of popular mobilization from the early People's Republic tend to be revived. However, it stands out as problem that the one-party Frelimo state structure prevails at the sub-district township level. Although most places seem to have a formal separation between the party cell structures on the one hand, and the township secretary (*secretario do bairro*) based on *grupos dinamizadores* on the other, most ordinary people do not see the difference. This means that people who do not feel close to the Frelimo party are alienated from municipal affairs. A solution to this might be posed by further democratization, as demonstrated by a municipality in the south, the town of Mandlakaze. Here, transfer of powers and resources to a township leader (*presidente do bairro*) elected by a secret vote is expected to lead to the mobilization of more citizens' resources (e.g. through revitalization of the institution of 'voluntary work' and community projects such as construction of new primary schools), as well as to a better and more transparent management of municipal resources. Likewise, incorporation of township representatives in the regular deliberations of the executive municipal council would strengthen the planning and implementation capacity of the latter.

The municipalities seem to have regained momentum after a very troubled start, with extremely low participation in the local elections in June 1998. After that, there was a 'honeymoon' year that produced better local services, many visible improvements and a more positive attitude to the new municipal authority among most citizens. However, after this period popular participation had to be institutionalized in a manner that makes the municipalities effective tools of government *by* and *for* the people.

Concluding Remarks

We must acknowledge Frelimo's sincere commitment to improving people's lives, represented by remarkable achievements in the provision of social services in the aftermath of independence and, more recently, by substantial increases in the health and education budgets. On the other side it is obvious that people's perception of their problems and their own possible solutions were seldom taken into account. Participatory governance was never institutionalized and this has had a profound bearing on Frelimo's governance in the last three decades. Upon independence, nation-building based on uniformity and modernization became first priorities which, in the context of limited physical and human resources, downgraded the solution of people's more immediate concerns. After the return to peace, while some events suggest that a trend towards more openness is in place, a certain level of resistance to participation still exists.

Participation is an essential element of pro-poor governance and should be sought after by creating institutional mechanisms that favour and promote it. The government of Mozambique, partly because of its overloaded agenda, partly because of the lack of participatory tradition, has not yet been able to take advantage of the social forces in a way that favours pro-poor governance. There is an attentive civil society that can, under the right conditions, provide extremely valuable contributions to the policy formulation process and to implementation and monitoring. These resources are currently underexploited and local NGOs and social movements have to fight to make their voices heard. Indeed, a higher level of openness would not only improve policy effectiveness and ownership at the societal level, but would also contribute significantly to social stability and enhance the government's legitimacy. Last but not least, participation might lead to empowering people, thus effectively contributing to combat one of the root causes of poverty. If Mozambique wants its governance structures to be effectively pro-poor, and in general provide its population with the opportunities of 'A Better Future',[63] it will have to change its approach in relation to people's and civil society's participation in policy-making and decisions concerning the allocation of resources. While acknowledging that the government has been successful in creating the circumstances favourable to poverty alleviation, it has been less effective in establishing governance mechanisms which promote accountability to the supposed beneficiaries and in ensuring that poor people's interests and needs are taken into consideration in both policy-making and policy implementation.

In Mozambique's postcolonial history, the consultation process around the Land Law was unprecedented. It testifies to both the (so far, untapped) richness of Mozambican social capital and to the centrality of popular mobilization in generating pro-poor governance where democratic structures are in place. By contrast, the non-consultative and non-inclusive process characterizing the municipal reform produced a strong popular reaction in terms of mass abstention in the first local elections. Nevertheless, even in the municipal urban areas we have found ordinary people prepared to interact with public authorities, as long as the latter's purpose is to serve the people and not to amass wealth and power within political-administrative structures highly distrusted by the citizens.

The main political–structural differences between the two processes lie in the fact that the Land Law provoked already existing class interests and national civic networks, which preferred a result-oriented and constructive dialogue with the ruling party. The municipal reform, however, struck more localized interests, and the opposition parties tried to capitalize on growing public disappointment with the way decentralization was proceeding. Instead of initiating a mass-based movement for a rectification of the municipal reform, the opposition parties subsumed popular discontent in their own tactics of confrontation with the ruling party.

The Land Law-related mass campaign has succeeded not only in obtaining radical changes in a law crucial to poverty reduction, but also in institutionalizing the participation of civil society organizations in the policy-making process, an essential condition for bringing the institutions closer to the intended beneficiaries. An 'entry point' has been created: a national committee (*Campanha Terra*) aiming at the dissemination of information to rural families. This, it is hoped, will lead to a dissemination of information to other areas and sectors and at all levels of governance.

The land reform was much more participatory in its making, while the municipal reform is likely to produce important participatory effects in its implementation, once the municipalities have been established. There are already signs that the new local democratic bodies will create a dynamic where urban social questions – or issues of urban poverty – gain momentum in national policy-making.

Still the urban/rural divide is very important, illustrated above by the different 'natures' of the (rural) land reform and the (urban) municipal reform. Furthermore, the municipal reform might sharpen the urban/rural divide. The government's five-year plan (1995–99) to expand primary school networks, health centres and agricultural assistance has mainly benefited (some) rural areas. The urban areas are now 'compensated' from funds designed to give the new municipalities a sound financial start. Hence, we already see that non-municipalized rural towns lag far behind in the improvement of urban services and development of citizenship and participation. The *Fundo de Compensação* might institutionalize this discrimination in favour of the municipalized cities. The urban/rural divide was accentuated by the general elections of 3–5 December 1999 (Braathen 2000). A coherent policy at the national level to promote local democratic governance everywhere is missing, and likewise there are no attempts to embed the formal poverty alleviation policies and their framework into existing social movements or local institutions. The potential for pro-poor governance shown in this chapter is not fully utilized under the present politico-administrative and economic regime.

Notes

1. In the first five years after independence, school enrolment witnessed dramatic increases and the country's illiteracy rate was reduced from 93 per cent in 1975 to 70 per cent in 1980 (Graham 1993: 416). In the same years, Mozambique's health policy focusing on primary health-care, prevention and basic drugs was recognized by the WHO as an example for the rest of Africa and coverage of the population increased significantly.

2. The local level research was led by Einar Braathen: 'Projecto de Investigação sobre a Reforma de Governação Local' (PRIGOLO). The study was carried out from 1995 to 1999 with funding from the Norwegian Research Council (NFR), project no. 109746/730, and in collaboration with the Centro de Investigação e Documentação para o Desenvolvimento Integral (CIDDI, Beira)/Universidade Católica de Mocambique.

3. Between 1987 and 1991, aid represented around 70 per cent of GDP. It rose to more than 100 per cent for the period 1992–96 (World Bank 1998).

4. Over one million people died during wartime. Calculations made by the UN show that the cost of physical destruction during the 1980s amounted to 250 years' worth of exports at the 1992 level and to fifty times the annual influx of foreign aid (cited in Abrahamsson and Nilsson 1995).

5. See for example Migdal et al. (1994) and Evans (1995).

6. The economic policy reform included the liberalization of exchange rate, prices, interest rates and trade policies, tight control of monetary variables, high fiscal discipline, limited intervention in prices and wages administration and extensive privatization of the industrial, agricultural and service sectors, including the entire commercial banking sector, a fundamental step if the financial necessities arising from reconstruction are to be met (Addison 1998). The Bretton Woods institutions have been criticized for their lack of consideration of the problems specific to a country at war or emerging from a war, and for the mistargeting of the measures imposed. For example, Jeffrey Sachs (1996) has called the IMF's strict inflation targets a 'mistake' and demands for sharp cuts in money supply growth 'unnecessarily contractionary and unrealistic'. Sachs argues that in the case of Mozambique, 'reconstruction and rapid growth should take precedence over a rapid disinflation'. Abrahamsson and Nilsson (1996), Hanlon (1996), Osman (1998) and UNDP (1998a), each in their own way, advocate a more inward-oriented economic growth strategy, arguing that economic growth has not been sufficient to achieve equally important improvements in human development and that the economic structure in the making will not contribute significantly to poverty alleviation.

7. See Government of Mozambique (1998), World Bank (1998), EIU Country Report (1st quarter 1999).

8. www.imf.org/external/np/sec/nb/1999/nb9935.rtx. Debt reduction was essential: Mozambique's debt service was higher than expenditure on health and education. During 1995–97 it averaged $7.45 per person per year, while health and education spending was $5.04 or $6.76 according to the government and the IMF respectively.

9. See World Bank (1989) and World Bank (1990).

10. See UNDP (1997, 1998a), Greeley and Devereux (1999), Moore et al. (1999), Schneider (1999) among others.

11. *Social capital* 'refers to features of social organization, such as trust, norm, and networks, that can improve the efficiency of society by facilitating coordinated actions' (Putnam 1993: 167).

12. Evans (1996: 1130). These ideas have been further discussed in the context of Mozambique in Braathen (1997).

13. Expenditure on defence decreased from 25.9 per cent in 1987 to 14.5 per cent in 1997. Health and Education received 14.2 per cent in 1987 and 28 per cent in 1997. Source: UNDP (1998b: 34).

14. However, most of those sectoral plans were drafted when the results of the data collection exercise on poverty were still not available, which cast some doubts on the internal coherence of the plan with the SWAPs and the SWAPs with the overall objective of poverty alleviation.

15. The Grupo da Divida is a Mozambican coalition of NGOs advocating total debt cancellation. Their contribution was remarkable in so far as Mozambique benefited from the highest debt forgiveness among all the eligible countries so far.

16. Frelimo as a Leninist vanguard party never doubted it could effectively represent the interests of the poor and the oppressed; thus it never carried out exercises in participation and assessment of ambitions at local level. In some cases, such as the tremendous achievement in health and education in the 1970s, this arrangement worked quite well. In others, like the agricultural policies, the 'villagization' operation and the repression of traditional cults and values, this had a disastrous effect on people's commitment and the party-state's legitimacy (Geffray 1991). In all cases, these are clear indications that Frelimo is not used to give 'voice' to the people – leave alone civil society, which only recently emerged in Mozambique.

17. Personal communication.

18. The PRAP considers households' size a determinant of poverty and aims to reduce household size and dependency ratio via a new demographic policy and job creation. No mention is made of how this could be reconciled with the findings of the PPA, which highlighted that one of the causes of poverty, in rural people's perception, is precisely not to have relatives or people to mobilize during the peak agricultural season (Adam 1996: 5). In the PRAP there is little room for vulnerability to crises and no mechanisms for facing seasonal and transitory poverty, which emerged as a key issue from the PPA.

19. Toye (1999: 7).

20. Interview with an international NGO deputy director.

21. Oscar Monteiro, former Minister for State Administration, co-ordinator of the team that wrote the first National Human Development Report and prominent academic.

22. The 'assimilados' refer to indigenous people who were recruited into the Portuguese educational system, and later on became officials in the local colonial administration. They could apply for, and were usually granted, a limited citizenship status within the Portuguese metropol state.

23. 'Mimeosis' means imitation and is in new institutional theory an important mechanism – in opposition to coercion on the one side and deliberative political processes on the other – for providing structural isomorphism (similarity) between units at a macro- or large-scale macro- or global level. 'Individuals and organizations deal with uncertainty by imitating the ways of others whom we use as models' (Scott 1995: 45).

24. We owe this argument to Cahen (1999).

25. Gerschenkron (1962) made an influential theoretical explanation of how an *activist state*, in the European historical context, could help the 'latecomers' catch up with the advanced countries' developmental lead. This fitted neatly with the 1950s and 1960s radical anti-colonialism inspired by Lenin's theory of imperialism and the Chinese and Soviet experiences. Although Frelimo's leader Eduardo Mondlane was influenced by these ideas, his book *The Struggle for Mozambique* (Mondlane 1969/1995) shows that

inspiration from French and other European nationalist history was more important than the Russian Revolution. Hence, we hold that the influence of Latin-European and Jacobin state nationalism has been more influential than 'Marxism-Leninism' in Frelimo's development.

26. For a more detailed outline, see Rokkan and Eisenstadt (1973); and Flora (1992).

27. See Cravinho (1995); and Hall and Young (1997).

28. See Geffray (1991) and Saul (1993), who, in spite of different degrees of sympathy expressed for one of the parties of the civil war, agree on the political–internal factors that helped transform South African destabilization into a true civil war.

29. Hanlon (1990: 227). Also Abrahamsson and Nilsson (1995) seem to agree upon this.

30. Mamdani (1996). See the chapter by Camilo Bustillo-Perez in this book, which provides a critical discussion of the concept of the bifurcated state.

31. Mamdani (1996) presents a view of centralized and decentralized despotism.

32. See Bratton and van de Walle (1997). There was no labour or civic unrest (pp. 131–2), and Mozambique was the only example besides the Seychelles where donor pressure led to political liberalization (p. 182). However, one must acknowledge that donors' pressure found a fertile ground in a faction of Frelimo itself, which was committed to a negotiated solution with the rebels.

33. Currently including the Ministries of Agriculture, State Administration, Culture, Mineral Resources, Environment, Planning and Finance, and Justice, plus the Land Tenure Centre, FAO, the WB, USAID and two local NGOs, UNAC and ORAM.

34. Land campaign, in Portuguese. Campanha Terra is an informal coalition of development NGOs and associations aiming to disseminate the content of the Land Law.

35. Government of Mozambique (1998) 'Recenseamento Geral da População: Resultados Preliminares', Maputo, and DPDS, UEM and IFPRI (1998) 'Estimativas e Perfil da Pobreza em Moçambique', mimeo, Maputo.

36. Saad Filho (1997).

37. In Frelimo's post-independence Leninist programme, the large state farms and the co-operatives were essentially a means both to control the population and to transfer resources from agriculture to industry. Frelimo's democratic centralism de-legitimized popular tradition, culture and religion in the name of building a 'new' nation. Family agriculture was embedded in a thick layer of 'reactionary' social relations and was considered anti-scientific and retrograde; Frelimo could not encourage peasants to continue in this form of life which bore the legacy of colonialism.

38. See Cravinho (1995).

39. A number of conjunctural factors contributed to increasing Mozambican attractiveness for private foreign investment: tax holidays and custom exemptions, white settlers' flight from South Africa after the fall of the apartheid regime, the worsening tensions between white farmers and the Zimbabwean government, intense land pressure in southern Malawi.

40. Quan (1998).

41. Examples of the first kind are the exclusive use by peasants or investors of their own land. Of the second, the exclusive right of extension and purchase of a specific crop, as happens with cotton and tobacco.

42. Bill No. 19/97 of 1 October 1997 in force as of January 1998.

43. The group comprised UNAC, the National Peasant Union, ORAM, the

Association of Mutual Assistance, AMRU, the Rural Women's Union, CEA, the Centre for African Studies, CEP, the Centre for Population Studies, NET, the Centre for Studies in Land and Development, Action Aid, KEPA, the Centre of Cooperation Services for Development, MS, the Danish Association of International Cooperation, OXFAM UK/ Ireland, Oxfam's Joint Advocacy Program (Negrão 1999).

44. This section is based on results from the PRIGOLO research project (see note 2). Ten places from all the regions of the country have been investigated: Xai-Xai, Mandlakaze and Macia-Bilen in Gaza in the south; Beira, Chimoio, Gondola and Catandica in the centre; and Pemba, Montepuez and Chiure in Cabo Delgado in the north.

45. *Metical* no. 257 of 2 July 1998. *Mozambique Peace Process Bulletin*, 21 (21 July 1998): 'Local elections fiasco – only 15% turnout.' The following account is built on Braathen and Viig (1998).

46. The Law No.3/1994 on Municipal Districts passed the old one-party parliament in August 1994. Then the plan was to organize local elections in October 1995, one year after the presidential and legislative elections. The new government quickly postponed them to autumn 1996. The Frelimo majority bench in the new multiparty parliament forced through the second postponement, when it redesigned the whole municipal reform. The two last postponements were officially due to administrative and financial problems, but in reality the government wanted to gain time to respond to the grievances of the opposition who were very unhappy with the new design of the municipalities and the elections.

47. In the end, all but two parties joined the boycott campaign: the União Democratica, with a small group in parliament, and Partido Trabalhista, one of the smallest of the extra-parliamentary parties.

48. This solution was readopted for the 1999 general elections.

49. See Braathen (1994). This paper was based on the reports from the ten Norwegian UN Electoral Observers.

50. Ibid. In many districts, the District Electoral Commission was chaired by the district director of education. Although formally appointed by the Frelimo party, these chairmen were usually widely respected locally.

51. Three of the ten cities and towns in the sample were not going to take part in the forthcoming municipal elections. The respondents in the seven 'municipal' cities/towns were slightly better informed about the status of their city/town in the forthcoming elections.

52. See Putnam (1993: 112–13, 246–7) for definitions and discussions of civic virtue.

53. Araújo et al. (1998). This national survey on public opinion was commissioned by USAID and produced by the Centro de Estudos da População (CEP) of Universidade Eduardo Mondlane (UEM).

54. Ibid., pp. 5 and 241 ff.

55. For patrimonialization, see Médard (1996). The patrimonialized state is defined by the de facto *lack of distinction made between the public and private domain*. This implies a confusion between the public and the private, in spite of the fact that a structural differentiation between what is public and what is private might exist.

56. Cited in Weimer (1999: 136 ff.).

57. *Mozambique Peace Process Bulletin*, 21 (21 July 1998), p. 2.

58. For patrimonialization, see Médard (1996). The patrimonialized state is defined by the de facto lack of distinction made between the public and private domain. This

implies a confusion between the public and the private, in spite of the fact that a structural differentiation between what is public and what is private exists.

59. Cited in Weimer (1999: 21).

60. The mean of the two rural towns are 0.48 for Mandlakaze (median) and 0.34 for Catandica (the lowest score of discontent in our sample). However, they show patterns of discontent quite similar to those shown by the cities: highest discontent with indicators of public health, and lowest discontent with education.

61. This might be related to the fact that all the people in our sample are over eighteen (the age of the right to vote) and hence maybe are less concerned with the provision of education services. It might also be related to the fact that reconstruction of school buildings has been a major priority in donor-financed and government-financed development programmes.

62. We define civil society as citizen-based associations and organized interests in the local arena.

63. '*O Futuro Melhor*' (A better future) was Frelimo's slogan for the 1994 electoral campaign.

References

Abrahamsson, H. and A. Nilsson (1995) *Mozambique, the Troubled Transition*. London: Zed Books.

Adam, Y. (1996) 'A Pobreza em Moçambique Vista Pelos Pobres Eles Proprios'. Summary of the conclusions of the first phase of the Participatory Poverty Assessment, Maputo: mimeo.

Addison, T. (1998) 'Underdevelopment, Reconstruction and Transition in Sub-Saharan Africa', *Research for Action*, 45. Helsinki: WIDER.

Araújo, M. G. M. de, et al. (1998) *Inquérito Naçional de Opinião Pública*, Relatorio Final. Maputo: UEM/CEP.

Braathen, E. (1994) 'Voting for Peace. The First Multi-Party Elections in Mozambique'. Report presented to the Norwegian Institute of Human Rights, December.

— (1997) 'State Action, Social Capital and Poverty Alleviation. An Outline of a Decentralization Study of Mozambique'. Paper presented to the CROP, BIDPA and University of Botswana workshop on 'The Role of the State in Poverty Alleviation', Gaborone, 8–11 October 1997.

— (2000) *Mozambique: Parliamentary and Presidential Elections 1999. Nordem Observation Report*. Working Paper 2000 no. 10. Oslo: Norwegian Institute of Human Rights.

Braathen, E. and B. Viig (1998) 'Democracy without People? Local Government Reform and 1998 Municipal Elections in Mozambique', in *Lusotopie*. Paris: Éditions Karthala, pp. 31–8.

Braathen, E., M. Bøås and G. Sæther (eds) (1999) *Ethnicity Kills? The Politics of War, Peace and Ethnicity in Sub-Saharan Africa*. London: Macmillan.

Bratton, M. and N. van de Walle (1997) *Democratic Experiments in Africa: Regime Transitions in Comparative Perspective*. New York: Cambridge University Press.

Cahen, M. (1999) 'Transitions from War to Peace. Nationalism and Ethnicities: Lessons from Mozambique', in Braathen et al. (eds), *Ethnicity Kills?*, pp. 163–88.

Cravinho, J. (1995) 'Modernising Mozambique: Frelimo Ideology and the Frelimo State'. Unpublished Ph.D. Thesis, Oxford University.

Devereux, S. and A. Palmero (1999) 'Mozambique Country Report, fourth Draft', elaborated within the project 'Creating a Framework for Reducing Poverty: Institutional and Process Issues in National Poverty Policy' for the SPA Working Group on Poverty. Brighton: IDS, mimeo.

Evans, P. (1995) *Embedded Autonomy. States and Industrial Transformation.* Princeton, NJ: Princeton University Press.

— (1996) 'Government Action, Social Capital and Development', *World Development*, 24, 6, pp. 1,119–32.

Flora, P. (1992) 'Stein Rokkans Makromodell for Politisk Utvikling i Europa', in B. Hagtvedt (ed.), *Politikk mellom økonomi og kultur.* Oslo: Ad Notam Gyldendal.

Geffray, C. (1991) *A causa das Armas. Antropologia da Guerra Contemporanea em Moçambique.* Porto: Afrontamento.

Gerschenkron, A. (1962) *Economic Backwardness in a Historical Perspective.* Cambridge, MA: Belknap.

Goetz, A. and D. O'Brien (1995) 'Governing for the Common Wealth? The World Bank's Approach to Poverty and Governance', *IDS Bulletin*, 26, 2.

Government of Mozambique (1995a) 'Plano Quinquenal'. Maputo.

— (1995b) 'Estrategia de Alivio a Pobreza'. Maputo.

— (1998) 'A View of the Future'. Paper presented at a 1998 meeting of the Consultative Group for Mozambique, Maputo, September.

— (1999) 'Plano de Acção contra a Pobreza'. Maputo.

Government of Mozambique and IFPRI (1998) 'Inquerito aos Agregados Familiares'. Maputo.

Graham, L. S. (1993) 'The Dilemmas of Managing Transitions in Weak States: the Case of Mozambique', *Public Administration and Development*, 13, 4, pp. 409–22.

Greeley, M. and S. Devereux (1999) 'Getting It Right: Policy, Process and Poverty Reduction – An Overview of Six SSA Country Studies'. Paper presented at the research workshop 'Can Africa Claim the 21st Century?', Abidjan, 6–11 July.

Hall, M. and T. Young (1997) *Confronting Leviathan: Mozambique Since Independence.* London: Hurst and Company.

Hanlon, J. (1990) *Mozambique: The Revolution Under Fire.* London: Zed Books.

— (1996) *Peace without Profit.* Oxford: James Currey.

Herring, R. J. (1999) 'Comparative Conditions for Poverty Alleviation'. Paper presented at the DfID Conference on 2001 World Development Report, Eynsham Hall, Oxfordshire.

Hirschmann, Albert O. (1970) *Exit, Voice and Loyalty.* Cambridge, MA: Harvard University Press.

Hyden, G. (1999) 'Governance and the Reconstruction of Political Order', in R. Joseph (ed.), *State, Conflict and Democracy in Africa.* Boulder, CO: Lynne Rienner.

Kanbur, R. and L. Squire (1999) 'How Poverty Has Evolved: Exploring the Interactions'. Paper presented at the Symposium on the Future of Development Economics in Perspective, Dubrovnik, 13–14 May.

Katz, J. (1999) 'SPA V Report'. Paper presented at the research workshop 'Can Africa Claim the 21st Century?', Abidjan, 6–11 July.

Mamdani, M. (1996) *Citizen and Subject. Contemporary Africa and the Legacy of Late Colonialism.* Princeton, NJ: Princeton University Press.

Médard J.-F. (1996) 'Patrimonialism, Patrimonialization, Neo-Patrimonialism and the Study of the Post-Colonial State in Subsaharan Africa', in Henrick Secher Marcussen (ed.), *Improved Natural Resource Management: The Role of Formal Organisations in Informal Networks and Institutions.* Occasional Paper no.17, Roskilde University, Denmark.

Migdal, J., A. Kholi and V. Shue (eds) (1994) *State Power and Social Forces.* Cambrigde: Cambridge University Press.

Mondlane, E. (1969, 1995) *Lutar por Moçambique,* Colleccão nosso Chão. Maputo: CEA.

Moore, M., J. Leavy, P. Houtzager and H. White (1999) 'Polity Qualities: How Governance Affects Poverty'. Brighton: IDS, mimeo.

Negrão, J. (1999) 'Land and Rural Development in Mozambique – The Land Campaign in Mozambique'. Paper produced for the research project 'Creating a Framework for Reducing Poverty: Institutional and Process Issues in National Poverty'. Brighton: IDS, mimeo.

Osman, M. (1998) 'Globalisation and Peripheral Economies'. Paper presented at the Social Sciences Congress, Maputo, September.

Putnam, R. with R. Leonardi and R. Nanetti (1993) *Making Democracy Work. Civic Traditions in Modern Italy.* Princeton, NJ: Princeton University Press.

Quan, J. (1998) 'Issues in African Land Policy: Experiences from Southern Africa'. London: Natural Resources Institute, University of Greenwich.

Rokkan, S. N. and S. N. Eisenstadt (1973) *Building States and Nations.* Beverly Hills, CA: Sage.

Saad Filho, A. (1997) 'The Political Economy of Agrarian Transition in Mozambique', *Journal of Contemporary African Studies,* 15, 2.

Sachs, J. (1996) 'Towards a Growth-Orientated Economic Programme for Mozambique'. Paper for the conference 'Estrategias para acelerar o crescimento economico em Moçambique', Maputo, March.

Saul, J. S. (1993) 'Rethinking the Frelimo State', *Socialist Register.* London: Merlin Press, pp. 139–65.

Schneider, H. (1999) 'Participatory Governance: The Missing Link for Poverty Reduction', OECD Development Centre, Policy Brief no. 17. Paris: OECD.

Scott, Richard W. (1995) *Institutions and Organizations.* Thousand Oaks/London/New Delhi: Sage.

Serra, C. (1999) (ed.) *Eleitorado Incapturável. Eleiçoes Municipais de 1998 em Manica, Chimoio, Beira, Dondo, Nampula e Angoche. Maputo.* Maputo: Livraria Universitária.

Sobhan, R. (1998) 'How Bad Governance Impedes Poverty Alleviation in Bangladesh'. Technical paper no. 143. Paris: OECD Development Centre.

Toye, J. (1999) 'Nationalising the Anti-Poverty Agenda', *IDS Bulletin,* 30, 2.

UNDP (1997) *Governance for Sustainable Human Development.* New York: UNDP.

— (1998a) *Overcoming Human Poverty. Poverty Report 1998.* New York: UNDP.

— (1998b) *Relatorio Nacional do Desenvolvimento Humano 1998 para Moçambique.* Johannesburg: Creda Press.

— (1999) *Human Development Report 1999.* New York: UNDP.

Weimer, B. (1999) 'Abstaining from the 1998 Local Government Elections in Mozambique: Some Hypotheses', *L'Afrique,* 1999, pp. 125–45.

World Bank (1989) *Sub-Saharan Africa: From Crisis to Sustainable Growth.* Washington, DC: World Bank.

— (1990) *World Development Report.* Washington, DC: World Bank.

— (1998) *Rebuilding the Mozambique Economy: Assessment of a Development Partnership.* Washington, DC: World Bank.

14

Meeting the Challenge? The Emerging Agenda for Poverty Reduction in Post-apartheid South Africa

Julian May

In 1994 the first democratically elected government of South Africa committed itself to the Reconstruction and Development Programme (RDP), the policy framework through which, it was hoped, a broad transformation of South African society could be achieved. This document, and the subsequent RDP White Paper, proposed targets for development as well as the processes through which these targets were to be attained. Moreover, the RDP was seen to be a statement of intent, not only for government but also for other sectors of South African society, including the private sector, Non-governmental Organizations (NGOs) as well as local communities.

The first four years of the majority rule witnessed an intensive period in which the broad RDP goals and processes were used to formulate new policies, programmes and strategies of implementation. In addition, at a macro-economic level, national policies also have had to deal with the integration of South Africa into an increasing competitive and volatile global economy. At the same time, the legacy of the previous government's economic policies, including its debt burden, have had to be managed. The strategic shift in the implementation of the RDP in 1996, from being a specialized programme office to a function of line departments, also required a shift in the policy framework within which the RDP took place. Emphasis has increasingly been placed upon the preparation of sector-specific White Papers, policy documents and legislation, and less upon multi-sectoral policy statements such as the RDP White Paper. Furthermore, co-ordination of government policy has also shifted from a 'programme office' towards the use of a multi-year budgeting process as contained in the Medium-term Expenditure Framework in which targets are more carefully tied to the government's macro-economic strategy as contained in the Growth, Employment and Redistribution (GEAR) strategy.

As the ANC government enters its second term of office under the presidency of Thabo Mbeki, the emphasis of government activity appears also to have shifted from the formulation of policies and strategies, towards their implementation and evaluation. Despite concerns that the government has abandoned the RDP, at least at the level of rhetoric, this programme continues to guide most sectoral policies. This chapter tries to sketch out the agenda for poverty reduction that emerged between 1994 and 1998 and to assess how the implementation of this agenda will impact upon the continuing high levels of poverty in South Africa.

A Poverty Profile of South Africa

Since the mid-1960s the South African economy has suffered a prolonged deterioration in real growth, domestic savings and employment creation. As a result of this, the distribution of income-earning opportunities remains largely unchanged, with extremely limited prospects for the majority of South Africa's population. By 1995, the combined outcome of these trends resulted in an economy with very high income inequality, widespread poverty and high levels of unemployment. This is shown in Table 14.1.

TABLE 14.1 Poverty, inequality and unemployment (1995)

Indicator	%	Estimated population
Poverty rate total	49.9	19,700,000
Poverty rate in non-urban areas	70.9	13,700,000
Poverty rate in urban areas	28.5	6,000,000
Poverty share of non-urban areas	71.6	
African poverty rate	60.7	18,300,000
White poverty rate	1.0	44,000
Unemployment rate	29.3	4,250,000
Income share of poorest 40% of households	11.0	
National Gini Coefficient	0.52	

Source: Statistics South Africa (1997)

Approximately half of South Africa's population can be categorized as poor. Table 14.1 shows that most of the poor live in rural areas with the *poverty share* of rural areas (i.e. the percentage of poor individuals that live in rural areas) being equal to 72 per cent. The *poverty rate* in rural areas (i.e. the percentage of individuals classified as poor) is about 71 per cent, compared with 29 per cent in urban areas. Not surprisingly, 61 per cent of the African population is poor, and a mere 1 per cent of the white population is poor. The distribution of this poverty is by no means even across the provinces, as is shown in Table 14.2 which also shows the poverty gap in each province.

TABLE 14.2 Provincial distribution of poverty (1995)

Province	Households living in poverty (%)	Individuals living in poverty (%)	Poverty gap (R million)	Poverty gap as a % of GGP	Population that is non-urban (%)
Eastern Cape	40.4	50.0	3,303	11.4	63.4
Free State	56.8	64.0	3,716	15.7	31.4
Gauteng	29.7	41.0	917	0.6	3.0
KwaZulu-Natal	36.1	47.1	1,159	2.0	56.9
Mpumulanga	33.8	45.1	968	3.1	60.9
North West	15.4	21.1	1,551	7.3	65.1
Northern Cape	38.2	48.0	257	3.2	29.9
Northern Province	61.9	69.3	2,948	21.4	89.0
Western Cape	14.1	17.9	529	1.0	11.1
South Africa	35.2	45.7	15,348	4.0	46.3

Sources: DBSA (1998: 211) and Statistics South Africa (1998)

Table 14.2 shows that poverty rates are highest in the Northern Province and Free State, although the depth of poverty (the amount required to move all individuals above the poverty line) is highest in the Free State and Eastern Cape.[1] The total poverty gap (i.e. the amount that is needed annually to wipe out poverty through a perfectly targeted transfer to the poor) in 1995 was about R15 billion, or about 4 per cent of GDP. In the case of the Northern Province, the poverty gap amounts to 21 per cent of the provincial Gross Geographic Product. Table 14.2 also shows the high correlation between poverty and the percentage of the rural population within each province. This combination of a high poverty rate and deep poverty among the poor in rural areas means that 76 per cent of the total poverty gap is accounted for by poverty in rural households, although they make up less than 50 per cent of the population.

The adequacy of 'money-metric' poverty measures such as the above can be critiqued from a number of perspectives. Of these, one of the most damaging is that which notes that household income or expenditure can adequately reflect individual material well-being only if the household has access to a market at which it can purchase all goods at given prices (see the discussion in Ravallion 1996). Moreover, goods such as safe and available water and sanitation services are indivisible and have public good components that make it impossible for a single household to purchase marginally more of such goods. More generally, some analysts would argue that access to safe water, adequate shelter and so forth are better indicators of poverty and human possibility than are income- or expenditure-based measures.

Reflecting these various concerns, May et al. (1996) present a basic needs indicator for rural areas based on the type of shelter, water, sanitation and energy to which each household has access. In addition, the adequacy of food consumption is also shown, measured through the use of a caloric poverty line (see Table 14.3).

TABLE 14.3 Alternative measures of absolute poverty in rural South Africa

Poverty measures	Households which are poor (%)
Basic Needs Indicator (lowest rank on composite scale of housing, sanitation, water and energy)*	21.9
Nutritional Poverty Line (1,815 daily calories per adult equivalent)	44.6
Nutritional Poverty Line (2,100 daily calories per adult equivalent)	56.7

Source: PSLSD (1993)
Note: * Each component of the indicator was given equal weight and then summed.

This analysis found that 22 per cent of the rural African population falls into the lowest rank of a four-scale indicator (75 per cent of these households also fall below the income poverty line). The bulk of the households in this group live in homesteads with rustic or temporary roofing, such as plastic sheeting or cardboard, and have high occupation densities. These households use unprotected sources of water, do not have a toilet facility of any kind, and collect and use wood as their main energy source. Another 51 per cent of black rural households fall into the next highest basic needs category, meaning that they typically have access to a protected water source and an unimproved pit latrine, but have housing and energy sources similar to those of households in the lowest group. By way of contrast, only 3 per cent of all households resident in major metropolitan areas respectively fall into either of these two lowest basic needs categories.

The poor in South Africa are thus largely African, rural and women. Further, poverty extends beyond insufficient income, and includes other forms of deprivation including access to essential services and the marginalization of the rural population. Inequality and marginalization are an important aspect of this experience.

Poverty amidst plenty in South Africa The Gini Coefficient reported in Table 14.1 above reveals that South Africa follows Brazil in terms of income inequality with the second highest level among countries for which statistics are available. The income shares of deciles of households reveal the striking degree of inequality. The poorest 40 per cent of households, equivalent to 50 per cent of the population, account for only 11 per cent of total income, while the richest 10 per cent of households, equivalent to only 7 per cent of the population, accrue over 40 per cent of total income.

The heterogeneous nature of South Africa is further revealed if the outcomes of development are considered. In 1994, South Africa ranked eighty-sixth among countries for which a Human Development Index (HDI) had been measured. However, decomposing the HDI by province and race reveals great disparities in the level of human development in different parts of the country. The provinces of the Western Cape and Gauteng are considered to show a high level of human development, similar to that of Venezuela or Singapore. The Northern Province, on the other hand, has a low HDI, comparable with that of Zimbabwe or Namibia. White South Africans have a level of human development similar to that of Israel or Canada, while Africans score lower on the HDI than countries such as Egypt or Swaziland.

The development problematic of South Africa described more than a decade ago by Jill Nattrass as being that of 'poverty amidst plenty' thus remains appropriate to post-apartheid South Africa (Nattrass 1983: 12). Besides the social and political instability that the presence of extreme wealth alongside poverty brings, sufficient evidence exists to argue that the level of inequality in South Africa may dampen the country's economic growth rate (Bruno et al. 1996: 11; Eckert and Mullins 1989: 10). A high level of inequality could also reduce the impact of any improvements that might be achieved in employment creation and poverty reduction. If government policy is to meet the challenges of poverty depicted by Wilson and Ramphele (1989) as the legacy of apartheid South Africa, initiatives that improve the capabilities of the majority of South Africans are essential to achieve the very objectives of growth and development.

An Integrated Response

The government's response to sluggish economic growth, persistent poverty and high inequality, at least at the level of policy, appears to be an integrated approach that seeks to link economic growth with development. The flagship policy of the RDP went beyond a simple programme of action such as the multi-year plans often adopted by new democracies. Instead, the need for a fundamental transformation of the social, economic and moral foundations of South African society was repeatedly stressed as the rationale behind the programme (ANC 1994; GNU 1994). However, although this approach recognized the underlying development problematic of South Africa – that is, the need for structural transformation – the goals of the RDP are so broad as to be difficult to measure in a quantitative sense. Examples of these include:

• developing stable democratic institutions and participative practices
• establishing a prosperous, democratic and non-racial society
• addressing the moral and ethical development of society

On the other hand, at its most specific, in some documents the RDP committed government to some extremely detailed targets, such as the provision of a safe, clean water supply of 20–30 litres per capita per day within 200 metres (ANC 1994). In many instances, subsequent experience of implementation together with the fiscal realities have revealed the difficulties of adhering to such targets.

In June 1996, the government released the Growth, Employment and Redistribution (GEAR) strategy as a response to the country's vulnerable macro-economic situation. While not embodying any major departure from earlier government policy pronouncements, the GEAR strategy identified many of the structural weaknesses in the economy that inhibit growth and employment creation, and focused attention on market-based policy measures to address them. The GEAR strategy recognized that accelerated job creation is essential to achieving a sustained reduction in inequality, and that substantial job creation would require structural transformation to achieve higher and more labour-absorbing growth within the economy. The GEAR strategy clearly indicated the government's intention to alter the relative price of tradables and non-tradables to help increase the outward orientation of the economy, boost investment and increase the demand for labour, and focused its strategy for higher growth rates on several related elements, including:

• a reprioritization of the budget towards social spending
• an acceleration of the fiscal reform process

- the gradual relaxation of exchange controls
- the consolidation of trade and industrial reforms
- expansionary public sector restructuring
- structured flexibility with collective bargaining
- a social agreement to facilitate wage and price moderation

The South African government thus set itself the task of simultaneously reprioritizing the budget, reducing overall spending and improving targeting, while keeping the fiscal targets set out in the GEAR strategy. This is a huge task, made more complex by the reintegration of the South African economy into a globalizing international economy, and presents challenges for a long time to come. Some initial successes are already apparent: a reprioritization of expenditures has been achieved, and overall budget limits have largely been kept. Some successes have been achieved in reaching the poor. However, in the short to medium term, there will be certain costs and inefficiencies associated with organizational and systemic dislocations arising from fundamental shifts in policy. The attempt to refocus the budget and reduce costs simultaneously may yet prove difficult to achieve. As a result, the GEAR proposals concerning the size of the deficit and its impact on social expenditure remain areas of an unresolved controversy. Perhaps of greater significance, though, is the role played by the multi-year budgeting process through which the GEAR strategy is actually implemented.

By setting multi-year expenditure targets for the various government departments, the Medium-term Expenditure Framework (MTEF) is an important mechanism through which the GEAR strategy is to be implemented. As an example, the MTEF 1998 policy statement notes that capital expenditure financed by the national and provincial governments is projected to increase from about R14,369 million in 1998/99 to R16,348 million by the end of the MTEF period. Capital spending by public corporations is also expected to grow over this period, bringing the projected contribution of the public sector to gross domestic fixed investment to about R56,300 million in 2000/01, or about 7 per cent of GDP. In terms of the sectoral policies that make up government's agenda for poverty reduction, the main capital spending programmes on the national budget are envisaged as follows:

- expenditure on welfare services and social grants of R19.8 billion in 1998/99, R20.7 billion in 1999/00 and R22.2 billion in 2000/01
- transfers to local government for municipal infrastructure projects, rising from R583 million in 1998/99 to R990 million in 2000/01
- expenditure on health services of R25.1 billion in 1998/99, increasing to R28.1 billion in 2000/01 and a new hospital rehabilitation pro-

gramme, beginning with R100 million in 1998/99 and increasing to R500 million in 2000/01
* spending on land redistribution and land reform programmes of R685 million in 1998/99, increasing to R967 million in 2000/01
* allocations for various land and buildings projects on the public works vote of R1,665 million in 1998/99 increasing to R1,711 million in 2000/01
* capital spending on the transport vote amounting to R742 million in 1998/99, rising to R1,153 million in 2000/01, mainly for road projects
* spending on housing programmes and subsidies of over R 3.6 billion annually
* allocations to regional water schemes and related services of R1,247 million in 1998/99, increasing to R1,517 million in 2000/01 and capital spending on water schemes and related infrastructure of R1,537 million in 1998/99, increasing to R1,785 million in 2000/01
* allocations for poverty relief projects, rising from R500 million in 1997/98 to R800 million in 2000/01. In fact, the 1999/2000 budget actually made provision for R1.1 billion in poverty relief

However, despite the apparent focus on RDP objectives of the current MTEF, in a submission to the Portfolio Committee on Finance, IDASA analysts argue that deficit targets are crowding out social targets and that this situation will worsen over time. This is due to the retention of existing deficit targets in the face of slower than predicted growth rates. As a result of this, it is estimated that there will be R5 billion less available for non-interest expenditure in the later period of the MTEF than was anticipated at its launch in 1997/8 (IDASA 1998). The likely impact of this upon the successful implementation of the envelope of policies for the reduction of poverty requires a more detailed assessment of the various sectoral policies.

Sectoral Policies

Education The RDP placed considerable importance upon the development of South Africa's human resources through all forms of education and training, and the provision of schooling for children is the largest component of the government's responsibilities with respect to education. Among many others the RDP sets the following measurable targets:

* government must enable all children to go to school for at least ten years
* classes should not exceed forty students
* the structure of the education system, curricula and certification should be aligned with the national qualifications system

- the need for school buildings must be addressed by improved use of existing facilities and a school-building programme
- issues of equity in education must be addressed through curriculum development that pays attention to the education of African children especially in the areas of science, mathematics, technology, arts and culture

There has been intensive work undertaken on the development of policy for education which has been matched by government expenditure. The amount for education was the single largest amount, almost twice as much as the second largest (R44 million for health), and more than three times as much as the third largest (R27 million for the Constitutional Assembly) (*NGO Matters*, 2, 4 [April 1997], p. 9). The 1996/97 budget allocated a total of R34,133 billion of national and provincial departmental allocations to education, approximately one-quarter of the total budget. Between November 1995 and early 1997, education received a further R85 million in the form of Official Development Assistance from foreign governments. In 1996, R84.4 million in RDP funds were allocated to improve facilities and governance of schools. A further R1.2 billion was allocated to the Schools Building Programme. The Education Policy Reserve Fund, and the government's injection of an additional R200 million for textbooks, greatly assisted implementation in 1999. Government has also committed R300 million in financial aid to students for higher education.

However, in terms of outcomes, the picture is less promising for the formal education system. Matriculation results continue to show both poor performance overall and marked geographic (which in South Africa is a reflection of race) and gender differences. Only 55 per cent of the full-time 1996 students passed, and only 16 per cent with university entry endorsement. In 1998, just over 50 per cent of full-time students passed.

Thus, while education is relatively well-resourced, at least in monetary terms, it does not appear to have succeeded in delivering quality education on a broad basis. As an example, despite increasing enrolments by African children, uneven quality of teaching has resulted in ongoing marked racial differences in basic literacy and numeracy, even where there is similar attainment in terms of standard passed. Indeed, the Presidential Review Commission describes the situation within the Department of Education as being 'near-crisis'. The information presented above does suggest that, despite adequate current and future resources, little if any impact has actually occurred in key indicators of delivery, making it difficult to dis-agree with this finding. Reasons given by the commission for this apparent lack of delivery are mostly concerned with structural limitations. These include inadequate co-ordination, the impact of erratic restructuring and apparently dysfunctional actions at some levels. The development of greater management capacity, especially at a senior level, is identified as part of the solution. In terms of the national and provincial activities in ABET, a lack of person-power, authority and resources has hampered implementation.

Health The RDP explicitly recognized that health-care is only one way in which overall health status can be improved and raising the standard of living through improved income-earning opportunities, sanitation, water supply, energy sources and housing make up the overall strategy for improving health. More specifically, the aim set by the RDP was to ensure that all South Africans get better value for the money spent in the health sector, and generally to ensure that there was an improvement in the mental, physical and social health of the entire population.

Some specific targets set by the RDP included:

- ensuring that 90 per cent of pregnant women receive antenatal care
- ensuring that 75 per cent of deliveries are supervised and carried out under hygienic conditions by 1996, and by 1999, 90 per cent of deliveries should have been supervised
- providing such services at no charge at government facilities by 1997
- ensuring the right to six months' paid maternity leave and ten days' paternity leave
- providing an expanded and more effective programme of immunization which would achieve a coverage of 90 per cent by 1997
- retraining 25 per cent of district health personnel by the end of 1995 and 50 per cent by the end of 1997 on the Primary Health Care approach

The RDP also committed the government to a programme to combat the spread of sexually transmitted diseases and HIV and AIDS which was to include the active and early treatment of these diseases at all health facilities, plus mass education programmes involving media, schools and community organizations.

The White Paper for the Transformation of the Health System in South Africa accepted in April 1997 recognizes that the provision of health-care has had to confront the enormous disparities of the past. Policy has focused on reducing the cost of health-care to the least well-off, while increasing their access to health facilities, and has emphasized four processes:

1. Improving access to care through building or upgrading health facilities, through deploying health personnel into underserved areas and, most importantly, through the introduction of free care for certain health services and categories of patients.

2. Reducing the costs of health-care through reducing the costs of drugs (the National Drug Policy) and the establishment of a National Health Insurance system.
3. Improving health service delivery through an expanded immunization programme, the promotion of maternal health including the termination of pregnancy, and treatment of TB.
4. Improving preventative health-care through strengthening programmes for nutrition (the Integrated Nutrition Programme), hygiene and occupational health.

Free health-care is the policy that has probably made the most significant impact on improving access to health services for the poor to date. The PIR (Poverty and Inequality Report) reports on an evaluation of the free health-care (FHC) which found that health service utilization, particularly by the rural poor, had increased substantially and pregnant women had started attending antenatal clinics at an earlier stage. There was overwhelming support for the policy, but health personnel felt strongly that greater consultation and planning should precede the implementation of such extensive changes.

In general, the PIR concludes that the existing policies and programmes provide an excellent basis for addressing the challenges facing the health sector. In addition, practical steps have been taken to redress health sector inequities and to address poverty. In addition, the Presidential Review Commission comments that the Department of Health seems to have achieved a better balance between service delivery and internal transformation than other departments.

However, the PIR concludes that while the April 1996 extension of free primary care has improved financial accessibility, it does not directly address geographic and other aspects of access to primary care services, and the quality of care. Accessibility and quality of care improvements would include providing integrated, comprehensive primary care services (so that patients have a 'one-stop shop'), longer hours of opening, ensuring the routine availability of essential medicines, and empathetic staff attitudes.

The success of some policies has been marred by inadequate implementation strategies, which may be attributable to eagerness to make rapid changes. Linked to this, the Presidential Review Commission notes the need for a more effective communications strategy at the Department of Health.

There is also great variability between provinces. There have been some difficulties in moving from policy and programme development to implementation. This is partly due to inadequate management capacity, but also to structural obstacles and constraints. In particular, the Presidential Review Commission notes a lack of co-ordination between health and other departments and local authorities. At the hospital level, staff and other resource shortages continue to hamper the delivery of an effective health-care system. Health workers have claimed that the lack of resources and breakdown of management procedures have reached a point that is life-threatening, with dangerously few nurses, and bedlinen and medicines in short supply due to pilfering (*Mail and Guardian*, 26 February 1999).

Welfare The goal for welfare given by the RDP was to transform the existing social welfare policies, programmes and delivery systems so as to ensure basic welfare rights were provided to all South Africans. Redressing past imbalances would be achieved through a deliberate process of affirmative action in respect of those who had been disadvantaged in any way. The greatest coverage in terms of benefits to the poorest was stressed and social assistance in the form of cash or in kind was to be given to those most at risk. Delivery would be achieved through a restructured, integrated social welfare system at the different levels of government. Vulnerable groups targeted by the RDP for social welfare support included families with no income, women and children who have been victims of domestic and other forms of violence, young offenders and all those affected by substance abuse.

The welfare budget is the fourth largest vote in the government's budget, accounting for close on 10 per cent of the total. Welfare services and social security programmes form an integral part of the government's strategy for responding to poverty and inequality. The social component of the welfare budget is the largest (88.1 per cent) and impacts most directly on poverty and inequality, while the welfare services component of the budget (11 per cent) contributes towards human and social development. In 1993, approximately seven out of every hundred South Africans were in receipt of government social assistance of some sort and, currently, every month the DoW pays social grants to 2.9 million households. The proportion of income derived from social pensions is 28 per cent for the ultra-poor versus 5.8 per cent for the non-poor, with 22.4 per cent of rural incomes coming from transfers compared to 12.4 per cent in urban areas (DoW 1996; PSLSD 1993).

The welfare budget can thus be viewed as a designated budget to reduce income poverty and promote human development. Welfare policies and programmes are also designed to address transient poverty (short-term, temporary or seasonal poverty) as well as chronic poverty, which is long-term or structural. At the macro-economic level, the GEAR strategy acknowledges that social security, social services and related social development programmes are investments that contribute to social and economic gains and growth.

The 1998 MTEF report states that the key challenge for the welfare sector is to manage growth of expenditure on social security entitlement programmes while strengthening the funding of discretionary and developmental welfare services. The aim is to increase the share of spending allocated to developmental welfare services, which is currently less than 10 per cent of welfare and social security expenditure. A critical focus is ensuring an efficient management and delivery of social assistance grants, thereby contributing savings within the welfare budget.

The PIR concludes that welfare provision still bears the marks of apartheid inequalities, with people in disadvantaged and rural areas having very limited access, or no access at all, to the services of either government or welfare NGOs. However, there has been a conscious effort to target those categories that are most vulnerable.

A number of obstacles may interfere with the realization of the goals of social welfare of which budgetary constraints may be critical. Developmental social welfare might require a bigger staff complement than at present. Further examples of the effects of financial constraints are seen in the restriction of the flagship programme of the Department of Welfare to those not receiving any other forms of state assistance, and the controversy over the replacement of the more generous but restrictive state maintenance grant, with the more widely available child support grant.

The lack of, and difficulty in implementing, co-ordination of initiatives undertaken by the various government departments is an important challenge. Collaboration has often proven difficult, as government bureaucracies are not designed to facilitate inter-sectoral work. Finally, there are large numbers of needy people who must cope unassisted by the state as they fall outside the categories eligible for the specific benefits that are available.

Water and sanitation The RDP base document estimated that in 1994 there were more than 12 million people who did not have access to clean and adequate water and 21 million people who did not have access to adequate sanitation. In addition, surveys have suggested that, in 1994, only 21 per cent of households had access to piped water, and only 28 per cent had access to sanitation facilities (RDP 1995). In rural areas, more than 80 per cent of poor households had no access to piped water or to sanitation. Among rural African households, 74 per cent of all households need to fetch water on a daily basis. For 21 per cent of this population, the cartage distance is greater than 500m.

With respect to domestic water, the RDP set a short-term target to provide all households with clean, safe water supply of 20–30 litres per capita per day, and within 200 metres, as well as an adequate/safe sanitation facility per site through a national water and sanitation programme. Importantly, this was to be achieved though a tariff structure that would be affordable by communities in the rural areas. Finally, the RDP committed government to providing operation and maintenance systems that would ensure minimum disruption in service within two years.

To implement these goals, the Consolidated Municipal Infrastructure Programme targets the delivery of at least a basic level of services to all South Africans within ten years. In terms of the indicated packages proposed by the Municipal Infrastructure Investment Programme, this would imply access to an unreticulated water source, a VIP-type toilet, a secure biomass or non-grid electricity energy supply, all-weather road access to the settlement and on-site solid waste disposal. The indicative capital cost of this level of service provision was estimated to be R4,700 in 1997, with a running cost of R55 per household per month.

At a general level, there appears to have been some success in the implementation of these policies. Over 1,020 water supply projects have been identified, are underway or have been completed, bringing safe water to 8.9 million people and sanitation to about 100,000 people. Over 1,200,000 previously unserved people have already been supplied with water. As a result, the DBSA (1998: 30) estimates that an average of 1,000 people have gained access to clean water every day since 1994. However, delivery of domestic infrastructure shows considerable variation both in terms of actual delivery and the impact and sustainability of initiatives. For example, despite impressive progress made in the delivery of water, the DBSA (1998: 82) points to a high rate of failure in rural water schemes after construction. Moreover, the wastage of water remains a concern.

The PIR identified several problems in evaluating programmes for infrastructure provision which represent a threat to these programmes. Most important are the interlinked issues of low levels of service payments, subsidies and tariffs. The problem of low service payments confounds local government's capacity to deliver service that will be sustainable. Low payment levels for services compound a difficult financial situation for municipalities. A combination of factors, including the costs of incorporating former townships into municipal jurisdictions, low capacity for financial management in some areas, and inappropriate tariff and intergovernmental grant mechanisms, have resulted in an unsustainable financial situation. The White Paper on Local Government of 1998 draws attention to the broader problem faced by many local governments trying to implement a range of policies concerning domestic infrastructure. Here the issue of 'unfunded mandates' is stressed whereby powers are allocated to structures that lack the abilities and resources to execute them. This is exacerbated by the inability of many people to afford these services.

The solutions to overcoming these financial difficulties lie in improved financial management by municipalities, tougher measures for non-payers (including service cut-offs), closer monitoring of municipal finances by central and provincial government and the development of a culture of payment. As the effectiveness of the metering and billing system and the trust people place in it are major factors in payment, this also needs to be a major priority if more costs are to be recovered through payment for services

Energy The RDP estimated that only 36 per cent of South African households had access to electricity in 1994, which meant that some three million households were not electrified. This is supported by the PIR which argues that biomass fuels are used by about 16 million people, hydrocarbon fuels by about 21 million people and electricity by about 20 million. Given that the population of South Africa was around 38 million in 1994, it is apparent that many households continue to use more than one domestic energy source on a regular basis. Turning to social infrastructure, in 1994 it was also estimated that 86 per cent of the schools used by the African population and around 4,000 clinics were without electricity.

The RDP set the target of electrifying 2.5 million households, or 72 per cent of all households, by the year 2000. These RDP targets of 450,000 new connections per annum up to the year 2000 were not set by government, but were decided by the respective distributors and estimations by the electricity supply industry of what is achievable, in consultation with the relevant communities. The delivery of the Accelerated Electrification Programme is the responsibility of Eskom, local government in the form of transitional metropolitan councils and the Independent Development Trust (IDT).

The electrification programme set more detailed targets that include the electrification of at least 95 per cent of all urban dwellings by the year 2000. This will include all new houses to be built over the planning period. As far as social facilities are concerned, the aim is to electrify 9,500 of the 25,000 schools in South Africa that are without electricity. It is envisaged that the remaining 16,400 will be provided with power by means of photovoltaic cells (solar energy).

The Department of Mineral and Energy Affairs (DMEA) is responsible for policy formulation. The National Electricity Regulator (NER) was established by the DMEA in early 1995 with the task of promoting efficiency, electrification and controlling licences. It is also tasked with assessing and advising on such functions as the level of services offered, the efficiency of response to consumers and the provision of reader-friendly accounts. It has, through its licence controls, considerable power to ensure that minimum standards of electrification are being met. It does not, however, have the power to regulate or monitor the recipients of the electrification programme.

In many areas, local government plays a central role in the reticulation of electricity. If local governments are not delivering according to their mandate, the NER has the authority to call for the removal of the government representative. An electrification fund was made available for the first time in 1997; such a fund needs to be administered on a national level, and made available on a need basis. The NER is, at this stage, responsible for the devolution of funds to provincial and local authorities.

On the whole, transitional metropolitan councils have not been able to meet their targets. However, the IDT's rural development programme that includes the off-grid electrification of schools and clinics has achieved its goals. In 1995/96 Eskom reported that its contribution to the national electrification programme was well on track. It exceeded its target in 1996, and achieved this again in 1997. These connections are primarily in rural areas.

According to Eskom, the electrification programme adds approximately 800 new households to its customer base every working day. In rural areas, the DBSA (1998: 69) reports that the percentage of households with access to electricity has increased from 21 per cent in 1995 to 32 per cent in 1997. Approximately three million homes are expected to be connected between the initiation of the programme in the early 1990s and the year 2004.

Despite this pace of delivery, just under half of all South Africans still do not have access to electricity. Moreover, many of those who have access to electricity cannot take full advantage of it. Thus, for the next five to twenty years the poor are likely to continue to use wood fuel in particular, but also paraffin and coal.

A significant threat to the electricity drives is looming in the form of the continuing non-payment of electricity accounts from both consumers and local authorities. Eskom's outstanding arrears now amount to R1.2 billion. In addition, low take-up rates have restricted their ability to cross-subsidize, as they had originally planned. In 1997, Eskom made available R300 million to the industry, to facilitate the meeting of targets within the industry. The DBSA (1998: 69) notes that problems facing the electrification programme include: low consumption by newly connected customers, difficulties in determining the economic rationale for many electrification projects, and the ad hoc cross-sectoral integration with other types of infrastructure. Other problems relate to the fragmentation of the electricity distribution system.

Land reform Just over a quarter of African rural households (26 per cent) currently have access to a plot of land for the cultivation of crops (PSLSD 1993). Average land size for these households is 2.2ha. with poorer households having smaller amounts of land. This land is often of poor quality with limited water supplies. Estimates of land degradation in the rural poor areas of the country, for example, although not that reliable, indicate that at least 20 per cent is severely degraded (3.9 million ha.) and a further 40 per cent moderately degraded (5.2 ha.).

Enforcing segregation meant that large numbers of people were forcibly removed from 'Black Spots' into these bantustans. An estimated 475,000 people were removed from 'Black Spots' between 1960 and 1983, many of whom are eligible for restitution.

Marcus et al. (1996) report that about 68 per cent of South African's black rural households desire farmland, although the envisaged use of this land is not specified. Although figures are not available for non-agricultural land, it can be assumed that some of the 32 per cent who do not desire farmland do indeed want land for residential or other purposes.

The RDP set the following goals for land reform:

• to address effectively forced removals and the historical denial of access to land
• to ensure tenure for rural dwellers
• to supply residential and productive land to the poorest section of the rural population and aspirant farmers; specifically, 30 per cent of agricultural land within the first five years of the programme
• to remove all forms of discrimination in women's access to land

The land reform programme states that it was designed to:

• address the injustices of the past
• provide for a more equitable distribution of land ownership
• reduce poverty and contribute to economic growth
• ensure security of tenure for all
• support sustainable land-use patterns and facilitate rapid land release for development

In being operationalized, the land reform programme has been broken into three elements: redistribution, restitution, and tenure reform.

Redistribution aims to provide the disadvantaged and poor with land for residential and productive purposes and will benefit the urban and rural poor, labour tenants, farm workers and new entrants to agriculture. The Land Reform Pilot Programme (LRPP) was launched in 1994 and serves more or less as the prototype for the 'mainstream' land redistribution sub-programme that is soon to come into effect. The LRPP was subsumed within the mainstream land redistribution as of March 1996.

Restitution cases are dealt with through the Land Claims Court and Commission, established under the Restitution of Land Rights Act of 1994. Eligible cases are largely the victims of forced removals since 1913. In 1995, the Commission on Restitution of Land Rights was established and the Land Claims Court became operational.

Tenure reform seeks to improve the tenure security of all South Africans. This programme includes a review of current land policy, administration and legislation with a view to accommodating more diverse forms of land tenure. The Land Rights Act, 31 of 1996, makes provision for legally enforceable tenure rights under a diversity of forms of tenure. In addition, state land disposal and administration is dealt with through the implementation of the Development Facilitation Act, 67 of 1995.

The total budget for land reform for 1997/98 was (exclusive of roll-overs) R583 million, of which R64 million is for the restitution programme and R322 million for the redistribution.

In terms of the number of households to be affected and the amount of government money to be spent on land reform, the redistribution and tenure sub-programmes are likely to far exceed restitution. Although no reliable figures exist as to how many people have insecure tenure, it can be surmised that the majority of those living in the former bantustan and former South African Development Trust (SADT) areas can be characterized as having insecure tenure of one variety or another. This amounts to some 3.9 million black rural households. In addition, there are presently around 1.3 million households living in informal and squatter housing in and around urban areas, and roughly 800,000 permanent farmworkers and their on-farm households whose lodging is only as secure as their jobs. This yields a rough sum of around 6 million households. By contrast, land redistribution is unlikely to affect more than 1.5 million households over the next ten years. Land restitution, which is mandated by the constitution, is unlikely to affect more than 500,000 households, both urban and rural, over the same amount of time.

The PIR concludes that the progress of land reform in South Africa has been undeniably slow, due in part to the need to develop appropriate delivery mechanisms, as well as the complexity of existing and proposed tenure arrangements. However, delivery capacity has shown strong evidence of improving, not least because of the commitment of provincial and local government to play an expanded role.

Finally, now that many administrative and technical issues have been resolved, it is important that the Department of Land Affairs continue to expand capacity, both in terms of departmental staff and in terms of local support personnel. If capacity is expanded, however, it is expected that the land reform programme will come up against fiscal constraints at the present tiny level of funding. The fiscal resources comprised 0.3 per cent of the non-interest national government budget for 1996/97. This could be multiplied several-fold without having a significant impact on the overall government budget, while placing delivery on a much more satisfactory trajectory.

Labour Markets and Employment Generation

As already noted, almost 30 per cent of the labour force of South Africa, or 4.2 million people, were unemployed in 1994. Some two million of these were active work-seekers, with the balance being willing to work, but not actively in the job market. In addition, some 450,000 young people (a number which is expected to reach 600,000 within the next decade) enter the labour market each year from secondary and tertiary education.

The characteristics of unemployment in South Africa are such that Africans have a much higher rate of unemployment. Also, broad unemployment rates are higher in rural areas and for females. The smaller difference between narrow rural and narrow urban employment indicates that there are a far greater number of discouraged workers in rural areas. Age discrepancies in unemployment rates are also high. Broad unemployment among the youth stands at 60 per cent for youth below twenty compared to 12.5 per cent for people over age fifty-five.

The Presidential Jobs Summit was held on 30 October 1998 and emphasized a broad range of policy commitments including:

- the continued importance of sustainable and stable macro-economic and fiscal policies
- supply-side industry policy measures that encourage employment and investment
- new programmes to promote small, medium and micro-enterprises
- the enhancement of tourism capacity
- enhanced delivery of housing
- human resource development
- labour market policies dealing with job security, productivity and equity

In line with these areas of priority, the government has allocated about R5 billion towards special employment projects and labour-intensive infrastructure. These have included:

- the Community Based Public Works Programme (CBPWP) focusing on local infrastructure needs and
- the Working for Water Programme which targets improved water catchment management and access to water along with employment creation

- the Housing Subsidy Programme which provides standard capital subsidies for low-income housing projects (see Chapter 16)
- micro-enterprise support

The Community Based Public Works Programme was launched as a presidential lead project within the national public works programme. A grant of R250 million was allocated from the RDP fund to finance the CBPWP until the end of the 1996 fiscal year. The programme aims to contribute to infrastructural development through labour-based construction, especially targeting women. It creates temporary jobs while providing assets that add to income-generating capacity and improve the accessibility of remote communities. By the end of 1997, the programme had created 1,112 projects, mostly situated and providing employment opportunities to communities in the most impoverished areas. According to the 1997 evaluation the programme created 1.43 million days of work, with women and women-headed households filling over 41 per cent of those jobs.

The Working for Water Programme clears invading alien plants, such as wattles, pines and gums, from water catchment areas. Labour-intensive methods are used and as these projects are mainly located in areas of extreme poverty this is a valuable poverty relief initiative. Some 38,000 jobs have been created, mainly benefiting women. This is an investment in protecting water resources and the natural environment, while providing jobs and incomes to poor communities.

The key to the success of dedicated public works programmes as income providers to poor people is ensuring that they are well targeted. An evaluation of the Community Employment Programme (CEP), which is the component of the CBPWP implemented through the IDT, indicates that the programme had a significant impact on employment and was largely well targeted. For example, 79 per cent of workers employed were African, and 41 per cent were women. Furthermore, 61 per cent of the CEP projects were located in the three poorest provinces, KwaZulu-Natal, Eastern Cape and the Northern Province, and 88 per cent of CEP workers were drawn from rural areas. However, the evaluation found that the CEP workforce was dominated by the twenty-five to forty-five age groups, although rural areas contain larger numbers of youth and elderly. With respect to the education profile of the workforce it was found to have a close correlation with that of the poorest segment of South African society. Seventy per cent of the CEP workers had either no education or only primary education. While, overall, 48 per cent of the CEP workers were unemployed before the programme, 22 per cent were in full-time employment away from home, 11 per cent in part-time work and 5 per cent in domestic work.

Various programmes and institutions have been established to give effect to the government's strategy for the promotion of SMMEs.

Governance and Local Government

Local government has been described as the 'hands and feet' of reconstruction and development in South Africa. It is true that in the absence of effective local delivery bodies, the government is powerless to implement its policies and provide services. In many cases, local governments are responsible for the price and quality of a region's water, electricity and roads, and they control the use and development of land. In parts of the country they own substantial amounts of land. They purchase goods and services and pay salaries amounting to almost R50 billion. They set the agenda for local politics, and the way they operate sends strong signals to their own residents and to prospective migrants or investors. In essence, though, they implement policy and do not create it.

At the outset, local governments have encountered a number of problems:

- while local authorities in wealthier areas are often financially solvent and administratively competent, many local authorities in which the poor reside are neither sustainable nor economically viable; this is related to many issues including a rent boycott culture, inadequate private sector investment and the insolvency of black authorities
- the absence of local administrations in some areas, especially in rural communities
- poor service provision in townships
- community suspicion of government due to past experience with apartheid structures

Each of these problems forms part of the broader institutional context in which the development of local government structures is embedded and has slowed the process of building local government and the delivery of development.

The implementation of the Local Government Transition Act (1993) has revealed additional problems with the system of local government including:[2]

- the number of municipalities, the size of councils and problems associated with the demarcation between areas
- confusion between the two spheres of local government itself, namely local authorities and municipalities
- the relationship between the primary and secondary spheres of local

government, especially fiscal relations, is not always clear; this is complicated by the complexities involved in the flow of funds between the three spheres of government

- capacity constraints remain a serious problem and there is a need for cross-subsidization across municipalities; many local administrations also lack the skills required in a new and rapidly changing environment and the restructuring of local government training is still in its infancy
- the relationship between municipalities and civil society is still marked by confusion and uncertainty; moreover, the relationship between councillors and officials has also been less than satisfactory, largely a result of unclear and ill-defined lines of responsibility. The role of traditional authorities has also not been clarified
- financial weaknesses are among the greatest obstacles to the development of effective local government and this poor financial management and control is widespread; many municipalities, especially those serving poor communities, are struggling financially because of inadequate budgets allocated by central government, unrealistic budgeting, poor budget discipline, inadequate financial management and weak credit control

Finally, municipalities are expected to explore their new mandate and the latitude that it provides for innovative policies and programmes. With greater local autonomy, localities are required to find ways in which a balance between competition and co-operation can be achieved. This is problematic since a temptation will always exist to undermine other municipalities in the quest for investment. While some competition will improve both efficiency and innovation, if the regions do not work together, it is likely that all communities will lose out. The amalgamation of smaller authorities may be one way in which these problems, as well as capacity constraints, might be resolved. However, such amalgamation may lead to job loss and further political problems.

On the positive side, many local authority structures have responded in a credible fashion in the implementation of the projects undertaken as a part of the R1.3 billion Municipal Infrastructure Programme. By 1998, an estimated 6.5 million people had been reached by these programmes, and 242,000 people have been employed in the implementation of the various projects. In addition, some local governments have initiated innovative strategies for local economic development. At a more general level, it is also encouraging that most local authorities have recognized the need for change management. In other words, they have recognized the need to change existing mind-sets and institutional arrangements in order that development goals might be met. Many of the suggestions put forward in terms of changed management strategies have centred on the improvement of incentives and information.

Conclusion

The analysis above shows the extent of the challenge the government inherited on its election in 1994. Discriminatory policies against the majority of the country's population had resulted in both a high rate of poverty (the percentage of the population who are poor) and, more importantly, high levels of poverty (the average amount required by the poor to reach the poverty line). Furthermore, these policies also have resulted in an extremely high level of inequality which has been shown to be a factor inhibiting economic growth, promoting social disruption and limiting the impact of what growth does take place. Finally, the macro-economic consequences of previous actions have resulted in a high debt, inefficient and low investment and savings and high unemployment levels. These in turn have resulted in the government adopting fiscal discipline as a cornerstone of macro-economic policy which, despite efforts to reprioritize the budget, must limit its ability to deal with the poverty and inequality trap noted above. Resolving this paradox lies at the centre of government's success in achieving the goals of the RDP.

This chapter has attempted to bring together key information showing the levels of poverty and need in South African and the shortfalls in access to basic needs targeted for action by the RDP. This has been placed in the context of the current macro-economic situation of the country, and the policy framework that has been generated by the key national departments involved in the implementation of the RDP.

In general, expenditure, policy formation and, to a large extent, implementation, broadly correspond to the pro-poor approach adopted in the RDP. In most cases, government actions should have resulted in better access for the less well-off to education, health-care, housing and domestic infrastructure. The pace of delivery has undeniably not matched the delivery targets set by the RDP, but in terms of the principles and processes set for such delivery, in most cases these targets have been reached. There is of course one notable exception to this: the macro-economic framework proposed by the GEAR strategy, and it is not surprising that a good deal of criticism has focused on this exception. Certainly the lack of constructive debate with government around the macro-economic principles which informed the GEAR strategy is an area of contention. Moreover, given the apparent failure of trends predicted by GEAR to have emerged, the calls for such debate are defensible, whatever position is taken regarding role of consultation in forming macro-economic policy. To some extent, the Medium Term Expenditure Framework can offer a window for such engagement and seems an appropriate area for analysis; the IDASA Budget Information Service is an example of such analysis.

The chapter has also shown some of the blockages that have affected delivery. Of these, the slow place of institutional transformation is central. The fundamental shift required by the RDP was from institutions of exclusion and control to those based on democratic process and developmental governance. In many instances, delivery according to these RDP principles has required the creation of entirely new government directorates (monitoring and evaluation being a pertinent example) or the reorientation of existing government departments (the Department of Land Affairs is probably the most extreme example of this). In addition, two new spheres of government have had to be developed and their roles and responsibilities defined and allocated. Indeed, the drafting of a new constitution has required a fundamental transformation of the institutional framework of governance that has put in place social and economic rights for the rich and poor alike.

A second important reason for the slow pace of delivery lies with the reluctance of government to resolve blockages by increasing expenditure. Clearly, to the extent that departments have been unable to draw on additional resources, and had the capacity to manage this expenditure, delivery would have been slowed. The caveat is important since it is evident that many government departments have not been able to utilize the funds that were available. Increasingly, though, the capacity of departments will improve and, with it, the brake imposed by fiscal discipline may play a role in slowing delivery.

Finally, a third major area of concern relating to delivery relates to the *micro*-economic framework within which development takes place. Many of the reforms that have been adopted by the new South African government rely upon a mix of the 'market' for their implementation and the capacity of local communities and institutions to articulate needs and manage development processes. The Land Reform Programme is an example of this, although many other policies fall into the same category. However, in many cases, the expectations of policy fail to take account of the realities of market distortions, institutional failure and weak, fragmented communities. As a result, a mismatch between expectations and reality has emerged in terms of the micro-economic impact of macro-economic policies. This is an area of analysis that requires considerably more attention if the failure of good policy with sufficient resources is to be understood.

Notes

1. Comparing different data sets and poverty measures, Leibbrandt and Woolard (1999) have confirmed that this ranking of provinces is sound.

2. Similar problems have been identified in the Green Paper on Local Government.

References

African National Congress (ANC) (1994) *The Reconstruction and Development Programme.* Johannesburg: Umanyano Publications.

Bruno, M., M. Ravallion and L. Squire (1996) *Equity and Growth in Developing Countries, Old and New Perspectives on the Policy Issues.* Policy Research Working Paper no. 1563. Washington, DC: World Bank.

Department of Finance (1998) *Medium Term Budget Policy Statement* (2 November). Pretoria: Department of Finance.

Department of Welfare (DoW) (1996) *Report of the Welfare Reprioritisation Committee.* Pretoria: Department of Welfare, March.

Development Bank of Southern Africa (DBSA) (1998) *Development Report, 1998: Infrastructure, a Foundation for Development.* Midrand: DBSA.

Eckert, J. B. and D. Mullins (1989) 'Income Redistribution and Its Effects on the South African Economy', *Journal of the Study of Economics and Econometrics,* 13, 3, pp. 1–20.

Government of National Unity (GNU) (1994) *White Paper on Reconstruction and Development: Government Strategy for Fundamental Transformation.* Cape Town: Government Printer, September.

IDASA (1999) *Submission on National Budget 1999/2000 to the Portfolio Committee on Finance* (19 February). IDASA: Budget Information Service.

Leibbrandt, M. and I. Woolard (1999) 'A Comparison of Poverty in South Africa's Nine Provinces', *Development Southern Africa,* 16, 1, pp. 37–54.

Marcus, T., C. Eales and A. Wildschut (1996) *Down to Earth: Land Demand in the New South Africa.* Durban: Land and Agricultural Policy Centre and Indicator Press.

May, J., M. Carter and D. Posel (1996) *The Composition and Persistence of Poverty in Rural South Africa, an Entitlements Approach.* Land and Agriculture Policy Centre Policy Paper no. 15. Johannesburg: Land and Agriculture Policy Centre.

Nattrass, J. (1983) 'Plenty amidst Poverty, the Need for Development Studies'. Inaugural Lecture. Durban: University of Natal, 12 September.

PIR (1998) *Poverty and Inequality in South Africa.* Durban: Praxis Publishing.

Project for Statistics on Living Standards and Development (PSLSD) (1993) *Project for Statistics on Living Standards and Development.* http://www.uct.ac.za/depts/saldru/ SALDRU and World Bank, University of Cape Town.

Ravallion, M. (1996) 'Issues in Measuring and Modelling Poverty', *Economic Journal,* 106, 438, pp. 1328–43.

Statistics South Africa (1997) *Income and Expenditure Survey 1995.* http://www.statssa. gov.za/IES/IES.htm

— (1998) *Income and Expenditure Survey.*

Wilson, F. and M. Ramphele (1989) *Uprooting Poverty: The South African Challenge.* Cape Town: David Philips.

15

The South African Women's Budget Initiative: What Does It Tell Us about Poverty Alleviation?

Debbie Budlender

The budget is in many respects the single most important policy or law passed by any government, determining the resources to be allocated to each of its policies and programmes. Without the necessary resources, any policy, however 'good' in theory, will have limited success.

At least up until the mid-1980s, the annual March budget day in South Africa was perceived to be of interest mainly to white businessmen. The media analysed how the budget provisions – and in particular tax changes – would affect the businessmen in their lives as private taxpayers and as the 'leaders' (or controllers) of the economy. To the extent that the media mentioned the poor, they focused on increases – usually less than the rate of inflation – in old age pensions. Reports on pensions would typically be accompanied by case studies of, or comments from, white pensioners.

Some time in the mid-1980s the emerging union movement started providing comment on what the annual budget might mean for people other than businesspeople. Their input shifted the focus of the debate. To workers, indirect taxes such as general sales tax and VAT were as important as, if not more so, than direct taxes. And given that most workers were black and most businesspeople white, there were also new questions as to the extent to which the various allocations affected people from different race groups.

In 1994 the African National Congress (ANC) gained the majority of votes in the first democratic South African elections. The elections were conducted on the basis of party lists, with seats allocated to each party according to the proportion of total votes won at the national level and in each province. The ANC, after some debate, adopted a quota in its party list which ensured that at least one-third of its national parliamentarians would be women. Over 100 of the 400-odd parliamentarians in the first post-apartheid South African government were women – a remarkable increase on the less than 3 per cent of the final apartheid parliament. The first cabinet included three women ministers out of a total of twenty-seven, and three women deputy ministers out of a total of twelve. By mid-1996 there were a further five women deputy ministers and an additional woman minister. Importantly for our purposes, one of the new deputy ministers was Gill Marcus, previously chairperson of the parliamentary Joint Standing Committee on Finance (JSCOF).

Virtually all of the ANC women parliamentarians and ministers had a history in the anti-apartheid 'struggle', whether in the United Democratic Front, the internal or external wings of the ANC, uMkhonto we Sizwe, the trade unions, or elsewhere. Some had been members of women's organizations, or women's wings of these organizations. Within virtually all these formations there was ongoing debate as to the relative importance or ordering of the national liberation and women's struggles.

Many of the new parliamentarians in 1994 had been activists during the early 1990s with women who remained outside in the Women's National Coalition (WNC). The WNC was a broad-based movement which reflected the rapprochement and general euphoria of the immediate pre-election days. It included women from across the political spectrum, from all races and ages, and from across a wide span of classes. The primary practical aim of the WNC was to draw up a Women's Charter based on the demands and needs of as representative a sample of South African women as possible. This charter was drawn up and presented to the new leaders of post-apartheid South Africa. The broader aim of the WNC was to influence the pre-election negotiations and the drawing up of the interim constitution. This objective was achieved to the extent that the interim (and final) constitution entrenched equality as one of its fundamental principles.

The new parliamentarians stepped into their positions with high hopes of what they could and should achieve, and an awareness that there were many comrades and colleagues outside expecting them to achieve remarkable things. The Women's Charter, much like the Freedom Charter, was an aspirational document which asked for many things. Within a short time of coming into power, many people – women and men, parliamentarians and bureaucrats – realized that turning the apartheid ship around was no easy, or quick, task.

The Birth of the Women's Budget Initiative

It was against this background that the Women's Budget Initiative (WBI) was born. Within the JSCOF were a number of energetic and visionary women. One of these was Gill Marcus, the chairperson who, like many others, was determined that the standing committees of the new parliament would not act as rubber stamps as they had during apartheid.

Another was Pregs Govender, an ex-trade unionist of the female-dominated South African Clothing & Textile Workers Union, former co-ordinator of the Western Cape Workers College and, for a few years, co-ordinator of the WNC.

After the tabling of the first full budget under the new government in March 1995, the JSCOF added a poverty session to the normal budget hearings. Mamphela Ramphele, co-author with Francis Wilson of *Uprooting Poverty*, was asked to speak on the topic of women and the budget during this session. Mamphela Ramphele was, at the time, also the director of the Institute for Democracy in South Africa (IDASA), an NGO which incorporated a project focusing on analysis and advocacy around government budgets.

Some time after the first hearing, in mid-1995, a small group of parliamentarians got together with IDASA and individuals from other NGOs such as the Community Agency for Social Enquiry to discuss the possibility of a 'Women's Budget' project. The idea of the Women's Budget came from Australia. In that country the federal and state governments had, since the mid-1980s, each year tabled women's budget statements on budget day. These substantial documents, compiled by bureaucrats, set out how each agency's budget affected women and girls, either through targeted or general programmes.

The South African group recognized the enormity of the task ahead, and chose to treat the first year as an exploratory exercise. It was agreed that the analysis would focus on a small number of departments rather than the full range. Importantly, it was agreed that the chosen departments should not be limited to the social sectors traditionally seen as 'women's issues'. It was also agreed that the analysis should include taxation, so as to address revenue as well as expenditure. Finally, there would be a chapter on public service employment. This would deal with the widespread concern over the unrepresentative nature of the public service in terms of race and gender, and with the fact that women were largely absent from the higher decision-making echelons.

The South African initiative was different from the Australian in its location. Instead of being an exercise undertaken by the bureaucracy, in South Africa it was seen as an exercise in monitoring and advocacy. It was a statement that ANC parliamentarians and the NGOs involved in the initiative supported the broad thrust of government, but saw their task as ensuring that the government lived up to the ideals.

Three years after the launch of the WBI, the initiative has produced three books of sectoral analyses which between them cover all votes (allocations) of the national government and – to some extent – of the provincial government (see Budlender 1996, 1997, 1998). The books also contain chapters dealing with taxation, public sector employment, budget reform and inter-governmental fiscal relations. In addition to these three quite technical and detailed books, we have produced *Money Matters: Women and the Government Budget* (Hurt and Budlender 1998). This is a popularized version of the research, which provides simplified versions of selected chapters from the first two years' research at a level appropriate for a reader with grade 10 education.

The Women's Budget Initiative and Poverty

What has all this got to do with poverty? Pregs Govender's Preface to the first book is suggestive in this respect. She opens by quoting the words of Dora Tamana, a working-class veteran of the liberation struggle, as follows:

> You who have no food, speak
> You who have no homes, speak
> You who have no jobs, speak
> You who have to run like chickens from the vulture, speak

Govender goes on to note that while women are by no means a homogenous group, they 'are disproportionately represented among the poorest in our country. They are the majority of the homeless, the landless, the unemployed, the violated' (Govender 1996: 1).

The WBI is not concerned with women simply because they are women. It is, indeed, not concerned with all women. It is concerned with women to the extent that they are disadvantaged. And it recognizes that one of the primary elements in that disadvantage is economic, in the sense of poverty. It makes the link between the budget – the government's allocation of resources – and the current relative lack of control over resources of many women. One of the chapters of the first book presents a profile of South African women with a strong focus on their economic situation.

Rhonda Sharp, an academic who was involved in the early years of the Australian initiative, has developed an analytical framework which clarifies the different lenses through which one can analyse budgets from a gender perspective. She distinguishes between:

1. Expenditures specifically targeted to women, or gender issues. In South Africa this would include the Welfare Department's Flagship Programme for Unemployed Women with Young Children.
2. Expenditures which aim to address gender inequalities among public servants. This might include expenditures on crèche facilities for the children of public servants or training for women in male-dominated jobs.
3. Mainstream expenditures – all other allocations.

The third category includes by far the largest amount of money: about 99 per cent even in Australia, which has a significant number of gender-specific programmes. It is clearly the most important. And the question that is being asked of this category, is to what extent the expenditures and the programmes and policies that underlie them, exacerbate gender disparities or remedy them.

The term 'Women's Budget' has misled and confused many people. The initiatives do not draw up, or propose, a *separate* budget for women. They do not argue for a larger slice of the cake for women. Rather, they say that women make up just over half of all citizens of the country, and that their needs should be a primary consideration, or mainstreamed, in all budgetary decisions. Indeed, they argue that because women are generally more disadvantaged than men, and thus more in need of government assistance, their needs should be 'weighted' by more than their proportionate share of the population. At the same time we stress that the situation of women cannot be considered without examining that of men. Gender is about the relationship between women and men, and the position of the one group cannot be understood outside the context of the other, in much the same way as poverty cannot be understood, or addressed, without looking at the position of the rich people who own, control and benefit from the way the economy and society works.

The WBI's focus on disadvantage means that it is primarily concerned with black women. The close relationship between race and income in South Africa has had both advantages and disadvantages for the initiative. On the one hand, our racist history makes it unlikely that any South African researcher would ignore race in the way that some women's studies do elsewhere. On the other hand, as the race–class connection becomes blurred, as a few black people join the ranks of the wealthy, the focus on poverty can become diffused or confused.

In the WBI one aspect of this tension is apparent each time people are introduced to the idea for the first time. When asked what gender disparities they would look out for in different departments, the first response is almost always focused on the gender (and often race) composition of departmental staff. People want to know how many black and white women and men are employed, and how many of the different race–gender groupings are in management positions.

In the Women's Budget Initiative, we have acknowledged the importance of representivity in the public service. We know that having women in decision-making positions will not by any means guarantee gender-sensitivity, but feel that it increases the likelihood of some openness to the specific problems of women. We know that the presence of particular women in powerful positions has contributed to the success of our own initiative. We therefore do not oppose some analysis of staffing positions. However, we argue that representivity is of interest to this project primarily to the extent that it addresses the problems of (poor) beneficiaries 'out there' in the world, and ensures that delivery is gender-sensitive. Public servants, much as they may think otherwise, are generally not among those we would classify as our primary targets.

Our concentration on the poor and disadvantaged comes through in some way in sectoral analyses. Thus, for example, in education we are far more interested in what is happening (or *not* happening) in the adult basic education and training field, than in what is happening at the tertiary level. And in trade and industry, we are more interested in whether assistance is being provided to survivalist businesses, than in what is being done in respect of company ownership.

What Has Been Done

The WBI has succeeded beyond what would have been our wildest dreams when we first set out, very tentatively, in 1995. The initiative has gained widespread recognition both within the country and outside. It has provoked similar initiatives in a number of countries, with the most interest – gratifyingly for us – in other African countries. Uganda, Tanzania, Namibia and Mozambique already have initiatives, while several other countries have shown interest. Within the country, in the first year following the first Women's Budget, IDASA and the Youth Development Trust co-ordinated a Children's Budget. More recently a group of NGOs in the area of rural development has informed the Department of Finance of their intention to draw up a rural budget. And, importantly for this chapter, at the outset the SA NGO Coalition, the SA Human Rights Commission and the Commission on Gender Equality have announced that one of the most important outputs of their 'Speak Out on Poverty' hearings will be the compilation of a 'poverty budget' for 1999/2000.

The WBI itself, in response to a great number of requests, will take its first steps in looking at local government budgets during 1998/99, while contributing to past analyses of national and provincial budgets. In addition, in parallel to the parliamentary/NGO initiative, during 1997 the government embarked on its own, parallel women's budget exercise. This latter, which formed one of a number of pilots for the Commonwealth Secretariat, was co-ordinated by the Department of Finance. The first year of the pilot culminated in the tabling of a *Budget Review* on budget day in March 1998 which incorporated gender analysis in the traditional reports on departmental policies and budgets as well as (to a limited extent) in the other discussions.

Despite the apparent successes, there are many questions which those of us inside, as well as observers, can pose. One of the frequently posed questions concerns impact. People ask us whether, given that we say we are talking about concrete change rather than aspirations and ideals, we have effected any changes in the numbers of rands in the different pro-grammes and sub-programmes of the budget?

The answer is not simple. First, the WBI does not occur in a vacuum. From the beginning we have acknowledged the many other concurrent initiatives on which we have drawn, the strength we have gained from them, and the support we hope we have afforded their ventures. Besides the many initiatives in the field of gender, these other ventures include the forces inside and outside parliament and within government itself advoc-ating budgetary reform, transparency and accountability, as well as the increasing calls for far more attention to be paid to poverty. So, where we have seen changes, we cannot claim these for the WBI alone, but hope that we have been one of several forces which pushed this change along.

Having said that, we can point to some gains in programmes that we support, as well as some setbacks. For example, in terms of Sharp's first category – expenditures specifically targeted at gender or women's issues – the long awaited Office on the Status of Women was only allocated a director and a part-time secretary at the time of its establishment in early 1997. The Commission on Gender Equality, provided for in the con-stitution but also established only in early 1997, was in its first year not allocated enough even to cover the salaries of the commissioners. After much advocacy, in the 1998/99 budget the allocation was increased from R2.1 million to R10.0 million. The WBI was able to provide some support to the advocacy on the basis of its experience and skills in examining government budgets.

A second area in which the WBI has almost certainly had some impact is support for small, medium and micro-enterprises (SMMEs). Support for this sector was a professed priority for government from the start and largely reflected a desire to bring black people into the economy. The first year's WBI research included the Department of Trade and Industry, which is largely responsible for SMME support. The research pointed out the small amount allocated to the area as well as – and more im-portantly for women – that there was little attention to the micro- and survivalist end of the scale where women predominated. The research caught the attention of some of the key players, including the MP who soon after became the deputy minister. The point about survivalists is now widely acknowledged in the field. The problem at this stage is how to target this sector successfully. While the government budget allocation remains small, donors and others are keen to provide additional resources.

It seems, however, that the department is unable to spend what is available.

A third area in which our work has informed policy is in welfare grants for young children. Francie Lund was the author of the chapter on the Department of Welfare in the first book. Soon after, she was appointed to chair the Lund Commission, an investigation into the maintenance grant then available. The maintenance grant provided support for children, and some single parents (mainly mothers), up to age eighteen. Many in government were keen to cut the grant completely. They argued that this was necessary because of its limited reach, the fact that it reached very few African women and children and even fewer in rural areas, and because it was fiscally impossible to extend the grant to all who should be eligible.

The Lund Committee recommended a significant change in the form of support for poor children. The recommendation that eligibility be based on a less rigid definition of the family more appropriate to the diverse South African situation was widely accepted. Less acceptable were the recommendations in terms of the size of the grant (lower than previously), the abolition of the parental grant, and the lowering of the age limit from eighteen to six years. The WBI research was central in informing the committee's conclusions. Critics argue that the committee was too conservative in accepting that only a limited total amount would be made available for this grant and thus cutting the size and age group so as to be able to reach the many poor children who had until then not had access. The committee feared that by not accepting these limits, they would be party to the abolition of all child support of this nature.

The above examples could be supplemented with others. More generally, however, we argue that our impact cannot be simply measured in rands and cents in this way, particularly in the context of a tight macro-economic policy. The initiative has, we feel, contributed to an improvement in the sophistication of budgetary debate in both parliament and civil society. It has provided skills training in gender and budgetary analysis to the researchers, as well as to the many people who have worked with the project or been exposed to its approach in workshops, conferences and so on. It has contributed to the development of theory and practice in how to link policy and budget. It has contributed both through its own work, and through the impetus provided to others, in increasing the level of information on budgetary allocations and government performance.

The WBI has been one of the forces which have led to gender issues becoming much more prominent in economic debates. At the launch of the government-commissioned Poverty and Inequality Report, the 'women are impoverished' theme became something of a mantra. Similarly, and with good reason, the particular economic vulnerability of women was raised again and again by speakers in the 'Speak Out on Poverty' hearings organized by the SA NGO Coalition, the Human Rights Commission and the Commission on Gender Equality.

The WBI has also contributed to an increased recognition of unpaid labour, and the role this plays in underwriting many women's disadvantage. In the research workshops of the initiative we have talked a lot about the different roles which women and men play as producers, reproducers and community managers. We have become increasingly aware that it is women, more often than men, who have to juggle these roles over their lives as well as at any one time. This realization has led us to emphasize the unpaid reproductive work which women do in bearing and rearing children, seeing to the needs of other household members, as well as fetching water and firewood. We have spoken and written about the way this work constrains what women can do in terms of paid work. We have pointed out how many government policies, such as those of welfare and health, assume that women will continue to play this role and are, in this way, subsidized by them. We have talked and written about the need to accord value to this work so that it is factored into cost-benefit analyses of policies. We have, following Ingrid Palmer, referred to unpaid work as a tax which women pay 'before they come to market'.

Dangers

We have faced many hard choices in developing the project. This is inevitable with any new project. It is particularly challenging when one is operating in a deeply political sphere.

One of the choices involves audience. The three books which we have produced are not accessible to a wide South African audience. The authors have engaged in extensive research into their particular sector. They also draw on ideas about gender which are not common parlance. They are talking about a topic – economics – which instils fear into many people. And they are dealing with numbers, a subject area in which a great many South Africans feel inadequate. We have tried wherever possible to avoid the use of jargon, whether from the gender or sectoral lexicons. Nevertheless, what we produce is sometimes too complicated, and too turgid, for those outside government and even for those in parliament.

At the same time, the researchers can in no way pretend to know even a fraction of what those employed in the various departments do. Some part of this can be blamed on the lack of transparency of government, but we also cannot expect that a relatively short research project can yield an understanding equal to that of those who work daily in a particular sector. Nevertheless, the importance of the insights is proved by the fact that the researchers have been contacted by civil servants and ministers from a number of the departments, and called upon to assist in their ongoing work.

We see *Money Matters: Women and the Government Budget* as a partial response to the problem of reaching multiple audiences. We hope that this 'popular' book will make the topic less threatening, and allow readers to understand both the overall approach as well as some of the more important issues in the different sectors. We are also in the process of developing workshop materials which the Commission on Gender Equality, among others, has expressed interest in using in their own education work.

The initiative itself is spread across organizations, and relies on individuals who have other jobs. It does not have the human capacity to take the approach to women in organizations. There have, however, been many indications at workshops around the country that people are hungry to know more about the project. We are hoping that workshop materials will allow a wider range of people to incorporate sessions on budgets into their own workshops, or indeed run full workshops on the topic.

Inside and Outside: Two Legs

At the government end, we are hoping that the government initiative could address both the transparency issue and the need for greater involvement with the detail. But the outcome is far from certain and the Australian example reveals some of the potential dangers. In that country, the idea was introduced by 'femocrats' (feminist bureaucrats) who went into the bureaucracy after the electoral success of the Labour Party in the mid-1980s. These femocrats and their colleagues were advocates of change from within.

The Australian exercises were co-ordinated by their Office on the Status of Women. It was, however, the bureaucrats in the different agencies who were required to collect the information and analyse it before sending it through to the office. The office was aware that this approach would result in some skimpy reports, and some with whose analysis they would not agree. But they hoped that, over time, the understanding and sophistication of the bureaucrats would increase, and that this would influence budgets. This approach has obvious merits above an approach which centralizes the initiative in a few 'politically correct' and analytically sophisticated hands, but hands which have little real power to effect material change.

What the Australian initiative lacked was a strong link with gender activists outside government, either in parliament or in civil society. The Australian initiative at one stage had spread to all states, each of which produced tomes of varying thickness. Over time, however, many of these products became little more than public relations exercises for the government of what they had 'done' for women. Since the election of the more conservative government several years ago, the federal and many of the state initiatives have died completely.

In South Africa we hope that a two-legged approach might avoid some of these difficulties. We would like to maintain the extra-government approach in the form of an alliance between researchers, parliamentarians and advocacy groups within civil society. We feel that the detailed work of the researchers gives more weight and substance to the arguments of the advocates. At the same time, the advocacy work makes the research meaningful and prevents it lying unused and dusty on library shelves.

We hope that the initiative in government will run alongside, developing better systems that can provide better information for government and those outside to measure performance, understand whether policies are working, and so be in a position to propose changes. We expect government to monitor its own activities very carefully, and amend them where necessary. We hope that the talk about performance monitoring systems and incorporation of output and outcomes in budgeting will promote monitoring. And we hope that our vigilant presence will mean that the systems, outputs and outcomes will incorporate gender. We understand that we cannot expect government to criticize its own actions too vociferously, but hope, perhaps naïvely, that they will provide us with the information that will allow vociferous criticism and some sort of partnership in making improvements where this is necessary.

Reslicing the Cake or Increasing Its Overall Size

The non-government initiative has been criticized for not being radical enough. At the beginning of the project we took a decision to concentrate on redistribution of existing resources, rather than arguing repeatedly for 'more'. We did this partly because we saw the exercise as a more 'practical' refinement, in terms of short- or medium-term needs, of the aspirational and long-term Women's Charter demands. The second reason was that we did not feel it was right to argue that any particular sector should be bigger without having examined all other allocations so as to see where money could be freed up. We asked each researcher to suggest how allocations to different programmes within a sector could be shifted so as to be more gender-equitable and more pro-poor.

At a deeper level, then, we were operating more or less within the current budget 'envelope'. After the announcement of the GEAR strategy, some of our analyses suggested that the policy contained elements which had been detrimental to women in other countries. We also suggested that some of the objectives of GEAR might be incompatible: that the promise of job creation at the same time as cutting the budget deficit might work in a model, but not in the real world. We did not, however, push strongly that the budget deficit target be abandoned so as to provide more money for our favoured programmes. We adopted this 'conservative' approach in the hope that it could reach as great a number of ears as possible, that even those firmly committed to deficit reduction would see that the available money is not currently optimally distributed, rather than closing their ears before we had our say. We also believe that the approach forces us to focus more strongly on redistribution.

Limitations of the Research

For many readers, and particularly those with greater knowledge such as government bureaucrats, the research to date will be disappointing because of our lack of hard facts and figures. One of the early criticisms from people involved in budget-making and budget advocacy was that the book was about 'politics' rather than budgets. To us this criticism seemed strange, in that budgets are themselves inherently political. However, what these critics were saying was probably that our books had far more words than numbers.

One reason for this is that we argue – and we feel that our emphasis on this point is one of the more important contributions of the initiatives – that budgets should follow policy rather than vice versa. So, we argue, we must first examine whether policy is gender-sensitive, and then see whether the money follows that.

Another reason is that the requisite numbers are usually simply not available. Budgets in South Africa are published, and probably drawn up, at a very high level of aggregation. This limits all budget analysis. It makes any disaggregated analysis such as gender, location, or age, near to impossible. The government is aware of the need for more detailed information. Increasing the amount of information and indicators available is one of the most important aspects of the Department of Finance's ideas on budget reform, with its emphasis on performance monitoring. We welcome this move, but with some reservations. At times, it seems as if the whole country is indicator-mad. Collection of information is expensive in terms of money, human and other resources. We are eager advocates of greater information. But we also don't want to push information collection to the extent that it further impedes delivery.

South Africa provides a favourable context for initiatives such as the WBI. We have a constitution which entrenches equality. We have a government that is relatively open to ideas, partly at least because it is able to acknowledge the need for new policies, or changes in policies, without having to accept full responsibility for the current situation. There is a deep awareness of disadvantage and inequality, and a fairly widespread recognition that race is not the only cleavage. This awareness is spread throughout society, and is prevalent among cabinet ministers as well as among many government bureaucrats. The support of someone like Deputy Minister Gill Marcus is based not only on a commitment to gender equality, but also on a recognition that the WBI provides a method to promote accountability and a focus on the disadvantage.

This is a very different situation from some other countries in which there have been attempts to introduce the initiatives. In other countries such an initiative can be met by denials that inequality exists or, alternatively, claims that women choose to be discriminated against, that it is 'our culture', and so on. In many countries there will be resistance from government to what is perceived as interference or pressure from outside. South Africa is fortunate in these respects too.

The South African government, like others, is not always open to criticism and there are plenty of examples of well-intended comment being greeted by defensiveness if not outright hostility. Nevertheless, factors such as the strong (and incestuous) links between government and the civil society from which many of the current government policy-makers hail and the stated commitment to transparency assist in muting resistance. The WBI has the added advantage over some other initiatives of strong involvement by parliamentarians who clearly have some right to 'interfere'. Further, the ongoing nature of the project and our policy of sticking to solid research rather than broad slogans have won recognition from some who might at first have doubted the worth of the work.

At the same time, South Africa is also faced with a great many challenges, and there is always tension around which receive attention. For many people, gender is still seen as a 'frill' or add-on, which must be abandoned when resources are constrained.

Some economists – including those from the World Bank – argue that gender inequity is expensive, in that it produces outcomes which are less than optimally efficient by not using to the full all the available resources. The arguments and examples often focus on areas such as education and health. In the case of education, for example, many advocates of women's education emphasize the falling birth rates which usually accompany increased levels of female education rather than the direct benefits to the woman concerned.

More radical economists adopt a wider view of efficiency. By expanding the view of the economy to include the care economy and (unpaid) reproductive activities, these economists take into account a wider range of costs and benefits of policies and programmes. Ingrid Palmer goes as far as to say that there is never a conflict between gender equity and economic efficiency, if one talks about social efficiency, and looks at social rather than individual costs (Palmer 1997).

The Bank, or some of those who work for it, have recently started openly advocating the development of women's budgets in other countries. The advocates single out the South African model as the one to follow. In their arguments, however, they stress the economic rationality of these and other initiatives to develop women rather than tackling questions of social justice.

Gender inequity is wrong both because it can be inefficient, and because it is 'not fair'. In South Africa, if not in all countries, 'fairness' must rank high among government considerations. The WBI does not base its arguments solely, or even mainly, on economic efficiency. It argues that governments need to focus their attention and available resources on those who are most in need of assistance. In South Africa, as in most (all?) other countries, those most in need of assistance are poor people. This grouping includes a disproportionate number of women.

References

Budlender, D. (ed.) (1996) *The Women's Budget*. Cape Town: IDASA.

— (ed.) (1997) *The Second Women's Budget*. Cape Town: IDASA.

— (ed.) (1998) *The Third Women's Budget*. Cape Town: IDASA.

Govender, P. (1996) 'Foreword', in Budlender (ed.), *The Women's Budget*, pp. 1–13.

Hurt, K. and D. Budlender (1998) *Money Matters: Women and the Government Budget*. Cape Town: IDASA.

Palmer, I. (1997) 'Social and Gender Issues in Macro-Economic Policy Advice' in J. Frieberg-Strauss, F. Diaby-Pentzlin, K. U. Freitag and M. Gutierrez (eds), *Gender and Macro Policy*. Sechborn: Deutsche Gesellschaft fur Technische Zusammenarbeit, pp. 1–12.

16

Redressing Urban Poverty in Post-apartheid South Africa

Christian M. Rogerson

Context

Over the past decade, the worsening problem of urban poverty in Africa has attracted the attention of an increasing number of researchers (Rakodi 1995; Moser 1995, 1996, 1998; Moser and Holland 1997). In redressing urban poverty, the asset vulnerability framework provides a useful conceptual base for approaching an understanding of anti-poverty policy formulation (Moser 1998). International research highlights that poverty is not always a static condition among individuals, households or communities (Moser 1996). Instead, it is recognized that while some individuals or households are permanently poor, others become impoverished, as a result of general life-cycle changes, specific events such as the illness of a main income-earner, or a deterioration in external economic conditions (Rakodi 1995). Accordingly, because individuals and households are moving into and out of poverty, researchers suggest the adoption of the dynamic concept of vulnerability in order to understand these processes of change (Rakodi 1995; Moser 1996, 1998; May 1998). Vulnerability is closely linked to asset ownership. It is appreciated that vulnerability to poverty is countered by the asset bases of the poor and by the management of their complex asset portfolios, particularly in times of crises (Moser 1996, 1998).

The definition of the asset base of the poor has been much disputed (Moser 1998). Nevertheless, at least four broad categories of assets have been identified: human capital (such as labour, education, health), social and institutional assets (household relations, trust, access to decision-making), natural resources (land, water, common property) and human-made assets (housing, productive infrastructure, social infrastructure) (May 1998: 7–8). Overall, the more assets that individuals, households and communities have or secure access to, and the better these assets are managed, the less vulnerable they are; the greater the erosion of their asset base the greater their insecurity and associated poverty (Moser 1998).

From the perspective of this asset vulnerability framework, therefore, poverty is characterized by not only a lack of assets and the poor's inability to accumulate an asset portfolio but also by an inability to devise an appropriate coping or management strategy (Rakodi 1995; Moser 1996). The key issues in anti-poverty strategies are therefore to build up the asset base of the poor and to expand better their capabilities to manage their existing package or portfolio of assets (Moser 1998).

Within the broader international context of urban poverty studies, South Africa is distinguished by its dismal history of denial of access to the majority of the country's citizens (South Africa 1997a). In many respects, apartheid planning served to make the poor 'invisible' by displacing them geographically. The poor were shifted to the margins, both of urban areas and more importantly to the spatial margins of the country as a whole, thus to focus the core of South Africa's poverty in the rural areas. With the march of urbanization, the impact of violence, and the breakdown and subsequent collapse of discriminatory controls on access to the cities, the question of urban poverty and of the associated inequalities of South Africa's cities becomes of rising policy significance (Rogerson 1996; May 1998). In common with trends of poverty observed in the rest of sub-Saharan Africa, the growing importance of urbanization is linked to a rapidly increasing proportion of the poor being situated in urban rather than rural areas (World Bank 1996: 38).

The aim in this chapter is to use the conceptual framework of the asset vulnerability framework to interpret the question of urban poverty alleviation in South Africa and of national strategies which address the poor. In the National Poverty and Inequality Report on South Africa it was disclosed that although South Africa is classed as an upper-middle-income country in per capita terms, the majority of the country's households experience poverty or vulnerability to being poor (May 1998). Moreover, the poverty rate (i.e. the percentage of households classified as poor) for all urban households was calculated as 24.4 per cent. In relative terms the incidence, depth and severity of urban poverty are shown to be highest in South Africa's small towns, followed by secondary cities and lowest in the country's four metropolitan areas (Woolard 1997). In absolute terms, the greatest burden of urban poverty in South Africa occurs, however, in the metropolitan areas, more especially in the shackland informal settlements that have burgeoned over the past two decades (Rogerson 1996). The unemployed, women-headed households and communities of international migrants are strongly represented among South Africa's urban poor. Nevertheless, it is important to recognize the group of the 'working poor' and that almost half of South Africa's urban poor are engaged in some form of wage or salaried employment (Bhorat et al. 1997; May 1998).

It is the task here to analyse the existing challenge of urban poverty in post-apartheid South Africa and to examine certain key aspects of on-going poverty alleviation programmes. Addressing the challenge of urban poverty in South Africa will demand the mainstreaming of policy interventions at all three tiers of government: national, provincial and local (Rogerson 1999a). The essential goal in this investigation, however, is to concentrate on issues of national level programme interventions for urban poverty alleviation in South Africa. The chapter is structured into two sections of discussion. First, the focus is on the rethinking, which has occurred at national level, of approaches to urban policy and urban poverty in South Africa. In the second section, attention shifts to examine the implementation of certain key national government programmes which are designed to contribute towards urban poverty eradication. More specifically, the concern is with a set of strategies that can assist in strengthening the asset base of the urban poor in South Africa. Although there are a number of national government programmes which impact upon the poor (May 1998), the focus is here specifically upon policies to augment the use of the poor's labour through stimulating the small enterprise economy and for the expanded provision of shelter to the poor.

Rethinking Urban Policy and Urban Poverty in South Africa

Over the last decade, there has been considerable rethinking about South African urban policy in general and urban poverty issues in particular. During the 1980s, within the NGO sector, and in the early 1990s ANC policy documents, poverty in general and to a lesser extent urban poverty enjoyed a degree of policy prominence. For example, one of four policy guidelines suggested in the conclusion of an Urban Foundation study was that there should be 'a special focus on state assistance to raise the living standards of the poor' (Urban Foundation 1990: 4). The ANC's Reconstruction and Development Programme (RDP) document also placed considerable emphasis upon urban poverty within a conceptual framework of an 'integrated and sustainable programme', the first of such programmes being 'meeting basic needs'. It refused to be drawn into what it saw as a false dichotomy between 'growth' which is 'commonly seen as a priority which must precede development' and 'development' which is portrayed as 'a marginal effort of redistribution to areas of urban and rural poverty'. In short, the RDP sought a developmental programme for the country which emphasized a new paradigm that cross-cut stale debates emanating from the apartheid era (McCarthy and Hindson 1997).

The form that this paradigm took was open to different interpretations, but by the time the new government gazetted its Urban Development

Strategy in 1995, the emphasis in the urban policy component of government thinking had begun to shift from seeing housing and basic services as the leading policy instrument for a country faced with pronounced socio-economic disparities, towards job creation as the key urban priority (South Africa 1995). Likewise, NGOs such as the Centre for Development and Enterprise (CDE) and the National Business Initiative (NBI) also tended to portray South African cities as centres deserving of economic policy emphases in a context of global competitiveness (CDE 1996). Overall, however, it is counter-productive to draw too sharp a distinction between growth-oriented and poverty-related development strategies, particularly in metropolitan areas. In this respect, the emphases of the government's 1995 Urban Development Strategy were broadly correct, albeit perhaps biased towards the metropolitan areas (McCarthy and Hindson 1997).

The Urban Development Framework (South Africa 1997a) seeks a more balanced approach through its association with the parallel efforts to formulate a Rural Development Framework. Significantly, the Urban Development Framework seeks to accommodate the growth and job-creation orientation of new South Africa's macro-economic strategy (GEAR) with the more redistributive and 'people development' association of the RDP. It does so through incorporation of the need to stimulate local economic development and enhanced global competitiveness of South African cities, arguing that there is no necessary contradiction between the emphasis on growth in current national macro-economic policy and the earlier emphasis on redistribution (South Africa 1997a: 11). Indeed, unless South Africa's urban areas are investor friendly, and unless they lead the expansion of employment opportunities, it will be almost impossible to achieve any of the other socially worthy objectives of the democratically-elected government (McCarthy and Hindson 1997: 32). This is not, however, to gainsay the crucial importance of policies to address poverty alleviation in urban areas. To choose one example, given that urban crime is now perhaps the most important constraint upon investor confidence; and given also that much urban crime is a product of urban poverty, there is a potentially strong complementarity between urban economic growth and poverty alleviation strategies. Moreover, in the long run, redistribution without growth and job creation is unsustainable, offering only temporary poverty alleviation and longer-term reversion to possibly deeper and more intractable impoverishment (McCarthy and Hindson 1997).

Overall, this shift in policy focus towards jobs, employment and economic priorities can be explained, to a large extent, by the imperatives of a new and emerging understanding of a changed demographic situation in South Africa. What is evident from a range of demographic analyses and the preliminary findings of the 1996 census is that South Africa's population is not growing as rapidly as once previously thought (South Africa 1997b). Combined with evidence of more moderate shifts of the population towards South African large metropolitan areas (CDE 1995), this means that expectations of the anticipated sizes of South African cities are significantly lower than was envisaged during the 1980s, and correspondingly that the scale of anticipated urban poverty is lower than some alarmist projections had suggested. In policy terms, what this meant, in some circles, is a temptation to return to First World concepts of 'mopping up' urban poverty, rather than a more Third World 'active assimilation of the poor' model. But, when population and economic projections of the 1990s are compared, it is evident that the 'mopping up' model is unrealistic, and the 'active assimilation of the poor' model still highly relevant in South Africa, suggesting that a combination of the two may prove optimal (McCarthy and Hindson 1997: 29).

It should be emphasized that the greatest share of South Africa's population increase is still expected to occur in the metropolitan areas (CDE 1995). Such projections underscore the need to keep the national developmental focus on the economic prospects offered by the metropolitan areas, as is reflected in the government's 1995 Urban Development Strategy and the 1997 Urban Development Framework. However, it serves also as a warning signal not to neglect the current realities and future prospects of urban poverty. In many respects, the recent downwards estimates of both existing urban populations and the scale of urban poverty are fortunate because, despite considerable recent efforts, the rates of delivery of urban housing, jobs and services have not kept pace with previous projections of population growth. This constraint upon the capacity of post-apartheid society to deliver has caused a degree of pessimism in several quarters. Nevertheless, current demographic data and projections make the urban poverty and development challenge appear more manageable (CDE 1995). Seen from a metropolitan perspective, therefore, these centres appear to benefit from a new 'dynamic equilibrium' in national demographic and income trends (McCarthy and Hindson 1997). Overall, it is recommended that within the metropolitan areas the policy focus is most appropriately centred upon the expansion of job opportunities coupled with housing and service provision. Poverty alleviation foci can be targeted upon localized areas, for example of (often) female-headed households in shackland settlements.

The opposite side of this new 'equilibrium', however, is that small towns and secondary cities appear to deserve a special focus in policy formulation for urban poverty alleviation. It is clear that small towns and secondary cities carry a weighty burden of urban poverty in South Africa. The problematic of rural and small-town development are inextricably interwoven. To a large degree, the majority of small towns exist only to service rural populations and agricultural needs (CDE 1996; Nel 1997). Where these populations and needs decline, so too do the towns in the longer term. At the same time, successful rural and agricultural development cannot materialize unless integrated with the type of services and opportunities that can be found in or near small towns. Accordingly, to the extent that urban policy is concerned with urban poverty, one adjustment to policy would be to prioritize the cases of (most) small towns and (many) secondary cities as deserving of the greatest emphasis. In extreme cases whole small towns or secondary cities may have to be considered in poverty alleviation terms.

Any attempt at spatially demarcating the urban poverty challenge is, however, a crude analysis and must be supplemented by a-spatial considerations. For the poorest section of the urban population unaddressed basic needs cover all or most facets of living and working. Typically, this means that not only jobs and incomes, but also housing, services, education and health facilities are absent or inaccessible. Urban policies therefore need to be coupled to wider policy frameworks in order to address this totality of needs if the poor are to move out of their existing circumstances. It is recommended therefore that what is required in South Africa is an integrated set of programmes which are designed both to strengthen the assets of the urban poor and to enhance their geographically marginal access to existing livelihood opportunities, thus to overcome the inherited apartheid legacies.

Programmes to Strengthen the Asset Base of the Poor

It is evident that in strengthening the assets of the poor, there are a number of spheres of national government policy which can reduce their vulnerability to poverty. Among several policies, health, education, crime prevention and infrastructure delivery are clearly key target areas in improving the assets of the poor in terms of their human and social capital as well as access to productive capital (see Abrahams and Goldblatt 1997; Budlender 1997a, 1997b; Louw and Shaw 1997; Pieterse 1997; May 1998 for discussion).

In the context of addressing core issues of urban poverty, the focus narrows to evaluate two specific kinds of policy intervention which potentially may serve either to strengthen directly the assets of South Africa's urban poor or to improve their range of choice with respect to alternative coping strategies. First, the critical issues surrounding programmes for urban housing provision are detailed. Second, the array of government initiatives which have been introduced to promote the development of the small, medium and micro-enterprise economy (SMMEs) as a sphere for urban labour absorption are investigated.

Strengthening Productive Assets: Housing Provision

The international experience confirms that housing is a critical asset for the urban poor (Moser 1996: 7). A situation of insecure housing increases the poor's vulnerability whereas secure housing is a productive asset which can serve to cushion the poor against the crushing impacts of poverty. Not only does it provide shelter and space for human development but its security encourages households to invest further in it. Home-owners may rent out rooms, sell part of their plot, or as a last resort, sell all of their property. A secure house is an important source of credit, providing recognized collateral for loans. Households also use their housing as a base for home enterprises, which provide women in particular with opportunities for economic activity (Moser 1996, 1998).

Overall, policies and programmes that focus on housing as an asset can assist households to become less vulnerable, offering them a greater number of choices and opportunities for development. For housing to impact positively on the urban poor, it needs specifically to target them by asserting their rights and ensuring their achievement. In terms of detailed strategies for housing as an asset, there is a fundamental need to provide security of tenure and, if possible, the provision of essential services (water, sanitation, electricity) to promote the productive use of the home. In addition, the manner of housing delivery should reinforce and promote the social relationships of trust and reciprocity within the community. It should afford the poor choices and opportunities that best suit their particular circumstances. Lastly, given that they represent the majority of the urban poor, women should not be specifically discriminated against in their access to housing and instead should be specifically supported (Smit and Williamson 1997: 8).

Historically, the housing sector in South Africa has not been performing well. The problems of the housing sector exist, in part, on the supply side and others on the demand side. Supply-side constraints include under-investment in terms of share of the national budget, the limited capacity of the construction sector, institutional bottlenecks and the fear of risk among financial institutions. In addition, another key factor is that the design of South Africa's cities is wasteful, inefficient, inequitable and costly to manage. On the demand side, apartheid policies had significant effects in terms of African housing demand. Affordability constraints due to low incomes, high unemployment, circular migration, a history of prohibition on African home ownership, spatial inefficiencies of high transport costs and limited access to credit from the formal finance sector are some of the factors constraining effective housing demand among the majority of South Africans.

Severe inequality was an outcome that characterizes South Africa's underperforming housing sector (see Goodlad 1996). For whites the average floor area per person is about 33 square metres whereas for Africans it is 9 square metres in formal housing and a meagre 4–5 square metres in informal housing. Currently, the urban poor reside in a diverse range of shelter conditions, including hostels, backyard shacks, garages and out-buildings, spontaneous informal settlements, planned site-and-service schemes and upgrading projects; state-owned rental housing, inner-city flats and employer-owned housing. Informal housing is the most prevalent means by which the poor access shelter; about one-third of existing stock in urban areas is informal and in South Africa's economic heartland, Gauteng, an estimated 80 per cent of newly-built housing is informal, manifest either as unplanned informal settlements or backyard shacks (Smit and Wiliamson 1997: 10). Importantly, many of these forms of accom-modation are regarded as illegal, have insecure tenure and are characterized by limited services, overcrowding and inadequate or deteriorating physical conditions. Socially, the housing situation contributes to considerable dis-satisfaction and dysfunctional behaviour, including criminality and violence. Overall, it is clear that the housing situation in South Africa does not offer the poor an asset that can reduce their vulnerability and promote their socio-economic development (Smit and Williamson 1997: 11). In order to address circumstances of poverty and inequality in housing, it is important to have a framework that is robust and flexible enough to accommodate variety and to provide a set of programmes that address specific concerns.

THE POLICY FRAMEWORK AND KEY PROGRAMMES Issues of housing featured strongly in the reconstruction and development commitments of South Africa's first democratic government (Goodlad 1996). The essence of current national housing policy is represented in a 1994 White Paper, a Record of Understanding between government and the Association of Mortgage Lenders, several implementation manuals, reports by the Depart-ment of Housing (DOH)'s task team and finally, a proposed Housing Bill. The national housing vision is sketched in the White Paper as follows:

> Government strives for the establishment of viable, socially and economically integrated communities situated in areas allowing convenient access to eco-nomic opportunities as well as health, educational and social amenities, within which all South Africa's people will have access on a progressive basis to: a permanent residential structure with secure tenure, ensuring

privacy and providing adequate protection against the elements; and potable water, adequate sanitary facilities, including waste disposal and domestic electricity supply. (South Africa 1994)

Moreover, the White Paper specifies a two-part national housing goal, namely to increase the housing sector's share of government budget from its current 1 per cent to 5 per cent and to increase delivery incrementally to 350,000 units per annum within five years and to produce at least one million units over those five years (South Africa 1994).

The approach taken to housing in post-apartheid South Africa is that the aim 'was to create an environment in which the state facilitated delivery rather than engaged directly in provision, and in which market and community involvement was maximised' (Goodlad 1996: 1636). South Africa's housing strategy combines elements of both welfare and market models and 'although some international influences are apparent it has no close similarity to any other nation state's strategy' (Goodlad 1996: 1644). Overall, the Department of Housing views housing as a variety of processes through which stable and sustainable public and private residential environments are created for households and communities. It recognizes that the environment within which a house is situated is as important as the house itself in satisfying the needs and requirements of occupants. The policy framework is articulated around several substantive areas or programmes.

The most far-reaching and important is the national subsidy scheme which is administered through provincial housing boards and provides a one-off, capital subsidy for land, housing and infrastructure to those beneficiaries earning less than R3,500 per month. The subsidy scheme represents a compromise between popular demands for the state to deliver complete houses for all and a concern to spread housing benefits widely (i.e. a compromise between width and depth). The maximum lump sum subsidy (which is available for the very poor) is R15,000 which in most contexts is insufficient to cover the costs of a serviced site and a 40-square-metre top structure. Thus households must augment the subsidy with a loan (or from their own savings) or embark on an incremental housing process where only a rudimentary shelter can be provided at the outset. Another feature of the subsidy system is its concern with ensuring that private sector delivery agents are not squeezed out by 'unfair competition' from the public sector. The housing subsidies can be accessed through a variety of approved routes, namely: individual subsidy, a project-linked route and an institutional (such as housing association) route. Subsidies are targeted at new housing starts although top-up subsidies can be accessed where state investments in prior projects are below the amount of subsidy on offer (Smit and Williamson 1997). In addition, there are also funds available through the Discount Benefit Scheme to allow beneficiaries to purchase their government-owned houses as well as a hostels redevelopment programme.

A second key area of intervention concerns an expansion of housing credit to the poor through making the enormous resources in the finance sector available to the majority of the populace. This issue is addressed by attempting to gain the co-operation of private sector finance institutions by assuming some of the risks usually taken by the private sector. The most significant risk interventions are the creation of a mortgage indemnity scheme; the formation of Servcon which endeavours to 'normalize' the existing lending environment by offering special arrangements to those who have defaulted on loan repayments; the product defect warrant scheme in which housing developers must provide guarantees against defects; and the National Urban Reconstruction and Housing Agency which uses guarantee funds to mobilize bridging and end-user finance for purposes of low-income housing. In addition, the National Housing Finance Corporation was launched to mobilize wholesale finance for the housing sector with a special focus on facilitating the activities of the non-traditional lending sector (such as stokvels) (Smit and Williamson 1997).

Other intervention points include the establishment of housing support centres which will provide a range of support activities such as training, materials production and consumer education. Such centres are a recognition that the subsidies are insufficient on their own to allow the building of a formal house on a serviced site and, given that formal finance is unlikely to be made available to those earning less than R1,500 per month, much housing activity will be incremental and will require support. Several initiatives have been launched also to facilitate the speeding of the development process, the most important being the Development Facilitation Act, which focuses on streamlining processes of township establishment, tenure delivery and rapid land development for urban residents (South Africa 1997a: 15).

Finally, the housing policy framework seeks to rationalize the institutional environment in order both to achieve delivery and to circumvent political conflicts. The constitution defines housing affairs as the concurrent responsibility of both central and provincial governments. In principle central government is empowered to set parameters for provincial housing policy formulation and, beyond the observance of such parameters, provinces are constitutionally empowered to either adopt policy developed by central government or to formulate new policy. In practice, few provinces have attempted to formulate distinct provincial policies. Nevertheless, in certain instances some significant departures from central government policy have been implemented. In the Free State, the provincial government rejected the notion of incremental housing and set a 40-square-metre minimum standard for top structures as prerequisite for subsidy approval. The net effect has been that the very poor simply cannot access housing subsidies. In another departure, the Free State and certain other provinces allow local authorities to subsidize the provision of serviced sites and to use housing subsidies for top structures only; in addition, the Free State permits local authorities to use subsidy money as bridging finance (at zero interest), a situation not permitted in the private sector unless firms are working through a local authority, effectively as contractor not developer (Smit and Williamson 1997).

The result of these departures has been 'to make it very difficult for the private sector to operate as packagers and initiators of projects in some provinces', thus placing added burdens on already overstretched local authorities who lack the capacity to take the leading role. At root, the problem arises because of central government's failure to distinguish those parameters of housing policy which are in the national interest from those which are open to provincial interpretation. It is recommended, in line with the Ministerial Task Team, that, apart from specifying what are the national-level parameters, steps be taken to operationalize housing policy-making and accountability at provincial level; in other words provinces should be encouraged to formulate their own policies and then to take responsibility for such policies (Smit and Williamson 1997: 26).

ASSESSING THE POLICY FRAMEWORK AND HOUSING PROGRAMMES
The fact that housing has been a very public barometer of government performance has resulted in a range of criticisms and assessments of the workings of housing policy that have emanated from different ideological stances (Smit and Williamson 1997). From the perspective of orthodox Marxists, within two and a half years after its adoption, the whole policy framework and associated set of programmes is asserted to be an embarrassment and a complete failure with the whole thrust of policy described as 'market-centred'. By contrast, the lobbyists of 'make-the-market-work' offer a different set of criticisms, particularly concerning the inappropriate design of housing subsidies and linkages to financial markets.

In this assessment the impact of current housing policy and practice is evaluated in so far as it addresses the inter-related challenges of poverty and inequality. In general, the new policy must be acknowledged as marking a highly significant break with the apartheid past, placing at centre-stage the poor and issues of low-income housing (Smit and Williamson 1997: 33). First, a pro-poor housing policy framework has been set in place which demonstrates a strong commitment to address the housing needs and aspirations of the poor and to confront apartheid legacies and imbalances, particularly as manifest in increased allocations to housing (5 per cent) in the national budget. Second, the poor population is specifically targeted through the housing subsidy system. Indeed, despite its faults and teething problems, the new subsidy system is a considerable departure from and improvement upon that established during the apartheid era. The DoH has unequivocally shifted away from the form of housing support of the apartheid period and committed itself to a non-discriminatory housing programme that is primarily directed towards assisting the poor in accessing housing opportunities. It is clear, however, that non-discriminatory practices and gender equality are still goals to be attained with respect to poor women's access to housing (Parnell 1996). Evidence exists that women still suffer discrimination under the workings of the new subsidy scheme and that gaps exist in the current housing subsidy that must be filled 'to ensure that gender equality becomes a reality rather than simply a statement of intent' (Smit and Williamson 1997: 35).

Overall, the implementation of policy has demonstrated both achievements and failures which will need to be addressed in order to optimize the government's impact in future on reducing poverty and inequality in the housing sector. At the centre of controversy is the provincial target for the One Million Houses Programme and the very slow delivery of housing opportunities. As of end-June 1997 more than 590,000 subsidies had been approved and 248,100 sites built or currently under construction. The critical gap was between approvals and completions of houses (Goodlad 1996). Since 1997 there is mounting evidence of an improvement in the tempo of housing starts and completions (Fraser-Moleketi 1998). Indeed, in the 1998/99 financial year it was reported that most provincial governments across South Africa had spent their full allocations for housing rather than having significant year-on-year roll-overs in their budgets. This situation is seen as indicating that the pace and progress in the actual delivery of houses to the poor is showing marked signs of improvement (Chalmers 1999).

The bulk of subsidies have been allocated to households earning under R800 per month and, if the present trends continue, 'most of the funds allocated to the subsidy scheme will eventually reach a significant proportion of South Africa's poor' (Smit and Williamson 1997: 37). One of the main advantages of the capital subsidies is that they give the poor an immediate asset rather than a liability which would be the case in alternative suggestions for changing to a system of making loans at well below market rates.

The most common subsidy is the project-linked subsidy which delivers a very basic shelter, a plot of approximately 250 square metres with secure tenure and a combination of infrastructure services (Abrahams and

Goldblatt 1997; Bierman 1999). Project-based subsidies are allocated to developers who undertake new construction or in situ upgrade projects with the amount of subsidy determined by the number of qualifying beneficiaries in each of four subsidy income bands (Swamy and Ketley 1997: 33). The subsidy is paid directly to the developer in stages and the developer reduces the end-cost of the provided dwelling by an amount that is equivalent to the subsidy allocated to the beneficiary. By end-June 1997, 525,000 project-linked subsidies were approved as opposed to only 42,000 individual subsidies, which are paid directly to individuals who then deal directly with a builder or seller. Until recently, little interest was attracted to institutional subsidies but recently government has promoted this form of subsidy in terms of developing social housing. Making use of this form of subsidy, potentially between 15,000 and 30,000 new rental units will become available. Geographically, most housing projects occur in and around urban areas; significantly, the rate of subsidy approvals has varied between provinces with Eastern Cape and KwaZulu-Natal the worst performers. Delays in subsidy approval in these regions result in the erosion of the subsidy by inflation, reducing its impact on assisting the poor (Smit and Williamson 1997: 38).

A positive feature of evolving policy and housing programmes is that they allow for a considerable variety of housing delivery systems which, if carefully selected and well-managed, can assist in addressing the diverse needs and aspirations of the poor. The DoH has recognized the presence of the diversity of processes by poor individuals and communities in addressing their housing needs. Within the current context, the most favoured are upgraded and serviced sites, which ensure the basic health and safety of residents, deliver secure tenure and facilitate access to end-user finance, all of which are significant for reducing the vulnerability of the poor. In addition, these delivery systems are accompanied by support-oriented mechanisms, most importantly the housing support centres, designed to facilitate the self-help process. Although surveys of housing project beneficiaries disclose dissatisfaction with aspects of the housing process, particularly of lack of amenities, costs and inadequacy of information, many commented on the positive improvements in their lives that the subsidy provided in the form of taps, sanitation and, most importantly, a feeling of ownership and security (Smit and Williamson 1997: 41).

Overall, an evaluation of current housing initiatives from a poverty and inequality perspective points to its success in at least four major respects. First, it represents a significant departure from previous subsidy policies that favoured the relatively affluent, whites and males; the intended beneficiaries (i.e. those with less than R1,500 per month) are being reached (Swamy and Ketley 1997: 33). Second, it is beginning to impact upon the poor, providing them with a basis for shelter which is secure and ensures basic standards of health and safety. Third, the poor are being provided with a tangible asset that will furnish a buffer against poverty and reduce their vulnerability to changing circumstances. Lastly, it must be acknowledged that although the government's housing programme got off to a slow start due to capacity problems and long lead times (up to two years for planning and infrastructure provision), the latest indications are that the tempo of delivery is beginning to accelerate (Fraser-Moleketi 1998: 13).

Despite these achievements, there remain certain identifiable areas where a reconsideration of policy and an improvement in existing programmes can be effected. First, the overwhelming emphasis given to rapid delivery obscures other aspects which are essential in addressing poverty and inequality (Smit and Williamson 1997; Tomlinson 1999). Of several issues that need attention, the most important relate to gender equality, the formalization of tenure in existing informal settlements, and the greater promotion of community processes and of people-centred development in the housing sector (Smit and Williamson 1997: 43). Second, attention needs to be given to the question of providing protection against a danger of 'downward-raiding' of low-income subsidy beneficiaries by higher-income groups (Bond and Tait 1997: 20). Although the solutions to this problem are not immediately apparent, 'measures for addressing downward raiding do need to be incorporated into contemporary policy' (Smit and Williamson 1997: 30). Third, equally important is that contemporary policy must be more aggressive as regards ensuring access to land for the poor, which can be 'the most critical element for overcoming poverty in a city' (South Africa 1997a: 15). In particular, it is necessary to guard against the reproduction of apartheid-style ghettos of the poor which are segregated along class rather than racial lines (Bond and Tait 1997: 26). Indeed, Tomlinson (1999) argues that any spatial implications that might slow down the spending on housing programmes have been disallowed with the consequence that most new developments have occurred on the urban periphery.

Fourth, the important issue of rental housing has been overlooked in South Africa's national housing programme. A number of recent studies have highlighted the crucial role of rental housing for poor households in South African urban areas and argued for the incorporation of rental housing into current housing policies and programmes (see Gilbert et al. 1997; Watson and McCarthy 1998). Fifth, there is a danger that the housing programme as it is currently functioning is primarily driven by developers who are attracted to building houses on cheap, uncontested land far from jobs and social services (Tomlinson 1999). As argued by Bierman (1999), the functioning of the present housing system serves to reinforce peripheral, dispersed, low-density forms of shelter development which are often not co-ordinated with infrastructure development programmes. Sixth, it is important that the functioning of the existing housing subsidy scheme be monitored, particularly in light of alternative suggestions for modifying the subsidy and integrating it into formal financial markets (Smit and Williamson 1997). Finally, in view of the high numbers of immigrants in the urban poor of South Africa, new research suggests that there is 'a need for clear and unambiguous housing policies for non-citizens in South Africa' and that 'the South African government should consider a pro-active rather than a reactive, approach to the issue' (McDonald 1998: 2).

Strengthening the use of labour: SMME development The question of improving the urban poor's access to productive income opportunities is of critical significance for poverty eradication and inequality reduction in South Africa. In strengthening the productive use of labour, it is crucial to assess the policy directions and workings of the set of national pro-grammes geared to the enhancement of the SMME economy. Overall, the set of programmes for assisting the SMME economy potentially offer a basis for addressing urban poverty through strengthening existing coping strategies or by offering alternative livelihoods for those individuals and households engaged in the survival informal economy. In addition, it presents the potential for redressing apartheid inequalities through upgrading micro-enterprise development and the condition of the emerging SMME economy which is dominated by historically disadvantaged communities (Rogerson 1999b).

At the outset, however, it is acknowledged that the urban SMME economy is not an homogeneous entity; rather it is segmented into three sets of enterprises: (1) survivalist enterprises of the informal economy; (2) a segment of growth-oriented micro-enterprise; and (3) the formal SMME economy presently dominated by established white-owned enter-prise. It is grossly misleading to conceive all participants in the urban SMME economy as potentially successful entrepreneurs. The majority of the population working in the SMME economy are unable or unlikely ever to make a transition away from the struggle for meagre survival, 'con-strained by a number of factors which constantly reinforce their position at the bottom of the pile' (Horn 1995: 35). Worst affected are women, shackled by patriarchy and the responsibilities of child-care which limits both their choice of skills and their capacity to pursue further training. Although some participants may grow towards micro-enterprise and formal SMMEs, most will stay behind and remain poor, becoming trapped in a range of casual work relationships within the structures of the dominant formal economy (Rogerson 1997). Forms of casual work include short-term or temporary wage work, disguised wage work (such as commission sellers and home-workers) and dependent work (common among street traders with dependency based on credit relationships). This situation points to a need for introducing a set of supportive programmes aimed to transcend the particular environmental constraints that relegate women to the poorest niches of the urban SMME economy (Horn 1995). An integrated policy framework is required to take account of the set of specific factors which ghettoize women's participation in the SMME economy largely to the area of survivalist enterprise; suggested intervention programmes concern the organization and regulation of informal workers, the redesign of social security systems, extension of child-care provision and a monitoring system on SMME programmes that would allow a clear assessment of its impact on survivalist enterprise.

ASSESSING THE POLICY FRAMEWORK Existing government policy intervention for SMMEs represents a complex package of programmes (Rogerson 1999b). An important concern relating to the national SMME policy surrounds problems that arise from the internal contradictions and diverse objectives that underpin the current policy framework (Manning 1996). The national government views SMMEs as key instruments for attaining several different objectives: employment generation, income re-distribution and the enhancement of competitiveness, particularly of small-scale manufacturing operations. As Manning (1996: 68) observes: 'Not only are these very divergent policy objectives, but the policy instruments required to effect them are equally divergent (ranging from technology support, R & D support, to literacy and numeracy training, and access to basic information).' While it must be acknowledged that each of the policy objectives is both valid and critical in relation to issues of poverty eradication and inequality reduction, 'policy-makers necessarily have to impose a hierarchy of importance upon them, in order to decide on the distribution of resources' (Manning, 1996: 68). Although the total budgetary cut for SMME programmes needs to be reassessed and radically adjusted upwards, it is clear that before this takes place government should carefully reassess the directions and emphases in the SMME programme in order that transparent guidelines be determined to enable more appropriate targeting of funds and support programming.

In terms of existing principles for intervention, a reassessment is necessary based upon current and new evidence. The conventional wisdom surrounding the equation of SMME promotion necessarily with employment creation must be queried. The broad evidence in support of the perception of SMMEs as important quantitative sources of employment is somewhat weak. Equally important is the question of the *quality* of the jobs that are generated through the SMME economy. Increasingly, it is suggested that the quality of employment in the SMME economy is poor with especially poor wage and working conditions among groups of primarily women home-based workers and the most severe work conditions occurring in survivalist enterprises.

Although the SMME strategy undoubtedly will contribute to redressing severe racial inequalities inherited from the apartheid period, it must be cautioned that while SMMEs 'do represent one vehicle for redressing racial income inequalities, it would be dangerous for policy-makers to rely on SMMEs as the main agent for economic redistribution' (Manning 1996: 65). First, reliance on SMMEs to redistribute wealth 'does not tamper with the core economic power of South Africa, most of which is concentrated in the hands of the large white-owned corporations'. Second, as the majority of African-owned businesses presently are very small and yield only limited incomes to their owners, they alone 'cannot be expected to significantly shift the patterns of income distribution'. Finally, even if SMMEs are a successful channel of wealth to African entrepreneurs, this will not necessarily translate into reduced income inequality; instead, one unintended outcome may be the enrichment of a limited number of African entrepreneurs at the expense of the majority.

ASSESSING THE SMME PROGRAMMES At the core of urban SMME programmes are the policy interventions introduced by the new institutions and structures set up to implement the national SMME strategy; the key actors are Ntsika Enterprise Promotion Agency (NEPA) and Khula Enterprise Finance (Rogerson 1999b). In launching the implementation of programmes proposed in the White Paper on Small Business, national government severely underestimated several vital institutional factors: (1) the problems of establishing the set of new support institutions; (2) the capacity of these new support institutions to establish and implement a wide range of new policy initiatives; and (3) the capacity of the existing NGO network in South Africa to become involved in the highly ambitious set of programmes that were implemented both as regards financing and non-financial support for SMMEs in South Africa (Patel et al. 1995). Overall, in light of institutional constraints, the continual proliferation of new programmes (however worthy and innovative) for SMME development is itself a cause for concern.

These institutional problems provide important background to assessing the workings of the SMME programmes launched by NEPA and Khula. At the heart of NEPA's interventions is the establishment and accreditation of a network of local business service centres (LBSCs) which are to deliver a package of non-financial business support and 'real services' to SMMEs. The first assessments of functioning LBSCs reveal a diverse range of experiences. But the broad conclusion must be that the activities of LBSCs should be further supported as they make a real contribution towards poverty eradication as well as the reduction of racial economic inequalities. Although some LBSCs' prime target is the more established SMMEs, a focus on poverty eradication and economic empowerment of historically disadvantaged communities is a feature of most accredited LBSCs. Certain blockages exist in the network and operations of LBSCs that demand policy attention as regards fine-tuning the programme; the training programmes of several LBSCs perpetuate women's concentration in certain traditional activities such as sewing, dressmaking and knitting; skills shortages exist; the outreach of small town LBSCs into surrounding rural areas often is weak; few linkages of LBSCs occur to local government and more widely to Local Economic Development planning initiatives; the existing network is too sparse and must be extended geographically; and, finally, there is a need to link LBSCs and their non-financing support services to the co-ordinated extension of financial support for SMMEs, especially in cases of LBSCs situated outside metropolitan areas where the demand for their services often is restricted by the absence of NGOs operating in the financial sphere (Rogerson 1997: 19).

Improvements need to be effected also in the important activity of expanding access to financing for SMMEs. The Khula lending programme has been in operation only since January 1997; Khula officials none the less concede that the volume of loans that have been made to NGOs is currently insufficient to meet the needs of the SMME community. Moreover, the present reach of the programme is geographically uneven and must be deepened. Another bias inherent in the present programme is towards funding the more established SMMEs rather than survivalist enterprises. The major problems appear to lie in the lack of suitable NGOs or other Retail Financial Intermediaries operating as lenders and that the existing distribution of financing NGOs introduces considerable spatial biases into accessing finance. Khula's establishment of a credit guarantee facility potentially will be of greatest assistance to more established formal SMMEs or some larger micro-enterprise rather than for survivalist enterprise. Nevertheless, the impact of this programme so far has been limited by the reluctance of commercial banks to participate in the programme, an issue which may require government intervention (Rogerson 1997, 1999b).

A range of other yet newer SMME initiatives introduced by NEPA potentially can impact on urban poverty or redressing inequality. The newly-inaugurated Manufacturing Advice Centres largely will serve growth objectives through seeking to strengthen the competitiveness of more established SMMEs. Of greater significance on a long-term basis for affecting inequality and reducing poverty is the enactment of initiatives to enhance the access of SMMEs to both government and large private sector procurement/linkage programmes. The issue of public procurement is particularly crucial in light of international experience which suggests that 'public procurement policy represents a powerful instrument which governments could use to stimulate inter-firm collaboration' (Manning 1996: 240). Once again, for survivalist enterprises, the domain of the very poor, the impact of expanding the role of SMMEs through sub-contracting and government tenders will be limited, as the greatest positive effects potentially will accrue to the group of more established SMMEs with the capacity to deliver goods and services of the required quality and quantity (Rogerson 1997).

Outside national programmes, sight must not be lost of the potentially significant role of local government intervention for assisting SMME development (Rogerson 1999a). In particular, for groups of survivalist enterprise engaged in street hawking or the running of spazas, the activities of local government can exert a profound impact upon the economic health of these kinds of enterprise and of the coping strategies of poor households (Rogerson 1997). The establishment of formal markets, land-use zoning and infrastructure provision, among others, are key areas of local government intervention which can impact positively upon the workings of particularly survivalist informal enterprise. In addition, the local planning and support of periodic markets is an attractive and inexpensive poverty-redressing policy intervention for SMME upgrading, not only in small towns but also as components in integrated projects for urban reconstruction. Another linked set of local interventions can relate to the potential of promoting agriculture as more than a mere safety-net for the urban poor (Rogerson 1998). Especially in the peri-urban areas of secondary cities and small towns, the potential for promoting the poor's greater access to natural resources and of establishing an active peri-urban agricultural sector requires serious investigation and support measures designed to improve the poor's access to cultivable land (Task Team et al. 1997).

Overall, it is evident that an examination of potentials for this range of possible local interventions to support SMME development, including for survivalist enterprise, be stressed as part of the developmental responsibilities of local government and incorporated in the design of local economic development strategies. It must be reiterated that the activities of local government rather than national SMME programmes may be most critical interventions for urban poverty reduction (Rogerson 1999a). Nevertheless, as indicated earlier, several existing NEPA and Khula initiatives merit further financial support, extension and fine-tuning in order to boost micro-enterprise development and to expand the ranks of emerging entrepreneurs and integrate them into the mainstream economy.

Conclusion

It has been argued that an overriding priority for a pro-poor urban strategy in South Africa is to set in place a coherent set of policies and co-ordinated programmes which are designed to strengthen the asset base of the urban poor (Rogerson 1999a).

In addressing the challenges of urban poverty, it is clear that sustained labour-intensive macro-economic growth is among the most critical pre-conditions for poverty reduction in South African urban areas (particularly the metropolitan centres) because it will create expanded income opportunities for the poor while furnishing resources to the public sector both for a range of targeted interventions and for sets of social programmes designed to enhance human capital.

To some extent, the foundations for successful initiatives to redress urban poverty in post-apartheid South Africa have already been laid in present government policies and programmes concerning urban reconstruction and development. In particular, the expansion of the present national housing policies and programmes and of the range of existing initiatives to support the SMME economy will contribute towards an enhancement of the asset base of the urban poor. Nevertheless, it is evident that there are certain areas of policy in which further improvements may be effected, that fine-tuning of existing programmes must be made in order comprehensively to combat and redress urban poverty in South Africa.

In the final analysis, there is a need for achieving a stronger integration of pro-poor policies across a range of sectors that impact upon strengthening the assets of the poor and for redressing urban poverty. The goal of integration is contingent upon South Africa introducing certain integrative institutional structures which are designed to co-ordinate both policy formulation and implementation in many areas that impact upon the reduction of poverty (see May 1998).

References

Abrahams, G. and M. Goldblatt (1997) *Access to Urban Infrastructure by the Poor: Progress in the Public Provision of Infrastructural Assets*. Unpublished report prepared for the Project on Poverty and Inequality.

Bhorat, H., F. Cassim and L. Torres (1997) *Poverty in the Labour Market*. Unpublished report prepared for the Project on Poverty and Inequality.

Bierman, S. (1999) *Service Trade-Offs Theme Paper*. Unpublished paper prepared for the Project on Spatial Guidelines for Infrastructure Investment and Development, Pretoria.

Bond, P. and H. Tait (1997) 'The Failure of Housing Policy in Post-Apartheid South Africa', *Urban Forum*, 8, 1, pp. 18–40.

Budlender, D. (1997a) *Women and Gender.* Unpublished report prepared for the Project on Poverty and Inequality.

— (1997b) *Education and Training.* Unpublished report prepared for the Project on Poverty and Inequality.

CDE (Centre for Development and Enterprise) (1995) *Post-Apartheid Population and Income Trends: A New Analysis.* Johannesburg: CDE.

— (1996) *South Africa's Small Towns: New Strategies for Growth and Development.* Johannesburg: CDE.

Chalmers, R. (1999) 'Provinces Upbeat on Housing Expenditure', *Business Day* (Johannesburg), 16 January.

Fraser-Moleketi, G. (1998) *Government's Response to the Poverty and Inequality Report.* Address presented at the Conference on Poverty and Inequality, Midrand, 12 June.

Gilbert, A., A. Mabin, M. McCarthy and V. Watson (1997) 'Low Income Rental Housing: Are South African Cities Different?', *Environment and Urbanization,* 9, 1, pp. 133–47.

Goodlad, R. (1996) 'The Housing Challenge in South Africa', *Urban Studies,* 33, 9, pp. 1629–45.

Horn, P. (1995) 'Self-Employed Women's Union: Tackling the Class–Gender Intersection', *South African Labour Bulletin,* 19, 6, pp. 34–8.

Louw, A. and Shaw, M. (1997) *Stolen Opportunities: The Impact of Crime on South Africa's Poor.* Unpublished report prepared for the Project on Poverty and Inequality.

McCarthy, J. J. and D. Hindson (1997) *Urban Policy and Urban Poverty.* Unpublished report prepared for the Project on Poverty and Inequality.

McDonald, D. (1998) *Left Out in the Cold?: Housing and Immigration in the New South Africa.* Migration Policy Series no. 5. Cape Town: Southern African Migration Project.

Manning, C. (1996) *Market Access for Small and Medium-Sized Producers in South Africa: The Case of the Furniture Industry.* Unpublished PhD Dissertation, University of Sussex, Brighton.

May, J. (ed.) (1998) *Poverty and Inequality in South Africa.* Durban: Praxis.

May, J. and C. M. Rogerson (1995) 'Poverty and Sustainable Cities in South Africa: The Role of Urban Cultivation', *Habitat International,* 19, pp. 165–81.

Moser, C. (1995) 'Urban Social Policy and Poverty Reduction', *Environment and Urbanization,* 7, 1, pp. 159–71.

— (1996) *Confronting Crisis: A Comparative Study of Household Responses to Vulnerability in Four Poor Urban Communities.* Washington, DC: World Bank.

— (1997) *Poverty Reduction in South Africa: The Importance of Household Relations and Social Capital as Assets of the Poor.* Unpublished report. Washington, DC: World Bank.

— (1998) 'The Asset Vulnerability Framework: Reassessing Urban Poverty Reduction Strategies', *World Development,* 26, pp. 1–19.

Moser, C. and J. Holland (1997) *Urban Poverty and Violence in Jamaica.* Washington, DC: World Bank.

Nel, E. (1997) *Poverty and Inequality in South Africa: The Small Town Dimension.* Unpublished report prepared for the Project on Poverty and Inequality.

Parnell, S. (1996) *The Housing Budget.* Paper presented at the Women's Budget Initiative Workshop, Cape Town, 10 March.

Patel, L., C. Cachalia and T. Pelser (1995) *Report on Non-Governmental Organisations and Poverty Alleviation in South Africa.* Unpublished report prepared for the World Bank.

Pieterse, E. (1997) *Social Capital and Community Initiatives*. Unpublished report prepared for the Project on Poverty and Inequality.

Rakodi, C. (1995) 'Poverty Lines or Household Strategies: A Review of Conceptual Issues in the Study of Urban Poverty', *Habitat International*, 19, 4, pp. 407–26.

Rogerson, C. M. (1996) 'Urban Poverty and the Informal Economy in South Africa's Economic Heartland', in *Environment and Urbanization*, 8, 1, pp. 167–81.

— (1997) *SMMEs and Poverty in South Africa*. Unpublished report prepared for the Project on Poverty and Inequality.

— (1998) 'Urban Agriculture and Urban Poverty Alleviation in South Africa', *Agrekon*, 37, 2, pp. 171–88.

— (1999a) 'Local Economic Development and Urban Poverty Alleviation: The Experience of Post-Apartheid South Africa', *Habitat International*, 23, 4, pp. 511–34.

— (1999b) 'Small Enterprise Development in Post-Apartheid South Africa: Gearing up for Growth and Poverty Alleviation', in K. King and S. McGrath (eds), *Enterprise in Africa: Between Poverty and Growth*. London: Intermediate Technology Publications, pp. 83–94.

Smit, D. and A. Williamson (1997) *The Housing Sector*. Unpublished draft report prepared for the Project on Poverty and Inequality.

South Africa, Republic of (1994) *A New Housing Policy and Strategy for South Africa*. Pretoria: Government Printer.

— (1995) *Urban Development Strategy of the Government of National Unity*. Pretoria: Government Printer.

— (1997a) *Urban Development Framework*. Unpublished report, Department of Housing, Pretoria.

— (1997b) *Census '96: Preliminary Estimates of the Size of the Population of South Africa*. Pretoria: Central Statistics.

Swamy, G. and R. Ketley (1997) *South Africa: A Review of Public Expenditures Efficiency and Poverty Focus*. Unpublished discussion paper presented at the Second Workshop of the Project on Poverty and Inequality, Durban, 10–11 April.

Task Team of the Department of Agriculture, the Rural Strategy Unit and the World Bank (1997) *Free State Mission on Rural Investment*. Glen: Rural Strategy Unit.

Tomlinson, R. (1999) *Coming to Terms with the Location of Housing and Infrastructure Grant Funding*. Unpublished paper prepared for the Project on Spatial Guidelines for Infrastructure Investment and Development, Pretoria.

Urban Foundation (1990) *Policy Overview: The Urban Challenge*. Johannesburg: Urban Foundation.

Watson, V. and M. McCarthy (1998) 'Rental Housing Policy and the Role of Household Rental Sector: Evidence from South Africa', *Habitat International*, 22, 1, pp. 49–56.

Woolard, I. (1997) *A Comparison of Urban Poverty*. Unpublished report, Data Research Africa, Durban.

World Bank (1996) *Taking Action for Poverty Reduction in Sub-Saharan Africa: Report of an Africa Region Task Force*. Washington, DC: World Bank.

Index

Zed Titles on Poverty

Many Zed Books titles on international and Third World issues deal, one way or another, with the question of poverty. The following titles, however, deal with the question specifically.

Brian C. Aldrich and Ravinder S. Sandhu (eds), *Housing the Urban Poor: A Guide to Policy and Practice in the South*

Michel Chossudovsky, *The Globalization of Poverty: Impacts of IMF and World Bank Reforms*

Siddharth Dube, *In the Land of Poverty: Memoirs of an Indian Family, 1947–97*

David Gordon and Paul Spicker (eds), *The International Glossary on Poverty*

Rajni Kothari, *Poverty: Human Consciousness and the Amnesia of Development*

John Madeley, *Big Business, Poor Peoples: The Impact of Transnational Corporations on the World's Poor*

Suzanne Thorbek, *Gender and Slum Culture in Urban Asia*

For full details of this list and Zed's other subject and general catalogues, please write to: The Marketing Department, Zed Books, 7 Cynthia Street, London N1 9JF, UK or e-mail: sales@zedbooks.demon.co.uk

Visit our website at: http://www.zedbooks.demon.co.uk